Dik Bakker and Martin Haspelmath (Eds.)
Languages Across Boundaries

Languages Across Boundaries

Studies in Memory of Anna Siewierska

Edited by
Dik Bakker and Martin Haspelmath

DE GRUYTER
MOUTON

ISBN 978-3-11-033103-5
e-ISBN 978-3-11-033112-7

Library of Congress Cataloging-in-Publication Data
A CIP catalog record for this book has been applied for at the Library of Congress.

Bibliografische Information der Deutschen Nationalbibliothek
The Deutsche Nationalbibliothek lists this publication in the Deutschen Nationalbibliografie; detailed bibliographic data are available in the internet http://dnb.dnb.de.

© 2013 Walter de Gruyter GmbH, Berlin/Boston
Cover image: Stacey McDonald, AsspocketProductions.etsy.com
Portrait Anna Siewierska (p. vii): Z. Chomeniuk, Gdynia
Typesetting: Frank Benno Junghanns, Berlin
Printing: Hubert & Co. GmbH & Co. KG, Göttingen
♾ Printed on acid-free paper
Printed in Germany

www.degruyter.com

Preface

On Tuesday 19 July 2011, Anna and I finished a co-authored article on suppletion in person forms. It was the 19th article we had written together; we were not to know that it would be the last. A few days later, we flew to Hong Kong in order to attend the 9th Conference of the Association for Linguistic Typology (ALT), of which Anna was president at the time. During earlier discussions by the ALT board, Anna had managed to convince her colleagues that the 2011 conference should be held in Asia rather than in Europe or the Americas, and preferably in China. She saw the enormous potential for the ALT in that part of the world, especially after a very successful trip we had made to universities in Beijing, Xi'an and Shanghai two years earlier. After the conference, we left Hong Kong for Hanoi and set out on a tour of Vietnam, a country that Anna had long wanted to visit. Towards the end of our holiday, on 6 August 2011, near the town of Dalat, a truck that was overtaking in the opposite direction ran into our minibus, hitting the exact part of the vehicle where Anna was sitting. She died in my arms, on the way to the hospital, just 55 years young, taking with her all that she still had to give to the world, as a linguist, a teacher and a wonderful human being.

On 27 April 2012, the Max Planck Institute for Evolutionary Anthropology in Leipzig, where Anna had been a visiting scholar on several occasions over the previous decade, organized a one-day memorial workshop for her. The workshop brought together many of the most prominent figures in the field of linguistic typology and functional linguistics, who came to pay tribute to Anna, to her work, her role in linguistics and above all to her. As a further tribute, it was proposed to put together a joint special issue of *Folia Linguistica* and *Linguistic Typology*, the respective journals of the Societas Linguistica Europaea (SLE) and the ALT, two organizations of which Anna had been the president and an active member, and in nearly every of whose conferences she had loyally participated over the previous twenty years. However, De Gruyter Mouton, the publisher of both journals, suggested that it would be a better idea to compile a book and to distribute it to the combined membership of SLE and ALT, which together numbers around 1400 linguists from around 75 countries all over the globe.

The result is in your hands. This book contains thirteen chapters (co-)authored by nineteen leading scholars in the field – Anna's peers, many of whom she also counted as personal friends. She first met most of them at meetings of the European Science Foundation's EUROTYP project (1990–1995) or at the biennial conferences of the ALT, which were the natural sequel to it. Johan van der Auwera chaired a EUROTYP group, as did Anna, and both were part of the EUROTYP core group. Bernard Comrie was an advisory member of this group and later regularly invited Anna over to the Max Planck Institute in Leipzig. Marianne Mithun was Anna's predecessor as president of the ALT and Johanna Nichols her successor, while Christian Lehmann took over from Anna as president of the SLE. Balthasar Bickel, Martin Haspelmath and Volker Gast organized Syntax of the World's Languages conferences in 2004 and 2008, while Anna organized the 2006 conference in Lancaster. Grev Corbett and (during his Manchester years) Bill Croft were her closest typological colleagues in England. Through Bill, Anna met Sonia Cristofaro, with whom she shared many a conference, many a linguistic discussion and many a chat over the years, both on professional occasions and privately. Andrej Malchukov she met several times at the Max Planck Institute in Leipzig; with him she co-organized an SLE workshop and co-edited a book on impersonal constructions. Andrej Kibrik was encouraged by Anna to write a book proposal for the Oxford typology series, which resulted in his monograph *Reference in Discourse*. Giorgo Iemmolo was invited by Anna for a stay at Lancaster University. Alena Witzlack-Makarevich worked with Anna, Giorgio and Balthasar on the Referential Hierarchies in Morphosyntax project (RHIM, 2009–2012). Denis Creissels invited Anna to Lyon.

Together, these colleagues and friends have written the chapters of this book, which discuss some of Anna's favourite topics in linguistics: typological hierarchies, ditransitives and above all, since her seminal 2004 book on the subject, person forms and person marking. I am extremely grateful to these colleagues, who constitute, in my view, the cream of linguistic typologists, and whose names will probably never be found together again as contributors to a single volume. The book also contains the article that Anna and I finished before we left on that fateful journey, as well as a comprehensive bibliography of her work. So she is also very much present here herself.

I am also very grateful to De Gruyter Mouton, and above all to our friends in their linguistics section in Berlin. It was they who suggested the idea for the book and took care of its production, generously contributing to the expenses involved. I would also like to express my gratitude to the boards of both the SLE and the ALT, who immediately agreed to cover the remaining costs, thus making it possible to distribute the book among the linguistic community on an unparalleled scale.

Finally, I am greatly indebted to my co-editor Martin Haspelmath, without whom the book would not have been what I hope it is now. I first met Martin in 1987 when he was still an MA student. This was at the 14th International Congress of Linguists, in what was then East Berlin. It was at the same conference that I first met Anna.

Borders meant little to Anna. She was born in Poland, in Gdynia, but for long periods, she lived and worked in other countries: Australia, the Netherlands and

England. Her real world was that of languages, which cannot be stopped by borders. May this volume find its way to bookshelves and libraries all over the planet, to linguists of all lands, and so help to perpetuate her memory, her work and her dreams.

Dik Bakker

Contents

Preface —— v
Contributors —— xi
Bibliography of Anna Siewierska —— xii

Matthew Baerman and Greville G. Corbett
Person by other means —— 1

Balthasar Bickel, Giorgio Iemmolo, Taras Zakharko,
and Alena Witzlack-Makarevich
Patterns of alignment in verb agreement —— 15

Bernard Comrie
Human themes in Spanish ditransitive constructions —— 37

Denis Creissels
The generic use of the second person singular pronoun in Mandinka —— 53

Sonia Cristofaro
The referential hierarchy: reviewing the evidence in diachronic perspective —— 69

William Croft
Agreement as anaphora, anaphora as coreference —— 95

Volker Gast and Johan van der Auwera
Towards a distributional typology of human impersonal pronouns, based on data from European languages —— 119

Beate Hampe and Christian Lehmann
Partial coreference —— 159

Martin Haspelmath
Argument indexing: a conceptual framework for the syntactic status of bound person forms —— 197

Andrej A. Kibrik
Peculiarities and origins of the Russian referential system —— 227

Andrej L. Malchukov
Alignment preferences in basic and derived ditransitives —— 263

Marianne Mithun
Prosody and independence: free and bound person marking —— 291

Johanna Nichols
The origin and evolution of case-suppletive pronouns: Eurasian evidence —— 313

Anna Siewierska and Dik Bakker
Suppletion in person forms: the role of iconicity and frequency —— 347

Index —— 397

Contributors

Matthew Baerman
University of Surrey
m.baerman@surrey.ac.uk

Dik Bakker
Universities of Amsterdam & Lancaster
d.bakker@uva.nl

Balthasar Bickel
University of Zürich
balthasar.bickel@uzh.ch

Bernard Comrie
Max Planck Institute for Evolutionary Anthropology
comrie@eva.mpg.de

Greville G. Corbett
University of Surrey
g.corbett@surrey.ac.uk

Denis Creissels
University of Lyon
denis.creissels@univ-lyon2.fr

Sonia Cristofaro
University of Pavia
sonia.cristofaro@unipv.it

William Croft
University of New Mexico
wcroft@unm.edu

Volker Gast
University of Jena
volker.gast@uni-jena.de

Beate Hampe
University of Erfurt
beate.hampe@uni-erfurt.de

Martin Haspelmath
Max Planck Institute for Evolutionary Anthropology
haspelmath@eva.mpg.de

Giorgio Iemmolo
University of Zürich
giorgio.iemmolo@uzh.ch

Andrej A. Kibrik
Institute of Linguistics RAN
and Lomonosov Moscow State University
aakibrik@gmail.com

Christian Lehmann
University of Erfurt
christian.lehmann@uni-erfurt.de

Andrej L. Malchukov
Max Planck Institute for Evolutionary Anthropology
andrej_malchukov@eva.mpg.de

Marianne Mithun
University of California, Santa Barbara
mithun@linguistics.ucsb.edu

Johanna Nichols
University of California, Berkeley
johanna@berkeley.edu

Anna Siewierska
University of Lancaster

Johan van der Auwera
University of Antwerp
johan.vanderauwera@ua.ac.be

Alena Witzlack-Makarevich
University of Zürich
witzlack@spw.uzh.ch

Taras Zakharko
University of Zürich
taras.zakharko@uzh.ch

Bibliography of Anna Siewierska

Monographs

Siewierska, Anna. 1980. *The passive: a comparative study*. M.A. Thesis, Monash University.
Siewierska, Anna. 1985. *Word order and word order rules*. Ph.D. dissertation, Monash University.
Siewierska, Anna. 1984. *The passive: a comparative linguistic analysis*. London: Croom Helm.
Siewierska, Anna. 1988. *Word Order Rules*. London: Croom Helm.
Siewierska, Anna. 1991. *Functional Grammar*. London: Routledge.
Siewierska, Anna. 2004. *Person*. Cambridge: Cambridge University Press.
Siewierska, Anna. 2008. *Ren cheng fan chou = Person*. Di 1 ban. (Yu Yan Xue Fan Chou Yan Jiu Cong Shu). Beijing Shi: Beijing da xue chu ban she.

Edited volumes

Lehmann, Christian & Dik Bakker, Östen Dahl & Anna Siewierska (eds.). 1992. EUROTYP Guidelines of the Committee on Computation and Standardization. *Working Papers of the European Science Foundation's EUROTYP Project*.
Siewierska, Anna (ed.). 1997. *Constituent order in the Languages of Europe* (Empirical Approaches to Language Typology/EUROTYP 20-1). Berlin & New York: De Gruyter Mouton.
Siewierska, Anna & Jae Jung Song (eds.). 1998. *Case, grammar and typology: in honor of Barry J. Blake*. (Typological Studies in Language 38) Amsterdam: Benjamins.
Baker, Paul, Andrew Hardie, Tony McEnery & Anna Siewierska (eds.). 2000. *Proceedings of the Third Discourse Anaphora and Reference Resolution Colloquium* (2000). UCREL Technical Papers Volume 12 Special Issue. Department of Linguistics, Lancaster University.
Siewierska, Anna & Hawkins, John A. (eds.). 2003. *Performance principles of word order*. (Working Paper (ESF Eurotype) 2).
Siewierska, Anna & Willem B. Hollmann (eds.). 2007. *Ditransitivity*. Special issue of *Functions of Language*.
Siewierska, Anna (ed.). 2008. *Impersonal constructions in grammatical theory*. Special Issue of *Transactions of the Philological Society*.
Malchukov, Andrej & Anna Siewierska (eds.). 2011. *Impersonal constructions: a cross-linguistic Perspective*. (Studies in Language Companion Series, 124). Amsterdam: Benjamins.

Articles

1983

Siewierska, Anna. 1983. Another theory of the passive that doesn't work. *Linguistics* 21(4). 557–571.

1984

Siewierska, Anna. 1984. Phrasal discontinuity in Polish. *Australian Journal of Linguistics* 4(1). 57–71.
Siewierska, Anna. 1984. Relational Grammar and exceptions to the passive. *Zeszyty Naukowe Wydzialu Humanistycznego Uniwersytetu Gdanskiego* 4. 27–39.

1987

Siewierska, Anna. 1987. Postverbal subject pronouns in Polish in the light of topic continuity and the topic/focus distinction. In Jan Nuyts & Gerard de Schutter (eds.), *Getting the Word into Line: on word order and functional grammar*, 147–161. (Functional Grammar Series 5). Dordrecht: Foris Publications.

1988

Siewierska, Anna. 1988. Postposed subject pronouns in Polish. *Kwartalnik Neofilogiczny* 35(3). 315–330.

Siewierska, Anna. 1988. The passive in Slavic. In Mat Shibatani (ed.), *Passive and Voice*, 243–289. Amsterdam: Benjamins.

Siewierska, Anna. 1988. Automatyczne rozumienie jezyka naturalnego w oparciu o analizy skladniowe (Syntacitic based parsing strategies). *Archiwum Computer Studio Kajkowski* 2. 3–23.

1990

Siewierska, Anna. 1990. Fronting strategies in English. *Zeszyty Naukowe Wydziału Humanistycznego Uniwersytetu Gdańskiego* 9. 9–29.

Siewierska, Anna. 1990. The source of the dative perspective in Polish pseudo-reflexives. In Mike Hannay & Elseline Vesters (eds.), *Working with Functional Grammar: Descriptive and Computational Applications*, 1–14. Dordrecht: Foris Publications.

1991

Bakker, Dik & Anna Siewierska. 1991. A data base system for language typology. *Working Papers of the European Science Foundation's EUROTYP Project* 2(2). 1–42.

Siewierska, A. 1991. An overview of word order in Slavic languages. *Working Papers of the European Science Foundation's EUROTYP Project* 2(1). 66–99.

1992

Siewierska, Anna. 1992. Layers in FG and GB. *Layered Structure and Reference in a Functional Perspective*, 409–432. Amsterdam: John Benjamins.

Siewierska, Anna. 1992 (1993). Pragmatic functions and the pragmatics of word order in FG: the case of Polish. *Proceedings of the international congress of linguists* 15(1). 280–282.

Siewierska, Anna. 1992. Niet-subject-argumenten in Bantu talen: een FG analyse (Non-subject arguments in Bantu: an FG analysis). *Taal en Tekstwetenschap* 10(1). 23–42.

Lehmann, Christian, Dik Bakker, Osten Dahl & Anna Siewierska. 1992. *EUROTYP Guidelines*. Committee on Computations and Standardization. *Working Papers of the European Science Foundation's EUROTYP Project*.

1993

Bakker, Dik & Anna Siewierska. 1993. A contribution to constituent order explanations. *Working Papers of the European Science Foundation's EUROTYP Project* 2(5). 126–144.

Bakker, Dik & Anna Siewierska. 1993. Computerprogramma's voor taaltypologie [Computer programs for language typology]. *Gramma/Taal en Tekstwetenschap* 2. 235–255.

Siewierska, Anna. 1993. On the interplay of factors in the determination of word order. In Joachim Jacobs, Arnim von Stechow, Wolfgang Sternefeld & Theo Vennemann (eds.), *Syntax: An International Handbook of Contemporary Research*, Vol. 1, 826–846. Berlin: Walter de Gruyter.

Siewierska, Anna. 1993. On the ordering of subject agreement and tense affixes. *Working Papers of the European Science Foundation's EUROTYP Project* 2(5). 101–126.
Siewierska, Anna. 1993. Semantic functions and theta-roles: convergences and divergences. *Working Papers in Functional Grammar* 55. Amsterdam: University of Amsterdam.
Siewierska, Anna. 1993. Syntactic weight vs information structure and word order variation in Polish. *Journal of Linguistics* 29(2). 233–265.
Siewierska, Anna. 1993. Subject and object order in written Polish: some statistical data. *Folia Linguistica* 27(1–2). 147–170.

1994

Siewierska, Anna. 1994. The relationship between affix and main clause constituent order. In Brigitta Haftka (ed.), *Was determiniert Vorstellungsvariation? Studien zu einem Interaktionsfeld von Grammatik, Pragmatik und Sprachtypologie*, 63–76. Opladen: Westdeutscher Verlag.
Siewierska, Anna. 1994. Word order and linearization. In R. E. Asher & J. M. Y. Simpson (eds.), *The Encyclopedia of Language and Linguistics*, 4993–4999. Oxford: Pergamon.

1995

Siewierska, Anna. 1995. On the coding of grammatical relations. In P. H. Franses, A. de Klein, J. van Kuppevelt, V. Mamahdou en J. van der Zee (eds.), *Van frictie tot wetenschap: Jaarboek Vereniging van Akademie-onderzoekers*, 107–116. KNAW.

1996

Siewierska, Anna & Dik Bakker. 1996. The distribution of subject and object agreement and word order type. *Studies in Language* 20(1). 115–161.
Siewierska, Anna. 1996. Word order type and alignment type. *Sprachtypologie und Universalienforschung* 49(2). 149–176.

1997

Siewierska, Anna. 1997. The formal realization of case and agreement marking: a functional perspective. In Anne-Marie Simon-Vandenbergen, Kristin Davidse & Dirk Noël (eds.), *Reconnecting language: morphology and syntax in functional perspectives* (Current Issues in Linguistic Theory 154), 181–210. Amsterdam: John Benjamins.
Siewierska, Anna. 1997. Introduction. In Anna Siewierska (ed.), *Constituent order in the Languages of Europe*, 1–18. Berlin & New York: De Gruyter Mouton.
Siewierska, Anna. 1997. Variation in major constituent order: a global and a European perspective. In Anna Siewierska (ed.), *Constituent order in the Languages of Europe*, 475–551. Berlin & New York: De Gruyter Mouton.
Siewierska, Anna & Ludmila Uhlířová. 1997. An overview of word order in Slavic languages. In Anna Siewierska (ed.), *Constituent order in the Languages of Europe*, 105–149. Berlin & New York: De Gruyter Mouton.
Siewierska, Anna, Jan Rijkhoff & Dik Bakker. 1997. Appendix – 12 word order variables in the languages of Europe. In Anna Siewierska (ed.), *Constituent order in the Languages of Europe*, 783–812. Berlin & New York: De Gruyter Mouton.

1998

Siewierska, Anna. 1998. From passive to inverse. In Anna Siewierska & Jae Jung Song (eds.), *Case, grammar and typology: in honor of Barry J. Blake*, 229–246. Amsterdam: Benjamins.

Siewierska, Anna. 1998. Languages with and without objects: the Functional Grammar approach. *Languages in Contrast* 1(2). 173–190.
Siewierska, Anna. 1998. Polish main clause constituent order and FG pragmatic functions. In Mike Hannay & A. Machtelt Bolkestein (eds.), *Functional Grammar and verbal interaction*, 243–266. Amsterdam: Benjamins.
Siewierska, Anna. 1998. Nominal and verbal person marking. *Linguistic Typology* 2(1). 1–53.

1999

Siewierska, Anna. 1999. From anaphoric pronoun to grammatical agreement marker: Why objects don't make it. *Folia Linguistica* 33(1–2). 225–251.
Siewierska, Anna. 1999. Reduced pronominals and argument prominence. In Miriam Butt & Tracy Holloway (eds.), *Proceedings of the LFG 99 Conference*, 119–150. Stanford: CSLI Publications.

2000

Siewierska, Anna. 2000. On the origins of the order of agreement and tense markers. *Historical Linguistics 1995: selected papers from the 12th International Conference on Historical Linguistics, Manchester, August 1995*, vol. General Issues and Non-Germanic Languages, 377–392. (Current Issues in Linguistic Theory 161). Amsterdam: Benjamins.
Siewierska, Anna. 2000. Annotated bibliography of typology. In *Annotated Bibliography of English Studies*. Vol 108. Theoretical Linguistics. Amsterdam: Swets and Zeitlinger.

2001

Siewierska, Anna. 2001. Order correlations between free and bound possessors: perspectives from diachronic change. In Walter Bisang (ed.), *Aspects of typology and universals*, 133–152. (Studia Typologica 1). Berlin: Akademie Verlag.
Siewierska, Anna. 2001. On the argument status of cross-referencing forms. In Maria Jesus Pérez Quintero (ed.), *Challenges and developments in functional grammar* (Revisita Canaria de Estudios Ingleses 4). 215–236.

2002

Bakker, Dik & Anna Siewierska. 2002. Adpositions, the lexicon and expression rules. In Ricardo Mairal Usón & María Jesús Pérez Quintero (eds.), *New perspectives on argument structure in Functional Grammar*, 125–178. Berlin & New York: De Gruyter Mouton.
Siewierska, Anna. 2002. Word order. In Neil J. Smelser & Paul B. Baltes (eds.), *International Encyclopedia of the Social and Behavioral Sciences*: Amsterdam/Lausanne/New York/Oxford/Shannon/Singapore/Tokyo: Elsevier. 16552–16555.

2003

Siewierska, Anna. 2003. Reduced pronominals and argument prominence. In Miriam Butt & Tracy Holloway (eds.), *Nominals: Inside and Out*, 119–150. Stanford: CSLI Publications..
Siewierska, Anna. 2003. Person agreement and the determination of alignment. *Transactions of the Philological Society* 101(2). 339–370.

2004

Bakker, Dik & Anna Siewierska. 2004. Towards a Speaker model of Functional Grammar. In J. Lachlan Mackenzie & Maria de los Angeles (eds.), *A New Architecture for Functional Grammar*, 325–364. Berlin & New York: De Gruyter Mouton.

Hengeveld, Kees & Jan Rijkhoff & Anna Siewierska. 2004. Parts-of-speech systems and word order. *Journal of Linguistics* 40(3). 527–570.
Siewierska, Anna. 2004. On the discourse basis of person agreement. In Tuija Virtanen (ed.), *Approaches to Cognition through Text and Discourse*, 31–46. (Trends in Linguistic Studies and Monographs 147). Berlin & New York: De Gruyter Mouton.

2005

Siewierska, Anna & Dik Bakker. 2005. The agreement cross-reference continuum: Person marking in Functional Grammar. In Casper de Groot & Kees Hengeveld (eds.), *Morphosyntactic expression in Functional Grammar*, 203–248. (Functional Grammar Series 27). Berlin & New York: De Gruyter Mouton.
Siewierska, Anna. 2005. Gender in personal pronouns. In Martin Haspelmath, Matthew S. Dryer, David Gil, & Bernard Comrie (eds.), *World Atlas of Language Structure*, 182–185. Oxford: Oxford University Press.
Siewierska, Anna. 2005. Alignment of verbal person marking. In Martin Haspelmath, Matthew S. Dryer, David Gil, & Bernard Comrie (eds.), *World Atlas of Language Structure*, 406–409. Oxford: Oxford University Press.
Siewierska, Anna. 2005. Verbal person marking. In Martin Haspelmath, Matthew S. Dryer, David Gil, & Bernard Comrie (eds.), *World Atlas of Language Structure*, 414–417. Oxford: Oxford University Press.
Siewierska, Anna. 2005. Third-person zero of verbal person marking. In Martin Haspelmath, Matthew S. Dryer, David Gil, & Bernard Comrie (eds.), *World Atlas of Language Structure*, 418–421. Oxford: Oxford University Press.
Siewierska, Anna. 2005. Order of person agreement markers. In Martin Haspelmath, Matthew S. Dryer, David Gil, & Bernard Comrie (eds.), *World Atlas of Language Structure*, 422–425. Oxford: Oxford University Press.
Siewierska, Anna. 2005. Passive constructions. In Martin Haspelmath, Matthew S. Dryer, David Gil, & Bernard Comrie (eds.), *World Atlas of Language Structure*, 434–437. Oxford: Oxford University Press.

2006

Hollmann, Willem B. & Anna Siewierska. 2006. Corpora and other methods in the study of Lancashire dialect. *Zeitschrift für Anglistik und Amerikanistik* 54(1). 21–34.
Siewierska, Anna & Dik Bakker. 2006. Inclusive and exclusive in free and bound person forms. In Filimonova, Elena (ed.), *Clusivity: Typology and case studies of the inclusive-exclusive distinction*, 149–176. (Typological Studies in Language 63). Amsterdam: Benjamins.
Siewierska, Anna & Dik Bakker. 2006. Bi-directional vs. uni-directional asymmetries in the encoding of semantic distinctions in free and bound person forms. In Terttu Nevalainen, Juhani Klemola & Mikko Laitinen (eds.), *Types of variation: diachronic, dialectal and typological interfaces*, 21–52. (Studies in Language Companion Series, 76) Amsterdam: Benjamins.
Siewierska, Anna. 2006. Word order and linearization. In Keith Brown (ed.), *Encyclopedia of Language and Linguistics*, 13(2). 642–649. Oxford: Elsevier.
Siewierska, Anna. 2006. Linguistic typology: where functionalism and formalism almost meet. In Anna Duszak & Urszula Okulska (eds.), *Bridges and barriers in metalinguistic discourse*, 57–76. Berlin: Peter Lang.

2007

Bakker, Dik & Anna Siewierska. 2007. Another take on the notion Subject. In Mike Hannay & Gerard J. Steen (eds.), *Structural-functional studies in English grammar: in honour of Lachlan Mackenzie*, 141–158. (Studies in Language Companion Series 83). Amsterdam: Benjamins.

Bakker, Dik & Anna Siewierska. 2007. The implementation of grammatical functions in Functional Discourse Grammar. *Alfa – Revista de Linguistica* 52. 269–292.

Hollmann, Willem B. & Anna Siewierska. 2007. A construction grammar account of possessive constructions in Lancashire dialect: some advantages and challenges. *English Language and Linguistics* 11(2). 407–424.

Siewierska, Anna & Dik Bakker. 2007. Bound person forms in ditransitive clauses revisited. *Functions of Language* 14(1). 103–125.

Siewierska, Anna & Willem B. Hollmann. 2007. Introduction. *Functions of Language* 14(1). 1–7.

Siewierska, Anna & Willem B. Hollmann. 2007. Ditransitive clauses in English with special reference to Lancashire dialect. In Mike Hannay & Gerard J. Steen (eds.), *Structural-functional studies in English grammar: in honour of Lachlan Mackenzie*, 85–104. (Studies in Language Companion Series 83). Amsterdam: Benjamins.

2008

Siewierska, Anna. 2008. Ways of impersonalizing: pronominal vs. verbal strategies. In María Ángeles Gómez-González, J. Lachlan Mackenzie & Elsa González Álvarez (eds.), *Current Trends in Contrastive Linguistics*, 27–61. (Studies in Funtional and Structural Linguistics 60). Amsterdam: Benjamins.

Siewierska, Anna. 2008. Introduction: Impersonalization from a subject-centred vs. agent-centred perspective. *Transactions of the Philological Society* 106(2). 1–23.

2009

Siewierska, Anna & Dik Bakker. 2009. Case and alternative strategies: word order and agreement marking. In Andrej Malchukov & Andrew Spencer (eds.), *The Oxford Handbook of Case*, 290–303. Oxford: Oxford University Press.

Bakker, Dik & Anna Siewierska. 2009. Weighing semantic distinctions in person forms. In Johannes Helmbrecht, Yoko Nishina, Yong-Min Shin, Stavros Skopeteas & Elisabeth Verhoeven (eds.), *Form and function in language research: papers in honour of Christian Lehmann*, 25–56. (Trends in Linguistics 210). Berlin & New York: De Gruyter Mouton.

Siewierska, Anna. 2009. Semantics. In Jonathan Culpeper, Francis Katamba, Paul Kerswill, Ruth Wodak, and Tony McEnery (eds.), *English language: description, variation and context*, 186–201. London: Palgrave.

Siewierska, Anna. 2009. Person asymmetries in zero expression and grammatical function. In Franck Floricic (ed.), *Essais de linguistique générale et de typologie linguistique offerts au Professeur Denis Creissels à l'occasion de ses 65 ans*, 425–438. Paris: Presses de L'École Normale Superieure.

2010

Siewierska, Anna, Jiajin Xu & Richard Xiao. 2010. Bang-le yi ge da mang (offered a big helping hand): a corpus study of the splittable compounds in spoken and written Chinese. *Language Sciences* 32(4). 464–487.

Siewierska, Anna. 2010. From third plural to passive: Incipient, emergent and established passives. *Diachronica* 27(1). 73–109.

Siewierska, Anna. 2010. Person forms. In Jae Jung Song (ed.), *The Oxford Handbook of Linguistic Typology*, 322–343. Oxford: Oxford University Press.

Siewierska, Anna. 2011. Implicational universals. In Patrick Colm Hogan (ed.), *The Cambridge Encyclopedia of the Language Sciences*, 279–281. Cambridge: Cambridge University Press.

2011

Hollmann, Willem B. & Anna Siewierska. 2011. The status of frequency, schemas, and identity in Cognitive Sociolinguistics: A case study on definite article reduction. *Cognitive Linguistics* 22(1). 25–54.

Siewierska, Anna & Maria Papastathi. 2011. Third person plurals in the languages of Europe: typological and methodological issues. *Linguistics* 43(2). 575–610.

Siewierska, Anna. 2011. Overlap and complementarity in reference impersonals: Man-constructions vs. third person plural-impersonals in the languages of Europe. In Andrej Malchukov & Anna Siewierska (eds.), *Impersonal Constructions: A Cross-Linguistic Perspective*, 57–90. (Studies in Language Companion Series 124). Amsterdam: Benjamins.

Yan, Yi & Anna Siewierska. 2011. Referential impersonal constructions in Mandarin. In Andrej Malchukov & Anna Siewierska (eds.), *Impersonal Constructions: A Cross-Linguistic Perspective*, 547–580. (Studies in Language Companion Series 124). Amsterdam: Benjamins.

2012

Siewierska, Anna & Dik Bakker. 2012. Three takes on grammatical relations: a view from the languages of Europe and North and Central Asia. In Pirkko Suihkonen & Bernard Comrie (eds.), *Argument structure and grammatical relations: a crosslinguistic typology*, 295–323. (Studies in Language Companion Series 126). Amsterdam: Benjamins.

2013

Siewierska, Anna. 2013. Functional and Cognitive Grammars. In Keith Allan (ed.), *The Oxford Handbook of The History of Linguistics*, 485–502. Oxford: Oxford University Press.

Siewierska, Anna & Dik Bakker. 2013. Passive agents: prototypical vs. canonical passives. In Greville Corbett et al. (eds.), *Canonical morphology and syntax*, 151–189. Oxford: Oxford University Press.

Ponsford, Dan, Willem Hollmann & Anna Siewierska. 2013. Sources of BET. *Functions of Language* 20(1). 90–124.

Siewierska, Anna & Dik Bakker. 2013. Suppletion in person forms: the role of iconicity and frequency. This volume.

Reviews by Anna Siewierska

McCawley, James D. 1989. Adverbs, Vowels and Other Objects of Wonder. *Studies in Language* 11(2). 479–485.

Givón, T. 1992. Syntax. A Functional Typological Introduction. *Forum der Letteren* 33(4). 308–311.

Payne, Doris L. 1992. The Pragmatics of Word Order. Typological Dimensions of Verb Initial Languages. *Journal of Linguistics* 28. 256–260.

Klaiman, M. H. 1993. Grammatical Voice. *Linguistics* 31. 398–401.

Nichols, Johanna. 1994. Linguistic Diversity in Space and Time. *Linguistics* 32. 148–153.

Payne, Doris L. 1995. Pragmatics of Word Order Flexibility. *Journal of Linguistics* 31. 458–463.

É. Kiss, Katalin (ed.). 1998. Discourse Configurational Languages. *Journal of Linguistics* 34(1). 257–261.
McGregor, William B. 2000. Semiotic Grammar. *Functions of Language* 7(1). 168–172.
Haspelmath, Martin, Ekkehard König, Wulf Oesterreicher & Wolfgang Raible (eds.). 2004. Language typology and language universals: an international handbook. *Journal of Linguistics* 40(3). 683–687.
Butler, C. S. 2005. Structure and Function – A Guide to three Major Structural-Functional Theories. 1&2.
Falk, Yehuda N. 2008. Subjects and Universal Grammar. *Journal of Linguistics* 44(1). 530–534.

Reviews of Anna's books

Pinkster, Harm. 1987. Review of The Passive. A Comparative Linguistic Analysis. *Journal of Linguistics* 23(1). 247.
Gebruers, Rudi. 1994. Anna Siewierska on functional grammar. *Functions of Language* 1(1). 129–144.
Blake, Barry. 1999. Constituent order in the languages of Europe. *Journal of Linguistics* 35. 645–650.
Haverkort, Marco. 1999. Constituent order in the languages of Europe. *Studies in Language*. 23(3). 700–709.
Robinson, S. 2000. Case, typology and grammar: In honor of Barry J Blake. *Language* 76(2). 468.
Vogel, Petra Maria. 2001. Case, typology and grammar: In honor of Barry J. Blake. *Studies in Language*. 25(1). 167–173.

Obituaries

Cornillie, Bert, Ruth Wodak & Johan van der Auwera. 2011. In memoriam Anna Siewierska (25 December 1955 – 6 August 2011). *Folia Linguistica* 45(2). 549–554.
Abraham, Werner, Balthasar Bickel, Bernard Comrie & Ekkehard König. 2011. Anna Siewierska (1955–2011). *Studies in Language* 4. 737–738.
Blake, Barry J, Willem Hollmann, Nigel Vincent & Anne Wichmann. 2012. Obituary for Anna Siewierska (1955–2011). *Functions of Language* 19(1). 2–3.

Forthcoming

Siewierska, Anna. (to appear). Passive agents: Canonical vs. Prototypical Passives. In Greville Corbett et al. (eds.), *Towards a Canonical Typology*. Oxford: Oxford University Press.
Siewierska, Anna. (to appear). Semantics. In J. Culpeper, F. Katamba, P. Kerswill, T. McEnery & R. Wodak (eds.). London: Palgrave.
Siewierska, Anna. (to appear). The syntagmatic iconicity of person forms: a comparison across Languages. In W. Kubinski & D. Stachowiak (eds.), *Beyond Philology*.
Siewierska, Anna. (to appear). Historical and universal-typological linguistics. In Linda R. Waugh, John E. Joseph and Monique Monville-Burston (eds.), *Cambridge History of Linguistics*. Cambridge: Cambridge University Press

Matthew Baerman and Greville G. Corbett
Person by other means[1]

1 Introduction

As Anna Siewierska notes (2004: 8) 'the universality of person as a grammatical category is sometimes called into question.' And indeed, in some languages, an interesting minority, it is not obvious whether there is a person feature as part of the morphosyntactic system or not. We find conflicting analyses of individual languages, and there are instances of intriguingly similar systems being analysed differently, because of distinct traditions. Cross-linguistically there is a relatively short list of features which are genuinely morphosyntactic; that is, they are referred to by rules of syntax and by rules of inflectional morphology. Person is often such a feature, being referred to by rules of agreement, and being relevant to verbal inflection. Such morphosyntactic features are to be distinguished from purely morphological features, such as inflectional class, which allow generalizations across lexemes but which are not accessible to rules of syntax. While languages in which person is straightforwardly a morphosyntactic feature are numerous and well-known, we are concerned here with languages where its expression is bound up with that of another feature, namely gender, so that its status is far from certain. We consider several such instances, from different linguistic and geographical areas.

Consider first this paradigm, traditionally laid out, of verb agreement forms from Archi, a Daghestanian language of the Lezgic group.

(1)   Gender-number markers for the verb 'be' in the present tense in Archi (Kibrik et al. 1977a: 55, 63)

GENDER	NUMBER	
	SINGULAR	PLURAL
I (male human)	w-i	b-i
II (female human)	d-i	
III (some animates, all insects, some inanimates)	b-i	Ø-i
IV (some animates, some inanimates, abstracts)	Ø-i	

---

[1] The support of the European Research Council (grant ERC-2008-AdG-230268 MORPHOLOGY) and of the Arts and Humanities Research Council (grant AH/I027193/1 From competing theories to fieldwork) is gratefully acknowledged.

There are four gender values, glossed with the Roman numerals I-IV, with the semantic assignments indicated. For some agreement targets the markers may be prefixal, as in 1), for others infixal, and there are interesting syncretisms. Agreement is always with the absolutive argument but not all verbs show agreement. Here are examples with a verb which has infixal agreement:[2]

(2)   bošor   a<w>χu
      man(I)[SG.ABS] <I.SG>lie.down.PFV
      'the man lay down'

(3)   kɬele   a<b>χu
      man(I)PL.ABS   <I/II.PL> lie.down.PFV
      'the men lay down'   (Marina Chumakina, fieldwork)

Bošor 'man' in (2) above belongs to gender I, and it has a suppletive plural, kɬele. Comparable examples can be given for the other gender values. By and large gender agreement is simply a matter of matching the gender of the controller. The traditional paradigm has no mention of person, and in the singular part of the paradigm, it indeed plays no role, since personal pronouns take the expected gender-number agreement:

(4)   zon   d-irχ:ʷin
      1SG.ABS II.SG-work.IPFV
      'I work' (woman speaking)   (Kibrik et al. 1977b: 117)

In (4) we may label the pronoun as first person singular, but there is no evidence for person on the verb, which is gender II singular. That is, the verb agrees, in gender and number, but shows no evidence of person. The same is found with the second person singular pronoun:

(5)   un   hanžugur   da-qˤa?
      2SG.ABS what.way   II.SG-come.PFV
      'How did you get here?' (to a woman)   (Kibrik et al. 1977b: 121)

---

[2] For examples (2), (3), (6) and (7) we thank Marina Chumakina and our Archi consultants, especially Bulbul Musaeva, Zumzum Magomedova and Dzhalil Samedov.

The third person pronouns, singular and plural, have the expected gender and number agreements (four genders, two numbers). Now consider the first and second person pronouns in the plural:

(6) nen   aχu
    1PL.EXCL.ABS [III/IV.PL]lie.down.PFV
    'We lay down.'

(7) ž^{w}en   aχu
    2PL.ABS   [III/IV.PL]lie.down.PFV
    'You (plural) lay down.'   (Marina Chumakina, fieldwork)

The agreement form is that of the genders III and IV in the plural. Yet the first and second person pronouns are used practically always of humans.[3] This is indeed a curious relation between gender and person. One analysis, that of Kibrik et al. (1977a), treats the pronouns as irregular lexical items; their irregularity is seen in terms of gender. If this were an isolated pattern it might indeed be best to treat it as a lexical peculiarity. But rare though it is, it does turn up in other languages in the world, which suggests that something more systematic is going on. To make comparison clearer, consider the table in (8a) below, in which the paradigm in (1) is reconfigured with person agreement information factored in. Recall that in Archi genders I and II are for nouns with human referents, genders III and IV are for non-humans. In the singular there is only gender agreement (with no indication of person). In the plural, however, first and second person take the same form as the non-human genders. Now compare the Archi paradigm (8a) with one from Ingush (8b). (Archi is from the Daghestanian branch of Nakh-Daghestanian and Ingush from the Nakh branch.) Though the forms and inventory of genders are somewhat different, the pattern is essentially the same, with first and second person plural taking the same agreement form as (one set of) inanimates. (Note that the names that Nichols uses for the non-human genders are simply based on their typical agreement forms in the singular and the plural.)

---

[3] Pronouns may be omitted in Archi, and to date we have no evidence that the pronouns of interest, as in (6) and (7), behave any differently from the others in this respect.

(8) a. Archi 'be.PRS'   b. Ingush 'be.PRS' (Nichols 2011: 143, 431)

	SINGULAR	PLURAL	
I (MASC)	w-i	1	
II (FEM)	d-i	2	ø-i
III	b-i	III	
IV	ø-i	IV	
		I (3 MASC)	b-i
		II (3 FEM)	

	SINGULAR	PLURAL	
MASC	v-y	J/J	j-y
FEM	j-y	1	d-y
J/J		2	
B/B	b-y	B/D	
B/D		D/D	
D/D	d-y	B/B	b-y
3 MASC			
3 FEM			

Now consider the paradigms in (9) below, from much further afield: (9a) is from Tucano (Tucanoan, Columbia), and (9b) is from Krongo (Kadugli, Sudan).[4] Again we find first and second person taking the same agreement form as inanimates, though in these cases it is not restricted to the plural: in Tucano number is not distinguished at all for these values, and in Krongo the plural is not sensitive to gender.

(9) a. Tucano 'do' (West & Welch 2004: 37)   b. Krongo 'saw' (Reh 1985: 186)

	SINGULAR	PLURAL
1		
2	wee-ʔe	
3 NEUT		
3 MASC	wee-mí	wee-má
3 FEM	wee-mó	

	SINGULAR	PLURAL
1		
2	n-àasàlà	
3 NEUT		k-àasàlà
3 MASC	àasàlà	
3 FEM	m-àasàlà	

---

4 Another possible representative of this sort of system is Andoke, a language isolate of Columbia. Witte (1977: 55) gives the paradigm for the word (or part of speech) he terms the *copulative*, in which third person arguments show six gender distinctions. First and second person arguments take the same agreement forms as the third person neuter. However, Landaburu (1979: 112f, 159), who calls this the *assertif*, gives a fuller but at the same time rather different picture. The forms which correspond to those given by Witte are morphologically analyzed as a lexical base plus suffixed demonstrative pronoun, but in addition he gives forms with the first and second person (singular and plural) suffixed too, yielding full person agreement. Unfortunately, none of the examples in Witte's text would involve first or second person agreement anyway, so it is impossible to know what to make of this discrepancy.

It seems clear that both gender and person are involved in the paradigms in (8) and (9), but how can we account for the unusual configuration that they share? If we take the Nakh-Daghestanian examples as a point of departure, this suggests a fundamental asymmetry between gender and person in these paradigms. The inflectional markers are primarily gender markers; indeed, in most of the languages of this family they are EXCLUSIVELY gender markers. From that perspective these paradigms are made up of gender markers whose distribution has been perturbed by values of person. We therefore suggest the following possible interpretation of the interaction of gender and person in the Nakh-Daghestanian, Tucano and Krongo paradigms:

- In each paradigm there are only gender-number forms, but no person forms as such.
- In each paradigm there is a default form, which serves for the neuter (or one of the non-human genders).
- Gender agreement is restricted to third person arguments in part of the system (the plural in Archi) or all of the system.
- First and second person, since they lack gender agreement, take the default form.
- Person marking is thus a by-product of this restriction on the distribution of gender agreement.
- On this interpretation, the patterns in (8) and (9) are a result of gender agreement being restricted to third person arguments. This mirrors the familiar restriction of pronominal gender distinctions to third person (Siewierska 2004: 104–105), which is found in these languages as well, so it appears that this pattern is not entirely arbitrary. On the other hand, it is very rare, so that the mere fact that we may have a ready explanation at hand is not enough to show that the pattern itself is more than an accident. A useful next step, therefore, will be to look at comparative evidence, particularly from the Tucanoan family. This evidence suggests that the proposal, based on the restriction of gender agreement, may be on the right track.

2 Tucanoan evidence

The basic elements of the system described above are found through the whole Tucanoan family, but with numerous subtle and not-so-subtle variants. In some cases these provide further support for the analysis proposal above. In other cases, they caution against an overly facile interpretation of the data. Two key elements of our proposal find support in the Tucanoan languages. First, that a person-based restriction on gender agreement is a distinct notion from person agreement. Second, that the characteristic shape of these paradigms is due to the interplay of forms with gender agreement and an underspecified 'elsewhere' form.

Evidence that we can treat apparent person marking as the surface manifestation of a person-based restriction on gender agreement comes particularly from Orejón (Western Tucanoan, southern branch). Before highlighting the relevant points, it should be noted that Orejón differs from the languages presented so far, in that there are only two genders, masculine and feminine, and nouns which denote inanimates take masculine agreement. With that in mind, consider first the indicative present-future paradigm in (10a) below. This is in effect the two-gender analogue of the Tucano paradigm, with gender agreement in the third person singular, and one form for the rest of the singular. Contrast this with the corresponding interrogative paradigm in (10b). Each paradigm comprises four suffixes which, while not identical (two of the four differ slightly), are clearly morphologically related. But the striking fact is that their distribution is different: while in the indicative the gender-agreeing suffixes are restricted to the third person singular, in the interrogative their range is extended to the second person singular. This can be seen even more clearly in the past tense paradigms (10c,d), which have only three forms each: two gender-agreeing forms, and a single form for the rest. The indicative and interrogative paradigms thus have different configurations of person syncretism, as a consequence, we would contend, of differing restrictions on gender agreement.

(10) Orejón suffixes (Velie & Velie 1981: 123f)

a. indicative present-future

	FEM	MASC
1SG	-yi	-yi
2SG	-yi	-yi
3SG	-ko	-hɨ
PL	-yo	-yo

b. interrogative present-future

	FEM	MASC
1SG	-yi	-yi
2SG	-ko	-kɨ
3SG	-ko	-kɨ
PL	-ye	-ye

c. indicative past

	FEM	MASC
PL	-bɨ	-bɨ
1SG	-bɨ	-bɨ
2SG	-bɨ	-bɨ
3SG	-go	-gɨ

d. interrogative past

	FEM	MASC
PL	-de	-de
1SG	-de	-de
2SG	-go	-gɨ
3SG	-go	-gɨ

Note, however, that the nature of these restrictions is not entirely clear. It is tempting to see them as morphosyntactic, in the way that the restriction on plural agreement to animate arguments, also a characteristic of the Tucanoan languages, surely is. In at least some languages, however, we cannot treat the restriction as morphosyntactic. Consider Tucano again. Many verbal constructions involve a nominal form, termed gerundive in the description. The nominal form marks gender-number using suffixes identical to those found on nouns, as in (11) below.[5] This gerundive forms a periphrastic construction together with an auxiliary verb (the verb 'do' shown above in (9a)). But while the auxiliary displays the apparent person-based restrictions on gender agreement, the gerundive does not. The result is a periphrastic construction, such as that shown in (12) below, whose individual members display different gender agreement patterns. If we treat this as a single agreement domain, then clearly the gender restriction is morphological and not morphosyntactic.

(11)   Tucano nominal forms (West & Welch 2004: 37, 81, 85)

   a. gerundive 'wash'   b. comparable suffixes on nouns

	SINGULAR	PLURAL
MASC	coe-gɨ	coe-rã
FEM	coe-go	
NEUT	coe-ro	

   acaweré-gɨ   'male relative'
   acaweré-go   'female relative'
   acaweré-rã   'relatives'
   acá-ro   'box'

(12)   Tucano present progressive paradigm (gerundive + auxiliary) 'is washing'; the non-agreeing default form of the auxiliary is shown in boldface (West & Welch 2004: 37)

	SINGULAR		PLURAL
1 MASC	coe-gɨ	**wee-ʔe**	
2 MASC			
3 MASC	coe-gɨ	wee-mí	coe-rã wee-má
1 FEM	coe-go	**wee-ʔe**	
2 FEM			
3 FEM	coe-go	wee-mó	
3 NEUT	coe-ro	**wee-ʔe**	

---

[5] The noun system includes a large number of different singular and plural suffixes, but gerundive inflection is limited to this set of four. Note that inanimate count nouns typically have a distinct plural form (e.g. *acá-ri* 'boxes'), but always take singular agreement.

In most other Eastern Tucanoan languages the auxiliary element is suffixed to the nominal form; this means that the morphological unity of the construction is even more apparent, as in the non-past conjectural paradigm of Carapana in (13) below. Note here that the syncretic auxiliary form is simply zero.

(13)   Carapana non-past conjectural 'work' (Metzger 2000: 154)

	SINGULAR	PLURAL
1 MASC	paa-ɨ	paa-rã
2 MASC	paa-ɨ	
3 MASC	paa-ɨ-mi	
1 FEM	paa-o	
2 FEM	paa-o	
3 FEM	paa-o-mo	
3 NEUT	paa-ro	

The second key element of our proposal is that the non-gender-agreeing form should be treated as a default form. This of course is an easy way to explain away forms with an eclectic paradigmatic distribution, but there are some positive indications. First, if there is any zero exponence in the paradigm, it realizes the non-gender-agreeing cells. This was already apparent in (13), and can be more clearly seen in Macuna in (14), also from the Eastern Tucanoan branch, where the first person/second person/third person neuter form has no suffix.

(14)   Macuna present 'fall' (Frank, Smothermon & Smothermon 1995: 48)

	SINGULAR	PLURAL
1	kedia	
2	kedia	
3 NEUT	kedia	
3 MASC	kedia-bĩ	kedia-bã
3 FEM	kedia-bõ	kedia-bã

Still, in spite of what is often assumed, there is no necessary connection between zero exponence and underspecification. Perhaps more telling then is the evidence from Cubeo (Eastern Tucanoan, as is Tucano). In (15) below, consider first the middle paradigm (15b), illustrating the so-called class I unmarked evidential forms. *Class I* and *class II* refer to tense-aspect distinctions whose actual interpretation depends on the lexical class (stative/dynamic) of the verb. The shape of the paradigm is exactly that of the Tucano paradigm shown above in (9a). In Cubeo, there is a suffix -*wɨ* found in the first and second person, and the third person neuter. The other two paradigms (15a) and (15c) have a form -*awĩ*, which is similar to -*wɨ*, and which we speculate is related, though the evidence is uncertain.[6] On the assumption that -*wɨ* and -*awĩ* can be equated, the differences in their distribution are interesting to consider. In the class II paradigm in (15a), the range of this affix is restricted by dedicated suffixes for first person singular and first person plural (exclusive), while in the assumed remote past (15c), this suffix is used throughout. This pattern can be understood if we think of -*wɨ*/-*awĩ* as being unspecified both for person and gender, and so being used as an 'elsewhere' form just in case no more specific suffix has been assigned.

(15) Cubeo (Chacon 2012: 270, 272f)

a. class II tense-aspect

	SINGULAR	PLURAL
1 MASC	-ka-kɨ	-ka-rã
1 FEM	-ka-ko	-ka-rã
2	-awĩ	-awĩ
3 NEUT	-awĩ	-awĩ
3 MASC	-ãbe	-ibã
3 FEM	-ako	-ibã

b. class I tense-aspect

	SINGULAR	PLURAL
1	-wɨ	-wɨ
2	-wɨ	-wɨ
3 NEUT	-wɨ	-wɨ
3 MASC	-bi	-bã
3 FEM	-biko	-bã

c. assumed remote past

-kēbã-awĩ

The Cubeo data also illustrate an additional complication to our account. If we contrast the class II paradigm to the class I paradigm, we see a spreading of gender agreement from the third person to the first person. Superficially we might compare this to the behaviour seen above in the interrogative paradigms in Orejón in (10b), where gender agreement is extended from the third person to the second, but there is an important difference. In Cubeo there is a bona fide first person marker -*ka*, which in turn serves as a host for gender markers, which are in

---

6 Chacon (2012) equates the forms in (15a) and (15c), while Maxwell & Morse (1999: 43f) in their description give the form of the assumed remote past as -*kebã-wɨ*, and explicitly relate its terminal -*wɨ* with that found in (15c), thus equating (15b) and (15c). Combining these views suggests that the idea that there is a diachronic relationship between all three is not implausible.

fact distinct from the gender markers found in the third person. The extension of gender marking to the first person thus seems to depend on the 1st person suffix -*ka*, and is not an independent phenomenon.

Thus, not all variant gender-person configurations in the Tucanoan languages can be attributed to the same factors. A particularly striking deviation is found in the Wanano (Eastern Tucanoan, northern branch) paradigm shown in (16a) below, which is practically the mirror image of the Tucano paradigm in (9a): it has gender agreement ONLY in the first and second person. But judging by the suffixes, this paradigm has a different origin. The Wanano suffixes correspond not to the verbal suffixes of Tucano, but to the nominal gerundive suffixes in (11a) (shown again in 16b)[7], which distinguish gender only, not person. The major differences in Wanano with respect to Tucano are that (i) the suffix -*ro*, which is neuter in many of the other Eastern Tucanonan languages, has been generalized as a gender-neutral third person singular suffix (paralleling the gender-neutral use of -*ro* in the noun system; see Stenzel 2004: 128), and (ii) the plural has a parallel first/second versus third person split, mirroring the contrast in the noun system between the plural suffix for higher animates (-*na*) versus general animate -*a*; see Stenzel (2004: 138).

(16)   a. Wanano 'sell.FUT' (Waltz 1976: 30)   b. Tucano gerundive 'wash'

	SINGULAR	PLURAL
1 MASC	ta-*cɨ*-hca	ta-*na*-hca
2 MASC		
1 FEM	ta-*co*-hca	
2 FEM		
3	ta-*ro*-hca	ta-*a*-hca

	SINGULAR	PLURAL
MASC	coe-*gɨ*	coe-*rã*
FEM	coe-*go*	
NEUT	coe-*ro*	

Both the singular and plural forms of Wanano are of particular interest because they manifest person marking through morphology which originally was unconnected with person distinctions, and they do so through means distinct from that seen in the other examples in this article.

---

[7] The resemblance between Wanano -*co*, -*cɨ* and -*ro* and Tucano -*go*, -*gɨ* and -*ro* is clear. Wanano -*na* and Tucano -*rã* are also likely to be related (Tucano /r/ is actually realized as a nasalized flap in this environment; Welch & West 1967: 16, 20).

3 Comparing the data

The similarity of the patterning cross-linguistically and its correspondence with familiar patterns of pronominal gender distribution could suggest that this phenomenon has extra-morphological motivation. We might look for some sort of syntactic or semantic restriction on gender marking in these languages. However, it is not at all clear what level it would operate on, and the Tucano evidence presented in (12) suggests it is after all morphologically stipulated.

In many of the examples given above the only evidence for morphosyntactic person is the asymmetrical distribution of gender marking. This might be taken as a reason not to posit a person feature at all. This claim has been made specifically for Archi (Kibrik et al. 1977a: 55, 63–64). Let us go back to the Archi paradigm in (1), since the data appear clear-cut and have been discussed in the literature. Archi has no marker that is unique to person; all the markers in (1) are part of the gender-number system, and so the claim in Kibrik et al. (1977a), following Kibrik (1972), appears reasonable. Nevertheless this point of view has been contested; Chumakina, Kibort & Corbett (2007), following Corbett (1991: 127–128, 272) suggest that a morphosyntactic feature person is required for Archi. There are two main arguments. The first is the additional complexity required in the gender system. Kibrik postulates two extra values of the gender feature to allow for the agreement of the first and second person pronouns (these take, as we saw, gender I (masculine) or gender II (feminine) according to the speaker or hearer, and in the plural they take the form of interest here, equivalent to the non-human plural). Since these are combinations of gender across the singular-plural divide which are not otherwise found in the gender system, two additional gender values are required by Kibrik. However, it is possible if unusual for the personal pronouns to be used of non-humans, in which case genders III and IV are found in the singular, which means that there are two further possible featural specifications for the first and second person pronouns. In other words, an analysis which avoids postulating a person feature in Archi proves relatively costly in terms of the gender system. The stronger argument concerns resolution – the rules determining the agreements with conjoined noun phrases. If we treat Archi as having a gender feature but no person feature, the resolution rules need to be complex and are typologically rather strange. They involve ranking the gender values into a hierarchy which has no motivation except to allow the necessary reference to the personal pronouns. If we allow a person feature the resolution rules are straightforward and typologically normal (see Corbett 2012: 239–251 for more detail). Hence, taking these points into account, it is arguable that the Archi forms given in (1) realize a morphosyntactic system which includes a person feature, in addition to gender and number.

There is an interesting comparison in Dargi, another member of the Daghestanian family, as shown in (17).

(17) Akusha Dargi (Daghestanian; van den Berg 1999: 154, 157)[8]

a. 'gender' markers   b. intransitive imperfect endings   c. 'come' (imperfect

SINGULAR	
MASC	w-
FEM	r-
NEUT	d-, ‹r›, -r

PLURAL	
1	
2	d-, ‹r›, -r
NEUT	
3 MASC	b-
3 FEM	

+

1SG	-asi
2SG	-adi
3	-i
1PL	-eħeri
2PL	-adari

→

	FEM	MASC	NEUT
1SG	r-aš-asi	w-aš-asi	
2SG	r-aš-adi	w-aš-adi	
3SG	r-aš-i	w-aš-i	
1PL	d-aš-eħeri		d-aš-i
2PL	d-aš-adari		
3PL	b-aš-i		

If we look just at (17a), the situation is comparable to that in Archi, except that Akusha Dargi has three genders rather than four. We might hesitate to propose a person feature perhaps. On the other hand, the inflections given in (17b) clearly justify a person feature. When the two are found together, as in (17c), it would surely be perverse to have a person feature to account for the distribution of the suffixes but not for that of the prefixes. These data in turn may make us rethink our view of Archi.

There are indeed difficult issues here. If for Archi we accept a morphosyntactic person feature, we have done so in the absence of any unique form. Now non-autonomous *values* of features are well-known. For instance, Zaliznjak (1973: 69–74) discusses values of the case feature which have no unique form, but where excluding a given value would create odd rules of government (verbs would have to govern different cases in the singular and plural). Non-autonomous *features* are a bigger step; and yet the syntax of Archi does appear to require a morphosyntactic feature person, for which the morphology has no unique form.

---

[8] For simplicity we give paradigms for agreement with a single argument. For the complexity of the transitive paradigm, where the two markers behave differently, see van den Berg (1999).

4 Conclusion

An obvious but no less important conclusion is that all of these systems need careful analysis. We should not assume that a person feature comes for free, merely because it is widespread; we should justify its use for each language. Equally the lack of a unique person form should not make us immediately jump to the opposite conclusion.

We have seen instances of a strange pattern, where a default form in the gender system also serves within the person system. The fact that a similar pattern recurs in languages very distant both geographically and genealogically suggests that it is a significant one. There is even a possible explanation for it, based on common patterns found in personal pronouns. And yet when we compare carefully within each family the apparently simple pattern becomes less simple, and the analyses without a person feature become less attractive. The issues are genuinely difficult, since proposing a non-autonomous feature is normally something we would wish to avoid. Thus even on the fringe of the person system there remain some intriguing issues.

Abbreviations

1 first person, 2 second person, 3 third person, ABS absolutive, EXCL exclusive, FEM feminine, IPFV imperfective, MASC masculine, NEUT neuter, PFV perfective, PL plural, PRS present, SG singular.

References

Chacon, Thiago Costa. 2012. *The phonology and morphology of Kubeo: The documentation, theory, and description of an Amazonian language*. Ph.D. Thesis, University of Hawai'i at Mānoa. (http://www.etnolinguistica.org/tese:chacon-2012)

Chumakina, Marina, Anna Kibort & Greville G. Corbett. 2007. Determining a language's feature inventory: Person In Archi. In Peter K. Austin & Andrew Simpson (eds.), *Endangered Languages* (special issue of *Linguistische Berichte*, number 14), 143–172. Hamburg: Helmut Buske.

Corbett, Greville G. 1991. *Gender*. Cambridge: Cambridge University Press.

Corbett, Greville G. 2012. *Features*. Cambridge: Cambridge University Press.

Frank, Paul S., Jeffrey Smothermon & Josephine Smothermon. 1995. *Bosquejo del macuna: Aspectos de la cultura material de los macunas, fonología, gramática*. Bogotá: Associación Instituto Lingüístico de Verano.
(http://www.sil.org/americas/colombia/pubs/abstract.asp?id=928474518998)

Kibrik, Aleksandr E. 1972. O formal′nom vydelenii soglasovatel′nyx klassov v arčinskom jazyke. *Voprosy jazykoznanija* 1. 124–131.

Kibrik, Aleksandr E., S. V. Kodzasov, I. P. Olovjannikova and D. S. Samedov. 1977a. *Opyt strukturnogo opisanija arčinskogo jazyka: I: Leksika, fonetika*. (Publikacii otdelenija strukturnoj i prikladnoj lingvistiki, 11). Moscow: Izdatel'stvo Moskovskogo universiteta.

Kibrik, Aleksandr E., S. V. Kodzasov, I. P. Olovjannikova & D. S. Samedov. 1977b. *Arčinskij jazyk: Teksty i slovari*. (Publikacii otdelenija strukturnoj i prikladnoj lingvistiki, 14). Moscow: Izdatel'stvo Moskovskogo universiteta.

Landaburu, Jon. 1979. *La langue des Andoke (Amazonie colombienne)*. Paris: SELAF.

Maxwell, Michael B. & Nancy L. Morse. 1999. *Gramática del cubeo*. Bogotá: Editorial Alberto Lleras Camargo. (http://www.sil.org/americas/colombia/pubs/abstract.asp?id=928474519056)

Metzger, Ronald G. 2000. *Marĩ yaye mena carapana, yaia yaye mena español macãrĩcã tuti = Carapana-español, diccionario de 1000 palabras*. Bogotá: Editorial Alberta Lleras Camargo. (http://www.sil.org/americas/colombia/pubs/abstract.asp?id=928474518918)

Nichols, Johanna. 2011. *Ingush grammar*. Berkeley: University of California Press. (http://www.escholarship.org/uc/item/3nn7z6w5)

Reh, Mechthild. 1985. *Die Krongo-Sprache (Nìinò Mó-Dì): Beschreibung, Texte, Wörterverzeichnis*. Berlin: Dietrich Reimer Verlag.

Siewierska, Anna. 2004. *Person*. Cambridge: Cambridge University Press.

Stenzel, Kristine Sue. 2004. *A reference grammar of Wanano*. Ph.D. Thesis, University of Colorado. (http://www.etnolinguistica.org/tese:stenzel-2004)

Van den Berg, Helma. 1999. Gender and person agreement in Akusha Dargi. In Greville G. Corbett (ed.) *Agreement* (special issue of *Folia Linguistica* 33(2)). 153–168.

Velie, Daniel & Virginia Velie. 1981. *Vocabulario orejón*. Lima: Ministerio de Educación and Instituto Lingüístico de Verano. (http://www.sil.org/americas/peru/show_work.asp?id=16766)

Waltz, Nathan. 1976. *Hablemos el guanano: Gramática pedagógica guanano-castellano*. Bogotá: Ministerio de Gobierno. (http://www.sil.org/americas/colombia/pubs/abstract.asp?id=928474518795)

Welch, Betty & Birdie West. 1967. Phonemic system of Tucano. In Viola G. Waterhouse (ed.), *Phonemic systems of Colombian languages*, 11–24. Norman: Summer Institute of Linguistics of the University of Oklahoma.

West, Birdie & Betty Welch. 2004. *Gramática pedagógica del tucano*. Bogotá, D.C., Colombia: Fundación para el Desarrollo de los Pueblos Marginados. (http://www.sil.org/americas/colombia/pubs/abstract.asp?id=928474518808)

Witte, Paul. 1977. Functions of the Andoke copulative in discourse and sentence structure. In Robert E. Longacre & Frances Woods (eds.) *Discourse grammar: Studies in indigenous languages of Colombia, Panama, and Ecuador* (part 3), 253–288. Dallas: Summer Institute of Linguistics. (http://www.sil.org/acpub/repository/21893.pdf)

Zaliznjak, Andrej A. 1973. O ponimanii termina 'padež' v lingvističeskix opisanijax. In Andrej A. Zaliznjak (ed.) *Problemy grammatičeskogo modelirovanija*, 53–87. Moscow: Nauka. [Reprinted in: Andrej A. Zaliznjak. 2002. *Russkoe imennoe slovoizmenenie: s priloženiem izbrannyx rabot po sovremennomu russkomu jazyku i obščemu jazykoznaniju*, 613–647. Moscow: Jazyki slavjanskoj kul'tury.]

Balthasar Bickel, Giorgio Iemmolo, Taras Zakharko, and Alena Witzlack-Makarevich
Patterns of alignment in verb agreement[1]

1 Siewierska's Problem

A highly productive inquiry in typology concerns the alignment of argument roles, especially the identical vs. different treatment of the three core roles S, A, and P by the rules of case assignment and agreement marking. With regard to case marking, determining alignment is straightforward: one can simply check which argumental NPs are assigned the same case markers. With regard to agreement, the issue is more complex. Whereas argumental NPs exist independently of case marking, agreement consist of two components: (i) whether or not it exists (i.e. whether certain argument features like person, number of gender, show up at all in the verb morphology), and (ii) if agreement exists, how its markers align roles. In many cases, the answers to these question are still straightforward and one can easily observe that the agreement markers of, e.g., Latin show accusative alignment.

However, when expanding the typological scope, one often runs into what we call here "Siewierska's Problem": argument marking in agreement is often complex and does not allow simple answers. As a matter of fact, the analysis of an agreement system as being primarily ergative, accusative or neutral heavily depends on which criteria one employs. As Siewierska (2003) notes in her seminal article on the determination of the alignment of agreement in ditransitive constructions, in some instances the consideration of different criteria gives rise to conflicting classifications, i.e. the criteria may not converge in identifying a unique alignment type. Siewierska (2003: 342) considers the following four criteria that apply to the determination the alignment of agreement:[2]

---

[1] Earlier versions of this article were presented at the Anna Siewierska Memorial Workshop in Leipzig, April 27, 2012, and at the conference "Syntax of the World's Languages IV" in Dubrovnik, October 1–4, 2012. We thank the audiences for helpful comments and questions. We are also grateful for very useful comments and suggestions on a first drft by Dik Bakker and Martin Haspelmath. Author contributions: B.B., G.I. and A.W.-M. conceived and designed the study and all contributed to the writing. B.B. conducted the statistical analysis. All authors were involved in discussion and interpretation of the results. G.I. and A.W.-M. contributed to data analysis and coded agreement data. T.Z. did most of the data extraction and aggregation work. We thank Lennart Bierkandt and Kevin Bätscher for help in data collection and encoding

[2] A further criterion, not considered by Siewierska (2003), concerns the host(s) of agreement marker(s), i.e. auxiliaries, lexical verbs, etc. We will not consider this criterion here either.

1. *Trigger Potential:* which argument(s) do and which do not trigger agreement marking (i.e. does agreement exist at all)?
2. *Form:* which argument(s) are covered by the markers with the same phonological form?
3. *Position:* which arguments trigger agreement in the same position relative to the verbal stem and/or relative to each other (e.g. pre, post, etc.)?
4. *Conditions:* which arguments trigger agreement under the same condition?

As observed by Siewierska, often these four factors converge in establishing an overall agreement pattern, as, e.g., in German in (1) below, where all the criteria listed above give a consistent alignment pattern. In terms of Trigger Potential, German displays accusative alignment: only S and A trigger agreement. When we take into consideration the Form and Position criteria, we see that they comply with the Trigger Potential characterization: with respect to the Form criterion, the system is consistently accusative, with S and A marked differently from P, since P is never overtly marked in German verb agreement.[3] Likewise, with regard to the Position criterion, we have again S=A≠P, since agreement is realized by means of an overt suffix only for S and A.

(1) German

a. *Ich   schlaf-e.*
   1SG.NOM   sleep-1SG.S/A
   'I sleep.'

b. *Du   schläf-st.*
   2SG.NOM   sleep-2SG.S/A
   'You sleep.'

c. *Er   schläf-t.*
   3SG.M.NOM sleep-3SG.S/A
   'He sleeps.

d. *Ich   seh-e   sie.*
   1sg.nom   see-1SG.S/A 3SG.F.ACC
   'I see her.'

---

3 Here and in the remainder of the paper, we simplify. We only consider default lexical classes and do not discuss deviating valency classes such as experiencer verbs. Also see below on this point.

  e. *Du* *sieh-st* *mich.*
    2SG.NOM see-2SG.S/A 1SG.ACC
    'You see me.'
  f. *Er* *sieh-t* *dich.*
    3SG.M.NOM see-3SG.S/A 2SG.ACC
    'He sees you.'

However, in many other languages these criteria diverge in defining the alignment of agreement, thus giving rise to discrepancies. The situation can be illustrated with English: most English verbs in the present indicative are marked with the suffix -s when the subject is third person singular and are unmarked otherwise, as in (2):

(2) a. *They like sailing.*
  b. *He like-s sailing.*

With respect to the Trigger Potential criterion, the English present indicative agreement system can be characterized as exhibiting accusative alignment. However, when the distribution of zero versus overt agreement markers is taken into account (i.e. the Form criterion), S/A is marked differently from P only in the third person singular, whereas the alignment is neutral (S=A=P) in the rest of the paradigm, as none of the argument roles triggers an overt agreement marker.

More complex discrepancies arise in systems with multiple markers per argument. An illustration of such a system comes from the imperfective agreement paradigm found in Tirmaga (Surmic; Bryant 1999), which has three slots of agreement marking: one prefix and two suffix slots. Table 1 shows the paradigms separately for each of the three roles S, A, and P.

Table 1. Agreement paradigms for S, A, and P in the Tirmaga Imperfective aspect

Person	pf	sf1	sf2	pf	sf1	sf2	pf	sf1	sf2
1s	k-	—	-i	k-	—	-i	—	-aɲ	—
1pi	k-	—	—	k-	—	—	—	-ey	—
1pe	k-	—	-(G)o	k-	—	-(G)o	—	-ey	—
2s	—	—	-i	—	—	-i	—	-aɲ	—
2p	—	—	-(G)o	—	—	-(G)o	—	-oŋ	—
3s	—	—	—	—	—	—	—	—	—
3p	—	—	-(G)ɛ	—	—	-(G)ɛ	—	—	—
		S			A			P	

The application of the criteria to the Tirmaga paradigm provides conflicting evidence on the alignment pattern. When one considers the Trigger Potential criterion, the resulting alignment is neutral, since all the three roles S, A, and P display some kind of agreement marking, at least in part of the system. With regard to the Position criterion, Tirmaga shows accusative alignment, since S and A are marked in the prefix ('pf') slot and in the second suffix ('sf2') slot respectively, as opposed to the markers for P, which occupy the first suffix ('sf1') slot. Under the Form criterion, finally, one considers the phonological shape of individual markers and asks which argument roles are marked by identical vs. distinct markers. The Form criterion does not establish a unique alignment pattern in the Tirmaga paradigm: the prefix position shows accusative alignment in the first person (S and A is marked with *k-* and thus differently from P), whereas other persons have zero exponence which covers all roles alike, thereby constituting neutral alignment. In the first suffix slot non-third person argument is accusatively aligned due to the suffixes *-aɲ, -ey, -oŋ*, whereas the absence of overt markers for the third person arguments establishes neutral alignment. In the final suffix slot, there is again a number of markers (*-i, -(G)o, -(G)ɛ*) which establish the accusative alignment, whereas arguments of those referential categories which have zero exponents for all three argument roles (i.e. the first person plural inclusive and the third person singular) align neutrally. The alignment patterns established on the basis of these three criteria and the observed discrepancies are summarized in (3).

(3) Tirmaga agreement alignment
    a. *Trigger Potential:* S=A=P
    b. *Form:* S=A≠P, S=A=P
    c. *Position:* S=A≠P

With the exception of Siewierska (2003), discrepancies like these have received little attention in the typological literature or in the description of individual languages. This article intends to explore the distribution and influence of such discrepancies in the determination of the alignment in agreement systems, focusing specifically on discrepancies between alignments in terms of Trigger Potentials and alignments in terms of Form. We explore two research questions:

1. How frequent and how strong are these discrepancies cross-linguistically?
2. Do these discrepancies have an impact on our generalizations about the distribution of alignment systems?

We begin by describing the database used for this study and then address these questions in turn.

2 Data, analysis and coding methods

We surveyed 260 languages and coded their agreement systems for alignment patterns as part of the AUTOTYP database of grammatical relations.[4]

Unlike Siewierska (2003), whose focus was on person agreement only, we also considered instances of gender, number and honorificity agreement. To keep our dataset manageable in size, however, we treated gender-differentiating agreement markers as if they were just one marker, i.e. we did not track the difference between for example third person masculine vs. feminine agreement, but simply third person gender agreement. We considered a particular person-number-gender combination as overtly marked if it is overtly marked for at least one gender.

Also departing from Siewierska, we only looked at grammatical agreement in the sense of Bickel & Nichols (2007), i.e. we only coded verbal markers of argument properties that can in principle co-occur with a coreferential noun phrase in the same clause (regardless of whether this co-occurrence is frequent or rare in discourse). Grammatical agreement in this sense corresponds to what Siewierska (2004) treats as the union of syntactic and ambiguous agreement. Cliticized or incorporated pronouns that cannot co-occur with co-referential noun phrases were not analyzed as instances of agreement.

For coding alignments, we considered only the coding of S, A, and P argument roles and excluded arguments of ditransitive verbs from our present purview. S, A, and P are defined by numerical valency and semantic entailment properties of lexical predicates, following earlier proposals of ours (Bickel & Nichols 2009, Bickel et al. 2010, Bickel 2011a, Witzlack-Makarevich 2011). We furthermore limited our attention to lexical predicates that qualify as open, default classes of their language and excluded predicates with non-canonical agreement patterns, other special behavior, or lexical constraints of any kind.

We analyzed the alignment of agreement systems under the two criteria of (i) Trigger Potential, i.e. which argument(s) trigger(s) agreement; and (ii) identity of Morphological Marking, which implies identity of both phonological form and morphological slot.[5] The formulation of the second criterion is similar to Siewierska's Form and Position criteria but departs from her original proposal in so far as we took into consideration individual slots in which given phonological forms appear in the string of morphemes, rather than a binary prefix vs. suffix distinction.

---

[4] The dataset used in this study is available for download at http://www.spw.uzh.ch/autotyp/available.html

[5] An alternative approach would be to take into account just phonological properties, abstracted, if possible, across positions. While possible and interesting, we leave the exploration of this alternative for another occasion.

The two criteria basically equate the Trigger Potential with syntax and Morphological Marking with morphology, allowing us to frame the question in terms of possible discrepancies between how argument roles are aligned in agreement syntax as opposed to agreement morphology. Agreement syntax in this sense refers to whether or not the verb – or more generally, any predicate complex that heads a clause – registers features contained in S, A or P and therefore systematically interacts with these arguments. If a specific argument does not trigger agreement at all (e.g., P arguments in German), this means that the verb does not interact with this argument at all in the syntax. Such questions of verb-argument interaction are fundamental for the organization of syntax, typically requiring specific modeling in formal theories.

This conceptualization of Trigger Potentials and Morphological Marking as two dimensions of agreement does not match traditional grammar, where they are not kept separate. For data like those from Tirmaga in Table 1, one would traditionally focus on the form and position of markers and argue that the paradigms show (mostly) accusative alignment. The fact that all three arguments behave alike in triggering agreement would not be considered an interesting fact. For other languages, however, traditional grammar would focus precisely on triggering behavior and not consider form and position criteria. For German for example, one would traditionally say that only S and A arguments trigger agreement; one would not say that German is accusatively aligned because S and A have overt agreement markers whereas P shows zero markers. Applying different criteria in Tirmaga and in German is typologically inconsistent, as Siewierska has noted.

Furthermore, it is essential to keep apart cases (i) where an argument has a Trigger Potential but the morphology happens to be zero in a specific category (such as third person singular in Tirmaga) and (ii) where an argument never triggers agreement (like German P arguments). In type (i), the grammar of the verb has to check for the presence of specific features in all arguments, and as a result, the verb enters a specific morphosyntactic relationship with all arguments.

The same morphosyntactic relationship does not exist between the verb morphology and arguments that never trigger verb agreement, i.e. in type (ii). In other words, there is a fundamental difference between accusative alignment in a language like Tirmaga and accusative alignment in a language like German, and this difference can only be captured by following Siewierska's innovation and consider Trigger Potentials independently of Morphological Marking.

Trigger Potential is a notion that is uniquely tied to agreement: it is only for agreement that it makes sense to ask whether there exists a specific syntactic relationship between the verb and features of a specific set of arguments. There is no equivalent of this in case assignment: the syntactic relationship that is marked by case exists independently of case assignment, as argumental NPs always bear a syntactic relationship to the predicate since they are assigned a semantic role by it. The relationship is not **established** by the presence of case morphology, and so one would not say that P arguments in, say, Thai bear no syntactic relation to the verb just because there is no case marking. Instead, case morphology can be said to **mark** the existing relationship. As a result of this, the absence of case morphology is equivalent to zero marking and not to the absence of syntactic relationships. Therefore, in contrast to agreement marking, case marking can be fully determined by considering Morphological Marking; the Trigger Potential has no role to play here.

When looking at Morphological Marking in agreement, we considered which roles trigger overt agreement morphology per referential category (i.e. per every person/number combination) in every relevant morphological slot in the predicate. Consider the data in (4) from the Uto-Aztecan language Pipil:

(4) Pipil (Uto-Aztecan; Campbell 1985)

    a. *ni-panu*
       1SG.S/A-pass
       'I pass'

    b. *ni-mits-ita-k*
       1SG.S/A-2SG.P-see-PST
       'I saw you'

    c. *ti-nech-ita-k*
       2SG.S/A-1SG.P-see-PST
       'You saw me'

    d. *panu*
       [3S/A-]pass
       'he passes'

    e. *ki-neki*
       [3S/A-]3SG.P-want
       'he wants it'

    f. *ni-k-neki*
       1SG.S/A-3SG.P-want
       'I want it'

If we consider the morphological realization of agreement in the first prefix slot in Pipil, we observe a S=A≠P alignment for the first person singular: there is *ni-*

'1sS/A' for S in (4a) and for A in (4b), but zero exponence for the first person singular P role in this slot, as (4c) shows; first person singular P is instead marked in the second slot (*-ne* in (4c)). The situation is identical for the first person plural and for the second person. However, when we consider the morphological marking of the third person within the first prefix slot, we observe that three roles behave alike (S=A=P), in that none of them shows up with an overt morphological trace in this slot (be it a dedicated marker or a portemanteau affix, cf. (4d–f)). The markers in the first prefix slot here only register first person (4f)). This is different for the second prefix position, filled by *mits-* in (4b), and *ki-* in (4e) and (4f). Here one obtains S=A≠P alignment, since the markers that appear in this slot encode the P argument, as opposed to S and A, which leave no overt morphological trace in this slot.

The situation is again different in the suffix position. Here we have neutral alignment for singular arguments, since this category never results in overt morphology across all persons. For plural arguments, however, there is an opposition between overt marking of S and A (cf. *-t* in (5a) and (5b)) vs. no marking for P (5c), again across all persons:

(5)   Pipil (Uto-Aztecan; Campbell 1985)

    a.   *panu-t*
        [3S/A-]pass-PL.S/A
        'they pass (S)'

    b.   *tech-ita-ke-t*
        1PL.P-see-PST-PL.S/A
        'they saw us (A)'

    c.   *ni-kin-ita-k*
        1SG.S/A-3PL.P-see-PST[-PL.P]
        'I saw them (P)'

The example of Pipil also shows that alignment can differ across referential categories. In the first prefix we get S=A=P for the third person and S=A≠P elsewhere; in the suffix slot, we get S=A=P in the singular and S=A≠P in the plural. The second prefix slot, by contrast, shows consistent S=A≠P alignment for all referential categories.

In case a language has multiple allomorphs of agreement markers (e.g. conditioned by inflectional classes), we proceeded as follows: morphologically overt allomorphs were encoded as the same marker for the present purposes. If one of the allomorphs has zero exponence, we considered the size and productivity of individual inflectional classes. Only the major pattern of marking – either in terms of the number of inflectional classes or, where the information is available, in terms of the class size – was considered. For instance, for Latvian three conjugation classes with several subclasses are differentiated. Class II (also referred to as "long") and the overwhelming majority of verbs in Class I (called "short") have zero exponence for the second person singular present, whereas the verbs of Class III ("mixed") use the suffix -*i* in this context. As the most productive and numerous class is Class II, the exemplar paradigm selected for Latvian has no overt marker in the second person singular present (cf. Holst 2001, Mathiassen 1997, Nau 1998).

For easy data entry, we only coded overt markers. The distribution and semantics of zero exponents was then automatically inferred with the help of an ancillary database that tracks all referential features that an agreement system is sensitive to. Thus, in the case of the Pipil first prefix slot, zero exponence of S/A agreement for third person forms is not explicitly coded in the database, but it can be inferred from the list of the referential types of Pipil which includes three persons and two numbers. The same holds for the singular arguments in the suffix slot.[6] Since agreement systems sometimes undergo splits conditioned by temporal-aspectual properties of the clause (e.g. past vs. non-past, perfective vs. imperfective) we tracked the effects of these conditions in the database and considered the affected alignment patterns as individual datapoints. We refer to these patterns as constituting agreement 'systems' within a language in the following. The database thus contains a total of 289 systems from 260 languages.

3 Does it make a difference?

There are many languages where the alignment of Trigger Potentials deviates from the alignment of Morphological Marking. The extent of such discrepancies can be quantified by counting how often Morphological Marking shows alignment that is identical to the alignment of the Trigger Potential. In the English present tense, for example, one marker (-s) differs and one marker (zero) is identical with the alignment of the Trigger Potential (which is S=A≠P), resulting in an identical alignment proportion of .5 for this system. The histogram in Figure 1 shows the frequency of identical alignment proportions binned into ten intervals running from [0,.1] to [.9,1]. The rightmost interval consists almost completely of systems with no discrepancy at all (111 systems with an identical

---

[6] All data processing, analysis and visualization was done in R (R Development Core Team 2012), with the added packages lattice (Sarkar 2010) and vcd (Meyer et al. 2009).

alignment proportion of 1, compared to 2 systems with a proportion between .9 and 1); the leftmost interval contains 19 systems with no identical alignment at all and 46 systems with identical alignment proportions greater than 0 and smaller or equal to .1.

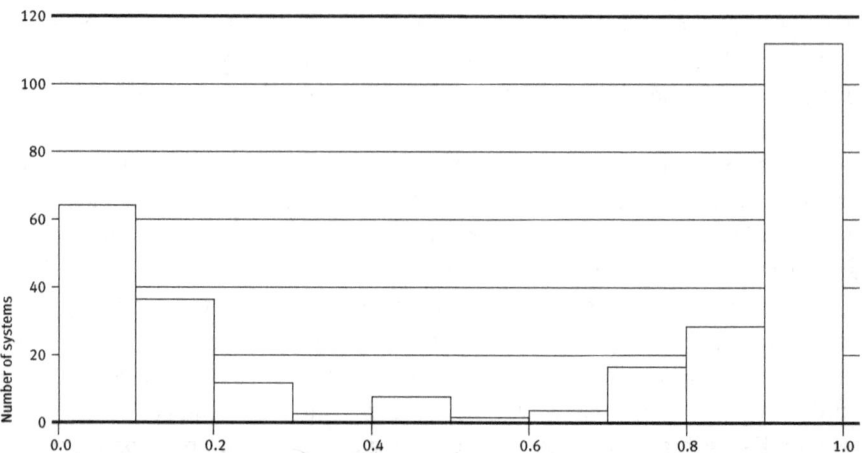

Figure 1. Histogram of the proportions of identical alignment between agreement morphology and trigger potentials in each system (N=289).

In total, almost two thirds ($N = 178$) of the 289 systems in our database show at least some kind of discrepancy between alignments in terms of Trigger Potentials and alignments in terms of Morphological Marking. The histogram furthermore shows that discrepancies tend to be severe: 43% ($N = 125$) show an identical alignment value below (or equal to) .5. These findings suggest that Siewierska's Problem is a serious one. It is imperative that typologies of alignment in agreement be clear on whether they refer to trigger potential or to agreement morphology and apply criteria consistently across languages. The two ways of looking at alignment differ substantially. While this is an important insight with many practical consequences for typology's day-to-day business, the theoretically more pressing question concerns the source and consequences of such discrepancies between syntax and morphology. We take up this issue in the following.

4 Sources of the discrepancies

Two causes of discrepancies are trivial. First, if a referential type, e.g. third person singular, is always zero-marked (i.e. in any role) in a particular slot, its alignment is neutral, while overt markers can be distributed both according to neutral as well as according to any other alignment pattern. Second, tripartite alignment (S≠A≠P) is logically possible only with Morphological Marking. Trigger Potentials can never have this type of alignment: if all roles trigger agreement this leads to neutral (S=A=P) alignment, no matter how diverse the morphological shapes and positions may be; if only a subset triggers agreement, this leads to accusative (S=A≠P), ergative (S=P≠A) or horizontal (S≠A=P) agreement, again regardless of the morphological structure. This situation can be illustrated with the morphology of second person agreement in the Mayan language Ch'orti':

(6)   Ch'orti' (Mayan; Quizar 1994)

   a. *i-wayan.*
      2SG.S-sleep
      'you sleep (s)'

   b. *a-ira-en.*
      2SG.A-see-1SG.P
      'you see me (A)'

   c. *in-ira-et.*
      1SG.A-see-2SG.P
      'I see you (P)'

In the incompletive aspect there are two dedicated markers for the second person singular S (6a) and A arguments (6b). The P argument is not marked with a prefix, but with a suffix instead (6c). Thus, although the individual markers are different for the three argument roles S, A, and P, in terms of Trigger Potential the alignment is neutral, since all three argument roles equally trigger agreement.

Excluding all instances of zero exponence and of tripartite alignment in morphology brings down the proportion of systems with at least one discrepancy to 122 (42%) out of 289 systems (from 178 or 62%, cf. above). These remaining discrepancies are empirical observations, and not logically derivable from how alignment is defined. In other words, it could well be the case that languages would tend to favor similar alignments in the morphology as in the syntax, perhaps in response to iconicity principles. In that case, we would expect, for example, that neutral alignment in the syntax would tend to go together with neutral alignment in the morphology, so that we would find neutral markers in most morphological slots. Systems like this are apparently rare. What comes closest corresponds to what is sometimes called hierarchical agreement. A case in point is agreement prefixes in Plains Cree. Here, categories like second person trigger agreement in all three roles, and these roles receive exactly the same morphological marking (the prefix *ki-*):

(7)   Plains Cree (Algonquian; Dahlstrom 1991)
    a. *ki-pimipahtā-n.*
       2-run-SG.S/A/P
       'you (SG) run (S)'
    b. *ki-pēhtaw-i-n.*
       2-hear-2>1-SG.S/A/P
       'you (SG) hear me (A)'
    c. *ki-pēhtaw-iti-n.*
       2-hear-1>2-SG.S/A/P
       'I hear you (SG) (PL.P)'

But this seems to be very strongly disfavored worldwide and markers tend to differentiate roles, leading thus to discrepancies.

Discrepancies can arise independently in every slot of the agreement morphology and in every referential category: while in Cree, the alignment of the prefix slot is identical to the alignment of the Trigger Potential for the first and second person, the suffixes show various discrepancies. Consider, for example, the distribution of the second person plural suffix *-nāwāw* in one of the suffix slots (suffix slot 5):

(8)   a. *ki-pimipahtā-nāwāw.*
       2-run-2PL
       'you (PL) run (S)'
    b. *ki-wāpam-i-nān.*
       2-hear-2>1-1PL
       'you (PL) see us (A)'
    c. *ki-wāpam-iti-nāwāw.*
       2-hear-1>2-2PL
       'I see you (PL) (P)'

Whereas the S and P arguments of this referential type are marked with *-nāwāw*, as in (8a) and (8c), the A argument of the same referential type is not marked in this slot; instead we find a first person suffix -nān (8b). This results in ergative alignment.[7]

In general, each agreement category in each slot allows for maximally four types of how overt morphology can align roles (S=A=P, S=A≠P, S≠A=P, S=P≠A) if we exclude tripartite alignment (following the reasoning above). Therefore, the range of logically possible opportunities for discrepancies rises with the number of agreement categories and agreement slots. For instance, Jero (Opgenort 2005) has 11 referential categories for the S argument (three person categories, three number categories and an inclusive vs. exclusive distinction in the first person of both dual and plural). Each of the marking of the A argument of these 11 types can be conditioned by the P arguments which again are of these 11 types (e.g. A of the first person singular when acting on the second person singular P, A of the first person singular when acting on the second person plural P, etc.). In the same fashion, the marking of the P argument across all 11 referential types varies with respect to the A argument and its referential types. To calculate alignment we take an S argument of a particular referential type and compare it with the A argument of the same referential type under one of the 11 conditions and with the P argument of the same referential type under one of the 11 conditions (Witzlack-Makarevich 2011, Witzlack-Makarevich et al. 2011). This results in 11^3 alignment statements per agreement slot. Jero has 3 slots relevant for agreement and the number of alignment statements for each of them is theoretically 11^3, that is, $11^3 \times 3 = 3993$ alignment statements in total. The actual number of alignment statements is, however, somewhat lower than this amount of combinatorial possibilities, as particular referential categories or referential category combinations are non-existent or belong to a different (e.g. reflexive) paradigm. Nevertheless, there is still a very large space of opportunity for discrepancies, easily extending into several thousands when there are many categories and a complex system of morphological slots.

Interestingly, languages seem to exploit these possibilities to a substantial extent: Figure 2 plots the proportion of discrepancies, i.e. alignment statements that differ between Morphological Marking and Trigger Potential, per system against the number of category/slot combinations that are distinguished by that system. The data are limited to nontrivial cases of non-identical alignments, i.e. following the reasoning above, we consider here only overt morphology and exclude tripartite alignment.[8] The plot suggests that the opportunity space

---

[7] See Witzlack-Makarevich et al. (2011) on deriving basic alignment types from systems with hierarchical and coargument conditioned systems of alignment.
[8] Note that a language like English counts as having 1 agreement category in the non-past (third person singular), i.e. we counted the number of overtly marked categories, not the number of feature values in oppositions.

for discrepancies becomes heavily, and often fully, exploited with systems that contain more than 6 categories (67% discrepancies with 7 categories in 6 systems, 34% with 8 categories in 17 systems, 88% with 9 categories in 8 systems etc.). Systems with fewer categories tend to show alignments that match the alignment of agreement trigger potentials either completely (displayed in the graph as thin horizontal lines at 0% with systems of 1, 2, 4 or 5 categories) or to a large extent (12.5% discrepancies with 3 categories in 8 systems, 14% with 6 categories in 14 systems).

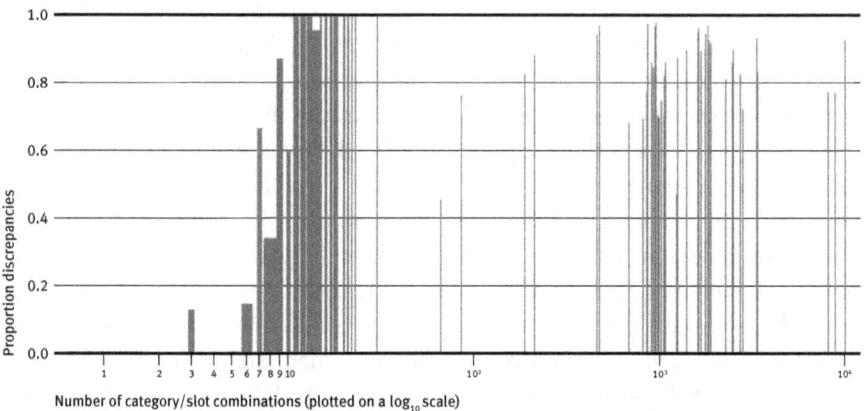

Figure 2. Proportion of alignment discrepancies in overt agreement morphology vs. agreement trigger potentials (y-axis) in correlation with the number of category/slot combinations defined per agreement system (x-axis, plotted on a $\log_{10}$ scale). Barwidth is proportional to the count of systems (from the total of N=289) within each given number of category/slot combinations.

It is not immediately clear why languages exploit the opportunity space for discrepancies so strongly. One possibility is that complex morphological systems may have developed through repeated accretion of freshly grammaticalized markers, each giving rise to new alignment patterns somewhere in the system. For example, if a language develops P agreement based on accusatively-marked pronouns, one expects the morphology to keep the emerging agreement markers separate and in a different position from older agreement markers. The result would be neutral alignment in terms of trigger potentials, but S=A≠P alignment in the morphological structure for this position. This is a plausible scenario and can be observed, for example, throughout Romance. The question whether this is a universally valid scenario, however, must be left for detailed research on the extent to which agreement systems reflect layered grammaticalization of case-marked pronouns. For now, we conclude that richer paradigms lead to more discrepancies and that 7 categories represent the critical threshold for this.

5 Implications for typological generalizations

Another question that arise from our findings concerns the kinds of alignment where discrepancies are concentrated. Table 2 gives an overview of the distribution of alignments types in overt Morphological Marking and among Trigger Potentials, excluding again non-tripartite alignment. The strongest deviation, alone accounting for 51% of the total χ^2-deviation (284.41), comes from the increased proportion of neutral alignments among agreement Trigger Potentials (with 41% as compared to 14% in the morphology). While these discrepancies are not logically necessary, they reflect the widespread pattern in agreement systems illustrated by the Tirmaga, Pipil and Ch'orti' examples above: although there is agreement morphology for all three arguments, the morphology makes distinctions, mostly aligning A with S.

Table 2. Proportion of alignments in overt morphology compared to trigger potentials, excluding tripartite alignment ($N = 289$)

	S=A=P	S=A≠P	S=P≠A	S≠A=P
Morphological Marking	0.14	0.37	0.21	0.28
Trigger Potential	0.41	0.55	0.03	0.01

The flip side of this is a heavily increased proportion of ergative and S≠A=P alignments in Morphological Marking (together 49% vs. 4% in Trigger Potentials). This could potentially challenge the relatively well-established principle that verb agreement is strongly biased against S≠A alignment patterns (e.g. Siewierska 2004). Given the discrepancies we noted above, it is possible that such an anti-ergative bias only holds for relatively simple agreement systems where discrepancies are more limited (cf. Figure 2).

Figure 3 appears to confirm this suspicion since more complex systems (to the right on the graph) indeed tend to have a lower proportion of S=A(=P) alignments, i.e. more S≠A patterns. Decreased S=A(=P) proportions are less common among simpler systems (to the left of the graph), where the only notable exception consists of a few radically ergative systems with one single agreement category (e.g. gender agreement in Nakh-Daghestanian, represented here by 5 systems[9]).

---

[9] The only other cases in our database are ergative agreement in Nias (Austronesian) and in Hurrian, and S-only agreement in Tuvaluan (Austronesian), which results in S≠A=P alignment.

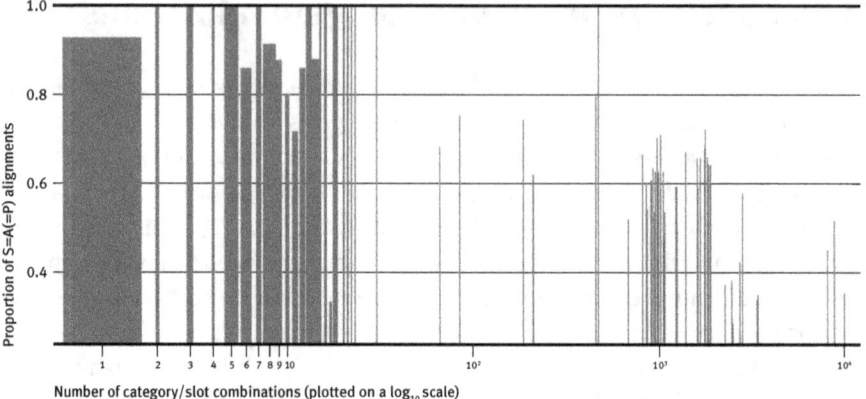

Figure 3. Proportion of S=A(=P) alignments in overt agreement morphology (y-axis) in correlation with the number of category/slot combinations defined per agreement system (x-axis, plotted on a $\log_{10}$ scale). Barwidth is proportional to the count of systems (from the total of N=289) within each given number of category/slot combinations.

However, as shown by the thin bar widths on the righthand side of Figure 3, more complex systems are much rarer than simpler systems (at least in our database, but we believe this to be fairly representative of worldwide distributions). Also, they tend to be concentrated only in a few families: in our database of 289 systems, there are only 4 families (Algonquian, Nilotic, Tacanan and the Kiranti group of Sino-Tibetan) and the family-level isolate Ainu which contain at least one system that is complex in the sense that it contains at least 60 category/slot combinations.[10] When one surveys the proportions of S=A(=P) alignments in these systems (see the Appendix for a complete list), one notices that they hardly ever fall below 50%. This reflects a general trend, also found in families with members showing moderate complexity: Table 3 lists the mean proportions of S=A(=P) (and if applicable, standard deviations) for all families where this mean is below 1. There are only seven further families that have mean proportions of S=A(=P) below or equal 0.5, i.e. families that show a possible trend favoring ergative alignments. Nakh-Daghestanian and Algonquian are the only families in the table where this trend is relatively compact and suggestive of a family-wide feature. The other families in Table 3 with mean proportions below or equal 0.5 either show large standard deviations (Mayan, Macro-Ge) or are represented only by single members (Hurrian, Zuni, Muskogean).

---

[10] 60 is a reasonable threshold for calling a system 'complex' because there is a natural gap in Figure 3 between systems up to 30 and systems with more than 60 categories/slot combinations.

Table 3. Mean proportions μ of S=A(=P) in overt morphology below 1 in families, ordered by proportions. N (cat. comb) shows the range of number of category/slot combinations across all members of the family in our database

Family	N (systems)	N (cat./slot comb.)	μ	std. dev.
Hurrian	1	1	0.00	
Nakh-Daghestanian	5	(1,1)	0.00	0.00
Zuni	1	6	0.00	
Mayan	11	(8, 17)	0.39	0.49
Algonquian	10	(2266, 10047)	0.40	0.09
Macro-Ge	2	(4, 6)	0.50	0.71
Muskogean	1	8	0.50	
Kiranti	29	(457, 1889)	0.63	0.10
Tacanan	1	66	0.68	
Ainu	1	85	0.75	
Sepik	5	(1, 9)	0.80	0.45
Austronesian	16	(1, 14)	0.81	0.40
Nilotic	5	(1, 210)	0.87	0.18
Indo-European	1	(1, 13)	0.95	0.22

This suggests that decreased S=A(=P) proportions are limited to only few families and is hardly ever a dominant trait of entire families. Given this, we expect that paradigm complexity has little impact on the universal trend towards S=A alignment in agreement morphology, i.e. that the correlation noted in Figure 3 only reflects effects in very few languages and systems and is not a robust principle of typology. To test this hypothesis, we applied Bickel's (2011b, in press) Family Bias Method to our data. This method estimates statistical signals for diachronic biases from their expected synchronic results: if S=A alignments outnumber S≠A alignments significantly (under binomial testing) in a family, a change towards S=A alignments in this family was more likely than a change away from it (either because the proto-paradigm(s) showed S=A, which then hardly ever got lost, or because S=A was not there and then it was innovated early or often in the family). If there is no significant synchronic preference, by contrast, no signal can be inferred because, in this case, there was either no diachronic bias towards a particular structure, or the difference in biases was too small to leave a signal, or the family is too young to allow a signal to show up. Using extrapolation methods, signals for diachronic biases can also be estimated for isolates and small families.[11]

---

[11] The method is implemented in and available as an R package (Zakharko & Bickel 2011). We used the method with the default settings of the package.

In order to find out whether paradigm complexity has an effect on diachronic biases towards or against S=A alignments in agreement morphology, families were grouped into simple (between 1 and 5 categories), moderately complex (between 6 and 30 categories or category combinations) and highly complex (above 60 categories or category combinations). The choice of cut-off points is arbitrary but it is based on the fact that 6 categories is the first point (after 1) at which S=A proportions fall below 1.0 in Figure 3 and that, as noted earlier, there is a gap between systems with up to 30 and systems with more than 60 category combinations.[12]

Figure 4 summarizes the results. Almost all families are diachronically biased towards S=A(=P) alignments in their agreement morphology, and this preference is observed to a comparable extent across degrees of paradigm complexity.[13] The summary figure also includes the results of a separate analysis of diachronic biases in trigger potentials (rightmost bar), and the preference for S=A(=P) alignment is in the same ballpark here as well. We can conclude that agreement systems strongly prefer S=A(=P) alignments in both Morphological Marking and Trigger Potential. Deviations from this are limited to a few groups and languages with high (such as Algonquian) and moderate complexity (such as Mayan).

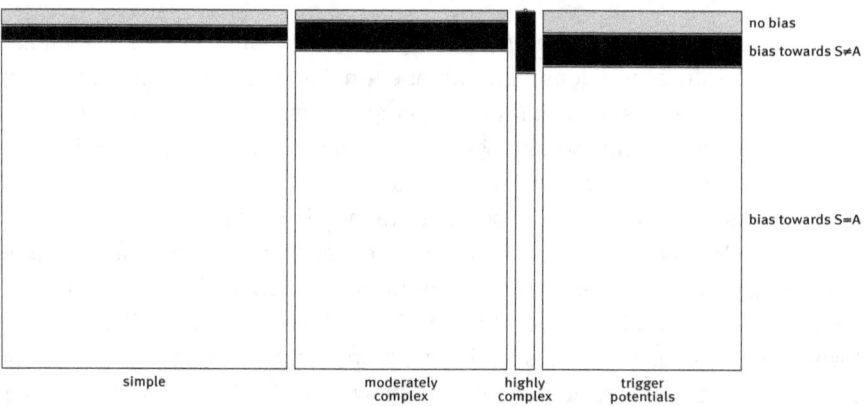

Figure 4. Proportion of estimated diachronic family biases towards S=A(=P) vs. S≠A alignments in Morphological Marking across different degrees of paradigm complexity, and among agreement Trigger Potentials. Tile sizes are proportional to frequencies (Meyer et al. 2009); a small circle indicates zero counts.

---

12 When families were diverse with regard to these categories of complexity (e.g. Indo-European or Austronesian, cf. the range of category counts in Table 3), we split the family into smaller groups that fell consistently into one or the other group. Whenever possible, such groups were based on known genealogical subgroups, as defined in Nichols & Bickel (2009).
13 A likehood ratio χ^2 test comparing a loglinear model with vs. without an interaction between bias direction x complexity type suggests independence: $\chi^2_\Delta = 2.29$, $df = 2$, $p = .32$.

6 Conclusion

Siewierska (2003) raised an important issue for typologies of alignment. Looking at alignment patterns in agreement systems in terms of the type of roles that can trigger agreement in the syntax (i.e. Trigger Potential) leads to very different characterizations than when one examines alignment patterns for specific agreement markers in specific morphological positions (i.e. Morphological Marking). Discrepancies are in fact severe, and it is imperative that typology carefully distinguish between different notions of alignment in agreement systems. Some of the sources of these discrepancies are trivial and have to do with the logic of determining alignments. However, we also observed (Section 4) that a substantial proportion of discrepancies is empirical in nature: agreement morphology could in principle be more in line with agreement syntax. At present it is not clear to us why morphological systems should exploit the possibility for discrepancies as strongly as they do, but we suspect that this has to do with the complex histories of grammaticalizing layer after layer in agreement systems. Such a scenario would explain why discrepancies become stronger the more complex paradigms are in terms of the number of referential categories and category combinations they are sensitive to.

While the study of discrepancies that Siewierska called for gives new insights into possible historical scenarios on how alignment patterns have developed in agreement systems, it could in principle challenge received universal principles on preferred alignments in such systems. As we showed in Section 5, however, confounding effects are severely limited: there are only very few language families in the world where there seems to have been a bias away from S=A and towards S≠A alignments, and this is true regardless of whether one looks at agreement syntax or agreement morphology. There is a slight preference for S≠A alignments in more complex paradigms, but it is only in a handful of language families that this is a significant and diachronically relevant trend (e.g. in Algonquian). In all other families, there is a very strong overall bias towards S=A, even when paradigms are exceedingly complex, as, for instance, in Kiranti.

Abbreviations

1 first person, 2 second person, 3 third person, ACC accusative, F feminine, IND indicative, INDEP independent indicative, M masculine, NOM nominative, NSNPST non-simple non-past, PRS present, PST past, PL plural, SG singular, SNPST simple non-past.

Appendix

Proportion of S=A(=P) in overt morphology and number of category/slot combinations per system in families where at least one system has more than 60 combinations

Family	Language	System	Pr(S=A)	N (category/slot comb.)
Ainu	Ainu		0.753	85
Algonquian	Arapaho	INDEP	0.287	2495
Algonquian	Atikamekw	INDEP.NPST	0.450	8117
Algonquian	Blackfoot	INDEP	0.578	2817
Algonquian	Cheyenne	INDEP.PRS.IND	0.338	3354
Algonquian	Cree (Plains)	INDEP	0.517	8845
Algonquian	Menomini	INDEP	0.372	2266
Algonquian	Micmac	INDEP.IND	0.353	10047
Algonquian	Munsee	INDEP.NPST	0.381	2467
Algonquian	Ojibwa (Eastern)	INDEP.PRS	0.350	3391
Algonquian	Passamaquoddy	INDEP.PRS	0.421	2726
Kiranti	Athpare	IND	0.676	1761
Kiranti	Bahing	NPST.IND	0.626	951
Kiranti	Bahing	PST.IND	0.540	859
Kiranti	Bantawa	IND	0.589	1621
Kiranti	Belhare	IND	0.721	1772
Kiranti	Camling	IND	0.503	1247
Kiranti	Chintang	NPST.IND	0.658	1822
Kiranti	Dumi	NPST.IND	0.479	1057
Kiranti	Hayu	NPST.IND	0.519	682
Kiranti	Hayu	PST.IND	0.665	811
Kiranti	Jero	IND	0.536	941
Kiranti	Koyi	NPST.IND	0.602	850
Kiranti	Koyi	PST.IND	0.605	901
Kiranti	Kulung	NPST.IND	0.633	922
Kiranti	Kulung	PST.IND	0.606	903
Kiranti	Kõic	NPST.IND	1.000	471
Kiranti	Kõic	PST.IND	0.794	457
Kiranti	Limbu	NPST.IND	0.640	1889
Kiranti	Limbu	PST.IND	0.642	1847
Kiranti	Lohorung	NPST.IND	0.592	1238
Kiranti	Lohorung	PST.IND	0.592	1238
Kiranti	Old Thulung (Mukli)	NPST.IND	0.626	1052
Kiranti	Old Thulung (Mukli)	PST.IND	0.625	989
Kiranti	Puma	NPST.IND	0.656	1668

Family	Language	System	Pr(S=A)	N (category/slot comb.)
Kiranti	Thulung (Mukli)	NPST	0.708	1016
Kiranti	Thulung (Mukli)	PST	0.701	973
Kiranti	Wambule	IND	0.535	1071
Kiranti	Yakkha	IND	0.656	1606
Kiranti	Yamphu	IND	0.670	1391
Nilotic	Nandi	NSNPST	1.000	10
Nilotic	Nandi	SNPST	1.000	8
Nilotic	Teso		0.742	186
Nilotic	Turkana		0.619	210
Tacanan	Reyesano		0.682	66

References

Bickel, Balthasar. 2011a. Grammatical relations typology. In Jae Jung Song (ed.), *The Oxford Handbook of Language Typology*, Oxford: Oxford University Press.

Bickel, Balthasar. 2011b. Statistical modeling of language universals. *Linguistic Typology* 15. 401–414.

Bickel, Balthasar. in press. Distributional biases in language families. In Balthasar Bickel, Lenore A. Grenoble, David A. Peterson & Alan Timberlake (eds.), *Language typology and historical contingency: studies in honor of Johanna Nichols*, Amsterdam: Benjamins (pre-print available at http://www.spw.uzh.ch/bickel-files/papers/stability.fsjn.2011 bickelrevised.pdf).

Bickel, Balthasar & Johanna Nichols. 2007. Inflectional morphology. In Timothy Shopen (ed.), *Language typology and syntactic description*, 169–240. Cambridge: Cambridge University Press (Revised second edition).

Bickel, Balthasar & Johanna Nichols. 2009. Case marking and alignment. In Andrej Malchukov & Andrew Spencer (eds.), *The Oxford Handbook of Case*, 304–321. Oxford: Oxford University Press.

Bickel, Balthasar, Manoj Rai, Netra Paudyal, Goma Banjade, Toya Nath Bhatta, Martin Gaenszle, Elena Lieven, Iccha Purna Rai, Novel K. Rai & Sabine Stoll. 2010. Ditransitives and three-argument verbs in Chintang and Belhare (Southeastern Kiranti). In Andrej Malchukov, Martin Haspelmath & Bernard Comrie (eds.), *Studies in Ditransitive Constructions. A Comparative Handbook*, 382–408. Berlin & New York: De Gruyter Mouton.

Bryant, Michael Grayson. 1999. *Aspects of Tirmaga grammar*. University of Texas at Arlington dissertation.

Campbell, Lyle. 1985. *The Pipil language of El Salvador*. Berlin & New York: De Gruyter Mouton.

Dahlstrom, Amy. 1991. *Plains Cree Morphosyntax*. Garland Publishing.

Holst, Jan Henrik. 2001. *Lettische Grammatik*. Hamburg: Helmut Buske Verlag.

Mathiassen, Terje. 1997. *A Short Grammar of Latvian*. Columbus, Ohio: Slavica Publishers.

Meyer, David, Achim Zeileis & Kurt Hornik. 2009. vcd: visualizing categorical data. R package (http://www.R-project.org).

Nau, Nicole. 1998. *Latvian*, vol. 217 Languages of the World/Materials. München: Lincom Europa.
Nichols, Johanna & Balthasar Bickel. 2009. The AUTOTYP genealogy and geography database: 2009 release. Electronic database, http://www.uzh.ch/spw/autotyp.
Opgenort, J. R. 2005. *A Grammar of Jero*, vol. 5/3 Brill's Tibetan Studies Library: Languages of the Greater Himalayn Region. Leiden: E. J. Brill.
Quizar, Robin. 1994. Motion verbs in Ch'orti'. *Función* 15–16.
R Development Core Team. 2012. *R: a language and environment for statistical computing*. Vienna: R Foundation for Statistical Computing, http://www.r-project.org.
Sarkar, Deepayan. 2010. lattice: Lattice Graphics. R package version 0.18-8. http://CRAN.R-project.org/package=lattice.
Siewierska, Anna. 2003. Person agreement and the determination of alignment. *Transactions of the Philological Society* 101. 339–370.
Siewierska, Anna. 2004. *Person*. Cambridge: Cambridge University Press.
Witzlack-Makarevich, Alena. 2011. Typological variations in grammatical Relations. University of Leipzig dissertation.
Witzlack-Makarevich, Alena, Lennart Bierkandt, Taras Zakharko & Balthasar Bickel. 2011. Decomposing hierarchical alignment: participant scenarios as conditions on alignment. 44th Annual Meeting of the Societas Linguistica Europaea, Logroño, September 8.
Zakharko, Taras & Balthasar Bickel. 2011. familybias: Family bias estimation. R package, http://www.spw.uzh.ch/software.html.

Bernard Comrie
Human themes in Spanish ditransitive constructions

1 Basic principles of flagging and indexing of objects in Spanish[1]

In order to discuss the various kinds of objects that can occur with monotransitive and ditransitive verbs in Spanish, I use the terminology of (1), in particular the "abbreviations" P, R, and T.

(1) P patient-like argument of a monotransitive verb
     R recipient-like argument of a ditransitive verb
     T theme-like argument of a ditransitive verb

In Spanish, the flagging (case marking, including by means of prepositions) and indexing (representation in the morphosyntactic structure of the verb) of full noun phrases in these three grammatical relations is complex. Starting with P, we can establish a general rule as in (2).

(2) A full noun phrase P may appear with or without the preposition *a* 'to' (Differential Object Marking); the preposition *a* is used if P is both human and referential ("personal *a*").

The statement on the occurrence of personal *a* in (2) is an oversimplification, for instance in that personal *a* may be found with some non-human animates and even under certain circumstances with inanimates, and there are idiosyncrasies with regard to referentiality (e.g. the quintessentially non-referential pronoun *nadie* 'no one' requires personal *a*), but it will suffice for present purposes; a fuller account in English can be found in most larger reference grammars of Spanish, e.g. Butt and Benjamin (1995: 312–318). In examples (3) and (4), the P is

---

[1] Different versions of the present article have been presented to various audiences, including in Spanish-speaking countries. I am grateful to all those who provided comments and native-speaker judgments, and also to Concepción Company Company and Rosa María Ortiz Ciscomani for material they made available to me.

inanimate, and therefore does not take personal *a*, whether referential (as in (3)) or not (as in (4)).

(3) *Busco   el   libro.*
    seek.1SG the   book
    'I am seeking the book.'

(4) *Busco   libros.*
    seek.1SG books
    'I am seeking books.'

In (5) and (6), the P is human; in (5), it is also referential, and therefore takes personal *a*, while in (6) it is non-referential, and does not take personal *a*.

(5) *Busco   a-l   médico.*
    seek.1SG   to-the   doctor
    'I am seeking the doctor.'

(6) *Busco   médicos.*
    seek.1SG   doctors
    'I am seeking doctors.'

In the varieties of Spanish examined here, P is never indexed in the verb (for instance, through doubling by means of a clitic pronoun), except in cases of dislocation, where the noun or prepositional phrase is no longer part of the basic clause structure.[2]

The rule for flagging R in a ditransitive construction can straightforwardly be stated as in (7).

(7) R always requires the preposition *a*.

Note that this applies both to referential Rs as in (8) and to non-referential Rs as in (9).

(8) *Dieron   libros   a   sus   vecinos.*
    gave.3PL   books   to   their   neighbors
    'They gave books to their neighbors.'

---

[2] Especially in Southern Cone (of South America) varieties of Spanish, such as that of Buenos Aires, a P flagged with personal *a* may be resumed by a clitic pronoun in the verb structure, e.g. *lo vi a Juan* 'I saw John'. Such varieties are not represented in the corpus for this article.

(9) *Dieron libros a vecinos.*
 gave.3PL books to neighbors
 'They gave books to neighbors.'

It is usual, however, for R to be doubled by means of a dative clitic pronoun. Examples like (8)–(9) are judged to be unnatural, or at least bookish, in many varieties of Spanish. The artificial example (9) was in fact extracted from the naturally occurring example (10), which does include the dative clitic pronoun *les* 'to them'.

(10) *Les dieron libros a vecinos que terminan sus estudios.*
 CLIT.DAT.3PL gave.3PL books to neighbors REL finish-3PL their studies
 'They gave books to neighbors who are finishing their studies.'
 http://www.launion.com.ar/?p=61116, dated 2011 Sep 22, consulted 2012 Apr 06

Incidentally, this provides a reasonably robust test to distinguish between R and directional complements, the latter also being flagged with the preposition *a* but not triggering clitic doubling; compare (11) with the R *Ana* and (12) with the directional complement *México*.

(11) *Le envié la carta a Ana.*
 CLIT.DAT.3SG sent.1SG the letter to Ana
 'I sent the letter to Ana.'

(12) *Envié la carta a México.*
 sent.1SG the letter to Mexico
 'I sent the letter to Mexico.'

The flagging of non-human Ts in ditransitive constructions is straightforward, as can be seen in (8)–(12): just like Ps in monotransitive constructions, they receive no overt flagging. I return to the treatment of human Ts in section 2.

So far, I have restricted myself to the flagging and indexing of full noun phrases. Object pronouns in Spanish are normally clitic, being attached to the verb. In the third person non-reflexive, Spanish distinguishes accusative (for P and T) and dative (for R) clitic pronouns, while in the first and second persons and in the reflexive no such distinction is made, as seen in (13).

(13) Spanish clitic pronouns

	ACC	DAT
1SG		me
2SG		te
1PL		nos
2PL		os
3REFL		se
3SG.M	lo	le
3SG.F	la	le
3PL.M	los	les
3PL.F	las	les

A number of comments are in order with reference to (13).

First, the second person forms given in (13) are familiar. Morphologically third person forms serve as polite forms referring to the addressee, and thus distinguish accusative from dative. In Latin America, the morphologically third person forms given in (13) are the only forms to refer to a plural addressee, and the second person plural form *os* is not used. In earlier periods of the language, the morphologically second person plural clitic *os* was also used as a polite singular, and this usage is still found in order to stylize dialogue of the period, as in (31) and (33) below.

Second, some varieties of Spanish neutralize or at least partially neutralize the distinction between accusative and dative third person pronouns, for instance using *le* as the accusative with human Ps. However, none of the varieties comprising the corpus for the present study is of this type (except perhaps for occasional examples that do not affect the crucial points to be made). In varieties that do have this neutralization, which removes one of the criteria for keeping T and R apart in ditransitive constructions, one might well expect there to be some differences in possible combinations of flagging and/or indexing for human R and T, but this falls outside of the scope of this article.

Third, when both R and T are third person clitic pronouns, the R is expressed as *se*, as in (14). Historically at least, the basic use of *se* is as a third person reflexive pronoun, and the use of *se* to replace other third person dative clitic pronouns is often referred to as "spurious *se*". Note, however, that in an example like (14) *se* can also be interpreted as reflexive (coreferential with the subject).

(14) *Se los dieron.*
3REFL CLIT.ACC.3PLM gave.3PL
'They gave them [sc. the books] to him/her/them/themselves.'

Fourth, there are heavy constraints on the expression of T by means of first or second person clitic pronouns (cf. Haspelmath 2004, including a cross-linguistic perspective), and no examples occur in my corpus. This means that the effective combinations of dative and accusative clitics are dative *me, te, nos, os,* and *se* (the latter with reflexive and non-reflexive interpretations) and accusative *lo, la, los,* and *las*. The order in these combinations is always dative before accusative.

2 The treatment of human themes

Spanish in most respects has indirective alignment of ditransitive constructions, for instance in that the T of the ditransitive construction takes the same set of accusative clitic pronouns as the P of a monotransitive construction, distinct from the dative set of clitic pronouns used for R of the ditransitive construction, and in that only P and T but not R can appear as the subject of a corresponding passive. This neat alignment pattern is complicated by the behavior of full noun phrase Ps, which, as shown in (3)–(6) above, sometimes take the preposition *a* (like R) and sometimes do not. It is time to consider the behavior of T. In the examples given so far of ditransitive constructions, a full noun phrase T has not been marked with the preposition *a*, but all Ts so far have been inanimate, so absence of *a* is expected.

We may now turn to the vexed question of human, more specifically referential human Ts in Spanish ditransitive constructions, i.e. the translation equivalents of sentences like *King Charles of France gives his daughter Gisela in marriage to Duke Rollo of Normandy*. There is clearly a potential problem, since if both T and R are full noun phrases in a ditransitive construction, both might be expected to be flagged with personal *a*, leading to possible confusion of two objects, T and R, flagged overtly and identically. On the other hand, omitting personal *a* on a human referential T might not be considered an ideal solution, given that occurrence of personal *a* is obligatory for human referential Ps and the general indirective alignment of Spanish ditransitive constructions.

It is often said in grammatical descriptions of Spanish that in such cases, where both T and R of the same verb would be expected to be flagged with *a*, then the *a* should at least preferentially simply be omitted from the T (e.g. Butt and Benjamin 1995: 315), and somewhat embarrassingly for me as one of the co-authors Malchukov et al (2010: 7–8) reiterate this description: "the T is normally not marked by *a* (in the presence of an R marked by *a*), even in the unusual case when T is animate". As we will see, this claim is incorrect. This is sometimes even taken further by claiming that T is never flagged with personal *a* in ditransitive constructions, which would mean that Spanish has alignment as in (15) below, so-called active or split P alignment (Siewierska 2003: 348–355), whereby some Ps (P_T, those without personal *a*) and all Ts are flagged alike, while other Ps (P_R, those with personal *a*) and all Rs are flagged alike.[3]

(15)   T   R
        P_T P_R

Elicitation turns out not to be particularly helpful or reliable in finding out what the state of affairs actually is in Spanish ditransitive constructions with human Ts. I have encountered native speakers of Spanish who readily accept examples where both T and R are flagged with personal *a* (and who have wondered aloud how else one could express this idea) and native speakers who have vehemently denied that such combinations are possible. Moreover, there seems to be no clear regional or other correlation with these different judgments. In other words, one is confronted by precisely the kind of situation where an analysis of actual usage is a must whatever methodological principles one might otherwise adhere to. But before turning to the corpus analysis, a couple of other points are worth mentioning.

First, there is absolutely no constraint against combining a P flagged with personal *a* and a directional complement flagged with *a*, as in (16).

(16) *Envié   a   mi hermana a   Caracas.*
      sent.1SG to my sister   to Caracas
      'I sent my sister to Caracas.'

Second, there are of course previous studies on the subject of human Ts in ditransitive constructions, with perhaps the most influential, including outside the Spanish-speaking world, being those by Company (1998, 2001, 2003). Company gives (17), where the T, though human and referential, lacks personal *a* as fully acceptable, but (18), with personal *a*, as less acceptable.[4]

---

3 Although I will be arguing that Spanish does not, at least not straightforwardly, illustrate split P alignment in its ditransitive construction, this in no way detracts from the clear recognition of this alignment pattern as a typological possibility in Siewierska's work. Moreover, the detailed corpus analysis of English dialect ditransitive constructions in Siewierska and Hollmann (2007) was a model for the present study. Note that Siewierska illustrates split P alignment exclusively with examples where the choice between P_T and P_R depends on the lexical verb selected; the extension to cases where the determining factor is the nature of the P is mine.

4 The judgment "??/*" comes from Company (1998: 553), while Company (2001: 20) marks the same example as "??". The absolute judgment is perhaps less important than the relative judgment that (18) is judged considerably less acceptable than (17). In these articles, Company cites examples of other changes (e.g. common versus proper noun) that can modify the acceptability judgments.

(17) El   maestro presentó   su   mujer a   los alumnos.
    the   teacher presented.3SG   his wife   to the students
    'The teacher presented his wife to the students.'

(18) ??/*El maestro presentó   a su   mujer a   los alumnos.
    the   teacher presented.3SG   to his wife   to the students
    'The teacher presented his wife to the students.'

These judgments are often presented (e.g. by Malchukov et al 2010: 7–8) as evidence in favor of split P alignment. However, Company's judgments are considerably more differentiated. Thus, she presents (19) as fully acceptable, although it combines both T and R flagged by personal *a*; the only difference between (19) and (18) is that (19) has R doubled by a dative clitic pronoun, which as was noted in section 1 is normal practice in most varieties of Spanish.

(19) El   maestro les   presentó   a su   mujer a   los alumnos.
    the teacher CLIT.DAT.3PL   presented.3SG   to his wife   to the students
    'The teacher presented his wife to the students.'

In order to try and advance our understanding of the flagging of human Ts in Spanish, I noted down examples encountered in my leisure reading of Spanish. Relevant examples were found in the works listed in (20) below, plus a couple of examples that happened to catch my eye, appearing on the title page and first inside page of the popular Peruvian magazine *¡Hola! Perú* (No. 40, 2011), which I did not otherwise read. With the exception of the magazine, all are works of fiction, with Falcones (2006) and Parra (2008) being historical novels dealing respectively with medieval Catalonia and nineteenth-century Mexico. The total number of pages, including also works that I read during the same period which did not furnish any examples, is probably around 2000 printed pages.

(20)   Falcones, Ildefonso: *La catedral del mar* (2006), Spain (Catalonia)
       Parra, Eduardo Antonio: *Juárez, el rostro de piedra* (2008), Mexico
       Rulfo, Juan: *El llano en llamas* (1953), Mexico
       Vargas Llosa, Mario: *Los jefes* (1959), Peru
       Vargas Llosa, Mario: *El hablador* (1987), Peru

My methodology was a simple one: While reading through the works in question, I noted down every sentence including a human T, noting also the page on which the example occurred to facilitate rechecking. Since my level of concentration varied during what was also reading for pleasure – "for fun and profit" might be more accurate – it is always possible that I may have missed an occasional example. An obvious question is why I did not use a more sophisticated method of accurately and automatically searching for relevant examples in an electronic corpus.[5] Unfortunately, neither Ts flagged with personal *a* nor those without provide any obvious element that can be searched for automatically. The preposition *a* is very frequent in Spanish and only a tiny proportion of hits on it would be relevant. Searching for the absence of *a* is clearly not feasible. Even a partial solution like searching for bare frequent proper names after a verb is problematic, since not only would it relate to a small proportion of human noun phrases, it would also run into problems with postverbal subjects, a frequent occurrence in Spanish. It should be noted that I systematically excluded one combination, namely with a reflexive clitic pronoun (including reflexively interpreted first and second person pronouns); such pronouns often receive idiomatic interpretations, and it is often unclear whether they should really be considered as Rs.[6]

The Appendix lists all the examples of full noun phrase human Ts that I found, with the above provisos, in the corpus, plus the two examples from *¡Hola! Perú*; each is accompanied by a translation, though not by an interlinear gloss. These examples, numbered (28)–(52) below, are classified according to various formal criteria, in particular whether arguments are full noun phrases or clitic pronouns, and whether or not the T has the preposition *a*. In what now follows, I present a selection of these examples (sometimes excerpted) with interlinear glosses, showing at least one example of each type and, where examples are found in more than one of the sources listed in (20) (though counting both Vargas Llosa short stories as one source), one example from each source.

It should be noted that overall human Ts are not frequent – a total of 25 examples, including the two from *¡Hola! Perú*. Moreover, their distribution is very uneven across the corpus, with by far the largest contributor being Falcones' *La catedral del mar*, with its medieval theme and 10 examples; I return to this point below.

First, we may consider examples where the T is a full noun phrase flagged with personal *a* and the R is a clitic pronoun. This is by far the most frequent subtype, with 18 examples (including the two from *¡Hola! Perú*):

---

[5] I am grateful to John Du Bois and Dan Slobin for discussion on this issue.
[6] I also excluded some examples that might be analyzed as having a human T and an inanimate R. None of these examples contains a clitic pronoun, which makes their analysis as ditransitive constructions with T and R questionable. Since all use personal *a* with the human T, the only effect would have been to increase the number of such examples.

(21)   Tú   no   me   vas   a   traer   a   nadie.
       you   NEG   CLIT.OBJ.1SG go.2SG to bring.INF to nobody
       'You aren't going to bring me anyone.'
       Parra: *Juárez*

(22)   la   esclava mora   le   bajaba   a Arnau
       the slave   Moorish CLIT.DAT.3SG brought.down.3SG   to Arnau
       'the Moorish slave girl brought Arnau down to him'
       Falcones: *La catedral*

(23)   Te   dio   a   su   hija.
       CLIT.OBJ.2SG   gave.3SG   to his daughter
       'He gave you his daughter.'
       Rulfo: *El llano*

(24)   Thalía   nos   presenta   a   Matthew   Alejandro.
       T.   CLIT.OBJ.1PL   present.3SG   to M.   A.
       'Thalía presents Matthew Alejandro to us.'
       ¡Hola! Perú

There are three examples with a human T lacking personal *a* and the R expressed as a clitic pronoun. However, in all examples there is at least a strong possibility that the T is non-referential, and therefore not expected to license personal *a*. In (50) the speaker is saying that he won't bring any servant woman. In (51), the identity of the messenger is unimportant, rather what is crucial is that the relevant information is sent. And in (49), neither the Valencian nor the author is interested in the identity of the woman – she is simply the first woman who comes to hand. Once we exclude these three examples as non-referential, all 18 remaining referential examples show human T flagged with personal *a*, suggesting that human referential Ts receive exactly the same flagging as human referential Ps.

Turning now to the examples where both T and R are full noun phrases, there are four examples where both T and R are flagged with personal *a*.

(25)   dieron   a   todas   las   mujeres   por   esposas
       gave.3PL   to all   the   women   for   wives

       a   los   de   la   compañía   de   almogávares
       to those   of   the   company   of   almogavars

       'they gave all the women as wives to those of the almogavars' company'
       Falcones: *La catedral*

(26) *Tasurinchi no va a devolver a la yaminahua a sus parientes.*
Tasurinchi NEG go.3SG to return.INF to the Yaminahua to her relatives
'Tasurinchi is not going to return the Yaminahua woman to her relatives.'
Vargas Llosa: *El hablador*

The small number of examples makes it difficult to extract significant generalizations, especially since three of the examples are from one source, Falcones' *La catedral del mar*, and might represent features of this particular author's style. However, contrary to what one would expect from Company's judgments on (17)–(19) above, as well as from the general preference to double Rs with dative clitic pronouns, in none of the examples is the R doubled by a dative clitic pronoun. In addition, however, to the small number of examples one also needs to take into account possible regional variation – neither Falcones (Spain) nor Vargas Llosa (Peru) represents Company's Mexican variety. In three of the examples the only order of the objects that makes sense seems to be T before R; in the fourth, (46), either order would make sense.[7]

Finally, there is one example where both T and R are full noun phrases and where T is not flagged with personal *a*, although this T is clearly referential – the old woman in question has high topic continuity in this part of the novel. This thus parallels Company's (17), and more generally split P alignment as in (15). But it is a minority pattern, including in the source where it is found, Falcones' *La catedral del mar*:

(27) *los soldados cedieron la anciana a Aledis.*
the soldiers yielded.3PL the old_woman to Aledis
'the soldiers handed over the old woman to Aledis.'
Falcones: *La catedral*

If in this context the author had wanted to say that Aledia saw the old woman, then only personal *a* would have been possible for the P: *Aledis vio a la anciana*.

One final point should be made in this section. The studies by Company (1998, 2001, 2003) and Ortiz (2003, 2005, 2011) suggest that the relative frequency of ditransitive constructions where both T and R are flagged with *a* has been decreasing over the history of Spanish. My work suggests that this is due to an overall decrease in reference to situations where both T and R are human. Table 1 extracts the relevant information from Ortiz (2005). This is thus not a change in relative frequency of alternative ways of expressing the same content, but rather

---

7 Enrique Palancar advises me that for him only the order T before R is possible in such sequences; this issue merits further investigation.

a decrease over time in the expression of a particular content. Apparently, in the Middle Ages it was more frequent to speak (or rather: to write in the attested genres) about human Ts than it is nowadays. It then comes as no surprise that the single largest contingent of my examples comes from Falcones' *La catedral del mar* with its medieval scenario.

Table 1. Number of ditransitive clauses with human T relative to total number of ditransitive clauses (adapted from Ortiz 2005: 198)

Century	Human T		Total
	Raw number	Percentage	
C13	33	10.4%	316
C14	41	35.7%	115
C16	53	9.3%	567
C19	9	2.4%	381
C20	5	1.8%	282

However, when situations with a human T are referred to, the relative percentage of flagging T with as opposed to without personal *a* has actually increased in recent centuries (though the raw numbers are very small, especially for the more recent period), as seen in Table 2, again presenting information extracted from Ortiz (2005).

Table 2. Number of human Ts without *a* in relation to those with *a* (adapted from Ortiz 2005: 198)

Century	T Ø, R *a*		T *a*, R *a*		Total
	Raw number	Percentage	Raw number	Percentage	
C13	26	79%	7	21%	33
C14	35	85%	6	15%	41
C16	47	89%	6	11%	53
C19	6	67%	3	33%	9
C20	1	20%	4	80%	5

3 Conclusions

Human Ts are relatively rare, although particular topics, such as introducing people socially, giving people in marriage, handing people over to judicial authorities, carrying babies, etc., can lead to a sudden local increase in frequency. The basic flagging of human referential Ts in modern Spanish, at least the varieties considered here, seems clearly to be with personal *a*. Omission of personal *a* appears as a less frequent option when R is also flagged with the preposition *a*, although even in this configuration flagging with personal *a* is more frequent – both this study and Ortiz (2005) end up with four examples to one. With respect to the occurrence of a dative clitic pronoun when both T and R are flagged with *a*, the present study gives the unexpected result that with this configuration the clitic pronoun is absent; this merits further investigation, based on a much larger sample.

I conclude that in general in Spanish, T is flagged in the same way as P, with the same kind of Differential Object Marking, i.e. Spanish has indirective alignment (T = P ≠ R), since R is always flagged with *a* and does not undergo Differential Object Marking. However, there is a less common (and apparently becoming even rarer) alternative of omitting personal *a* on a human referential T when the R is flagged with *a*, giving overall an alignment that appears to combine dominant indirective and recessive split P patterns.

A number of other languages share with Spanish the Differential Object Marking pattern whereby R and relevant P (high in animacy and/or referentiality) are flagged in the same way. A comparison of the behavior of animate/referential T across such languages would be an interesting cross-linguistic project.

Abbreviations

For P, R, and T, see example (1)

1 first person, 2 second person, 3 third person, ACC accusative, CLIT clitic, DAT dative, F feminine, INF infinitive, M masculine, NEG negative, OBJ object, PL plural, REFL reflexive, REL relative, SG singular.

Appendix

A. Human T with preposition *a*, R expressed only as clitic pronoun

Falcones: *La catedral*

(28) *Y todo lo soportaba por las dos veces a la semana en que la esclava mora le bajaba a Arnau*
'And he put up with all this for the two times a week that the Moorish slave girl brought Arnau down to him'

(29) *y la mora le traía al niño con más frecuencia*
'and the Moor brought the child to him more often'

(30) *Arnau fue incluido en el grupo de Ramon, a quien el prohombre lanzó una significativa mirada cuando le asignó al muchacho.*
'Arnau was included in Ramon's group, to whom the leader cast a meaningful glance when he assigned the lad to him.'

(31) *Excelencia ... os presento a Arnau.*
'Your Excellency ... I present Arnau to you.'

(32) *y le dieron por mujer a la que fue del señor de la Sola*
'and they gave him as wife the one who was señor de la Sola's'

(33) *Os concedemos en matrimonio a nuestra pupila Elionor*
'We grant our ward Elionor to you in marriage'

(34) *El propio rey te entregó a su pupila*
'The King himself gave you his ward'

(35) *Encarceladlo y traedme a su mujer y a sus hijos.*
'Imprison him and bring me his wife and children.'

(36) *La host de Barcelona ... os ordena entregarle a Arnau Estanyol, cónsul de la Mar.*
'The *host* [assembly of free citizens] of Barcelona orders you to hand over to it Arnau Estanyol, Consul of the Sea.'

(37) *entregadnos al cónsul de la Mar.*
'hand over to us the Consul of the Sea.'

Parra: *Juárez*

(38) *Tú no me vas a traer a nadie.*
'You won't bring me anyone.'

Rulfo: *El llano*

(39) *El señor cura nos encomendó le lleváramos a alguien que lo hubiera tratado de cerca*
'The priest entrusted us to bring to him someone who had had close dealings with him'

(40) *Te dio a su hija.*
'He gave you his daughter.'

Vargas Llosa: *Los jefes*

(41) *Le hice una señal y le mostré a Chunga*
'He made a sign to him and showed him Chunga'

Vargas Llosa: *El hablador*

(42) *le pidió que le diera como mujer a cualquiera de sus hijas*
'he asked him to give him as wife any of his daughters'

¡Hola! *Perú*

(43) *Thalía nos presenta a Matthew Alejandro.*
'Thalía presents Matthew Alejandro to us.'

(44) *Thalía y Tommy Mottola nos presentan a Matthew Alejandro.*
'Thalía and Tommy Mottola present Matthew Alejandro to us.'

B. Human T with preposition *a*, R expressed as full prepositional phrase

Falcones: *La catedral*

(45) *y dieron a todas las mujeres por esposas a los de la compañía de almogávares*
'and they gave all the women as wives to those of the almogavars' company'

(46) *cuando éste entró corriendo en la masía para presentar al nuevo barón a su familia.*
'when the latter ran into the farm in order to present the new baron to his family [or, conceivably: to present his family to the new baron]'

(47) *Nicolau no lo había recibido para amenazarle con denunciar a Arnau al magistrado municipal.*
'Nicolau had not received him in order to threaten him with denouncing Arnau to the municipal magistrate.'

Vargas Llosa: *El hablador*

(48) *Tasurinchi no va a devolver a la yaminahua a sus parientes*
'Tasurinchi is not going to return the Yaminahua woman to her relatives.'

C. Human T without preposition *a*, R expressed only as clitic pronoun

Falcones, *La catedral*

(49) *El valenciano buscó a otro noble, lo invitó al escenario y le concedió una mujer, la primera que encontró entre el público* [possibly non-referential]
'The Valencian looked for another nobleman, invited him onto the stage, and bestowed on him a woman, the first he found among the public.'

Parra: *Juárez*

(50) *Yo no le traería una sirvienta.* [non-referential]
'I wouldn't bring you a servant woman.'

Vargas Llosa: *El hablador*

(51) *Kachiborérine le mandó un mensajero* [probably non-referential]
'Kachiborérine sent him a messenger'

D. Human T without preposition *a*, R expressed as full prepositional phrase without clitic pronoun

Falcones, *La catedral*

(52) *El oficial se encogió de hombros y los soldados cedieron la anciana a Aledis.*
'The officer shrugged his shoulders and the soldiers handed over the old woman to Aledis.'

References

Butt, John and Carmen Benjamin. 1995. *A New Reference Grammar of Modern Spanish*. Second edition. Lincolnwood, IL: NTC Publishing Group.
Company Company, Concepción. 1998. The interplay between form and meaning in language change: Grammaticalization of cannibalistic datives in Spanish. *Studies in Language* 22. 529–566.
Company Company, Concepción. 2001. Multiple dative-marking grammaticalization: Spanish as a special kind of primary object language. *Studies in Language* 25. 1–47.
Company Company, Concepción. 2003. Transitivity and grammaticalization of object. The struggle of direct and indirect object in Spanish. In Giuliana Fiorentino (ed.), *Romance Objects: Transitivity in Romance Languages*, 217–260. Berlin & New York: De Gruyter Mouton.
Haspelmath, Martin. 2004. Explaining the Ditransitive Person-Role Constraint: a usage based account. *Constructions* 2/2004.
(http://elanguage.net/journals/constructions/article/view/3073/3052)
Malchukov, Andrej, Martin Haspelmath & Bernard Comrie. 2010. Ditransitive constructions: A typological overview. In Andrej Malchukov, Martin Haspelmath & Bernard Comrie (eds.), *Studies in Ditransitive Constructions: A Comparative Handbook*, 1–64. Berlin & New York: De Gruyter Mouton.
Ortiz Ciscomani, Rosa María. 2003. Non-diachrony of transitivity in Spanish. In Giuliana Fiorentino (ed.), *Romance Objects: Transitivity in Romance Languages*, 261–298. Berlin & New York: De Gruyter Mouton.
Ortiz Ciscomani, Rosa María. 2005. Los objetos concurrentes y la bitransitividad en el español en perspectiva diacrónica. In David Eddington (ed.), *Selected Proceedings of the 7th Hispanic Linguistics Symposium*, 192–202. Somerville MA: Cascadilla Proceedings Project. (www.lingref.com/cpp/hls/7/paper1098.pdf)
Ortiz Ciscomani, Rosa María. 2011. *Construcciones Bitransitivas en la Historia del Español*. (Publicaciones de Medievalia 38.) Mexico: Universidad Nacional Autómoma de México, Instituto de Investigaciones Filológicas and Hermosillo: Universidad de Sonora.
Siewierska, Anna. 2003. Person agreement and the determination of alignment. *Transactions of the Philological Society* 101. 339–370.
Siewierska, Anna and Willem Hollmann. 2007. Ditransitive clauses in English with special reference to Lancashire dialect. In Mike Hannay & Gerard J. Steen (eds.), *Structural-Functional Studies in English Grammar*, 83–102. Amsterdam & Philadelphia: John Benjamins.

Denis Creissels
The generic use of the second person singular pronoun in Mandinka[1]

1 Introduction

The term 'impersonal' has been applied to a heterogeneous range of phenomena loosely bound together by some kind of family resemblance, and it is extremely doubtful whether the traditional use of this term can be validated by a feature common to all and only the various phenomena traditionally called 'impersonal'.[2] This point will not be further discussed in this article, which is devoted to a particular kind of so-called R(eference)-impersonals, i.e. impersonals involving a reduction in referentiality.[3]

My interest in the coreference properties of pronouns expressing generalizations about humans or referring to unspecified humans, commonly called 'impersonal pronouns', was initially motivated by the hypothesis that the coreference properties of pronouns or pronoun-like forms such as French *on* or German *man* are different from those of semantically similar markers that do not originate from pronouns, like those occurring in generic or unspecified subject constructions originating from reflexive or passive constructions. The data I gathered showed that things are much more complex than I imagined at first, but at the same time convinced me that detailed descriptions of the coreference properties of various types of generic or unspecified human participants in individual languages may

---
[1] When I participated in the workshop on impersonals organized in 2008 by Anna Siewierska and Andrej Malchukov at the SLE meeting in Forli, I initially intended to present a paper on the generic use of the second person pronoun in Manding, but I realized that it was not possible to discuss this question properly without filling in some gaps in the data I had at my disposal, and I eventually presented a paper on the coreference properties of French *on*. Since in the meantime I did fieldwork in Senegal in order to gather material for a Mandinka grammar, when I was invited to contribute to a volume dedicated to the memory of Anna Siewierska, the choice of this topic was immediately obvious to me.
[2] On the typology of impersonal constructions, see Creissels (2007), Siewierska (2008), Malchukov & Ogawa (2011).
[3] Note however that precisely R-impersonals are problematic for an approach to impersonality in terms of departure from canonical subjecthood, since the pronouns or pronoun-like forms involved in some varieties of R-impersonals are not necessarily restricted to the syntactic role of subject, as can be seen from the example of English *you* (*Brushing **your** teeth is healthy*) or *one* (*Brushing **one's** teeth is helpful*).

contribute to a better understanding of R-impersonals in a cross-linguistic perspective.

It is cross-linguistically very common that second person pronouns or indexes, which canonically represent the addressee of the speech act, can also express generalizations over sets of human beings whose delimitation is generally left implicit and can only be inferred from the context, as in example (1), in which *you* expresses a generalization over human beings present in Los Angeles.

(1) *It is so smoggy in Los Angeles that* **you** *can barely breathe.*

This generalizing use of second person pronouns or indexes, usually termed 'impersonal', is particularly widespread among West African languages. Moreover, in some West African languages at least, the second person pronoun or index used in this function exhibits coreference properties somewhat unexpected, given what is known about the generic use of second person pronouns or indexes in more familiar languages, in which generic *you* can introduce generic referents but cannot refer back to generic referents already introduced by a noun phrase.

In this article, I provide a detailed description of the use of the Mandinka second person pronoun *í* in co-reference chains in which it refers back to non-specific noun phrases making explicit the domain within which the generalization applies. To the best of my knowledge, the situation I describe has never been analyzed before, either in Mandinka or in other languages, and none of the descriptive grammars of West African languages I have been able to consult mentions it, although it undoubtedly occurs in texts, not only in other Manding varieties (Bambara, Maninka, Dyula, etc.),[4] but also in languages whose genetic relationship with Mandinka is, at most, very remote, for example, Wolof.[5] This coincidence is important to observe, since it excludes the possibility that the situation described in this article might be due to phonetic changes in the history of Manding resulting in an accidental homonymy between two pronouns originally distinct, and calls for a functional explanation.

The article is organized as follows. Section 2 provides some basic information about Mandinka and Mandinka grammar. Section 3 presents the various strat-

---

[4] The Manding languages are a group of fairly mutually intelligible languages or dialects included in the western branch of the Mande language family. Bambara, Mandinka, Maninka, and Dyula, are the most widely spoken and best-known Manding varieties. The most recent classification of Mande languages, elaborated by Valentin Vydrin, can be found at http://mandelang.kunstkamera.ru/index/langues_mande/famille_mande/

[5] Mandinka belongs to the Mande language family, whereas Wolof is an Atlantic language. Mande and Atlantic were included by Greenberg in the Niger-Congo phylum, but the evidence for a Niger-Congo affiliation of Mande is rather slim.

egies used in Mandinka to express non-specific human participants. Section 4 describes the coreference properties of the second person singular pronoun in its generic use. Section 5 puts forward a possible grammaticalization path.

The Mandinka data presented here is entirely drawn from Mandinka texts gathered in Sédhiou (Senegal).[6] All the examples illustrating the coreference properties of the 2nd person singular pronoun used generically are natural discourse examples.

2 Some basic information about Mandinka and Mandinka grammar

Mandinka, spoken in Senegal, The Gambia, and Guinea-Bissau by approximately 1.5 million speakers, is the westernmost member of the Manding dialect cluster, included in the western branch of the Mande language family. The area where Mandinka is spoken largely coincides with the sphere of influence of the precolonial state of Kaabu.[7] Speakers of Mandinka call themselves *Mandiŋkóolu* (singular: *Mandiŋkôo*) and designate their language as *mandiŋkakáŋo*.[8] Rowlands (1959), Creissels (1983), and Creissels & Sambou (2013) constitute the main references on Mandinka grammar.

The most striking characteristic of clause structure in Mande languages is the extreme rigidity of the typologically unusual SOVX constituent order, and this is particularly true of Manding languages or dialects, including Mandinka. No operation such as focalization or questioning triggers a change in constituent order, and with the exception of some types of adjuncts, noun phrases or adposition phrases cannot move to topic position (at the left edge of the clause) without being resumed by a pronoun in the position they would occupy if they were not topicalized.

---

[6] This article has benefited from the support of the French National Research Agency (ANR) within the frame of the 'Sénélangues' project (ANR-09-BLAN-0326).

[7] According to oral traditions, the Kaabu kingdom originated as a province of the Manding empire conquered in the 13th century by a general of Sundiata Keita called Tiramakhan Traore. After the decline of the Manding empire, Kaabu became an independent kingdom. Mandinka hegemony in the region lasted until 1867, when the Kaabu capital (Kansala) was taken by the armies of the Fula kingdom of Futa Jallon.

[8] *Mandiŋkôo* is the definite form of a noun *mandiŋká* resulting from the addition of the suffix -*ŋká* 'people from...' to the toponym *Mandíŋ*, which primarily refers to the region that constituted the starting point of the Manding expansion. *Mandiŋkakáŋo* is literally 'language of the people from Manding'.

As a consequence of the rigid SOVX constituent order, Mandinka clause structure is characterized by a particularly clear-cut distinction between core arguments, which invariably precede the verb, and obliques, which with few exceptions obligatorily follow it, and can never be found between S and V.

Another important characteristic of Mandinka clause structure is that transitive and intransitive predications are formally differentiated by TAM and polarity marking. It is also remarkable that Mandinka has a total ban on null subjects or objects, with either an anaphoric or arbitrary interpretation – see Creissels (to appear) for a discussion of this aspect of Mandinka syntax.

As illustrated by example (2), in transitive predication, the subject and the object obligatorily precede the verb, and the subject obligatorily precedes the object. Declarative and interrogative transitive clauses always include a *predicative marker*, a portmanteau morpheme encoding aspectual and modal distinctions and expressing polarity, inserted between the subject and the object. Obliques (most of the time encoded as postposition phrases) follow the verb. The subject and the object bear no mark of their syntactic role and are not indexed on the verb.[9]

(2) a. *Jat-óo ye dánn-óo barama.*
    lion-DEF PF hunter-DEF hurt
    'The lion hurt the hunter.'

 b. *Dánn-óo ye jat-óo barama.*
    hunter-DEF PF lion-DEF hurt
    'The hunter hurt the lion.'

 c. *Ì yé bank-óo-lu táláa kabíil-oo-lú le téema.*
    3PL PF land-DEF-PL divide clan-DEF-PL FOC between
    'They divided the lands between clans.'

 d. *Kambaan-óo maŋ ber-ôo fáyí palantéer-óo kaŋ.*
    boy-DEF PF.NEG stone-DEF throw window-DEF on
    'The boy did not throw the stone into the window.'

 e. *Kew-ó ka a téerímâa máakóyí kód-óo to.*
    man-DEF IPF 3SG friend.DEF help money-DEF LOC
    'The man helps his friend financially.'

---

9 The abbreviations used in the glosses of Mandinka examples may be found towards the end of the article.

As illustrated by example (3) below, pronouns occupy the same positions as NPs representing the same participants, they have the same form in all their possible syntactic roles, and they do not express gender-like distinctions.

(3)   a. *Wul-óo ye díndíŋ-o kíisándí dimbáa ma.*
          dog-DEF PF child-DEF save fire.DEF OBL
          'The dog saved the child from the fire.'

    b. *A yé a kíisándí a ma.*
          3SG PF 3SG save 3SG OBL
          'He/she/it saved him/her/it from him/her/it.'

In intransitive predication, the subject precedes the verb. It bears no mark of its syntactic role and is not indexed on the verb. Obliques behave exactly in the same way in transitive and intransitive clauses.

As already mentioned above, in intransitive predication, some TAM-polarity values are not encoded by the same markers as in transitive predication:

- the predicative marker expressing 'perfective positive' has a different tonal structure in transitive predication (*máŋ*) than in intransitive predication (*mâŋ*);
- the negative copula used in the function of imperfective negative marker has a different tonal structure in transitive predication (*té*) and intransitive predication (*tê*);
- the predicative marker *yé* expressing 'perfective positive', used exclusively in the transitive construction, is in complementary distribution with a verbal suffix (*-tá*) expressing the same value in intransitive constructions – example (4a).

As illustrated by example (4b-c), in intransitive predication, the predicative markers common to transitive and intransitive predication and those which differ only in tone are inserted between the subject and the verb. The only TAM-polarity marker suffixed to the verb is *-tá* (perfective positive, intransitive).

(4)   a. *Yír-óo boyi-ta síl-óo kaŋ.*
          tree-DEF fall-PF road-DEF on
          'The tree fell down on the road.'

    b. *New-ó ka kómóŋ jíy-o kóno.*
          iron-DEF IPF rust water-DEF in
          'Iron rusts in water.'

c. *Kew-ô   mâŋ   kúmá   mus-óo   ye.*
   man-DEF PF.NEG talk   woman-DEF   BEN
   'The man did not talk to the woman.'

Not all semantically bivalent verbs are syntactically assimilated to prototypical action verbs. Some of them occur in a formally intransitive construction in which one of the two arguments is an *oblique argument* encoded as a postpositional phrase that differs in no way from postposition phrases in adjunct function, as shown in example (5).

(5) *Kew-ó   lafi-ta   kód-óo   la.*
     man-DEF want-PF money-DEF OBL
     'The man wants money.'

Note also that Mandinka does not have constructions of the type commonly termed 'double object constructions', which means that one of the arguments of semantically trivalent verbs must be encoded as a postposition phrase whose behavior is in no respect different from that of postposition phrases in adjunct function.

3 Unspecified human participants in Mandinka

At first sight, the situation of Mandinka with respect to the expression of non-specific (generic or unspecified) human participants is not particularly original. In addition to the possible use of indefinite determiners or agentless passive constructions (which however have the cross-linguistically rare feature of involving nothing that could be analyzed as passive morphology),[10] various semantic types of non-specific human participants can be encoded as *mǒo* (definite form of *mǒo* 'human being'),[11] *i* (low-toned) 'they', or *í* (high-toned) 'you (sg)'.

As illustrated by example (6a) below, *mǒo* is commonly used to express generalizations about human beings. From the point of view of Mandinka grammar,

---

[10] On the passive construction of Mandinka, see Creissels (to appear).
[11] In Mandinka, the definite form of nouns is formed by suffixing a low-toned *o* to the noun stem (for example, *kúlúŋ* 'boat' → *kúlúŋo*), but with stems ending with a vowel, the definite suffix interacts with the last vowel of the stem in various ways. In the case of stems ending with *aa* or *oo*, and optionally for those ending with *ee*, this interaction results in a purely tonal distinction between the bare noun stem and the definite form (for example, *báa* 'river' → *bâa*, *mǒo* 'human being' → *mǒo*, *kěe* 'man' → *kewô* or *kěe*), but depending on the context, the tonal distinction between the bare noun stem and the definite form may be neutralized by tone sandhi rules.

it would however not be justified to recognize the existence of a more or less grammaticalized impersonal pronoun *mŏo*, since morphologically, *mŏo* is the definite form of the noun *mŏo* 'human being', and syntactically, any Mandinka noun can be used in the definite form to express generalizations about other kinds of entities, as illustrated by *jatôo* (definite form of *jatá* 'lion') in example (6b).

(6) a. *Mŏo ka kúm-ôo fó le bii, săama a yé a báayi.*
person.DEF IPF word-DEF say FOC today tomorrow 3SG SUBJ 3SG cancel
'One says something today, and retracts tomorrow.'
lit. 'The man says a word today ...'

b. *Jat-ôo búka mŏo maa, fó a dáalámáayáa-ta.*
lion-DEF IPF.NEG[12] person.DEF attack unless 3SG be.wounded-PF
'Lions do not attack humans, unless they are wounded.'
lit. 'The lion does not attack the man ...'

As illustrated by example (7) below, the non-specific use of *i* 'they' includes the expression of unspecified participants with reference to habitual events, and vague reference in episodic contexts. Depending on the discourse context, *i* in the same sentences could be interpreted as referring to a specific group of people ('the people in question').

(7) a. *I ka kín-ôo tábí kaléer-óo le kóno.*
3PL IPF rice-DEF cook pot-DEF FOC in
'Rice is cooked in a pot.'
(alternative reading: 'The people in question cook rice in a pot')

b. *I yé a ñiniŋkáa a ka mêŋ jéle.*
3PL PF 3SG ask 3SG IPF REL laugh
'He was asked what he was laughing at.'
(alternative reading: 'The people in question asked him...)

As illustrated by example (8), as in other languages, the non-specific use of the second person singular pronoun in Mandinka is typically found in generalizations about humans in a given type of situation, often expressed as conditional sentences, and this use of the second person pronoun is widely attested in proverbs.

---

[12] Note that the first syllable of *búka* 'imperfective negative' cannot be isolated as a negative marker in a synchronic analysis of Mandinka, since there is no other case in which negation would be expressed via the addition of a syllable *bú*. The first syllable of *búka* may however be cognate with a negative marker found in other Mande languages – Creissels & Sambou (2013: 80).

(8) a. *Í sí jal-ôo jé,*
2SG POT griot-DEF see
'You may see a griot

a sí Suñjátá la kúw-o sáatá ñáa dóo ma, í
3SG POT Sunjata GEN matter-DEF explain way INDEF OBL 2SG
who tells you Sunjata's story in one particular way,

sí dóo fánáŋ jé, a sí a sáatá ñáa dóo ma.
POT INDEF also see 3SG POT 3SG explain way INDEF OBL
but later you may see another one who will tell it to you in another way.'

b. *Níŋ í máŋ féŋ sene, í búka féŋ káti.*
if 2SG PF.NEG thing cultivate 2SG IPF.NEG thing reap
'If one does not cultivate anything, one does not reap anything.'

c. *Níŋ í yé wóoró níŋ fulá kafu ñóoma,*
if 2SG PF six with two join together
'If one adds six and two,

wo mú jolú le ti?
DEM COP how.much FOC OBL
how much is it?'

d. *Níŋ í yé sól-óo barama, fó í yé sílá kút-ôo ñiniŋ.*
if 2SG PF leopard-DEF wound OBLIG 2SG SUBJ road new-DEF look.for
'If you wound a leopard, you must look for a new road.'

e. *Dol-ôo máŋ haráamu, níŋ í máŋ síira.*
wine-DEF PF.NEG be.forbidden if 2SG PF.NEG get.drunk
'Wine is not forbidden, if you do not get drunk.'

4 The use of generic *í* with a discourse antecedent

In French, generic *tu* 'you (sg)' can only refer back to another occurrence of generic *tu*, and generic *vous* 'you (pl)' can only refer back to another occurrence of generic *vous*, or to generic *on* (dedicated non-specific human index), and similar constraints can be observed in other European languages. By contrast, Mandinka *í* 'you (sg)' in its generic use may refer back to a variety of antecedents that could equally be resumed by 3rd person pronouns, without any difference in meaning.

When generic *í* 'you (sg)' introduces a generic referent, as in example (8) above, it cannot be substituted by *a* 'he, she, it', which could only be interpreted as referring anaphorically to some specific referent retrievable from the context. By contrast, in the examples quoted in this section, *í* referring back to a generic noun phrase can always be substituted by *a* 'he, she, it' without any difference in meaning, as illustrated by example (9).

(9) a. *Níŋ míŋ ŋa ń soosoo, í sí táa jee í yé a juubee.*
    if REL PF 1SG contradict 2SG POT go there 2SG SUBJ 3SG look
    lit. '[Anyone who contradicts me]ᵢ, youᵢ should go there and look at it.'
    'Anyone who does not believe me should go there and have a look at it.'

b. *Níŋ míŋ ŋa ń soosoo, a sí táa jee a yé a juubee.*
    if REL PF 1SG contradict 3SG POT go there 3SG SUBJ 3SG look
    lit. '[Anyone who contradicts me]ᵢ, he/sheᵢ should go there and look at it.'
    Same meaning as (a)

In example (10), generic *í* occurs in a conditional sentence similar to those in (8) above, with however the difference that the topic position at the left edge of the sentence is occupied by a generic NP equivalent to English 'any prince', coreferent with *í*.

(10) *Mansadiŋ wó mansadiŋ, níŋ í ñán-ta mansayáa-lá Mandiŋ,*
     prince INDEF prince if 2SG must-PF reign-INF Mande
     lit. '[Any prince]ᵢ, if youᵢ were doomed to reign over Mande,

Suusûu Súmáŋkúrú be í faa-la dóróŋ.
Suusuu Sumankuru COP 2SG kill-INF only
Suusuu Sumankuru would just kill youᵢ.'

'S.S. would kill any prince who was doomed to reign over Mande.'

In example (11) below, the antecedents of generic *í* are ordinary relative clauses in topic position. Such relative clauses are not inherently generic, and in other contexts, they could lend themselves to specific readings: 'the person whom love has killed' and 'the king whom I serve' respectively. They are interpreted here as generic because of the coreference relation with 2nd person *í*, which (in contrast with 3rd person *a*) can only refer back to generic antecedents.

(11) a. *Kanú ye méŋ faa, í mâŋ jífa.*
     love PF REL kill 2SG PF.NEG die.miserably
     lit. '[The person whom love has killed]ᵢ, youᵢ did not die miserably.'
     'If one is killed by love, one does not die miserably.'

b. Ńte bé mansâ mêŋ nóoma, í mâŋ ñánna kumbóo-la!
   1SG COP king REL after 2SG PF.NEG must cry-INF
   lit. '[The king that I serve]ᵢ, youᵢ must not cry!'
   'Whoever he may be, the king that I serve must not cry.'

In example (12), the antecedent of generic í is again a free relative in topic position, but it belongs to another type of relative clause, which is necessarily interpreted as non-specific: 'any person who tries to cut this tree'.

(12) Moo wó moo yé wo yír-óo sĕe faŋ-ó la,
     person INDEF person PF DEM tree-DEF cut cutlass-DEF OBL
     lit. '[Anyone who tried to cut this tree with a cutlass]ᵢ,

     í ká făa le.
     2SG IPF die FOC
     youᵢ would die.'

     'Anyone trying to cut this tree with a cutlass would die.'

In example (13), the antecedent of generic í is mŏo, definite form of the noun mŏo 'human being', the use of which to express generalizations over sets of human beings has already been illustrated by example (6) above.

(13) Wŏ tum-ôo, mŏo búka mansayáa sotó jaŋ,
     DEM time-DEF person IPF.NEG kingship.DEF get here
     lit. 'In those days, [the man]ᵢ did not become king here

     fó níŋ í táa-tá Mandiŋ.
     unless if 2SG go-PF Mande
     unless youᵢ went to Mande.'

     'In those days, one did not become king here without first going to Mande.'

In example (14), the antecedent moo wó moo 'anyone' is the subject of the clause to which the first occurrence of generic í belongs.

(14) Moo wó moo láa-tá í fáŋ na,
     person INDEF person trust-PF 2SG self OBL
     lit. '[anyone]ᵢ trusting in yourselfᵢ,

     í sí bulá ñiŋ túlúŋ-o to.
     2SG POT take.part DEM game-DEF LOC
     youᵢ may take part in this game.'

     'Anyone trusting in themselves may take part in this game.'

In example (15) too, the first occurrence of generic *í* has its antecedent (the relativizer *mêŋ*) in the same clause.

(15) Níŋ méŋ ye ñíŋ taamanseer-óo-lu súutée í bála,
 if REL PF DEM symptom-DEF-PL notice 2SG on
 lit. '[Anyone]ᵢ who notices these symptoms on youᵢ,

 í sí táa kátábáke í níŋ dókítár-óo-lu ye ñôo jé.
 2SG POT go quickly 2SG with doctor-DEF-PL SUBJ RECIP see
 youᵢ should go quickly to consult doctors.'

 'Anyone who notices these symptoms on themselves should go quickly to consult doctors.'

In example (16), in the same way as in several of the preceding examples, a free relative occupies the topic position at the left edge of the sentence, and generic *í* is included in the main clause. However, the antecedent of generic *í* is not the free relative, but *mŏo* 'the man', the subject of the relative clause.

(16) Mŏo ye mêŋ fíi, wǒ le ka fálíŋ í ye.
 person.DEF PF REL sow DEM FOC IPF grow 2SG BEN
 'What [the man]ᵢ has sown, this is what grows for youᵢ.'
 'One reaps what one has sown.'

In example (17), the antecedent of generic *í* in genitive function is *mŏo* 'the man' in subject function in the same clause.

(17) Mŏo ñán-ta í lá mus-óo mara-la báake
 person.DEF must-PF 2SG GEN wife-DEF look.after-INF carefully
 lit. [The man]ᵢ must look after yourᵢ wife carefully.'
 'One must look after one's wife carefully.'

An finally, example (18) illustrates the same syntactic configuration, but with generic *í* included in a topicalized noun phrase preceding *mŏo* 'the man' in subject position.

(18) Í báadíŋkéw-o, mŏo si sílá a la.
 2SG brother-DEF person.DEF POT be.afraid 3SG OBL
 lit. 'yourᵢ brother, [the man]ᵢ may be afraid of him.'
 'One may be afraid of one's own brother.'

To summarize, in Mandinka, generic *í* may refer back to non-specific noun phrases making explicit the domain within which the generalization applies (either the whole set of human beings, or a proper subset thereof), and there is no obvious syntactic restriction on the establishment of such coreference chains. Generic *í* may even precede the expression it is co-referential with.

In the generic use of *í* with a discourse antecedent, the selection of a particular semantic type of antecedent (non-specific noun phrases or relative clauses) seems to be the only thing that distinguishes the behavior of generic *í* from that of third person pronouns. When *í* 'you' introduces a non-specific human referent, as in example (8) above, it is of course not equivalent to *a* 'he/she/it', which in the absence of an overt antecedent is interpreted as referring to some specific entity whose identity is recoverable from the context. By contrast, when it resumes a non-specific noun phrase or relative clause, second person *í* can be replaced by third person *a* without any difference in meaning. Not surprisingly, generic *í* is particularly common in proverbs, and when working with consultants on proverbs such as that quoted above as example (16), I observed that the consultants indifferently quote the same proverbs with alternative formulations in which the same non-specific noun phrase or relative clause is resumed by either a second or a third person pronoun.

5 A possible grammaticalization path

In this section, I discuss a possible scenario according to which the reanalysis of a construction widely attested cross-linguistically may have resulted in coreference chains of the type described in Section 4.

Given the observations presented above, there is no difficulty in analyzing example (19) as involving a coreference chain in which a topicalized noun referring to a kind constitutes the antecedent of generic *í*.

(19) *Furêe,   níŋ í   yé í   nukuŋ í   kuubáa-lu   ma,*
corpse.DEF if 2SG PF REFL hide 2SG washer.DEF-PL OBL
lit. '[the corpse]$_i$, if you$_j$ hide from the persons who must wash you$_j$,

í   níŋ kós-óo   le ka táa alikiyáama.
2SG with uncleanness-DEF FOC IPF go next.world
you$_j$ go unclean to the next world.'

'A corpse hiding from those who must wash it goes unclean to the next world.'

There is however another possible interpretation of this sentence, since Mandinka has no vocative marker, and the same definite form is equally used in Mandinka for common nouns referring to kinds and for common nouns in vocative function. The noun in left-dislocated position in example (19) can therefore equally be understood as a pseudo-vocative directed to a virtual referent of *furée* 'corpse': 'Corpse, if you hide from those who must wash you, you go unclean to the next world!'

The beginning of example (20) below exhibits the same ambiguity, but the use of an imperative in the last part of this sentence shows that *díndíŋo* must be interpreted here as a vocative.[13]

(20)   *Díndíŋ-o,   níŋ   í   táa-tá   duláa   to,*
       child-DEF if   2SG   go-PF   place.DEF LOC
       'Child, if you go somewhere,

   níŋ   í   yé   keebáa   tará   jee,
   if   2SG   PF   old.person.DEF   find   there
   and if you find and old person there,

   kána   hórómántáŋyáa   sambá   a   kaŋ.
   SUBJ.NEG   disrespect.DEF   bring   3SG   on
   do not be disrespectful to them!'

Constructions with a second person pronoun coreferent with a pseudo-vocative directed to the potential referents of a noun are extremely common, cross-linguistically, as a possible discourse strategy for expressing generalizations, as illustrated in (21) by a famous verse from the pen of the French poet Charles Baudelaire, and in (22) by a Dutch proverb.

(21)   *Homme   libre,   toujours   tu   chériras   la   mer!*
       man   free   always   you   will.cherish   the   sea
       'Free man, you will always cherish the sea!'

(22)   *Als   de   vos   de   passie   preekt,   boer   pas   op   je   kippen!*
       when   the fox   the compassion   preaches   farmer   watch   on   your   chickens
       'When the fox preaches compassion, farmer watch your chickens.'

---

13 In Mandinka, the imperative singular is characterized by the absence of anything in the position normally occupied by a subject noun phrase. In the positive imperative, no predicative marker is present either, whereas the negative imperative is marked by *kána* 'negative subjunctive'.

Starting from that, it seems reasonable to suppose that the coreference chains involving generic *í* described in Section 4 originate from the reanalysis of such constructions. Example (18) illustrates the type of context in which, in a language in which nouns in vocative function are not formally distinct from topicalized nouns referring to kinds, a second person pronoun quite regularly resuming a pseudo-vocative directed to a virtual addressee in sentences expressing generalizations may be reanalyzed as resuming a non-specific noun phrase in topic function. This is probably what occurred in the history of Manding (or in the history of another West African language from which the construction may have spread to neighboring languages). The use of the second person pronoun as a resumptive pronoun taking non-specific noun phrases or relative clauses as its antecedents was subsequently extended to contexts in which the non-specific antecedent is not interpretable as a pseudo-vocative, as illustrated by the examples quoted in Section 4.

6 Conclusion

West African languages are rarely mentioned in general discussions of impersonality. In this article, on the example of the generic use of the second person singular pronoun in Mandinka, I have tried to show that West African language data may contribute to a better understanding of the phenomena traditionally grouped under the label 'impersonal', and in particular of so-called R-impersonals, by revealing possible connections that are not apparent in the languages for which the study of impersonality has a long-standing tradition.

Abbreviations

1 first person, 2 second person, 3 third person, BEN benefactive, COP copula, DEF definite, DEM demonstrative, FOC focalization, GEN genitive, INDEF indefinite, INF infinitive, IPF imperfective, LOC locative, NEG negative, OBL oblique, OBLIG obligative, PF perfective, PL plural, POT potential, RECIP reciprocal, REFL reflexive, REL relativizer, SG singular, SUBJ subjunctive.

References

Creissels, Denis. 1983. *Eléments de grammaire de la langue mandinka*. Grenoble: ELLUG.
Creissels, Denis. 2007. Impersonal and anti-impersonal constructions: a typological approach. Ms, University of Lyon. (http://deniscreissels.fr)
Creissels, Denis. To appear. Valency properties of Mandinka verbs. In Bernard Comrie & Andrej Malchukov (eds.), *Handbook of valency classes*.
Creissels, Denis & Pierre Sambou. 2013. *Le mandinka (mandinkakáŋo). Phonologie, grammaire et textes*. Paris: Karthala.
Malchukov, Andrej & Akio Ogawa. 2011. Towards a typology of impersonal constructions: A semanctic map approach. In Andrej Malchukov & Anna Siewierska (eds.), *Impersonal constructions, a cross-linguistic perspective*, 19–56. Amsterdam & Philadelphia: John Benjamins.
Rowlands, Evan C. 1959. *A grammar of Gambian Mandinka*. London: SOAS.
Siewierska, Anna. 2008. Introduction. Impersonalization: An agent-based vs. a subject-based perspective. Transactions of the Philological Society 106(2). 115–137. (*Special issue on Impersonal Constructions in Grammatical Theory*, guest-edited by Anna Siewierska.)

Sonia Cristofaro
The referential hierarchy: reviewing the evidence in diachronic perspective

1 Introduction

Through her work, Anna Siewierska has crucially contributed to expanding and systematizing our understanding of a number of grammatical phenomena related to the so-called referential hierarchy reported in (1), including for example zero as opposed to overt bound person marking, hierarchical alignment, alignment splits, and voice (Siewierska 1998, 2004, 2010b, to mention but a few).

(1) The referential hierarchy (Corbett 2000: 56, among others):

 1st person pronouns > 2nd person pronouns > 3rd person pronouns > kin > human > animate > inanimate

The referential hierarchy (also known as the topicality or animacy hierarchy) has been argued to reflect a variety of factors, including, for example, animacy, topicality, definiteness and natural attention flow (see Song 2001: ch. 3, for a review). These explanations, as is usually the case with typological explanations, have been proposed on synchronic grounds. If the cross-linguistic distribution of some construction is associated with some particular factor, and a plausible relation can be postulated between that factor and the properties of the construction, then the factor is assumed to be responsible for the distribution, independently of how the construction actually originated in individual languages. For example, as will be discussed in more detail in section 2, ergative systems are sometimes restricted to a right end portion of the referential hierarchy, e.g. nouns and third person pronouns as opposed to first and second person pronouns, or inanimate nouns as opposed to other NP types. This has been accounted for in terms of an inherent property of the relevant NP types, namely their relative likelihood of functioning as the initiators of an action, rather than in terms of the specific diachronic processes that gave rise to the ergative system in individual languages.

A recurrent feature of Anna Siewierska's work, however, is the emphasis placed on the possible relationship between the synchronic properties of the constructions being investigated and the diachronic origin of these constructions. For example, Siewierska (1998) investigates the possible diachronic relationship between ergative, passive, and inverse systems. Siewierska (2010a) relates the properties of different types of passive constructions to the source constructions from which they originated. Siewierska (2010b) checks several hypotheses about the development of zero third person bound pronominals against the cross-linguistic distributional patterns attested for these pronominals across different argument roles.

In this spirit, this article will investigate the possible diachronic origins of various phenomena that have been described in terms of the referential hierarchy, namely alignment splits, hierarchical alignment, and the presence vs. absence of a singular vs. plural distinction for different NP types. A number of diachronic processes that give rise to these phenomena, it will be argued, pose several challenges both for the explanations that have been proposed for the referential hierarchy on synchronic grounds, and for the very idea of a referential hierarchy, in the sense of a scalar alignment of particular NP types that is relevant for speakers and leads them to use different constructions for these NPs.

2 Some possible origins of alignment splits in case marking systems

As is well known (see, for example, Comrie 1989 and Dixon 1994), accusative alignment in case marking is sometimes limited to some left end portion of the referential hierarchy, for example first and second person pronouns as opposed to third person pronouns and nouns, pronouns as opposed to nouns, or pronouns and animate or definite nouns as opposed to inanimate or indefinite nouns. Ergative alignment, on the other hand, is sometimes limited to a right end portion of the hierarchy, for example inanimate nouns as opposed to animate nouns and pronouns, nouns as opposed to pronouns, or nouns and third person pronouns as opposed to first and second person pronouns.

An influential explanation that has been proposed for these patterns (for which see Dixon 1979 and 1994, Comrie 1989, DeLancey 1981, and Song 2001, among others) relates them to the use of overt, as opposed to zero marking for the two arguments of transitive verbs and the only argument of intransitive verbs (henceforth, A, P, and S arguments). It is assumed that speakers tend to use overt marking for particular argument roles only when these roles are more difficult to identify, and are therefore more in need to be indicated explicitly. In most instances of ergative and accusative systems, only one argument role is marked overtly, typically P in accusative systems and A in ergative systems. When these systems are limited to particular NP types, then, this is assumed to be because these NPs are less likely to occur in the role that is marked overtly in the system, hence, when they do, that role is more difficult to identify. Accusative systems are limited to certain NP types, for example first and second person pronouns, because these NPs are less likely to occur in the P role, possibly due to the inherent animacy of their referents. Ergative systems are limited to certain NP types, for example inanimate nouns, because these NPs are less likely to occur in the A role.

This explanation implies that speakers have some knowledge of the relative likelihood of different NP types occurring in particular argument roles, as mapped on the referential hierarchy, and this knowledge leads them to use overt marking for the less likely combinations of argument roles and NP types. However, the available diachronic data about the development of overt marking for particular combinations do not provide direct evidence in support of this scenario, and suggest some alternative hypotheses.

In several languages where ergative alignment does not apply to pronouns, the markers for A arguments presumably originated from a source relatively incompatible with pronouns. In some cases, for example, these markers can transparently be related to indexical elements, that is, demonstratives and (third person) pronouns. This has been shown to be the case for several Australian languages (McGregor (2006) and (2008)), as illustrated in example (2) for Bagandji.

(2) Bagandji (Australian; Hercus 1982: 63)

*Yaḍu-**duru**   gāndi-d-uru-ana.*
wind-DEM/ERG carry-FUT-3SG.SUBJ-3SG.OBJ
'**This wind** will carry it along / The wind will carry it along'

McGregor (2006) and (2008) accounts for this pattern by assuming that indexicals are initially used in apposition to nouns occurring in the A role to emphasize that these nouns exceptionally encode new or unexpected information. As a result, they are subsequently reanalyzed as endoding the A role (thus, for example, sentences such as 'X, this one, did Y' or 'X, he, did Y' become 'X ERG did Y'). Indexicals, McGregor (2006) argues, are not used with pronouns because pronouns represent given information, and this explains why the resulting A markers are not used with pronouns either.

Garrett (1990) raises similar arguments regarding languages where ergative alignment is restricted to inanimate nouns. Garrett shows that in some such languages, such as Hittite, specific markers for A arguments are likely to have developed through the reinterpretation of an instrumental marker in sentences with no overt third person A arguments, that is, sentences such as '(X) opened the door with the key' were reinterpreted as 'The key ERG opened the door'. As instrumentals usually do not apply to animates or pronouns (particularly first and second person ones), the resulting A markers are restricted in the same way.

To the extent that the diachronic reconstruction is correct, such cases provide no obvious evidence that the restrictions in the distribution of ergative systems are directly related to the lower likelihood of particular NP types occurring in the A role, and hence to the need to overtly indicate that role. The relevant ergative systems arise as specific markers for A arguments develop through the reinterpretation of preexisting markers in a system where A, P, and S arguments are originally undifferentiated. The reinterpretation is motivated in terms of the connection between the A role and the original function of the markers, for example the fact that the markers combine with A arguments to indicate new or unexpected information[1], or the fact that the markers encode meanings that imply the notion of agentivity, such as instrumental meanings. This is independent of the need to overtly signal the A role, and the restrictions in the distribution of the system are directly related to the restrictions in the distribution of the elements that give rise to the A markers, rather than the relative likelihood of the relevant NP types occurring in the A role. In fact, these restrictions are not found when the A markers originate from different sources, for example from possessive or oblique markers as nominalized or passivelike constructions of the type 'To X will be the Verbing of Y' or 'Y is Verbed by X' are reanalyzed as 'X ERG will Verb Y', 'X ERG Verbed Y' (see Gildea 1998, for Cariban languages, and Bubeník 1998 and Verbeke & De Cuypere 2009, among others, for Indo-Aryan languages). In such cases, the distribution of the source construction is unconstrained, and so is that of the resulting ergative systems. This is illustrated in (3)–(5), which show that these systems can apply, for example, to first and second person pronouns and animate nouns.

(3) Cariña (Cariban; Gildea 1998: 169)

A-eena-rɨ   i-'wa-ma.
2-have-NOMLZR   1-DAT/ERG-3.be
'I will have you' (from nominalized 'To me it will be your having')

(4) Kuikúro (Cariban; Franchetto 1990: 411, 409)

a. *Áiha u-ikucé-lâ   léha **e-héke.***
ASP 1-paint-PUNCT ASP 2-ERG
'You finished painting me'

---

[1] McGregor (2006, 2008) do not address the issue of why indexicals are not used with S arguments, which would yield an accusative, rather than an ergative pattern. To the extent that indexicals are originally used to mark new or unexpected information, however, this issue pertains to the relationship between this type of information and S arguments, rather than the rise of ergativity in itself.

b. ***I-ñomó-héke***   *titá*   *i-ta-lâ-ko.*
3-husband.PL-ERG there 3-HEAR-PUNCT-PL
'Their husbands there heard them'
[both from the same type of nominalized construction as (3)]

(5) Hindi (Indo-European; Verbeke & De Cuypere 2009: 5, 2)

     a. ***Laṛk-e=ne***   *bacch-e=ko*   *mār-a*   *hai.*
        boy-OBL=ERG child-OBL=ACC hit-ERG.M.SG be.AUX
        'The boy has hit the child'

     b. ***Maiṃ=ne***   *kītāb*   *paṛh-ī.*
        I=ERG   book   read-PERF.F.SG
        'I read a book'

Similar observations apply to accusative systems. In a number of cases where these are limited to pronouns, as illustrated by the Kanuri examples in (6a-b) below, or to pronouns and human, animate or definite nouns, the markers for P arguments presumably originated from the grammaticalization of a former topic marker, that is, sentences such as 'As for X, Y saw him' were reinterpreted as 'X ACC, Y saw him', and the resulting P marker was subsequently extended to non-topicalized objects. Synchronic evidence for this hypothesis comes from the fact that, in a large number of languages, such markers also function as topic markers. This is the case in Kanuri, as can be seen from (6c), and extensive cross-linguistic evidence is provided in König (2008) and Iemmolo (2010). Direct diachronic evidence of the grammaticalization process is also provided by several Romance languages (Iemmolo 2010, among others).

(6) Kanuri (Nilo-Saharan; Cyffer 1998: 52, 70)

     a. *Músa shí-**ga***   *cúro*
        Musa 3SG-OBJ saw
        'Musa saw him'

     b. *Káno-ro leji-ya*   *ráwanzá súr-in*
        kano-to go.3SG-DEPFUT uncle   see-IMPF
        'When she goes to Kano, she will see her uncle'

     c. *Wú-**ga***
        1SG-as.for
        'As for me'

As has long been recognized in the literature (Givón 1976, among others), topics have a tendency to be pronominal, human or animate, and definite. This means that topic markers will usually occur with pronouns and human, animate, and definite nouns. It is then to be expected that, if a P marker grammaticalizes from a topic marker, it will initially be restricted to these NP types, as has in fact been documented for Romance languages (Iemmolo (2010) and references therein). While these restrictions are exactly those described by the referential hierarchy, they cannot obviously be related to the need to disambiguate the P role due to the lower frequency of particular NP types occurring in that role. The accusative system develops as specific markers for P arguments arise through the grammaticalization of topic markers in a system where A, P and S arguments are originally undifferentiated. The grammaticalization process is arguably motivated by the fact that the topicalized element does indeed correspond to the P argument of the verb, so there is no direct evidence that this process originates from the need to disambiguate the P role.[2] The restrictions in the distribution of the system are a direct result of the restrictions in the original distribution of the topic marker, and they are not found when P markers develop from other sources. For example, as illustrated in (7) below, P markers may develop from the grammaticalization of 'take' verbs in serial verb constructions, that is, sentences such as 'take X (and) Verb (X)' are reinterpred as 'Verb X ACC' (see e.g. Li and Thompson (1974a) and (1974b) for Mandarin Chinese and Lord (1993) for several West African languages). Also, as illustrated in (8), P markers may originate from possessor markers in nominalized constructions of the type 'X is occupied with the Verbing of Y' as these are reanalyzed as 'X is Verbing Y ACC' (see Gildea 1998 for detailed data on such processes in several Cariban languages). In both of these cases, the source elements can apply to all NP types, and so do the resulting P markers. This can be seen from (7a-c) and (8), where the markers are used both with pronouns and with inanimate nouns.[3]

(7) Twi (Niger-Congo; Lord 1993: 66–79)
 [from an earlier description of the language]

 a. Ɔkɔm **de** me.
  hunger take me
  'Hunger takes me'

---

[2] A related question is why topic markers give rise to P, rather than A or S markers (though this process has also been decribed for some languages, see e.g. König (2008: 273–276) for !Xun). This, however, pertains to the relationship between topic markers and different argument roles, rather than any general relationship between accusative systems and particular NP types.

[3] Note that, in the Twi examples in (7b,c), the P marker attaches to a preceding A pronominal argument. Lord (1993) does not comment on this.

b. *Wǫ-de no yęę ǫsafohéne.*
    he-OBJ him make captain
    'They made him captain'

c. *O-de afoa ce boha-m.*
    he-OBJ sword put scabbard-inside
    'He put the sword into the scabbard'

(8) Wayana (Cariban; Gildea 1998: 201)

ï-pakoro-n iri-Ø pǝk wai.
1-house-POSS/OBJ make-NOMLZR occupied.with 1.be
'I'm (occupied with) making my house' [lit. 'my house's making']

3 Some possible origins of hierarchical alignment

Another phenomenon that has been described in terms of the referential hierarchy is so-called hierarchical alignment. This notion is usually used to refer to two distinct patterns, both pertaining to the different grammatical treatment of speech act (first and second person) vs. non speech act (third person) participants, as captured by the different ranking of these participants on the referential hierarchy (see Siewierska (2004: 51–57), Zúñiga (2006), and Lockwood and Macaulay (2012) for reviews and examples). The first pattern, usually called direct-inverse marking, is one whereby some languages use dedicated morphology to distinguish different combinations of speech act and non speech act participants in transitive clauses. Usually, one affix, the inverse, is used to indicate that a speech act participant is being acted upon by a non speech act participant, while the reverse situation where a speech act participant acts upon a non speech act participant is either not indicated overtly or indicated by means of a different affix, the direct. Direct and inverse affixes are also sometimes used in individual languages to indicate various combinations of speech act participants (first person acting on second, or vice versa) or non speech act participants (for example, third person obviative acting on third person proximate, or vice versa).

The second pattern referred to as hierarchical alignment pertains to the indexation of speech act and non speech act participants by means of bound person forms on the verb. In some languages, bound person forms index speech act participants in preference to non speech act participants independently of role, that is, first or second person participants are always indexed, while third person participants are either never indexed or indexed only when no first or second person participant is present.

Although individual analyses differ in their details, these patterns have been accounted for in terms of a general idea that speech act participants are somehow more prominent than non speech act participants, and represent natural agents and privileged points of view from which to describe events. As a result, they are accorded different treatment in terms of indexation, and the situation where a speech act participant is being acted upon by a non speech act participant is morphologically distinguished from the reverse, more natural situation (Comrie 1980, DeLancey 1981, and Song 2001: 170–178, among others). What is known about the origins of the distributional patterns involved in hierarchical alignment suggests, however, that at least some of these patterns may actually be unrelated to any difference in prominence between speech act and non speech act participants, and the relative degree of naturalness of particular participant combinations.

As far as direct-inverse marking is concerned, the available evidence about the origin of inverse affixes shows two major paths of development. In several North American languages, illustrated by Shasta and Nez Perce in (9) and (10) below, morphemes indicating that a non speech act participant acts upon a speech act participant are transparently related to cislocative elements meaning 'hither', 'here', or 'this way', and have been argued to have originated from these elements through a process whereby sentences such as 'He is Verbing hither' and 'May there be Verbing hither' are reinterpreted as 'He is Verbing me/you' and 'May you Verb me' (Mithun 1996).

(9) Shasta (Shastan; Mithun 1996: 420–422)

    a. *Kwáskak-**ak**.*
       they.ran-hither
       'They ran hither'

    b. *Rát·ayka-**mak**.*
       he.is.chasing-hither
       'He is chasing me'

    c. *Súmatahávk-**ak**.*
       I.make-angy-hither
       'I am making you angry'

    d. *Twári·čača·-m·**aak**.*
       you.look-hither
       'Why do you look at me?'

(10) Nez Perce (Sahaptian)

    a. *I-q́ínun-a.*
       3-see-PAST
       'He saw/looked'   (Rude 1991: 38)

    b. *I-q́ínun-**im**-a.*
       3-see-CISL-PAST
       'He looked this way'   (Rude 1991: 38)

    c. *Tiwíikin.*
       follow
       'I have followed you'   (Mithun 1991: 418)

    d. *Tiwíixn-**im**.*
       follow-CISL
       'You have followed me'   (Mithun 1991: 418)

The use of cislocative elements makes it possible to avoid direct reference to speech act participants, which is a quite common tendency cross-linguistically, particularly in directive speech acts where speakers are requesting action towards themselves (Heath 1996; Mithun 1996: 429; Siewierska 2004: 235–245). The relevant constructions, then, are naturally reinterpreted as indicating action upon a speech act participant. This process is one of context-induced reinterpretation. The use of the cislocative element is originally motivated by the fact that it contributes a specific component of the global meaning of the construction, and possibly by the need to avoid overt reference to a speech act participant.[4] Over time, the cislocative meaning is bleached and the cislocative element takes on a new meaning originally associated with the context as a whole. This is basically a mechanism of metonymization (Traugott and Dasher 2005), which is crucially related to the relationship between the original meaning of the cislocative and the global meaning of the context, rather than a perceived difference between speech act and non speech act participants, or the relative degree of naturalness of particular participant combinations.

---

4 This provides an explanation for the fact that not all languages that have inverse morphemes also have direct morphemes, which in the literature on hierarchical alignment (e.g. DeLancey 1981) has been assumed to be because of the higher naturalness of the situation where a speech act participant acts upon a non speech act participant. While the use of cislocative markers is motivated by the need to avoid overt reference to speech act participants, there does not appear to be any tendency to avoid reference to non speech act participants, so presumably these participants will be referred to explicitly, rather than implicitly through the use of elements that could give rise to direct markers (e.g. directional markers such as 'there' and the like.

Another possible source for inverse affixes are third person forms, possibly indefinites. This origin, for example, has been postulated by Fortescue (1997) for the so-called general or strong inverse prefix *ne-* in Chukchi, which is used in various combinations involving first, second, and third person objects. This is illustrated in (11), where the prefix is combined with the second person singular suffix *-gət* to indicate that a third person acts upon a second person singular. Jacques (2010, p.c.) also suggests that the Japhug Rgyalrong inverse suffix *-wy*, the use of which is illustrated in (12), might have originated from the third person pronoun *wə.

(11) Chukchi (Chukotan; Fortescue 1997: 382)

Ne-l?u-gət.
GENLINV-see-2SG
'He saw you'

(12) Japhug Rgyalrong (Sino-Tibetan; Jacques 2010: 129)

a. *Pɯ-mtó-t-a.*
AOR-see-PAT-1SG
'I saw him/her/it'

b. *Pɯ́-**wy**-mto-a.*
AOR-INV-see-1SG
'He/she/it saw me.'

In such cases, the use of inverse morphemes originates from the fact that they originally refer to a third person participant effectively involved in the action, so once again there is no obvious evidence that this use is related to the lower naturalness of the situation being described as opposed to one where a speech act participant acts upon a non speech act participant.

As far as indexation is concerned, bound person forms are known to originate from the affixation of corresponding independent forms, and many languages lack independent third person forms altogether (Mithun 1991, Siewierska 2004 and 2010b, among others). In these languages, if bound person forms develop from independent forms, the resulting indexation system may only be one with first and second but no third person forms. This seems to be a plausible origin for several indexation systems that display hierarchical alignment, because the relevant languages, as illustrated in (13)–(15) for Tangut, Diegueño, and Tiriyó, do not have independent third person pronouns (in the examples, '>' means 'acts upon').[5]

---

[5] The fact that some languages that display hierarchical alignment in indexation do have third person independent forms is not evidence against this hypothesis, because these forms often develop or become affixed after the affixation of first and second person forms (Mithun 1991).

(13) Person forms in Tangut (Sino-Tibetan)
Independent (Hwang-Cherng 2003: 607):

1 ŋa SG.FAM
  ŋa njɨ PL.FAM
2 nja SG.FAM
  nja njɨ PL.FAM
3 supplied by demonstratives

Bound (Watters 2002: 374, and references therein):
-ŋa 1SG.S, 1SG.A >3SG.P, 2SG.A>1SG.P, 2PL.A>1SG., 3SG.A>1SG.P, 3PL.A>1SG.P
-ni 1PL.S, 1PL.A>3SG.P, 2PL.S, 2PL.A>3SG.P
-na 2SG.S, 2SG.A>3SG.P, 3SG.A>2SG.P, 3PL.A>2SG.P

(14) Person forms in Diegueño (Yuman)
Independent (Langdon 1970: 145–146):

1 SG ʔən^ya
  PL ʔən^yawup
2 SG ma
  PL mən^yawup
3 supplied by demonstratives

Bound (Langdon 1970: 139–140):
n^y- 1A>2P, 3A>1P
ʔn^ym- 2A>1P
m- 2S, 3A>2P, 2A>3P
ʔ- 1S, 1A>3P

(15) Person forms in Tiriyó (Cariban)
Independent (noncollective; Meira 2006):

1 SG wï(i)
  PL.INCL kïmë
  PL.EXCL anja
2 ëmë
3 supplied by demonstratives

Bound (Gildea 1998: ch. 5; Meira 2006):
wɨ- 1S, 1A>3P
mɨ- 2S, 2A>3P
y(i)- 1S, 3A>1P
ə- 2S, 3A>2P

Sometimes, languages do have independent third person forms, but only indefinite ones (e.g. 'somebody', 'one' 'something', as opposed to 'he', 'she', 'it' and the like). This pattern, which has been described by Mithun (1991) and (1993) for several North American languages, may in principle also give rise to systems with only first and second person bound forms, because indefinite third person independent forms sometimes evolve into first and second person, rather than third person bound forms.⁶ As has been shown by Chafe (1990) and Mithun (1993), this happens when these forms are used to refer to a speech act participant in order to defocus attention from this participant. This is illustrated in (16) for Caddo, where the same prefix can be used to refer both to an indefinite third person and to first or second persons.

(16) Caddo (Caddoan; Chafe 1990: 60)

a. **Yi**-ʔi=ʔán-ah.
DEFOC.AG-catch-PERF
'One [of them] caught him'

b. **Yu**-t-háy=wa=yúh-ʔaʔ.
DEFOC.BEN-DAT-tell.PL-FUT
'He will tell us'

These facts suggest that hierarchical alignment in indexation is a result of what independent person forms existed in the language, that is, whether the language had any independent third person form at all and how these evolved, rather than the relative prominence of first and second participants as opposed to third.⁷

---

6 In other cases, indefinite third person independent forms evolve into bound forms with the same meaning, which gives rise to systems with indefinite, but no definite third person bound forms. This process usually takes place after the language has developed first and second person bound forms (Mithun 1991).

7 A related question is why languages tend to have first and second person independent forms, rather than third person ones. In principle, this might be related to accessibility (see Siewierska 2004: 173–185 for a critical appraisal of this notion). Pronouns tend to be used for first and second persons, rather than for third persons, because the former are more accessible than the latter. This implies a cognitive asymmetry between the various persons, as assumed in current explanations of hierarchical alignment patterns. Accessibility, however, does not account for why languages sometimes have indefinite, rather than definite third person pronouns, as indefinite third persons are presumably less accessible than definite ones. Also, as is observed by Mithun (1991), in languages that have only first and second person independent forms, third persons are usually referred to by zero, which is difficult to reconcile with the fact that third persons are less accessible than first and second persons, as zero marking is usually reserved for more accessible referents. A possible clue, however, is provided by the fact that pronouns originate from grammaticalization (Heine and Song 2011). Speaker and hearer are semantically specific notions, so

Diachronic evidence also provides a natural explanation for some facts about hierarchical alignment patterns that are difficult to account for in terms of the mechanisms that have been postulated to account for these patterns on synchronic grounds. In some languages, inverse morphemes are used to indicate that a second person acts upon a first person (see e.g. Haude 2006 for Movima). In other languages, however, they are used to indicate that a first person acts upon a second person, and in yet other languages, as can be seen from the Shasta examples in (9c–d) above, they can be used to indicate both of these situations. If one assumes that the use of inverse morphemes reflects the relative naturalness of the situation being encoded, then one has to assume that particular situations where a speech act participant acts upon another are not conceptualized as having the same degree of naturalness from one language to another,[8] and it is not clear why the morphemes are used to indicate reverse situations within the same language. These facts, however, are naturally accounted for by the origins of inverse morphemes. If the morphemes originate from a cislocative, then they are likely to be found in different situations involving speech act participants, because cislocative elements are compatible with any situation involving a speech act participant. If they originate from third person indefinite elements, then they may also be found in situations where a speech act participant acts upon another, because as was illustrated for Caddo in (16) above third person indefinites are also used in order to refer to speech act participants without overtly mentioning them.

4 Some possible origins of singular vs. plural distinctions

The referential hierarchy has also been used to describe the cross-linguistic distribution of singular vs. plural distinctions. As has been shown in the typological literature (Corbett 2000, among others), these distinctions are often limited to a

---

languages will have conventional strategies to convey these notions, which may eventually give rise to first and second person forms. The notion of third person, on the other hand, is just a component of a variety of other more specific meanings (e.g. 'John', 'cat', 'book' etc.). In most cases, these meanings are usually more central to the discourse context than the notion of third person in itself, so there is no particular reason why the various lexical items conveying these meanings should grammaticalize into third person.

8 This assumption is in fact implicit in much of the literature on hierarchical alignment in Algonquian languages (see Zúñiga 2006 and Lockwood & Macaulay 2012 for critical reviews), where different versions of the referential hierarchy are postulated for different languages depending on what person combinations are indicated by direct and inverse morphemes.

left end portion of the hierarchy, for example, first and second person pronoun as opposed to third person pronouns and nouns, pronouns and kin terms as opposed to animate and inanimate nouns, pronouns and human nouns as opposed to other nouns, or pronouns and animate nouns as opposed to inanimate nouns.

The most widespread explanation for these patterns is that number distinctions tend to be made in the domains where they are more relevant, and they are more relevant to the NP types towards the left end of the hierarchy, including for example first and second person pronouns, kin terms, and human or animate nouns, because these NPs encode animate referents, and these referents are inherently individuated (Comrie 1989, Corbett 2000, Croft 2003, Haspelmath 2005, among others).

This explanation, as repeatedly pointed out in the literature (Smith-Stark 1974: 665–666, Lyons 1999: 215), does not actually provide a comprehensive account of the distribution of singular vs. plural distinctions along the referential hierarchy. For example, these distinctions are sometimes made for particular nouns or NP types but not for other nouns or NP types whose referents involve the same degree of animacy and individuation, e.g. nouns such as 'man', 'child', 'sister' or 'woman', or kin terms in general, but not other human or animate nouns. Also, some languages have singular vs. plural distinctions for third person pronouns, which can refer to either animate or inanimate referents, but not for human or animate nouns, which never refer to inanimate referents. This suggests that animacy and individuation are at best responsible for just some aspects of the distribution of singular vs. plural distinctions. In what follows, a number of diachronic processes will be discussed pertaining to the development of these distinctions for different NP types. These processes, it will be argued, suggest that whether or not a singular vs. plural distinction is limited to particular NP types depends on what source constructions gave rise to the distinction, rather than any ranking of different NP types with regard to specific properties such as animacy or individuation.

As is well-known (see, e.g., Haspelmath 2005), many languages distinguish between singular and plural through the use of an overt morpheme for plural, and zero marking for singular. In many cases where the distinction is restricted to some particular NP type, the plural marker originates from the grammaticalization of an expression restricted to or typically used with that NP type. For example, plural markers restricted to humans or animates typically originate from expressions meaning 'people', as illustrated in (17) for Orkhon Turkic (see also Grierson 1883–1887, and Chatterji 1926 for similar patterns in several Indo-Aryan languages).

(17) Orkhon Turkic (Altaic): -*yun* / *gün* -PL, only for humans; cf. Uyghur (Altaic) *kün* 'people, folks', Mongolian (Altaic) *kümün* 'man, people' (Tekin 1968: 121)

Markers restricted to pronouns, or pronouns and human nouns, may originate from associative markers in expressions such as 'X and his peers, family, group', and associative meanings are typically relevant to pronouns and human nouns, rather than other NP types (Corbett (2000: 83–84)). This origin has been postulated, for example, for the plural markers of Ghanaian Pidgin English (Huber 1999) and Mandarin Chinese (Iljic 2001).

Plural markers may also develop from the grammaticalization of expressions such as 'all', 'several', 'many', and the like. These expressions are not restricted to particular NP types, and the distribution of the resulting plural markers is also unconstrained. This is illustrated in (18) and (19) for Tlingit and Magahi. In fact, languages sometimes have different plural markers. Some are derived from expressions pertaining to humans or animates, such as 'people', and are restricted to these NP types. Others are derived from expressions that can apply to all NP types, e.g. 'all', and are not so restricted. This pattern is illustrated in (20) for Maithili.

(18) Tlingit (Na-Dene; Swanton 1911: 169)

    a. *yuyā LAn-**q!***
       big whale-COLL
       'a big whale' (lit. 'a lot of whale')

    b. *ƚīngît/ gux/ hît, ƚīngît'-/ gux-/ hî'- **q!***
       man slave house man   slave house COLL
       'man/ slave/ house, many man together/ slaves/ houses'

(19) Magahi (Indo-Aryan; Grierson 1883–1887: 6–14)

    *ghar/ jannī/ ham **sab.***
    house woman I   all
    houses/ women/ we

(20) Maithili (Indo-Aryan; Yadav 1997: 70, 69)

    a. *ənḍit/ *bhəīs **lokəin***
       pundit buffalo people
       'pundits, *buffaloes'

    b. *jən/   gæ **səb***
       labourer cow all
       laborers, cows'

In all of these cases, singular vs. plural distinctions develop as specific plural markers arise through grammaticalization. The source elements, e.g. 'people', 'all', or associatives, typically involve the notion of plurality, and in a number of contexts the meaning components that they contribute in addition to this notion, while relevant to the situation being described, may be communicatively peripheral. For example, sentences such as 'mark where all the windows are' (as opposed, e.g., to 'all the windows are shuttered and most are double glazed'), or 'several/ a few/ a lot of people do that, but I don't' (as opposed to 'I blocked several people and they continue to have access to my discussions', 'a few people can get a lot done', 'a view shared by a lot of people') are normally used as equivalents of their unquantified counterparts, 'mark where the windows are' and 'people do that, but I don't'. Likewise, the meaning contribution of expressions such as 'people' is redundant when these expressions, as is often the case, are used in combination with terms referring to a group of human beings, e.g. 'the British people', 'the wizard people' or the like. It is then likely that the reinterpretation of particular expressions as encoding plurality is triggered by the reduced contextual prominence of their other meaning components. This is an instance of a process that Bybee, Perkins, and Pagliuca (1994: 81–87; 289–293) call generalization, which has been shown to be pervasive in grammaticalization (Heine, Claudi, and Hünnemeyer 1991, Bybee, Perkins & Pagliuca 1994, Hopper & Traugott 2003, Eckardt 2006, among others). This process is driven by the relative contextual prominence of the various meaning components of individual expressions, rather than by the relevance of the new meanings of these expressions for particular categories, for example the relevance of number distinctions for animate or individuated referents. The etymology of the various plural markers provides a ready explanation for their distribution across particular NP types, so relevance does not appear to play any obvious role in this distribution either.

Similar observations apply to some diachronic processes leading to the development of singular vs. plural distinctions for personal pronouns and kin terms. Contrary to nouns, pronouns usually originate from grammaticalization, and different lexical items, as illustrated in (21) below, may grammaticalize into different person and number forms. For example, humbling expressions such as 'servant' and the like, intensifiers, and proximal deictics give rise to first person singular forms, expressions such as 'people' give rise to either first or third person plural forms, and expressions such as 'man' and the like or distal deictics ('there') give rise to third person singular forms (Heine and Song (2011)). This is reflected by the fact that the singular and plural forms of pronouns, as opposed to those of nouns, are often suppletive (Daniel 2005).

(21) Lendu (Nilo-Saharan): *ku* 3SG < *ke* 'man', *ndrù, kpà* 'people, 3PL';
Zande (Niger-Congo) *kɔ* 3SG <**ko* 'man, male'(Heine and Song 2011: 26–28);
Ngiti (Nilo-Saharan): *àlɛ̃* 1PL.INCL < *alɛ* 'person' (Kutsch Lojenga 1994: 195)

While the way in which pronouns develop implies that they will often have distinct singular and plural forms, then, this does not hold for nouns.⁹ In this case too, the fact that singular vs. plural distinctions are limited to particular NP types, such as pronouns as opposed to nouns, is a result of how these distinctions originate, rather than any ranking of the relevant NP types with regard to some particular property.

In a number of languages where singular vs. plural distinctions are restricted to kin terms, the language has distinct singular and plural forms for verbs, and kin terms originate from verbal expressions, e.g. 'she whom you call daughter' or the like. In this case, the fact that kin terms display a singular vs. plural distinction not found for other NP types is a consequence of their verbal origin, rather than any inherent property of kin terms in themselves such as animacy. This pattern is attested in a number of North American languages, such as Jamul Tiipay. In this language, as illustrated in (22), both verbs and kin terms have reduplicated plural forms.

(22) Jamul Tipay (Yuman; Miller 2001: 72, 80)

   a. *nyay* / ***nyaay***
      hunt / hunt.PL
      'hunt / hunt.PL'

   b. *san* / ***saan***
      younger.sister / younger.sister.PL
      'younger sister/younger sisters'

Animacy and individuation do appear to be involved in some of the cases where a singular vs. plural distinction is restricted to particular NP types. For example, in a number of creoles and West African languages, plural forms are used to indicate individuated, as opposed to generic items (Holm 1988: 193, Baptista 2007). As animates are typically individuated, this may give rise to a situation where animates, as opposed to inanimates, are obligatorily marked for plural (see Kihm 1994: 133–134 for Kriyol). Likewise, in a number of North American languages, plural forms restricted to human or animates evolved from distributive

---

9 Interestingly, suppletive number forms are sometimes found for nouns whose referents often occur in groups, for example 'child', 'man', or 'woman', and in many languages these are the only nouns that distinguish between singular and plural (see e.g. Mithun 1988 on Central Pomo). This is naturally accounted for by assuming that, because of its frequency, the case where the referents of the relevant nouns occur in a group is designated by a distinct lexical item, which over time grammaticalizes into a suppletive plural form.

expressions such as e.g. 'man here and there', 'their respective wife(s)' or the like (Mithun 1999: 88–91, among others). This is illustrated in (23) below for Quileute, where a reduplicated form of nouns can be used to indicate both distribution (23a) and plurality (23b). The development from distributive forms to plural forms is a rather natural one, because distributive expressions typically involve plurality. Sapir (1930–1931: 257) and Mithun (1999: 90–91) argue that this development is favored by human and animate nouns because these nouns refer to individuated referents, so, when there is a plurality of these referents, these will be scattered over space, and the noun will carry a definite marker every time more than one is mentioned.

(23) Quileute (Chimakuan; Andrade 1933: 187)

    a. *tukô·yo'* / ***tut̲kôyo***
       snow / snow.DISTR
       'snow/snow here and there'

    b. *á't'cit* / *á'á't'cit*
       chief / chief.DISTR
       'chief/chiefs'

While in such cases the fact that human and animate nouns encode individuated referents does play a role in the distribution of singular vs. plural distinctions, this is related to specific properties of the relevant constructions (for example, the fact that they indicate individuated referents, or originate from distributive expressions), and need not be the case for other construction types.

5 Concluding remarks

A number of recent studies have questioned the validity of the referential hierarchy by showing that the predictions of the hierarchy are not fully borne out, that the patterns described by the hierarchy are areally and genealogically restricted, and that in some cases these patterns might be an epiphenomenal result of language-specific processes (Filimonova 2005, Bickel 2008, Bickel, Witzlack-Makarevich & Zakharko (draft)). However, the available diachronic evidence about the origin of alignment splits, hierarchical alignment, and the use of singular vs. plural distinctions for particular NP types poses some more general challenges for current explanations of the referential hierarchy. First, this evidence shows that the patterns that may be taken as evidence for the hierarchy (whatever their geographical or genealogical distribution) do not obviously originate from the mechanisms that have been postulated to account for these patterns on synchronic grounds, for example animacy, individuation, a perceived difference between speech act and non speech act participants, or the need to disambiguate particular argument roles. To the extent that the diachronic evidence pertains to specific source constructions in individual languages, this does not rule out that the mechanisms postulated on synchronic grounds may play a role in other languages where the relevant patterns originate from different source constructions. The diachronic evidence implies, however, that, contrary to the traditional view, the mere occurrence of these patterns in a language cannot be taken as evidence for these mechanisms, and that the number of cases where it is possible that they play a role is smaller than currently assumed (for a similar point of view, see Creissels 2008).

More importantly perhaps, the diachronic evidence shows that the various patterns captured by the referential hierarchy for some particular grammatical domain need not all originate from the same mechanisms, and that the same pattern may originate from different mechanisms in different languages. For example, different types of restrictions in the distribution of ergative systems originate from the reinterpretation of different source constructions (e.g. indexicals vs. instrumentals), and yet other processes of reinterpretation (such as the reinterpretation of topic markers into P markers) give rise to restrictions in the distribution of accusative systems. Inverse markers may originate from either cislocatives or third person forms, and this process is different from those presumably leading to the development of systems with no bound third person forms. The processes leading to singular vs. plural distinctions being restricted to particular NP types are not the same as the processes leading to these distinctions being restricted to some other NP type, and the same holds for different cases where these distinctions are restricted to the same NP type. For example, the fact that singular vs. plural distinctions are restricted to pronouns may be a result of the grammaticalization of distinct lexical items into either singular or plural pronominal forms, and the fact that they are restricted to humans may be a result of the development of plural forms from either distributives or expressions of multitude such as 'people'.

These facts suggest that, contrary to the traditional view, the referential hierarchy does not capture a ranking of different NP types with regard to some property that has psychological reality and leads speakers to use particular constructions, for example the relative likelihood of different NPs occurring in particular argument roles, the relative naturalness of different types of situations involving speech act and non speech act participants, or the relative degree of animacy or individuation of different referents. Rather, the hierarchy is best regarded as a descriptive schema that is general enough to capture the outputs of several independent diachronic processes.

The idea that the patterns described by the referential hierarchy (or other typological hierarchies, for that matter) are a result of the original distribution of specific source constructions provides a natural explanation for a number of facts that are not accounted for by existing explanations. First, this idea makes it unnecessary to account for exceptions to a particular pattern. As is well-known, typological hierarchies, including the referential hierarchy (Filimonova 2005), have a number of exceptions. If one assumes that the patterns described by some hierarchy originate from general principles related to inherent properties of the categories on the hierarchy, then one has to account for why these principles are contradicted in some cases. If the various patterns reflect the original distribution of their source constructions, however, then exceptional patterns will arise as a result of the reinterpretation of different source constructions. This is to be expected, because languages do not all have the same source constructions, and these may or may not undergo particular reinterpretation processes, as has been extensively shown in grammaticalization studies.

For example, contrary to the predictions of the referential hierarchy, singular vs. plural distinctions in Tlingit, as determined by the use of the plural marker exemplified in (18b) above, are more often made for inanimate, rather than animate nouns (Swanton 1911: 169). However, contrary to plural markers in other languages, which originate from expressions pertaining to humans or animates, the Tlingit plural marker was originally a collective with the meaning 'a lot of', as illustrated in (18a) above, and this type of expressions are recurrently used with inanimate nouns.

Similarly, as was pointed out in section 4, the idea that the distribution of singular vs. plural distinctions is related to animacy is at odds with the fact that in some languages the distinction is made for some NP types, e.g. third person pronouns or kin terms, but not for others that are associated with the same or a higher degree of animacy, e.g. animate nouns. This is naturally explained, however, by assuming that the distribution of singular vs. plural distinctions is actually determined by their source constructions. Sometimes, these distinctions develop from constructions pertaining to human or animate nouns, and they will be restricted to these nouns, at least initially. In other cases, they may develop from constructions restricted to other NP types (for example, from specific lexical items that grammaticalize into singular and plural pronominal forms, or from singular and plural verbal forms that are reinterpreted as kin terms), and they will be restricted to these NPs, regardless of animacy.

Also, existing accounts of the referential hierarchy and other typological hierarchies usually provide a direct explanation for the patterns where the distribution of a particular contruction is limited to some portion of the hierarchy, but not for those where this distribution is unconstrained, or those where the construction is not attested at all.[10] For example, the idea that speakers use overt marking for particular argument roles only when these roles are more in need of disambiguation provides an explanation for why accusative and ergative case marking systems are sometimes restricted to particular NP types, but does not explain why these systems may be used for all NP types, nor why A, P and S arguments may be undifferentiated (in fact, these two situations make for the majority of the world's languages, according to the data presented in Comrie 2008). These facts, however, follow naturally from the idea that the various patterns described by a hierarchy originate from the reinterpretation of several source constructions. Some source constructions will determine restrictions in the distribution of the resulting constructions (which however may be extended to new contexts in the course of time, thus yielding different distributional patterns). Other source constructions will yield unrestricted distributions from the beginning. Also, as individual source contructions need not be present or undergo reinterpretation in all languages, the resulting constructions will simply be absent from some languages.

Unlike traditional explanations, this analysis does not account for the nonoccurrence or the rarity of certain logically possible patterns, for example ergative systems restricted to a left end portion of the hierarchy, or singular vs. plural distinctions restricted to a right end portion. In principle, this phenomenon could be regarded as evidence that the various diachronic processes that lead to the development of the attested patterns reflect some more general principle of the type of those postulated in synchronic analyses, which allows for the development of the attested patterns, possibly through different diachronic mechanisms, and disallows the development of other logically possible patterns. The available diachronic evidence suggests, however, that the attested patterns are the result of context-induced processes of reinterpretation of highly specific source constructions, which is consistent with the large body of evidence about the development of grammatical categories that has been collected through grammaticalization studies (Bybee, Perkins & Pagliuca 1994, Heine 2003, among several others). This implies that any explanation about the non occurrence or the rarity of particular patterns should take into account what source constructions, if any, could give rise to these patterns, and how these constructions are usually reinterpreted in discourse, rather than just the patterns that are attested at the synchronic level.

These facts call for a shift in perspective in typological research. Typologists usually try to identify theoretically significant patterns based on synchronic

---

10 Such cases are sometimes accounted for in terms of competing motivations. For a critique of this approach, see Cristofaro (to appear).

distributions, for example, the distribution of particular alignment patterns or singular vs. plural distinctions across different NP types. While synchronically established types may be used as descriptive tools, however, it is crucial for typologists to obtain information about the history of individual constructions, and to shift from the comparison of synchronically established types to that of the diachronic processes that give rise to these types in individual languages.

Abbreviations

1 first person, 2 second person, 3 third person, ACC accusative, AG agent, AOR aorist, ASP aspect, AUX auxiliary, BEN beneficiary, CISL cislocative, COLL collective, DAT dative, DEFOC defocusing, DEM demonstrative, DEPFUT dependent future, DISTR distributive, ERG ergative, EXCL exclusive, F feminine, FAM familiar, FUT future, GENINV general inverse, IMPF imperfect, INCL inclusive, INV inverse, M masculine, NOMLZR nominalizer, OBJ object, OBL oblique, PAST past tense, PAT patient, PERF perfect, PL plural, POSS possessor, PUNCT punctual, SG singular, SUBJ subject.

References

Andrade, Manuel J. 1933. Quileute. In Frans Boas (ed.), *Handbook of American Indian Languages*, Volume 3, 151–292. Washington: Smithsonian Institution. Bureau of American Ethnology.
Baptista, Marlyse. 2007. Properties of noun phrases in Creole languages: a synthetic comparative exposition. In Marlyse Baptista & Jacqueline Guéron (eds.), *Noun Phrases in Creole Languages: A Multi-faceted Approach*, 459–479. Amsterdam and Philadelphia: John Benjamins.
Bickel, Balthasar. 2008. On the scope of the referential hierarchy in the typology of grammatical relations. In Greville G. Corbett & Michael Noonan (eds.), *Case and grammatical relations: papers in honor of Bernard Comrie*, 191–210. Amsterdam and Philadelphia: John Benjamins.
Bickel, Balthasar, Alena Witzlack-Makarevich & Taras Zakharko. Typological evidence against universal effects of referential scales on case alignment. Draft, University of Zürich.
Bubeník, Vit. 1998. *A historical syntax of late middle Indo-Aryan (Apabhraṃśa)*. Amsterdam and Philadelphia: John Benjamins.
Bybee, Joan, Revere Perkins & William Pagliuca. 1994. *The evolution of grammar.* Chicago and London: The University of Chicago Press.
Chafe, Wallace. 1990. Use of the Defocusing Pronominal Prefixes in Caddo. Anthropological Linguistics 32. 57–68.
Chatterji, Suniti K. 1926. *The Origin and Development of the Bengali Language.* Calcutta: Calcutta University Press.
Comrie, Bernard. 1980. Inverse verb forms in Siberia: Evidence from Chukchee, Koryak, and Kamchadal. *Folia Linguistica* 1. 61–74.

Comrie, Bernard. 1989. *Language universals and linguistic typology*. 2nd edition. Oxford: Basil Blackwell.
Comrie, Bernard. 2008. Alignment of Case Marking of Full Noun Phrases. In Martin Haspelmath, Matthew S. Dryer, David Gil & Bernard Comrie (eds.), *The World Atlas of Language Structures Online*. Munich: Max Planck Digital Library. (http://wals.info/feature/98)
Corbett, Greville G. 2000. *Number*. Cambridge: Cambridge University Press.
Creissels, Denis. 2008. Direct and indirect explanations of typological regularities: the case of alignment variations. *Folia Linguistica* 42. 1–38.
Cristofaro, Sonia. To appear. Competing motivations and diachrony: what evidence for what motivations? In Andrej Malchukov, Edith Moravcsik & Brian MacWhinney (eds.), *Competing motivations in grammar and cognition*. Oxford: Oxford University Press.
Croft, William. 2003. *Typology and universals*. 2nd edition. Cambridge: Cambridge University Press.
Cyffer, Norbert. 1998. *A Sketch of Kanuri*. Köln: Rüdiger Köppe.
Daniel, Michael. 2005. Plurality in Independent Personal Pronouns. In Martin Haspelmath, Matthew S. Dryer, David Gil & Bernard Comrie (eds.), *The World Atlas of Language Structures Online*. Munich: Max Planck Digital Library.
DeLancey, Scott. 1981. An interpretation of split ergativity and related patterns. *Language* 57. 626–657.
Dixon, Robert M. W. 1979. Ergativity. *Language* 55. 59–138.
Dixon, Robert M. W. 1994. *Ergativity*. Cambridge: Cambridge University Press.
Eckardt, Regine. 2006. *Meaning Change in Grammaticalization: An Enquiry into Semantic Reanalysis*. Oxford: Oxford University Press.
Filimonova, Elena. 2005. The noun phrase hierarchy and relational marking: Problems and counterevidence. *Linguistic Typology* 9. 77–113.
Fortescue, Michael. 1997. Eskimo influence on the formation of the Chukotkan Ergative clause. *Studies in Language* 21(2). 369–409.
Franchetto, Bruna. 1990. Ergativity and nominativity in Kuikúro and other Carib languages. In Doris Payne (ed.), *Amazonian linguistics: Studies in Lowland South America languages*, 407–428. Austin: University of Texas Press.
Garrett, Andrew. 1990. The Origin of NP Split Ergativity. *Language* 66. 261–296.
Gildea, Spike. 1998. *On reconstructing grammar: Comparative Cariban morphosyntax*. Oxford: Oxford University Press.
Givón, Talmy. 1976. Topic, pronoun and grammatical agreement. In Charles N. Li (ed.), *Subject and topic*, 149–189. New York: Academic Press.
Grierson, George A. 1883–1887. *Seven grammars of the dialects and subdialects of the Bihárí language*. Pt. III. Calcutta: Bengal Secretariat.
Haspelmath, Martin. 2005. Occurrence of nominal plurality. In Martin Haspelmath, Matthew S. Dryer, David Gil & Bernard Comrie (eds.), *The World Atlas of Language Structures Online*. Munich: Max Planck Digital Library.
Haude, Katharina. 2006. *A Grammar of Movima*. Ph.D. dissertation, Radboud University. (http://webdoc.ubn.ru.nl/mono/h/haude_k/gramofmo.pdf)
Heath, Jeffrey. 1996. Pragmatic skewing in 1<->2 pronominal combinations in native American languages. *International Journal of American Linguistics* 64. 83–104.
Heine, Bernd. 2003. Grammaticalization. In Brian D. Joseph & Richard D. Janda (eds.), *The Handbook of Historical Linguistics*, 576–601. Oxford: Blackwell.
Heine, Bernd, Ulrike Claudi & Friedericke Hünnemeyer. 1991. *Grammaticalization*. Chicago: University of Chicago Press.

Heine, Bernd and Kyung-An Song. 2011. On the grammaticalization of Personal pronouns. *Journal of Linguistics* 47. 1–44. Available on CJO 2011 doi:10.1017/S0022226711000016.
Hercus, Louise. 1982. *The Bagandji language*. Pacific Linguistics. Series B-67. Canberra: The Australian National University.
Holm, John A. 1988. *Pidgins and Creoles. Vol. 1, Theory and structure*. Cambridge: Cambridge University Press.
Hopper, Paul J. & Elizabeth C. Traugott. 2003. *Grammaticalization. Second edition*. Cambridge: Cambridge University Press.
Huber, Magnus. 1999. *Ghanaian Pidgin English in its West African context: a sociohistorical and structural analysis*. Amsterdam and Philadelphia: John Benjamins.
Hwang-Cherng, Gong. 2003. Tangut. In Graham Thurgood and Randy J. LaPolla (eds.), *The Sino-Tibetan Languages*, 602–620. London & New York: Routledge.
Iemmolo, Giorgio. 2010. Topicality and differential object marking: evidence from Romance and beyond. *Studies in Language* 34(2). 239–272.
Iljic, Robert. 2001. The origin of the suffix -men [Chinese character] in Chinese. *Bulletin of the School of Oriental and African Studies* 64. 74–97.
Jacques, Guillaume. 2010. The Inverse in Japhug Rgyalrong. *Language and Linguistics* 11. 127–157.
Kihm, Alan. 1994. *Kriyol syntax: the Portugese-based Creole language of Guinea-Bissau*. Amsterdam and Philadelphia: John Benjamins.
König, Christa. 2008. *Case in Africa*. Oxford: Oxford University Press.
Kutsch Lojenga, Constance. 1994. *Ngiti: a central-Sudanic language of Zaire*. Köln: Rüdiger Köppe.
Langdon, Margaret. 1970. *A Grammar of Diegueño. The Mesa Grande Dialect*. University of California Publications in Linguistics 66. Berkeley and Los Angeles: University of California Press.
Li, Charles N. & Sandra A. Thompson. 1974a. An explanation of word order change SVO→SOV. *Foundations of Language* 12. 201–214.
Li, Charles N. & Sandra A. Thompson. 1974b. Historical change of word order: a case study in Chinese and its implications. In John M. Anderson and Charles Jones (eds.), *Historical Linguistics. Volume 1*, 199–217. Amsterdam: North Holland.
Lockwood, Hunter T. and Monica Macaulay. 2012. Prominence Hierarchies. *Language and Linguistics Compass* 36. 431–446.
Lord, Carol. 1993. *Historical change in serial verb constructions*. Amsterdam and Philadelphia: John Benjamins.
Lyons, Christopher. 1999. *Definiteness*. Cambridge: Cambridge University Press.
McGregor, William B. 2006. Focal and optional ergative marking in Warrwa. Kimberley, Western Australia. *Lingua* 116. 393–423.
McGregor, William B. 2008. Indexicals as sources of case markers in Australian languages. In Folke Josephson & Ingmar Söhrman (eds.), *Interdependence of diachronic and synchronic analyses*, 299–321. Amsterdam: John Benjamins.
Meira, Sergio. 2006. *A Grammar of Tiriyó*. Berlin & New York: De Gruyter Mouton.
Miller, Amy. 2001. *A Grammar of Jamul Tiipay*. Berlin & New York: De Gruyter Mouton.
Mithun, Marianne. 1988. Lexical categories and number in Central Pomo. In William Shipley (ed.), *In Honor of Mary Haas*, 517–537. Berlin & New York: De Gruyter Mouton.
Mithun, Marianne. 1991. The develoment of bound pronominal paradigms. In Winfed P. Lehmann & Helen-Jo J. Hewitt (eds.), *Language Typology 1988*, 85–104. Amsterdam: John Benjamins.
Mithun, Marianne. 1993. Reconstructing the Unidentified. In Henk Aertsen & Robert J. Jeffers (eds.), *Historical linguistics 1989*, 329–347. Amsterdam and Philadelphia: John Benjamins.

Mithun, Marianne. 1996. New directions in referentiality. In Barbara Fox (ed.), *Studies in Anaphora*, 413–435. Amsterdam and Philadelphia: John Benjamins.
Mithun, Marianne. 1999. *The Languages of Native North America*. Cambridge: Cambridge University Press.
Rude, Noel. 1991. On the Origin of the Nez Perce Ergative NP Suffix. *International Journal of American Linguistics* 57. 24–50.
Sapir, Edward. 1930–1931. *The Southern Paiute Language*. Boston: American Academy of Arts and Sciences.
Siewierska, Anna. 1998. Passive-to-ergative vs inverse-to-ergative. In Anna Siewierska & Jae J. Song (eds.), *Case, Tyology and Grammar: In Honor of Barry J. Blake*, 229–246. Amsterdam & Philadelphia: John Benjamins.
Siewierska, Anna. 2004. *Person*. Cambridge: Cambridge University Press.
Siewierska, Anna. 2010a. From third plural to passive: Incipient, emergent and Established passives. *Diachronica* 27. 73–109.
Siewierska, Anna. 2010b. Person asymmetries in zero expression and grammatical function. In Franck Floricic (ed.), *Essais de typologie et de linguistique générale. Mélanges offerts à Denis Creissels*, 471–485. Paris: ENS.
Smith-Stark, T. Cedric. 1974. The plurality split. In *Papers from the Tenth Regional Meeting of the Chicago Linguistics Society*. 657–671.
Song, Jae J. 2001. *Linguistic typology: morphology and syntax*. Harlow, Essex: Longman.
Swanton, John. 1911. Tlingit. In Frans Boas (ed.), *Handbook of American Indian Languages. Vol. 1*, 159–204. Washington: Smithsonian Institution. Bureau of American Ethnology.
Tekin, Talât. 1968. *A grammar of Orkhon Turkic*. Bloomington: Indiana University Press.
Traugott, Elizabeth C. & Richard B. Dasher. 2005. *Regularity in Semantic Change*. Cambridge: Cambridge University Press.
Verbeke, Saartje & Ludovic De Cuypere. 2009. The rise of ergativity in Hindi: Assessing the role of grammaticalization. *Folia Linguistica Historica* 30. 1–24.
Watters, David E. 2002. *A grammar of Kham*. Cambridge: Cambridge University Press.
Yadav, Rawatar. 1997. *A reference grammar of Maithili*. New Delhi: Munshiram Manoharlal.
Zúñiga, Fernando. 2006. *Deixis and alignment*. Amsterdam and Philadelphia: John Benjamins.

William Croft
Agreement as anaphora, anaphora as coreference

1 Introduction[1]

In his contribution to this volume, Martin Haspelmath argues that the term "indexation" should be used for all bound person forms, and the terms "agreement" and "pronoun" should not be used for such forms. Part of his motivation for this proposal is to avoid fruitless debates on whether certain bound person forms are "arguments" (pronouns) or merely "agreement", in particular those bound person forms which sometimes occur with an independent noun phrase referring to the same referent, and sometimes do not (Haspelmath's "cross-indexes"). Haspelmath contrasts cross-indexes with gramm-indexes (bound person forms that must always cooccur with independent coreferring noun phrases) and pro-indexes (those that never cooccur with independent coreferring noun phrases). He notes, however, that the distinction between gramm-indexes, cross-indexes and pro-indexes is not sharp, and there is a continuum between the three (Haspelmath, this volume; § 6).

I basically agree with Haspelmath's proposal. Indeed, I made similar arguments myself (Croft 2001: 226–232), and in the second edition of *Typology and universals* (Croft 2003), I systematically replaced the term 'agreement' with 'indexation' (with thanks to Matthew Dryer for encouraging me to do so), albeit with a broader use than Haspelmath has, for reasons given in footnote 2. Some of Haspelmath's universals may need revision. For instance, Kanuri has optional indexes (Hutchison 1981: 139; see Croft 2001: 228), contrary to Haspelmath's universal C. Also, it is unclear whether the fusion of oblique adposition and index in the verb, as in Abkhaz (Hewitt 1979: 104), or the indexation of an argument that is governed by an oblique case, as in Marra (Heath 1981: 87), violates Haspelmath's universal A. But these cases are rare, and Haspelmath's universals (several of which are also Anna Siewierska's) are certainly very strong tendencies.

However, Haspelmath sees his proposal as a modest one: 'I propose that bound person forms should be **called** indexes, and I suggest that we should not

---

[1] I would like to thank Dik Bakker, Greville Corbett and Martin Haspelmath for discussion and comments on an earlier version of this article. None of them bear any responsibility for errors contained herein.

ask whether they are pronouns or agreement forms' (Martin Haspelmath, pers. comm.). Nevertheless, Haspelmath's terminological proposal does have implications for the theoretical analysis of bound person forms – implications that are made explicit in Croft (2001) and will be elaborated upon in this chapter. Haspelmath argues that cross-indexes should not be forced into the category 'pronoun' or 'agreement marker'; this dichotomy is forced upon the analyst only because of a further assumption, that 'arguments should not be expressed twice, but only by a single element' (Haspelmath, this volume, §5.4). I also agree that this assumption is inappropriate, and argued against it as well (Croft 2001: 228–229). But I would like to go further, and question another assumption behind the "pronoun"–"agreement marker" dichotomy as well, hence going beyond the critique in Haspelmath's contribution.

The assumption I would like to challenge is a supposed contrast between bound person forms, and also bound forms that index other properties of referents such as gender and number,[2] on the one hand, and independent pronouns on the other. In this analysis, bound person forms (and gender-number forms), are said to agree with another element. Hence agreement is a grammatical relationship or dependency relation between two elements in a sentence. In agreement, there are two grammatical entities, and the relevant grammatical features of one entity – in Corbett's now widely used term, the target – are determined by the inherent grammatical properties of the other entity – the controller. These are properties of what Corbett calls canonical agreement. (We return to the notion of a canonical type in section 6). I will call the analyis of agreement as a relationship between grammatical forms the **grammatical-dependency** analysis.

The grammatical-dependency analysis of agreement is found in different grammatical traditions, albeit formulated in various ways, and with various qualifications and hedges:

- "**Agreement** (or **concord**) is usually described as a relation between words that share a morphosyntactic feature." (Matthews 1981: 247, emphasis original)
- "Agreement is the phenomenon by which a word carries morphological features that originate **somewhere else**". (Bickel & Nichols 2007: 229, emphasis added; also cited by Haspelmath [this volume, §9]. The discussion following

---

[2] Haspelmath excludes bound nonperson markers, such as gender-number markers found on adjectival forms, from his definition of 'index'. In this chapter, I use a broader definition of 'index' than Haspelmath: one that includes forms that refer to properties of referents other than person. The arguments in the remainder of this chapter apply to those forms as well. All indexes, including nonperson indexes, refer to arguments (Lehmann 1982). The commonest diachronic source for all indexes, including nonperson indexes, are pronouns (personal or demonstrative, which themselves can overlap in function; see section 4).

this quote makes clear that 'somewhere else' means some other element in the sentence.
– Constituent B agrees with constituent A (in category C) if and only if the following holds true:
  1. There is a grammatical or semantic syntagmatic relation between A and B.
  2. A grammatical category C with a form paradigm of subcategories exists.
  3. A belongs to a subcategory c of C, and A's belonging to c is independent of the presence or nature of B.
  4. C is expressed on B and forms a constituent with it. (Lehmann 1982: 203)

In contrast, pronouns are referring expressions (Lyons 1977: 637), in the same way that noun phrases are, and their grammatical properties are a consequence of this fact. Pronouns themselves appear to be nonuniform. First and second person ('egophoric' (Dahl 2000: 39) or 'locuphoric' (Haspelmath, this volume)) pronouns refer to their referents (the speech act participants) independently of any other expression in the sentence, and hence are not grammatically dependent, as Haspelmath notes (this volume). Third person ('allophoric' (Dahl 2000: 39)) pronouns are often analyzed as "anaphoric". That is, they are referring expressions, not agreement markers; but their grammatical properties are nevertheless dependent on a previously occurring referring expression. Hence third person pronouns also have a grammatical-dependency analysis in this view; but first and second person pronouns are given an **independent-reference** analysis.

The problem in identifying (person) agreement markers with bound person forms is the widespread existence of cross-indexes, in Haspelmath's terms. In most uses of cross-indexes (and all uses of pro-indexes), there cannot be a grammatical dependency because there is no element for the index to be dependent on (Croft 2001: 226–230). As noted at the beginning of this chapter, Haspelmath, like myself, suggests that we abandon the assumption of unique expression of arguments (referents). I would make, and did make, a slightly stronger statement: 'all indexes refer' (Croft 2001: 229). In other words, indexes are best analyzed as referring expressions, like independent pronouns and noun phrases, an analysis also proposed by Anna Siewierska (Siewierska 2004: 173). This analysis can be applied to nonperson markers as well, following Lehmann's arguments that modifiers index the argument that contains them (Lehmann 1982: 215–233; note, again, that I use the term 'index' more broadly than Haspelmath does (see footnote 2)).

If we adopt the analysis of indexes as referring expressions, then the dichotomy between agreement markers and pronouns is weakened: indexes are like anaphoric pronouns. This is the position taken by a number of scholars, including Anna Siewierska. Barlow, in an analysis of agreement phenomena, concludes that 'there are many similarities and no major distinction between local [indexical] and anaphoric [pronominal] agreement' (Barlow 1988: 154). In Corbett's recent survey of agreement phenomena (Corbett 2006, esp. §7.6), he writes, 'there is no principled way to distinguish the agreement variation of the pronoun from that of other targets [i.e. forms with (bound) indexes, in the broad sense]' (Corbett 2006: 229). Siewierska states that '[m]ost scholars working on agreement acknowledge that there is no good basis for differentiating between person agreement markers [indexes] and anaphoric pronouns' (Siewierska 2004: 121; see also Siewierska 1999: 225).

Nevertheless, anaphoric pronouns are frequently given a grammatical-dependency analysis, not unlike the definitions of grammatical agreement given above, albeit loosened to allow for a relationship to an element in the preceding discourse but not in the same sentence. Yet the same problem is found in applying a grammatical-dependency analysis to anaphoric pronouns as in applying a grammatical-dependency analysis to (bound) indexes. Third person pronouns occur without their putative "antecedents", so-called "antecedentless anaphora". This phenomenon was the locus of a scholarly debate some years ago, and led to a proposal that third person pronouns should not be analyzed as grammatically dependent on another element in the sentence or the discourse (the usual meaning of "anaphoric"; but see section 4). Instead, they should be analyzed as independent referring expressions in their own right. In other words, third person pronouns are like first and second person pronouns in being independent referring expressions.

In this article, I take the two proposals – that so-called agreement markers and so-called anaphoric pronouns cannot be distinguished, and that anaphoric pronouns are independent referring expression, and so are like deictic (first and second person) pronouns – and combine them. That is, I argue for an independent-referring analysis of all forms that have been called indexes or pronouns.[3]

---

[3] One might ask if there is a grammatically relevant distinction between indexes and independent pronouns. Haspelmath (this volume) makes a sharp distinction between the two, based on the bound-free criterion. In an earlier version of this article, I argued that this distinction was not a sharp one, following Haspelmath's (2011) critique of definitions of wordhood. Haspelmath (pers. comm.) argues that the index-pronoun distinction is based solely on the bound-free distinction, which cannot be equated with the intuitive definition of a word (Haspelmath 2011: 39–40), and that the bound-free distinction among person forms is relevant to the universals listed at the end of Haspelmath (this volume). This may be true but it is not clear to me whether the universals are in fact valid (see the counterexamples to A and C mentioned above), or whether the sources on which the universals are based clearly distinguish indexes from pronouns solely by the criteria of boundness, or whether the universals are in fact best formulated in terms of bound vs. free or in terms of some other grammatical parameter(s). The main reason I am somewhat skeptical about the sharpness of the index-pronoun distinction is that pronouns grammaticalize into indexes, and grammaticalization is a gradual process.

Such an analysis requires some defense, because it is not entirely straightforward: the grammatical-dependency analysis does appear to be motivated by certain grammatical facts. In this article, I will argue for a cognitive-discourse analysis of indexes and pronouns, mainly in the form proposed by Cornish (1986, 1987, 1996, 1999), and adopted by Anna Siewierska (2004, chapter 5). There are also crosslinguistic universals such as the Agreement Hierarchy (Corbett 1979, 1983, 1991, 2000, 2006) that cut across indexes and pronouns, and support a unified cognitive-discourse analysis of indexes and pronouns as independent referring expressions.

2 'Syntactic agreement', 'semantic agreement', and the Agreement Hierarchy

In the grammatical-dependency analysis, agreement is analyzed as a relationship between two grammatical expressions in a construction, with grammatical features that must "agree" or match in some grammatically-expressed feature, as the term implies (cf. Lehmann's definition of agreement in section 1). That is, the properties of canonical agreement in Corbett's sense are taken as the benchmark for motivating the grammatical-dependency analysis.

As noted in §1 above, a similar grammatical-dependency analysis has been proposed for third person pronouns. Although there is no controller available in the immediate grammatical context, there is normally an antecedent that appears to serve as the controller. The grammatical-dependency analysis is that a reduced referential device such as a (third person) pronoun or an index must be dependent on another referring expression. In the grammatical-dependency analysis, agreement and anaphora are grammatically alike, even if not quite in the same way: both involve an asymmetric but grammatical dependency between two linguistic expressions.

In contrast, the independent-reference analysis of third person pronouns proposes that they are not dependent on another referring expression. In this analysis, the only relationship between the personal pronoun and its antecedent is *coreference*. Coreference implies that the full expression and the reduced expression – the personal pronoun – simply happen to refer to the same referent in the discourse. The use of a personal pronoun instead of a full referring expression occurs when the pragmatic conditions are right. Roughly, the pragmatic conditions are when the referent is sufficiently highly accessible (Givón 1983; Ariel 1988, 1990; Siewierska & Bakker 2005). In this analysis, the grammatical features of personal pronouns are determined by semantic properties of the referent.

In fact, there are two seemingly contradictory grammatical patterns that must somehow be reconciled for a more general theory of the use of pronouns and indexes. One observation supports the independent-reference analysis and the other supports the grammatical-dependency analysis, which are mutually inconsistent analyses of the same phenomenon.

The first pattern poses a serious problem for the indepedent-reference analysis of personal pronouns as pragmatically determined independently referring expressions. Personal pronouns may have their grammatical features determined by the grammatical features of an antecedent full expression rather than by inherent features of their referent. Corbett reports the Russian example (1), heard in May 1988 on Red Square in Moscow, in reference to a female guide:

(1)   Èkskursovod pered vami. On podnjal ruku.
       guide [MASC] before you   she [MASC] raised [MASC] hand
       'Your guide is in front of you. She (lit. 'he') has lifted (her) hand.
       (Corbett 1991: 232, 2006: 211)

The use of the masculine form of the third person pronoun *on* can only be explained by the fact that the antecedent noun *èkskursovod* is grammatically masculine. It is not a semantic property of the referent, who is female. If the third person pronoun were an indepedently referring expression, one might expect consistent use of feminine gender in situations like that found in (1).

Conversely, one also finds cases in which there is no "match" of grammatical features between the putative controller and the pronoun. For example, French titles (now largely obsolete) take feminine modifiers and predicates, even when they are used to refer to males. Personal pronouns referring to the titled person may, however, take the gender of the biological sex of the person:

(2)   *Sa* [FEM] *Majesté fut inquiète* [FEM], *et de nouveau il* [MASC] *envoya La Varenne à son ministre.*

       'His [FEM] Majesty was worried [FEM], and again he [MASC] sent La Varenne to his minister.'

       (J. & J. Tharaud, quoted by Grevisse 1964: 405, cited in Corbett 1979: 205)

If the third person pronoun "agreed" with its controller in the preceding clause, as expected in the grammatical-dependency analysis, then it would always be feminine. The masculine form supports the independent-reference analysis, in which the pronoun's form is determined by the properties of the referent (in this case, a male person). It poses a serious problem for the grammatical-dependency analysis.

Example (1) has been called 'syntactic agreement' and example (2) 'semantic agreement' (Corbett 1979: 203–204). In fact, 'semantic agreement' is a relationship between the target form and the referent of the controller, since the controller may have a different grammatical feature value, as in (2) where masculine 'semantic agreement' clashes with feminine noun gender. That is, 'semantic agreement' is found when the personal pronoun takes its grammatical features from semantic properties of the referent rather than grammatical properties of the putative antecedent expression. Example (2) also shows that one may have both 'syntactic agreement' and 'semantic agreement' in the same language, and indeed in the same utterance: the possessive modifier of *Majesté* (*Sa*) and its adjectival predicate (*inquiète*) are feminine in form ('syntactic agreement') while the third person pronoun *il* is masculine ('semantic agreement').

Table 1 gives the examples of syntactic and semantic agreement in several of Corbett's publications. In all of them, the semantic agreement features can be determined from the referent alone, without reference to the grammatical form of a putative antecedent expression.

Table 1. Examples of types of syntactic and semantic agreement.

Phenomenon/ Language	Syntactic agreement	Semantic agreement	Reference
conjoined NPs	subset (one conjunct)	entire set (cardinality)	Corbett 2006: 220–221
associative	subset	entire set (cardinality, person)	Corbett 2000: 191–194
collective nouns	collectivity	cardinality of individuals	Corbett 2000: 188–191
numerals	nonredundant/ special coding	cardinality	Corbett 2006: 208–209
Lena dialect of Spanish	lexical gender	collectivity (mass)	Corbett 2000: 192–193, fn 13
Arabic	lexical "number" (Fsg)	cardinality (pl)	Corbett 2000: 209–210
Lezgian pluralia tantum	lexical number	cardinality	Corbett 2000: 176
polite plurals	politeness	cardinality	Corbett 2000: 193–195
evaluatives (German, Bantu)	evaluation	biological sex/animacy	Corbett 1991: 228, 249–250
profession nouns, etc.	lexical gender	biological sex/animacy	Corbett 2006: 214
certain epithets	epithet	individual (sex)	Corbett 1983: 234; 2006: 222
Konkani	biological female sex	youth (age)	Corbett 2006: 215
Norwegian "pancake sentences"	object representing action/proposition	action/proposition	Corbett 2006: 223

As Corbett has documented in detail, these two types of "agreement" are found with (bound) indexes (in the broad sense) as well as with independent personal pronouns – something that might be unexpected if indexes and pronouns are sharply distinguished. For example, both masculine and feminine forms can be found in certain Russian constructions with an adjective modifying a noun that is grammatically masculine gender but refers to a female person:

(3)   *Ona xorošij   / xorošaja   vrač*
      she good [MASC] / good [FEM] doctor [MASC]
      'She is a good doctor.' (Corbett 1991: 238)

Corbett discovered a robust typological generalization: the alternation between syntactic agreement and semantic agreement is governed by a hierarchy of grammatical constructions, the Agreement Hierarchy, presented in (4) (Corbett 1979: 204):

(4)   attributive (modifier) – predicate – relative pronoun – personal pronoun

Crosslinguistically, either syntactic or semantic agreement is found in the target form in any of the constructional relations to the controller given in (4). But if syntactic agreement is found in a language in a particular construction on the Agreement Hierarchy, then syntactic agreement is found in that language in every construction to the left in the hierarchy. Conversely, if semantic agreement is found in a language in a particular construction on the Agreement Hierarchy, then semantic agreement is found in that language in every construction to the right in the hierarchy.

Corbett illustrates the operation of the Agreement Hierarchy in profuse detail (Corbett 1979, 1983, 1991, 2000, 2006, inter alia), and the reader is directed to those references for additional examples. One important point about the Agreement Hierarchy is that it, like many typological universals, operates both in cases where choice of syntactic vs. semantic agreement is categorical and in cases where the choice is variable, but one type of agreement is more/less frequent than the other. For example, in Serbo-Croatian, there is the survival of a dual agreement form for the numerals two, three and four; the corresponding semantic agreement is plural. For attributive modifiers, the syntactic dual survival agreement is categorical; at the other end of the Agreement Hierarchy, plural agreement is categorical for personal pronouns. For predicates and relative pronouns, either the dual survival agreement or plural agreement are possible. A text count, however, showed that the syntactic dual survival agreement was found in 82% of predicates but only 38% of relative pronouns (Corbett 1979: 206, citing Sand 1971: 55–56, 63). Hence, any explanation in terms of a motivating factor for the Agreement Hierarchy will have to be combined with a stochastic process in language use that may lead to conventionalization resulting in categorical usage. This is a fairly standard assumption in typological theorizing.

The possibility of either syntactic agreement or semantic agreement includes both indexes and third person pronouns. It provides strong evidence that indexes and third person pronouns form a natural class. The Agreement Hierarchy provides a robust crosslinguistic universal about the occurrence of semantic and syntactic agreement that covers both indexes and third person pronouns. Personal pronouns are included in the hierarchy along with various constructions that contain indexes. Hence we should expect that the analysis of semantic agreement and of syntactic agreement should be the same for personal pronouns and for bound indexes.

But what is the best analysis of semantic and syntactic agreement? Semantic agreement appears to favor the independent-reference analysis of pronouns, and syntactic agreement favors the grammatical-dependency analysis. These two analyses should apply to indexes as well, since indexes also exhibit both syntactic and semantic agreement, and indexes and pronouns together form the Agreement Hierarchy. The grammatical-dependency analysis of syntactic agreement is a common, perhaps the most common, analysis of indexes. The independent-reference analysis of indexes is less common, although as noted in section 1, it is suggested by Haspelmath and endorsed by Siewierska. These two analyses are, however, inconsistent with each other: one requires a grammatical dependency and the other lacks that same grammatical dependency.

3 Antecedentless pronouns

There is another phenomenon that poses an even more serious problem for the grammatical-dependency analysis of pronouns (and hence indexes). There may not be any expression in the relevant grammatical context for either an index or a personal pronoun to "agree" with. In attributive constructions and relative clause constructions, the supposedly agreed-with head noun may be absent (so-called headless phrases), leaving only an index on the modifier to refer to the head referent. In predication, the supposedly agreed-with subject or object argument phrase may be absent (so-called null anaphora), leaving only an index on the predicate to refer to the subject or object referent.

In many such cases, there is an antecedent referring expression in the discourse context, and the bound index may have a form matching that of the apparent antecedent, i.e. apparent syntactic agreement. A typical example is (5) from

Wolane, an Ethiopian Semitic language with masculine and feminine gender (Meyer 2006: 248):[4]

(5) ʔəndāč bɛ-žāgbɛ   y-dbeš-u-y-ān
     women INST-wooden_instrument 3PL-pound.IPV-PL-3SG.M.OBJ-AUX:NPST
     '(and then) the women pound it (tuber [MASC]) with a wooden instrument.'

The masculine singular object suffix -y refers to a tuber, mentioned three clauses earlier, which is grammatically masculine. These examples are ubiquitous in the languages that allow null anaphora (the vast majority of languages) and have bound forms that index referents (an overall majority of languages, based on the sample in Gilligan 1987).

But in the case of personal pronouns, and even with bound forms, the form indexing a referent may occur without an antecedent phrase in the discourse context, if the referent is sufficiently accessible in the broader context. These have been called antecedentless anaphoric pronouns. For example, if you and I have shared attention towards a woman nearby who is doing something strange, I may say to you, *What's she doing?*, without her having been mentioned in the previous discourse at all.

In the preceding example, the form of the personal pronoun matches the semantic properties of the referent (feminine singular). Most striking of all, though, antecedentless pronouns may occur in a form that does not match the semantic properties of the referent, but instead matches the syntactic properties of a referentially appropriate nominal form that nevertheless did not occur in the discourse context. This observation led to scholarly debate in the late 1980s and beyond (Bosch 1987, 1988; Cornish 1987, 1996; Dowty & Jacobsen 1989; Tasmowski-de Ryck & Verluyten 1982, 1987; Wiese 1983). Two invented examples using grammatical gender in French are given in (6)–(7) (Tasmowski-de Ryck & Verluyten 1982: 328):

(6) (John is trying to stuff a large table (*la table*, feminine) in the trunk of his car; Mary says:)
     Tu n'arriveras jamais à la [FEM]/*le [MASC] faire entrer dans la voiture.
     'You will never manage to get it into the car.'

(7) (same situation, but with a desk (*le bureau*, masculine))
     Tu n'arriveras jamais à le [MASC]/*la [FEM] faire entrer dans la voiture.
     'You will never manage to get it into the car.'

---

4 A list of abbreviations may be found at the end of the article.

These examples produce an analytical paradox. On the one hand, there is no textual antecedent, so presumably the only properties available to the speaker in choosing a pronoun form are those of the salient referent in the context. On the other hand, a pronoun form is chosen that can only be explained in terms of a linguistic expression that motivates that pronoun form.

The existence of examples such as *What's she doing?* mentioned above, as well as (6) and (7) and similar examples, has led a number of analysts, in particular Cornish, to abandon the analysis of third person pronouns as grammatically dependent on a linguistic expression in the discourse context. In other words, the independent-reference analysis is applied to all personal pronouns. Personal pronouns are independently referring expressions that have a certain pragmatic value as well as semantic and grammatical features associated with them. The only way to retain the grammatical-dependency analysis would be to posit virtual controllers, which is implausible and, as Haspelmath (this volume, § 5.1) points out, a Eurocentric analysis (and it does not even work for the European languages it was proposed for).

If the independent-reference analysis is adopted, then three major challenges to this analysis must be addressed. The first is a pragmatic characterization of the function of third person pronouns that distinguishes them in particular from deictic demonstrative pronouns (section 4). The second is a cognitive-discourse explanation as to how syntactic agreement is possible even without an antecedent expression (as well as when there is an antecedent; section 5). The third is to account for the distribution of syntactic and semantic agreement, in particular the Agreement Hierarchy, also in the cognitive-discourse theory (section 6). Note that meeting these challenges will allow, indeed require, us to extend the same analysis to indexes, thereby unifying the analysis of personal pronouns and indexes (in the broad sense).

4 A cognitive-discourse analysis of anaphoric pronouns

Cornish adopts a cognitive-discourse approach to the pragmatic status of referents in discourse, such that deixis and anaphora (as he continues to call it) are 'complementary procedures constructing, modifying and accessing the contents of mental models of an unfolding discourse within the minds of speaker and addressee (or writer and reader in the written form of language)' (Cornish 1996: 22). In other words, for Cornish the term 'anaphora' is dissociated from a grammatical-dependency analysis of pronouns. We will follow Cornish's use of 'anaphora' for the remainder of this article.

He goes on to propose the following definitions of the pragmatic distinction between deixis and anaphora (Cornish 1996: 22):

> Deixis, in this more cognitively-oriented conception..., serves prototypically to shift the addressee's attention focus from an existing object of discourse to a new one derived via the situational context of utterance. Anaphora, on the other hand, is a signal to continue the existing attention focus already established; the referents of (weakly stressed, phonologically non-prominent) anaphors are thus presupposed by the speaker to enjoy a relatively high degree of salience or focus level at the point in the text where they are used. So both anaphora and deixis operate at the level of memory organization, managing the latter by guiding the processing of incoming segments of a text.

Cornish uses the term 'anaphora' but has redefined it in cognitive terms, as continuation of the shared attention focus of the interlocutors. It is quite close to Ariel's definition of referent accessibility alluded to above (see also Siewierska 2004, ch. 5). The attention focus need not be established linguistically, by the use of a referring expression in the preceding discourse. It may be established through contextual salience in the case of antecedentless anaphora – no longer a contradiction in terms in Cornish's redefinition of anaphora. The contextual salience allowing for antecedentless anaphora may be available in the speech act situation or less directly via the shared knowledge or common ground of the interlocutors.

Cornish's definition of the contrast between deixis and anaphora provides a useful new perspective on the typology of demonstrative pronouns and third person pronouns. Grammatical descriptions of third person pronouns describe three broad types (Siewierska 2004: 5–6). In some languages, there are third person pronoun forms distinct from demonstrative pronoun forms. This is the case in English, and can be characterized as grammatically encoding the contrast in function between maintaining vs. shifting attention focus, as described in the quotation from Cornish above. In other languages, the demonstrative pronouns also serve as third person pronouns. In such languages, it may be the case that the pronoun form is used simply to refer to the focus of attention, whether it is the current focus of attention or a new focus of attention. That is, such forms neutralize the contrast described in the quotation above (though it is possible that there might be phonological and prosodic differences not reflected in the orthography or transcription). In still other languages, there simply are no third person pronouns. In these languages, the function of continuing the focus of attention is achieved by null expression, or null instantiation as it is called in construction grammar (Fillmore 1986; Lambrecht & Lemoine 2005), rather than by an overt grammatical form.

Cornish's analysis may also shed new light on the grammaticalization of demonstrative pronouns to third person pronouns. At a coarse-grained perspective, a demonstrative form used for shifting attention focus is extended in use to the situation of maintaining attention focus, and then the two functions are formally split by the phonological erosion of the maintaining-focus (anaphoric) form or by the introduction of a new or reinforced focus-shifting (deictic-demonstrative) form.

At a more fine-grained perspective, this dichotomy of functions will probably appear more complex, or at least the construal of particular situations as one or the other will be complex. For one thing, there is not necessarily a perfect match between form and function: Cornish allows for deictic interpretations of stressed personal pronouns (e.g. Cornish 1996: 32). Himmelmann (1996) proposes a four-way taxonomy of demonstrative-definite functions, but mainly examines the demonstrative modifier-definite article continuum. He notes that diagnostic contexts for distinguishing demonstrative pronouns and third person pronouns are rare in discourse (Himmelmann 1996: 211). But perhaps Cornish's analysis can be operationalized and allow for exploration of the grammaticalization path from demonstrative pronoun to third person pronoun.

5 The analysis of antecedentless anaphoric pronouns

The second major challenge to the analysis of third person pronouns and indexes as independent referring expressions is to explain how syntactic agreement is possible, even without an antecedent linguistic expression in the discourse. This challenge is the one that most exercised the scholars who debated the question in the 1980s.

Dowty & Jacobson proposed a semantic analysis for a class of entities in the world such as chairs: 'one of the actual properties of chairs is that the French word conventionally used to denote this class of objects is marked with the feminine gender feature' (Dowty & Jacobson 1989: 98). However, Dowty himself (n.d.) rejects this analysis, saying that it renders any semantic analysis of agreement as unfalsifiable. Pollard & Sag cite approvingly Chierchia's criticism that this approach seems 'extremely artificial' (Pollard & Sag 1994: 79 fn. 13, citing Chierchia 1988: 150).

Pollard & Sag themselves propose a pragmatic analysis: "For such languages, a different pragmatic constraint is evidently at work: roughly, an entity can serve as the anchor of an NP index only if the index's agreement features coincide with those of a common noun (of the language in question) that effectively classifies that entity at a level of granularity appropriate to the context". (Pollard & Sag 1994: 78; note that 'index' here refers to an abstract grammatical property in the syntactic representation framework of Head-driven Phrase Structure Grammar).

It is not entirely clear what is meant by "pragmatics" in Pollard & Sag's analysis. Barlow is more explicit. Following earlier proposals, he introduces discourse referents that are distinct from real-world referents and are associated with linguistic expressions such as pronouns or indexes (as noted in section 1 above, Barlow also unifies pronouns and indexes). A discourse referent has properties, some of which are semantic (i.e. properties of the real-world referent), others of which are not based on properties of the real-world referent such as grammatical gender (Barlow 1988: 182). This is a negative definition, however, and it would be desirable to find a more positive definition for the employment of syntactic agreement.

The main difference between Dowty & Jacobson's analysis, Pollard & Sag's analysis and Barlow's analysis is the shift from semantics to pragmatics to discourse. In all cases, in order for syntactic agreement to take place in antecedent-less anaphora, the referent must somehow be associated with a linguistic expression. The difference from the grammatical-dependency analysis of pronouns (and indexes) is that the linguistic expression associated with the referent need not have been produced in the discourse context. The analysis must be generalized to a linguistic expression that is part of the grammatical knowledge of the interlocutors and can be used to denote the referent intended by the speaker, whether or not it has actually been used in the preceding discourse context. As Bosch puts it, the discourse referent 'can always be accessed according to linguistic properties (such as gender or number) of expressions that have (**or could have**) occurred in discourse and that refer to the objects represented' (Bosch 1988: 219, emphasis added).

Perhaps the best description of the way in which a personal pronoun can employ a grammatical feature of a noun associated with the referent of the pronoun is given by Wiese: 'We may say that a pronoun **conforms** to nouns of the same gender or, more generally, that a pronoun has a certain **associative potential** due to formal lexical associations' (Wiese 1983: 392, emphasis original; see also Cornish 1987: 250). Wiese uses the term 'conform' to avoid the grammatical-dependency implications of 'agree'. He defines associative potential as delimiting the associated extension of the pronoun. In a cognitive-discourse perspective, one can think of potential as the range of potential construals afforded to a pronoun by virtue of its association with certain linguistic expressions (cf. potential for construal in Croft 2012: 16, 37, 135–136), for example due to the shared gender of the pronoun form and the associated linguistic expression. These construals will be illustrated in the following section.

6 The distribution of syntactic and semantic agreement

The analysis of a pronoun having an associative potential that can rub off on its discourse referent is supported by at least part of the response to the third challenge: using this analysis in an account for the distribution of syntactic and semantic agreement, including the Agreement Hierarchy. We begin with the most flexible aspect of their distribution, namely the alternation in personal pronouns.

Cornish gives a lengthy extract from a letter to *Le Monde* (J. Gattegno, 22 August 1979) about the minister of education (Cornish 1987: 253–254). The French word *ministre* is masculine, but the minister at the time was Mme Alice Saunier-Seïté. The first part of the letter discusses the role of the minister of education with respect to the universities in light of a recently-passed law, and uses masculine forms agreeing with the masculine word *ministre*. The second part of the letter discusses the actions of the specific minister serving at the time, and uses the feminine forms agreeing with the biological sex of the minister. Cornish argues that the first part of the letter uses masculine gender because the writer construes the minister as a role and the word naming that role is masculine, while the second part of the letter uses feminine gender because the writer construes the minister as an individual, who is female. In other words, choice of gender implies alternative construals of the referent derived in one case from the relevant word's gender (syntactic agreement) and in the other case from the biological sex of the referent (semantic agreement), even when a masculine antecedent phrase (*le ministre*) occurs in the discourse context.

A more striking example that Cornish provides is an extract from the film script *Le trou* by J. Becker and J. Giovanni:

(8) (Prison guard arrives with meal)

 First prisoner: *Qu'est que c'est?*
  'What is it?'
 Guard: *Le potage* [MASC] *du chef au vermicelle.*
  'The chef's vermicelli soup.'

 (The men have begun to eat)

 Second prisoner: *Elle* [FEM] *n'est pas mangeable.*
  'It is not fit to eat.'

(Cornish 1987: 256, from Rosenberg 1970: 58, note 20)

In this example, there is a full linguistic expression in the discourse context, *le potage*, which could serve as an antecedent to the pronoun in the second prisoner's utterance and motivate its gender choice. Instead, the second prisoner uses the feminine, which is presumably motivated by the gender of *soupe*, another term for soup. The difference is that *potage* construes the soup as more refined, whereas *soupe* construes the soup as a coarser dish – obviously, the way that the second prisoner construes it.

These examples show that a grammatical-dependency account of the grammatical features of a personal pronoun based on an antecedent relationship will fail, because the grammatical features of the personal pronoun are not always the same as that of the antecedent. Instead, these examples show that the grammatical features of the personal pronoun are motivated by a linguistic expression whose construal of the referent is part of what is being communicated by the speaker. In addition to the construal of a discourse referent in terms of a linguistic category and its associated grammatical features, a speaker may construe the referent as a referent "sui generis", that is, simply in terms of the referent's semantic properties – in other words, semantic agreement.

This phenomenon is similar to that described in Mathiot & Roberts (1979) for naturally occurring uses of English personal pronouns for various kinds of referents. Two examples they give involve an alternation between the inanimate/nonhuman pronoun *it* and the human pronouns *he/she*. In one example, a woman says of her bicycle, *I was going to give him a name. But after two blowouts what can I call it?* (Mathiot & Roberts 1979: 34). When the bicycle is construed as a normal, functioning, useful possession, the woman construes it more empathetically and uses a human (masculine) pronoun *him*. When the bicycle is not operating properly, the woman construes it as inanimate and uses *it*. In the other example a man who does odd jobs referred to a big ladder in the garage to his helper, *I take her out, you take it back in!* (Mathiot & Roberts 1979: 6). When the ladder is in his possession the man construes it more empathetically and uses the human (feminine) pronoun *her*; when it is in someone else's possession, he uses the inanimate pronoun *it*.

These are not examples of syntactic vs. semantic agreement: although *it* could be interpreted as semantic agreement, English nouns do not have nonsemantic gender. So the conventional semantic features of the English pronouns (human/nonhuman, also male/female in other examples given by Mathiot & Roberts) are being used to conceptualize the referent in different ways. As in the examples from French cited by Cornish, regardless of prior linguistic referring expressions, different grammatical forms of the pronoun are being used to convey more to the listener than just the identity of the real-world referent.

These examples using personal pronouns show that the grammatical "agreement" features of a pronoun can be used to evoke a grammatically appropriate noun and its conceptualization of the referent, or to evoke the referent itself and its semantic features, or even (as in the English examples from Mathiot & Roberts) to use conventional semantic features to reconceptualize the referent for the communicative purposes of the speaker. Since the conceptualization of the referent applies to a specific occasion in the discourse, the alternative possibilities of grammatical expression are better interpreted as a property of the discourse referent in the speaker's cognitive model, rather than a property of a referent in the real world.

What happens when we turn to person (and nonperson) indexes? What is the relationship between the often flexible conceptual use of personal pronouns with different agreement features, and the grammatical rules of modifiers, predicates and relative pronouns that conform to the Agreement Hierarchy? Is it possible to combine the conceptual-discourse analysis of personal pronouns with the different grammatical status of indexes on modifiers, predicates and relative pronouns in order to produce an independent-reference analysis of "agreement", instead of the more usual grammatical-dependency analysis?

The chief difference between personal pronouns on the one hand and the indexes occurring on modifiers, predicates and relative pronouns on other is that the latter are in a construction with another referring expression: the head noun for the modifier, the core argument(s) for the predicate, and the head noun of the relative clause construction. Thus, the interpretation of the index is determined in large part by the construction it occurs in.

The referring expression in the construction denotes the most accessible referent in that construction: head noun or core argument. Given the pronoun's definition as maintaining reference to a highly accessible referent, one would expect the index to be coreferential with that referring expression, since it denotes the most accessible referent in its context. One would also expect the index's grammatical features to share the same construal of the referent represented by the referring expression in the construction, since that referring expression is highly salient in its constructional context. This would be syntactic agreement. These two properties lead to the same outcome as the traditional analysis of agreement in the construction: the index refers to the same referent as its controller, and they match in their grammatical features. This corresponds to Corbett's Principle I for canonical agreement, that canonical agreement is redundant rather than informative (Corbett 2006: 11).

But it does not have to be this way. Corbett recognizes this, by also allowing for noncanonical agreement, that is, grammatical phenomena that deviate from the grammatical patterns of canonical agreement in various ways, without drawing a sharp line differentiating "agreement" from "not agreement". My analytical goal here is somewhat different, though not necessarily incompatible. I am seeking a general definition of the function of pronouns and indexes from which the more canonical or prototypical agreement facts fall out more or less naturally, but which allows for "noncanonical agreement". And I am in some sense starting from the opposite end from Corbett. Instead of taking redundant information of an index in a grammatical construction as the starting point (Corbett's canonical agreement), I am taking the function of anaphoric pronouns as the starting point and extending the cognitive-discourse independent-reference analysis of anaphoric pronouns to indexes.

Returning to the analysis: as seen in example (3) in section 3, semantic agreement may occur even in the case of attributive modification. That is, the index (in the broad sense) on the target form may express a grammatical feature that clashes with that of the head noun in attributive agreement; or with that of the argument in predicate agreement; or again that of the head noun in a relative clause construction. For this reason, one would not want to impose a feature-matching constraint on index and noun or argument. In effect, the index would be providing, or at least highlighting, different information about its referent than the full expression in the construction is doing. This is possible when the index is analyzed as an independent, albeit reduced, referring expression even in attributive constructions and argument structure constructions.

Of course, the construction itself may conventionalize a particular way in which the index may express features associated with the referent: the index may be required to exhibit syntactic agreement, or it may be required to exhibit semantic agreement. The result is crosslinguistic variation. This variation, whether categorically conventionalized or a usage frequency pattern, conforms to the Agreement Hierarchy, as we showed above.

Why does the Agreement Hierarchy rank the constructional contexts in the way that it does? The Agreement Hierarchy appears to reflect the degree of syntactic closeness or integration of the element to which the index is attached and the element which is the full(er) referring expression denoting the same referent. As Corbett puts it: "Attributive agreement represents agreement within the simple phrase, predicative agreement goes beyond the phrase but is restricted to the clause, the agreement of the relative pronoun goes beyond the clause but is restricted to the sentence, while the personal pronoun is not restricted to the sentence of the item controlling agreement." (Corbett 1979: 216)

We may offer a cognitive-discourse explanation for the centrality of the syntactic closeness/distance parameter underlying the Agreement Hierarchy. The construal of the referent represented by the fuller referring expression and hence the grammatical features invoking that construal will be less salient, the further the index is from the fuller referring expression in syntactic terms. And so semantic agreement – agreement with features predictable from the semantic properties of the referent alone, unrelated to the fuller referring expression – is more likely to occur, the further the index is from the referring expression. In other words, the Agreement Hierarchy should emerge as the natural consequence of the conventionalization, full or partial, of the relative likelihood of syntactic vs. semantic agreement of the indexes found in the different constructions based on the salience of the fuller referring expression in the index's constructional context.

Corbett observes that two other syntactic differences may lead to a shift from syntactic to semantic agreement. The first is what he calls real distance, namely the closeness of the element with the index to its controller (Corbett 1979: 220–221, 1991: 239–240, 2006: 168–170). Syntactic agreement is more likely to be found, the closer the target is to its controller. An example is the form of stacked modifiers in Chichewa with the head noun *ngwazi* 'hero', which is lexically Class 9/10 (a nonhuman noun class) but whose referent is human, which is normally Class 1/2. It is possible to have both syntactic and semantic agreement in the same construction, but only if the modifier with syntactic agreement is closer (Corbett 1991: 239, from Sam Mchombo, pers. comm.):

(9) ngwazi y-athu w-oyamba
 hero CL9-our CL1-first
 'our first hero'

(10) *ngwazi w-athu y-oyamba
 hero CL1-our CL9-first

Syntactic agreement is normally with the nearest conjunct for conjoined noun phrases, though there are some exceptions (Corbett 1991: 240). The explanation offered above for the distribution of syntactic and semantic agreement applies here as well.

The other syntactic difference in which there may be a shift from syntactic to semantic agreement is in the order of target and controller. If the target may precede or follow the controller, one can find syntactic agreement on a preceding target and semantic agreement on a following target, but not the other way around (Corbett 1979: 218–219, 2000: 192–193 fn. 13, 200–203, 214–216). A relatively straightforward example is modifier agreement in the Lena dialect of Peninsular Spanish. Certain nouns with a mass interpretation allow modifiers with either a grammatical gender agreement (masculine or feminine according to the noun) or a special semantic mass agreement form. Preceding modifiers take the syntactic gender agreement but following modifiers take the semantic mass agreement (Corbett 2000: 192–193 fn. 13, citing Hualde 1992):

(11) bwén-a šénte
 good-FEM.SG people.FEM
 'good people'

(12) šénte   bwén-o
      people.FEM   good-MASS
      'good people'

There is evidence that prenominal modifiers are more tightly integrated than postnominal modifiers (Croft 2009), although some of Corbett's other examples involve predicate agreement rather than modifier agreement. So it may be that this asymmetry in choice of syntactic vs. semantic agreement is due to the same factor as real distance and syntactic distance, and can therefore be accounted for in the same way.

7 Conclusion

I have argued for an analysis of both indexes (in the broad sense described in footnote 1) and third person (allophoric) pronouns as independent referring expressions, with respect to all of their grammatical properties. Both indexes and third person pronouns exhibit syntactic agreement as well as semantic agreement. Typological-universal patterns such as the Agreement Hierarchy include both, as argued for by a number of scholars. A cognitive-discourse analysis of third person pronouns, also argued for by a number of scholars, can be extended to indexes. All indexes refer. This analysis provides a uniform functional characterization of third person pronouns and indexes, and yields canonical agreement patterns as a natural consequence while accounting for a range of noncanonical agreement phenomena. Third person pronouns and indexes are analyzed as independently referring expressions, albeit reduced referential devices (Kibrik 2011: 39). This is not to deny that indexes are generally more reduced referential devices than personal pronouns are, nor to deny that this difference in degree has linguistic consequences of the sort described by Haspelmath in the appendix of his article (this volume).

The cognitive-discourse analysis of third person pronouns and indexes also allows us to treat person as a unified category. The cognitive-discourse analysis allows for an independent-reference analysis of third person pronouns as well as first and second person pronouns. The same independent-reference analysis applies to all persons as they are expressed in indexes bound to other word forms. Again, this is not to deny that the egophoric/locuphoric (first/second person) vs. allophoric (third person) distinction has linguistic consequences such as those described in Dahl (2000). But I would agree with Anna Siewierska that 'excluding the third person from the category of person...would severely skew our understanding of a number of facets of the category of person' (Siewierska 2004: 8).

Abbreviations

3 third person, AUX auxiliary, CL1 gender class 1, CL9 gender class 9, FEM feminine, INST instrumental, IPV imperfective, MASC masculine, MASS mass noun, NPST nonpast, OBJ object, PL plural, SG singular.

References

Ariel, Mira. 1988. Referring and accessibility. *Journal of Linguistics* 24. 65–87.
Ariel, Mira. 1990. *Accessing noun phrase antecedents*. New York: Routledge.
Barlow, Michael. 1988. *A situated theory of agreement*. Ph.D. dissertation, Stanford University. (Published by Garland Press, New York, 1992).
Bickel, Balthasar & Johanna Nichols. 2007. Inflectional morphology. In Timothy Shopen (ed.), *Language typology and syntactic description, vol. III: grammatical categories and the lexicon*, 169–240. Cambridge: Cambridge University Press.
Bosch, Peter. 1987. Pronouns under control? A reply to Liliane Tasmowski & Paul Verluyten. *Journal of Semantics* 5. 207–231.
Bosch, Peter. 1988. Representing and accessing focussed referents. *Language and Cognitive Processes* 3. 207–231.
Chierchia, Gennaro. 1988. Aspects of a categorical theory of binding. In Richard Oehrle, Emmon Bach & Deirdre Wheeler (eds.), *Categorial grammars and natural language structures*, 125–151. Dordrecht: Reidel.
Corbett, Greville G. 1979. The agreement hierarchy. *Journal of Linguistics* 15. 203–224.
Corbett, Greville G. 1983. *Hierarchies, targets and controllers: Agreement patterns in Slavic*. University Park, PA: Pennsylvania State University Press.
Corbett, Greville G. 1991. *Gender*. Cambridge: Cambridge University Press.
Corbett, Greville G. 2000. *Number*. Cambridge: Cambridge University Press.
Corbett, Greville G. 2006. *Agreement*. Cambridge: Cambridge University Press.
Cornish, Frances. 1986. *Anaphoric relations in English and French: a discourse perspective*. London: Croom Helm.
Cornish, Frances. 1987. Anaphoric pronouns: under linguistic control, or signalling particular discourse representations? *Journal of Semantics* 5. 233–260.
Cornish, Frances. 1996. 'Antecedentless' anaphors: deixis, anaphora, or what? Some evidence from English and French. *Journal of Linguistics* 32. 19–41.
Cornish, Frances. 1999. *Anaphora, discourse and understanding*. Oxford: Oxford University Press.
Croft, William. 2001. *Radical Construction Grammar: syntactic theory in typological perspective*. Oxford: Oxford University Press.
Croft, William. 2003. *Typology and universals*, 2nd edition. Cambridge: Cambridge University Press.
Croft, William. 2009. A typological asymmetry in noun phrase structure. Lecture presented at the Workshop on Noun Phrase Structure, University of Vigo, Vigo, Spain.
Croft, William 2012. *Verbs: aspect and causal structure*. Oxford: Oxford University Press.
Dahl, Östen. 2000. Egophoricity in discourse and syntax. *Functions of Language* 7. 37–77.
Dowty, David. n.d. Important note regarding "Agreement as a semantic phenomenon". (http://www.ling.ohio-state.edu/~dowty/papers/agreement-note.html, accessed 23 February 2012)

Dowty, David & Pauline Jacobson. 1989. Agreement as a semantic phenomenon. *Proceedings of the Fifth Eastern States Conference on Linguistics (ESCOL '88)*, ed. Joyce Powers & Kenneth de Jong, 95–108. Columbus: Ohio State University.

Fillmore, Charles J. 1986. Pragmatically-controlled zero anaphora. In Vassiliki Nikiforidou et al. (eds.), *Proceedings of the Twelfth Annual Meeting of the Berkeley Linguistics Society*, 95–107. Berkeley: Berkeley Linguistics Society.

Gilligan, Gary Martin. 1987. A cross-linguistic approach to the pro-drop parameter. Ph.D. dissertation, University of Southern California.

Givón, Talmy. 1983. Topic continuity in discourse: an introduction. In Talmy Givón *(ed.)*, *Topic continuity in discourse*, 1–41. Amsterdam: John Benjamins.

Haspelmath, Martin. 2011. The indeterminacy of word segmentation and the nature of morphology and syntax. *Folia Linguistica* 45. 31–80.

Haspelmath, Martin. 2013. Argument indexing: a conceptual framework for the syntactic status of bound person forms. This volume.

Heath, Jeffrey. 1981. *Basic materials in Mara: grammar, texts, dictionary*. (Pacific Linguistics, C60). Canberra: Research School of Pacific Studies, Australian National University.

Hewitt, B. G. 1979. *Abkhaz*. (Lingua Descriptive Studies, 2). Amsterdam: North-Holland.

Himmelmann, Nikolaus P. 1996. Demonstratives in narrative discourse: a taxonomy of universal uses. In Barbara Fox *(ed.)*, *Studies in anaphora*, 205–254. Amsterdam: John Benjamins.

Hualde, José Ignacio. 1992. Metaphony and count/mass morphology in Asturian and Cantabrian dialects. In Christiane Laeufer & Terrell A. Morgan (eds.), *Theoretical analyses in Romance linguistics: selected papers from the Nineteenth Linguistic Symposium on Romance Languages*, 99–114. Amsterdam: John Benjamins.

Hutchison, John P. 1981. *The Kanuri language: a reference grammar*. Madison: University of Wisconsin African Studies Program.

Kibrik, Andrej A. 2011. *Reference in discourse* (Oxford Studies in Typology and Linguistic Theory). Oxford: Oxford University Press.

Lambrecht, Knud & Kevin Lemoine. 2005. Definite null objects in (spoken) French: a Construction-Grammar account. In Mirjam Fried & Hans C. Boas (eds.), *Grammatical constructions: back to the roots*, 13–55. Amsterdam: John Benjamins.

Lehmann, Christian. 1982. Universal and typological aspects of agreement. In Hansjakob Seiler & Franz Josef Stachowiak (eds.), *Apprehension: Das sprachliche Erfassen von Gegenständen*, Vol. II, 201–267. Tübingen: Gunter Narr.

Lyons, John. 1977. *Semantics, vol. 2*. Cambridge: Cambridge University Press.

Matthews, Peter H. 1981. *Syntax*. Cambridge: Cambridge University Press.

Mathiot, Madeleine, assisted by Marjorie Roberts. 1979. Sex roles as revealed through referential gender in American English. In Madeleine Mathiot *(ed.)*, *Ethnology: Boas, Sapir and Whorf revisited*, 1–47. The Hague: Mouton.

Meyer, Ronny. 2006. *Wolane: descriptive grammar of an East Gurage language (Ethiosemitic)*. Köln: Rüdiger Köppe Verlag.

Pollard, Carl & Ivan A. Sag. 1994. *Head-driven Phrase Structure Grammar*. Chicago and Stanford: University of Chicago Press and the Center for the Study of Language and Information.

Rosenberg, Samuel. 1970. *Modern French ce. The neuter pronoun in adjectival predication*. The Hague: Mouton.

Sand, Diane E. Z. 1971. Agreement of the predicate with quantitative subjects in Serbo-Croatian. Ph.D. dissertation, University of Pennsylvania.

Siewierska, Anna. 1999. From anaphoric pronoun to grammatical agreement marker: why objects don't make it. *Folia Linguistica* 33. 225–251.
Siewierska, Anna. 2004. *Person*. Cambridge: Cambridge University Press.
Siewierska, Anna & Dik Bakker. 2005. The agreement cross-reference continuum: person marking in FG. In Kees Hengeveld & Caspar de Groot (eds.), *Morphosyntactic expression in Functional Grammar*, 203–247. Berlin & New York: De Gruyter Mouton.
Tasmowski-de Ryck, Liliane & Paul Verluyten. 1982. Linguistic control of pronouns. *Journal of Semantics* 1. 323–346.
Tasmowski-de Ryck, Liliane & Paul Verluyten. 1987. Control mechanisms of anaphora. *Journal of Semantics* 5. 341–370.
Wiese, Bernd. 1983. Anaphora by pronouns. *Linguistics* 21. 373–417.

Volker Gast and Johan van der Auwera
Towards a distributional typology of human impersonal pronouns, based on data from European languages

1 Introduction

1.1 Human impersonal pronouns

The topic of this chapter figured centrally in Anna Siewierska's research in the last few years before her unexpected and much too early death (see Siewierska 2008, 2010, 2011, Siewierska & Papastathi 2011).[1] Her interest in the topic seems to have emerged in the context of her work on the category of person, and her 2004 book on this category contains a number of interesting observations already (Siewierska 2004: Section 5.5). In her 2011 paper, Anna Siewierska uses the term 'R-impersonal' – with 'R' standing for (reduction in) 'referentiality' – for what we call HUMAN IMPERSONAL PRONOUN in this contribution. She describes this class of expressions as follows (Siewierska 2011: 57–58):

> R-impersonals have the appearance of regular, personal constructions but feature a subject which is human and non-referential. The non-referential human subject may be expressed lexically, pronominally or by the whole construction. The subject of lexical R-impersonals is typically the word for 'person' or 'people'.

Siewierska (2011: 58) uses example (1) from Abkhaz (quoted from Hewitt 1979: 157) to illustrate 'R-impersonals':

(1) Abkhaz

    a-way°ə̀ arə̀y a-š°q°ə̀ dàpx'ar ak'ə̀r ø-eylə̀-y-k'aa-we-yt'
    ART-person this ART-book he.read.it something it-PREV-he-learnt-DYN-FIN
    'If one reads this book, one will learn something.'

---

[1] We would like to thank several participants of the Anna Siewierska Memorial Workshop held at the MPI-EVA Leipzig on 27 April, 2012 for valuable comments and suggestions. We have particularly benefitted from comments made by the editors of this volume, Dik Bakker and Martin Haspelmath. Any mistakes or inaccuracies are of course our own responsibility. V. Gast wishes to acknowledge financial support from the German Science Foundation (DFG, GA 1288/6-1).

Impersonal pronouns deriving from nouns meaning 'man' are widespread in the languages of Europe, the most typical examples perhaps being provided by French (*on* as in example 2 below) and Germanic languages other than English (e.g. German *man*; see example 3). Similar expressions are also found in Slavic languages (e.g. Bulgarian *čovek*, as in example 4), where they are less widely distributed, however.

(2) French

   On ne vit qu'une fois.
   'You only live once.'

(3) German

   Man lebt nur einmal.
   'You only live once.'

(4) Bulgarian

   Čovek   samo   živee   vednăž.
   person only   live.3SG.PRS once
   'You only live once.'

English, while not having a 'man'-pronoun for contexts like those in (1)–(4) (anymore, see Fröhlich 1951, Meyer 1953, Jud-Schmid 1956), uses (quasi- pronominal) *people* in specific impersonal contexts:

(5) *People say he was mad.*

Pronouns based on a noun meaning 'man' or 'people' provide just one option of 'impersonalizing' an argument slot (see Section 1.2 below on the concept of 'impersonalization'). As the title of her 2011 paper shows – 'Man-constructions vs. third person plural-impersonals in the languages of Europe' – Anna Siewierska investigated such pronouns in comparison to impersonally used third person plural pronouns, or third person plural forms of verbs. A comparative study of such pronouns or verbs was published in Siewierska & Papastathi (2011), based on a translation corpus of nine European languages and on a typology proposed by Cabredo Hofherr (2006). '3pl impersonals' are characterized as follows (Siewierska & Papastathi 2011: 577–578):

> From the semantic perspective 3pl IMPs are constructions with a non-referential human subject which excludes the speaker and the addressee ... From the formal perspective 3pl

IMPs are constructions with a third person plural pronominal as subject which, in contrast to the typical usage of such third person plural pronominal subjects, lacks an overt antecedent in discourse.

Third person plural impersonals are found both with and without overt pronouns. While English requires overt *they* in examples like (6), Russian, as well as many other languages that allow pro-drop, does not use an overt pronoun in such cases (see example 7).

(6) *They're knocking on the door.*

(7) Russian (Siewierska & Papastathi 2011: 580)

Teper' starajutsja prepodavat' anglijskij jazyk   v mladšix klassax.
now   try.3PL   teach.INF   English language in younger classes
'Now they're trying to teach English in the lower grades.'

Anna Siewierska's work on R-impersonals/human impersonal pronouns has provided invaluable inspiration for our own studies on this topic. In van der Auwera et al. (2012), we present a comparative investigation of human impersonal pronouns in English, Dutch and German. In addition to 'man'- and 3pl-pronouns, we have taken other formal means of impersonalization into account, e.g. second person pronouns and impersonal pronouns deriving from a numeral meaning 'one', as in example (8).

(8) *You/one shouldn't drink and drive.*

In the present contribution we want to broaden the perspective further and, in a way, combine the typological approach taken by Siewierska (2011) and Siewierska & Papastathi (2011), who focus on fewer pronouns in more languages, with our own, so far Germanic-centred research on a broader range of formal devices for impersonalization. In so doing we aim to arrive at an integrated distributional typology of human impersonal pronouns, i.e., a typology which makes predictions about possible patterns of polysemy irrespective of the specific form or etymology of any given pronoun or construction. Like Siewierska & Papastathi (2011), we use the semantic map methodology as a way of representing distributional variation. Another parallel to the work done by Anna Siewierska and Maria Papastathi is that our research is also based on data from the three major Indo-European families represented in Europe. Given that, in addition to Germanic languages, we will consider selected Romance and Slavic languages, we will be dealing with strategies of impersonalization that we have not so far taken into account, e.g. middle markers such as Spanish *se* (see example 9), and impersonal modals like Russian (deontic) *sleduet*, illustrated in example (10).

(9)   Spanish

   Se   vive   solo una vez.
   mid live.3sg only one time
   'You only live once.'

(10) Russian

   Ètogo ne   sleduet   delat'.
   this   not should.IMPS.PRS   do.INF
   'One shouldn't do that.'

1.2 Defining human impersonal pronouns and impersonalization

One of the most striking features of human impersonal pronouns is that they do not introduce discourse referents. Therefore, they cannot be picked up anaphorically. For instance, *man* in example (11) cannot be interpreted as an antecedent of *er* 'he'.

(11) **Man hat geklopft. Er ist sehr verärgert.*
   IMPS has knocked   he is very angry
   Int.: 'Someone has knocked. He is very angry.'

Two instances of *man* co-occurring in a sentence are interpreted as instantiations of the same variable. Example (12a) is therefore interpreted as shown in (12b).

(12) a. *Wenn man   schnarcht, sollte   man sich entschuldigen.*
        if   IMPS   snores,   should IMPS MID apologize
        'If one snores, one should apologize.'

   b. $\forall x\ [\ x$ snores $\to x$ should apologize $]$

The inability to introduce discourse referents will be regarded as a defining property of human impersonal pronouns. We assume that such pronouns are used to fill an argument slot of a predicate without establishing a referential link to any discourse referent. Adopting analyses from the semantic literature (e.g. Moltmann

2006), we take it that human impersonal pronouns introduce a variable ranging over human entities without referring to any human referent in particular. This semantic definition of human impersonal pronouns – or, more generally speaking, of the impersonalization of argument positions – will briefly be explained in the following. For more information, the reader is referred to relevant work done from the perspective of argument structure (e.g. Blevins 2003) and in formal semantics (e.g. Moltmann 2006).

As is well known, argument terms (i.e., the constituents representing arguments in sentence structure) perform a double function (cf. Löbner 2002: Ch. 6, among many others): They refer to an entity or set of entities from the universe of discourse, and they express a predication about that entity. To use a classic example, *the man drinking a martini* in (13) refers to some real-world entity about which a question is asked ('Who is *x*'), and it expresses a property of that entity, i.e., that of '(being) drinking a martini'.

(13)   Who is the man drinking a martini?

As Donellan (1966: 366) has pointed out, "[i]f it should turn out that there is only water in the glass, one has nevertheless asked a question about a particular person, a question that it is possible for someone to answer". This shows, among other things, that reference and predication are, to an extent, independent, a point that becomes even clearer when we consider evaluative expressions such as *that idiot over there*.[2]

Human impersonal pronouns are thus regarded as argument terms that express predication without establishing reference. Put differently, they have an intensional interpretation, insofar as they restrict a (set of) argument(s) to human entities, but they do not have an extensional interpretation – they do not have or establish a referent. It is for this reason that they cannot be referred back to anaphorically (cf. example 11 above). Another property that follows from their non-referential nature is that human impersonal pronouns cannot be modified, as example (14) shows (see for instance Zifonun 2001: 235 on German *man*). This – like their inability to introduce discourse referents – differentiates them from (quantifying) indefinite pronouns like German *jemand* (cf. example 15).

(14)   Wenn man (*aus Apolda) stirbt, wird die Flagge auf Halbmast gesetzt.
         int.: 'If one (*from Apolda) dies, the flag is hoisted at half mast.

---

[2] See for instance Gast (2004) on the ascription of properties to a referent in the context of logophoricity.

(15) *Wenn jemand aus Apolda stirbt, wird die Flagge auf Halbmast gesetzt.*
'If someone from Apolda dies, the flag is hoisted at half mast.'

While most of the expressions dealt with in this chapter can reasonably be called 'pronouns', there are also cases for which a pronominal status is not entirely clear, e.g. the Bulgarian noun or pronoun *čovek* in example (4) above. In sentences containing a modal operator and an infinitive, as in example (10), one could assume an empty pronominal element (say, PRO in generative speech), but we will make the more semantically motivated assumption that there is an argument slot that is filled by a variable ranging over human referents. Rather than providing a definition of human impersonal pronouns like German *man*, French *on*, etc., we will thus define the concept of IMPERSONALIZATION, which we borrow from Blevins (2003) (although we use it in a slightly different way). Impersonalization is a process that applies to argument positions of predicates. It is defined in (16).

(16) IMPERSONALIZATION is the process of filling an argument position of a predicate with a variable ranging over sets of human participants without establishing a referential link to any entity from the universe of discourse.

As an example of impersonalization being achieved with a non-pronominal strategy, consider the German impersonal passive in example (17), which is equivalent to, and perhaps even synonymous with, example (18).

(17) *Es wurde die ganze Nacht getanzt.*
'There was dancing the whole night long.'
(lit.: 'It was danced the whole night long.')

(18) *Man tanzte die ganze Nacht.*
(lit.: 'IMPS was dancing the whole night long.')

Even though we define the topic of inquiry semantically, and independently of the specific types of strategies used for impersonalization, the chapter focuses on pronominal expressions, i.e., human impersonal pronouns. However, some non-pronominal strategies of impersonalization will also be taken into account, in particular impersonal modals and infinitives, which represent common strategies of impersonalization found in Slavic languages.

1.3 The structure of the article

We start in Section 2 with providing some background information on the diachrony and synchronic distribution of 'man'-pronouns, based on Giacalone Ramat & Sansò (2007) and Siewierska (2011). Section 3 presents a semantic map of third person plural impersonals proposed by Siewierska & Papastathi (2011). Section 4 contains some methodological remarks on semantic maps – more specifically, on 'connectivity maps' – and Section 5 introduces a connectivity map for human impersonal pronouns. The most important strategies of impersonalization found in the languages investigated by us are presented in Section 6. Section 7 contains some concluding remarks.

2 The diachrony and synchronic distribution of 'man'-pronouns

Giacalone Ramat & Sansò (2007) have claimed that 'man'-nouns tend to develop along the pathway shown in (19) (cf. also Siewierska 2011: 80). They often acquire a quasi-pronominal function in 'species-generic' contexts (a) and are then generalized subsequently to the other contexts in (b)–(d).

(19)   (a) species-generic
          → (b) human non-referential indefinite
             → (c) human referential indefinite
                → (d) human referential definite

The grammaticalization cline in (19) can be illustrated with data from Latin and Romance languages. 'Species-generic' stands for generically used nouns like Latin *homo* in (20).

(20)   species-generic: Latin (Giacalone Ramat & Sansò 2007: 100)

   Non solo in pane vivit homo.
   not only in bread lives man
   'Man does not live on bread alone.'

In a first step of grammaticalization, 'man'-nouns may come to be used in 'non-referential' contexts as in (21). In such contexts, the states of affairs expressed are non-veridical in the sense of Zwarts (1995, 1998)[3] and the pronouns do not come with an existential entailment (i.e., the existence of an individual to which the relevant predication applies is not implied).

(21) human non-referential indefinite: Old Italian
 (Giacalone Ramat & Sansò 2007: 101)

Cuando uomo truova la domolla nella via ...
When man finds the weasel on.the way
'When one finds a weasel on one's way... '
(↛ 'there is someone who finds a weasel on his way')

In a second step, 'man'-pronouns may be generalized to '(human) referential indefinite' uses, where they occur in veridical contexts and have existential quantificational force. A pertinent example from Modern French is given in (22).

(22) human referential indefinite (Creissels 2008: 8)

On a retrouvé ton porte-monnaie.
IMPS has found your purse
'Your purse has been found.'
(→ 'there is someone who found your purse')

Finally, 'man'-pronouns may acquire definite reference, more specifically, first person reference. As is well known, French *on* is commonly used in this function and, as a matter of fact, represents the default choice for expressing reference to the first person plural, as is illustrated in example (23).

(23) human referential definite (Giacalone Ramat & Sansò 2007: 105)

On a du pain pour nos vieux jours.
IMPS have part bread for our old day
'We've got bread for our old days.'

Grammaticalization paths like the one in (19) also have a synchronic interpretation. Given that synchronic distribution results from diachronic change, such

---

[3] An operator O is veridical if Op → p, otherwise it is non-veridical. A context in the scope of a non-veridical operator is also called 'non-veridical'. Note that the class of non-veridical contexts overlaps with the one of downward entailing contexts in the sense of Ladusaw (1979), but it is not co-extensive with the latter. For instance, specific modals are non-veridical, but not downward entailing.

clines can be regarded as 'semantic maps' (cf. Haspelmath 1997, van der Auwera 2013). They make predictions about possible patterns of polysemy in any given language. While the grammaticalization cline proposed by Giacalone Ramat & Sansò (2007) is only implicitly a semantic map, this device of representing distributional variation has explicitly been used in joint work by Anna Siewierska and Maria Papastathi on third person plural impersonals, to which we turn now.

3 A semantic map of third person plural pronouns

Siewierska & Papastathi (2011: 604) propose the semantic map shown in (24) for third person plural impersonals:

(24)

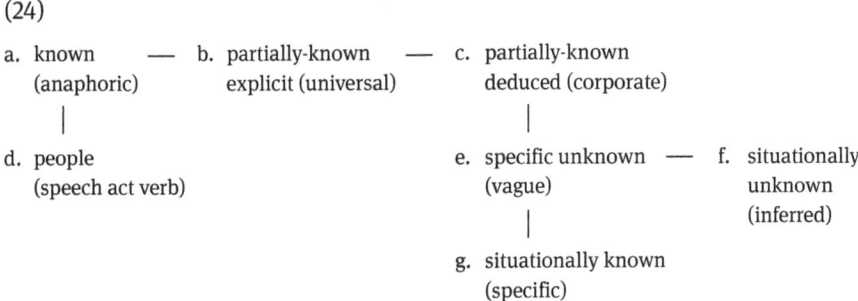

The map in (24) is best understood by considering some examples. Let us start from the left-center node, i.e., (d). As was mentioned in Section 1, in some contexts English uses *people* for impersonalization. Pronominal uses of *people* are particularly common in combination with speech act verbs, esp. *people say…* Alternatively, and with little difference in meaning or register, the third person plural pronoun *they* can be used in such contexts:

(25)　*They say that he was a drinker.* (d)

The top-left corner of the map represents common anaphoric uses of *they* (see example 26 below). Even though such uses are not 'impersonal' in any sense of that word, they are included in the map because they provide the lexical source of the impersonally used third person plural pronouns.

(26)　*Fred and Jack went home. They were tired.* (a)

The next node to the right, (b), stands for contexts in which the set of referents denoted by the impersonal pronoun is 'partially-known'. This means that the referents of the pronoun, while not having been introduced into the discourse, can be identified via some other constituent of the clause – in example (27) the prepositional phrase *in Spain*. They have universal – or better, 'generic' – reference insofar as they refer to (basically) all individuals to which the predicate '(being) in Spain' applies.

(27)   *In Spain, they eat late.* (b)

Node (c) stands for a type of impersonalization in which the extension of the entities referred to is restricted by the predicate of which they are an argument. It is in this sense that the referential restriction is 'deduced'. For instance, the set of referents that can change the tax laws, as in example (28), is quite restricted in reality. Such uses have also been called 'collective' (Kleiber 1994) and 'corporate' (Pesetsky 1996, Cabredo Hofherr 2006).

(28)   *They changed the tax laws last year.* (c)

The type of context instantiated by node (e) is 'vague' (cf. Cabredo Hofherr 2006: 243 for this term), insofar the set of persons referred to is 'unknown' (or perhaps irrelevant). Still, there is an existential entailment (in this sense, the use is 'specific'). Example (29) is a case in point.

(29)   *They've found his bike in the back of a barn.* (e)

In 'situationally unknown (inferred)' contexts, the event in question is not known to have taken place, but is merely inferred from (visual, acoustic, etc.) evidence. A pertinent example is provided in (30).

(30)   *They've been frying chips here.* (f)

The 'situationally unknown' use needs to be distinguished from (e) because there are languages that allow impersonal uses of third person plural pronouns or verbs in contexts of type (e), but not in contexts of type (f). For example, French *ils* is possible in specific unknown/vague contexts (see example 31a), but not in situationally unknown/inferred ones (see example 31b; this example is of course fine with an anaphoric reading).

(31)   a.   *Ils ont trouvé une moto dans la cour.*
            'They've found a motorbike in the courtyard.'

b. *Ici ils_{impersonal} ont mangé des fruits de mer.
    int.: 'Here they have eaten seafood.'
    (Cabredo Hofherr 2006: 243)

Finally, the 'situationally known/specific' use refers to examples like (32).

(32) They're knocking on the door. (g)

There is a 'physically present' and thus situationally accessible (singular or plural) agent, and a clearly perceptible event. Situationally known/specific uses of impersonal pronouns are most similar to (quantifying) indefinite pronouns like *someone*.

The semantic map in (24) can be regarded as a hypothesis about both diachronic developments in the genesis of impersonally used third person plurals and possible patterns of polysemy in this domain. The relevant pronouns start out from node (a) and then gradually extend their distribution. English *they* covers the entire map, as do the third person pronouns or verb forms of many other languages like Spanish, Russian, etc. However, there are also languages where third person pronouns have a more restricted distribution. For instance, it has been mentioned that French *ils* is not used in context (f).

As will have become apparent, there is a point of contact between the 'man'-cline presented in Section 2 and the semantic map introduced in this section: Node (c) on the 'man'-cline in (19) ('human referential indefinite') and node (e) on the third-person-plural-map ('specific-unknown/vague') were illustrated with the same type of example, i.e., (33) (= 22) for node (c) on the 'man'-cline, and (34) (= 29) for node (e) on the 3pl-map.

(33) On   a   retrouvé ton   porte-monnaie.
      Imps   has   found   your   purse
      'Your purse has been found.'
      (Creissels 2008: 8)

(34) They've found his bike in the back of a barn.

We will aim to show that the two maps can in fact be combined, and that the domain of human impersonal pronouns can be structured in terms of a few distributional parameters referring to the type of event description provided, and the type of quantification expressed. But before doing so, we will present our view of the concept of 'semantic map' in the next section.

4 Semantic maps

Even though the semantic map methodology is widely used in linguistic typology, there has been some controversy concerning the status and usefulness of (specific types of) semantic maps. We will therefore make some methodological remarks in this section before we present our own semantic map of human impersonal pronouns in Section 5. In Section 4.1, we briefly address the relationship between the two types of semantic maps that have played a prominent role in recent typological research ('connectivity maps' and 'proximity maps'). In Section 4.2, we provide a definition of connectivity maps and their components.

The discussion in Section 4.2 is somewhat technical, and the idea behind it is that of implementing the semantic map methodology in typological databases like TDIR (cf. Gast 2009) and, more generally speaking, in database systems like XLD (the 'Extensible Linguistic Database' system developed by Alexis Dimitriadis).[4] Readers who are not interested in matters of technical implementation, and who are familiar with the semantic map methodology may safely skip this section and go to Section 5.

4.1 Connectivity maps and proximity maps

In recent debates, a distinction is often made between (what we will call) connectivity maps and proximity maps. Connectivity maps are also called 'traditional', 'classical', 'first-generation', or 'implicational maps'. Proximity maps have also been called 'statistical', 'probabilistic', 'distance-based', and 'similarity maps' (see for instance Cysouw et al. 2010). Sometimes, the two types of maps or methods are regarded as complementary, and some authors seem to aim at determining which of them is 'better'. As has been argued by van der Auwera (2013), we believe that different types of semantic maps show different things, and have different merits. While it is (chronologically) true that proximity maps form the 'second generation' of semantic maps, and while they no doubt provide a useful heuristic alternative to the original type of map and represent a highly valuable addition to the 'typological toolbox' in general, we believe that they cannot replace connectivity maps, as we call the 'first-generation' maps of Haspelmath (1997), van der Auwera & Plungian (1998), among others.

Connectivity maps are hypotheses about possible patterns of polysemy which can be tested by sampling cross-linguistic data. They are also diachronic, as they represent distributional patterns that have resulted from specific types of

---

[4] See for instance http://languagelink.let.uu.nl/burs/docs/burs-design.pdf

historical developments. In other words, connectivity maps are hypotheses about (changes in) linguistic systems. They do not *per se* imply any claims with respect to the 'conceptual similarity' of the meanings or functions in question. While such claims have been made by cognitively oriented typologists like Kemmer (1993) and Croft (2001), connectivity maps can be used without any aspiration to 'cognitive reality' (cf. also Cristofaro 2010 for this point and for many pertinent examples).

Given that connectivity maps are hypotheses about possible linguistic systems, they are not (intended to be) generated 'bottom-up', i.e., they are not generated from raw data. They are informed by linguistic theory, and are regarded as means of testing and improving linguistic theories. This is what crucially distinguishes connectivity maps from proximity maps: Proximity maps provide an exploratory method and means of visualization for the generation of hypotheses, while connectivity maps *are* hypotheses.

We would also like to point out that, contrary to what has been claimed by proponents of the bottom-up/proximity approach, there is no difference in the degrees of 'mathematical well-formedness' or sophistication between connectivity maps and proximity maps. Croft & Poole (2008: 1) remark:

> ...the semantic map model, while theoretically well-motivated in typology, is not mathematically well-defined or computationally tractable, making it impossible to use with large and highly variable datasets.

This criticism is, in our view, not justified. Technically speaking, connectivity maps are graphs and as such perfectly well-defined. Graph theory is a well- established (and non-trivial) branch of mathematics (see for instance Diestel 2006 for an introduction), and there is no reason to assume that it is, in any way, less sophisticated than exploratory methods or visualizations in statistics. Given that connectivity maps are, technically speaking, graphs, they are, of course, 'computationally tractable', as is any graph. Connectivity maps can also be generated bottom-up from large amounts of data.[5] Since our approach is theory-driven and basically diachronic, however, we have refrained from applying a bottom-up approach of this type.

After these rather general comments on the semantic map methodology and on connectivity maps in particular, we will now proceed to provide a graph-theoretic definition of connectivity maps.

---

5 As in the case of proximity maps, more than one graph may be compatible with a given data set. In such cases, the various graphs need to be evaluated and compared (e.g. with respect to their predictive power). As in most cases, computers can help us solve problems, but they cannot solve the problems for us.

4.2 Defining connectivity maps

4.2.1 Components of the map

Technically speaking, a connectivity map can be defined as graph G which is constituted by a set of nodes N_G and a set of edges (pairs of nodes) E_G (note that the pairs in E_G are ordered, i.e., $\langle n_1, n_2 \rangle \neq \langle n_2, n_1 \rangle$):

(35) $G = \langle N_G, E_G \rangle$
 $N_G = \{n_1, n_2, n_3\}$
 $E_G = \{\langle n_1, n_2 \rangle, \langle n_2, n_1 \rangle, \langle n_2, n_3 \rangle, \langle n_3, n_2 \rangle\}$

The graph defined in (35) is based on the assumption that diachronic developments are possible in both directions (in other words, E_G is symmetric). It can be visualized as shown in (36). The nodes correspond to boxes, and the edges to lines between the boxes (the lines could alternatively be thought of as bidirectional arrows).

(36)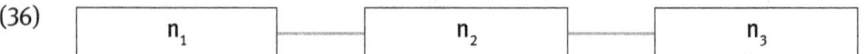

We will also need linguistic definitions of nodes and edges, in addition to the 'technical' ones. The nodes of a connectivity map are our *tertia comparationis* and are semantically or pragmatically defined. We will assume that the nodes of a connectivity map represent GENERALIZED UTTERANCE MEANINGS.[6] As becomes apparent from their name, generalized utterances meanings are generalizations over utterance meanings. Utterance meanings, in turn, are probably best defined in terms of their 'context change potential', using concepts from dynamic semantics (e.g. Heim 1982), with the notion of 'context' including linguistic as well as non-linguistic matters.

Generalized utterance meanings can be thought of as utterance types that are stripped of their lexical content. They can be represented as sets of feature-value pairs concerning properties of sentences such as the illocutionary force of the corresponding utterance, the (non-)veridicality of the proposition expressed, the (non-)instantiation of an event, TAM-features, etc. If we assume that the nodes n_1–n_3 in (35) above can be characterized in terms of two features F_1 and F_2 with the

---

[6] As Martin Haspelmath has pointed out to us, in the domain of lexical meanings we can simply use (nominal, adjectival, verbal) denotations as *tertia comparationis*, but in the case of highly context-dependent expressions like human impersonal pronouns the sentential environment needs to be taken into consideration.

values $\{a, b\}$ for F_1 and $\{x, y\}$ for F_2, they can alternatively be represented as shown in (37), and the corresponding graph can be visualized as in (38).

(37) $n_1 = \{<F_1, a>, <F_2, x>\}$
$n_2 = \{<F_1, a>, <F_2, y>\}$
$n_3 = \{<F_1, b>, <F_2, y>\}$

(38)

F_1: a	F_1: a	F_1: b
F_2: x	F_2: y	F_2: y

For the sake of simplicity, as well as for practical reasons, we will represent the nodes of a connectivity map in terms of '(generalized) diagnostic sentences', i.e., typical instantiations of the relevant generalized utterance meanings. For example, the sentences in (39) represent three types of context that will be of interest to our study of human impersonal pronouns. Note that these diagnostic sentences are still 'generalized' insofar as they contain an empty slot, x, for the marker whose distribution they indicate.

(39)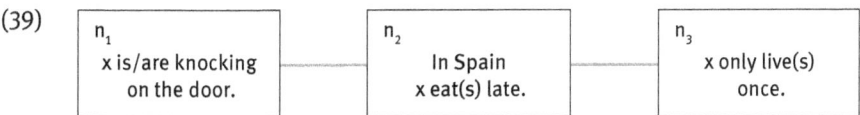

Having defined the nodes of the graph we also need to provide a linguistic interpretation of the edges. Given that we regard connectivity maps as representing (possible) diachronic developments, we will also interpret edges diachronically. Two nodes n_1 and n_2 are assumed to form an edge iff any given linguistic marker m can extend its distribution from n_1 to n_2 or vice versa without, at the same time, extending its distribution to any other node in N_G (the set of nodes constituting the graph).

4.2.2 Testing the map

One of the main purposes of a connectivity map is to predict possible patterns of polysemy. In other words, connectivity maps restrict the range of possible meanings or functions for any linguistic marker m. The distribution of a marker m can be represented as the set of nodes for which m can felicitously be used. For example, the distribution of English *they* relative to the three (generalized) utterance meanings shown in (39) corresponds to the set of nodes $\{n_1, n_2\}$. The function D_G – defined relative to a graph G – maps a linguistic marker m to its distribution, i.e., to the subset of nodes in N_G for which m can be used. This mapping is shown in (40), and it can be graphically represented as in (41), i.e., by highlighting the nodes in $D_G(m)$.

(40) $D_G(they) = \{n_1, n_2\}$

(41)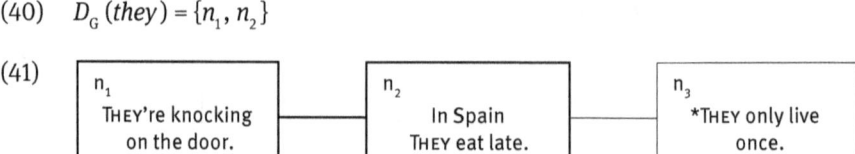

A connectivity map makes the prediction that any marker m which can be used to express an utterance meaning corresponding to some node n in N_G will be mapped by the function D_G to a set of nodes which form an uninterrupted chain in the graph G. Let us call this condition the CONNECTIVITY CONDITION. The connectivity condition can be (computationally) tested as follows: In a first step, we have to determine the subset of E_G (the set of edges in the semantic map/graph G) which contains only pairs containing nodes in $D_G(m)$. Let us call this set the 'test set' (TS_G) of m for a graph G. It is defined in (42). The test set is simply the set of edges/pairs $<n_i, n_j>$ from E_G such that both n_i and n_j are contained in the distribution of the linguistic marker m, i.e., $D_G(m)$.

(42) The test set
$TS_G(m) := \{<n_i, n_j> \in E_G \mid n_i \in D_G(m) \wedge n_j \in D_G(m)\}$

Let us now consider a hypothetical marker m which covers all nodes in N_G, i.e., $D_G(m) = N_G = \{n_1, n_2, n_3\}$ (cf. 43a). E_G is given in (43b). The test set of m (in E_G) is the set of pairs in (43c), as all edges in E_G contain nodes that are included in $D_G(m)$ (i.e., $TS_G(m) = E_G$).

(43) a. $D_G(m) = \{n_1, n_2, n_3\}$
      b. $E_G = \{<n_1, n_2>, <n_2, n_1>, <n_2, n_3>, <n_3, n_2>\}$
      c. $TS_G(m) = \{<n_1, n_2>, <n_2, n_1>, <n_2, n_3>, <n_3, n_2>\}$

In order to test the connectivity condition we have to check whether there is a direct connection between any one node contained in $D_G(m)$ on the 'test graph' $G_t(m)$ constituted by (the nodes of) $D_G(m)$ and (the edges in) $TS_G(m)$ ($G_t(m) = <D_G(m), TS_G(m)>$). For this purpose we can use the 'transitive closure' of $TS_G(m)$, i.e., the minimal transitive set containing $TS_G(m)$. The transitive closure of a set R is represented as R^+, so $TS_G^+(m)$ is the transitive closure of $TS_G(m)$. It is given in (44).

In addition to the edges of $TS_G(m)$ it contains the pairs $<n_1, n_3>$ and $<n_3, n_1>$, as n_1 and n_3 are connected (via n_2) in G.

(44) The transitive closure of the test set $TS_G(m)$
$TS_G^+(m) = \{<n_1, n_2>, <n_2, n_1>, <n_2, n_3>, <n_3, n_2>, <n_1, n_3>, <n_3, n_1>\}$

The set $TS_G(m)$ can be regarded as a list of all pairs of nodes that are connected – either directly or indirectly – on the graph constituted by the nodes covered by a given marker (i.e., $D_G(m)$) and the edges connecting members of $D_G(m)$ on the semantic map that is being tested.

In order to test whether the distribution of m conforms to the connectivity condition, we can now define a function that delivers the Cartesian square of $D_G(m)$ without the reflexive pairs (e.g. $<n_1, n_1>$). We will call this function the 'potential edge set' (E^p_G) of m, defined relative to a graph G. The potential edge set is simply the set of all possible edges (pairs of nodes) for a given set of nodes, as in (45).

(45) $E^p_G(m) := \{<n_i, n_j> \mid n_i, n_j \in D_G(m), n_i \neq n_j\}$

We can now test the connectivity condition by comparing the potential edge set $E^p_G(m)$ – the set of all possible edges on the map – to the test set $TS_G^+(m)$ – the set of all edges that result from adding indirectly linked nodes as pairs to $TS_G(m)$. The connectivity condition is met if and only if the two sets are identical:

(46) The connectivity condition
$E^p_G(m) = TS_G^+(m)$

The connectivity condition is satisfied by the marker m, as can be seen by comparing $E^p_G(m)$ in (47) to $TS_G^+(m)$ in (44) above.

(47) $E^p_G(m) = \{<n_1, n_2>, <n_2, n_1>, <n_2, n_3>, <n_3, n_2>, <n_1, n_3>, <n_3, n_1>\}$

The connectivity condition would not be satisfied by a marker m with the distribution $D_G(m) = \{n_1, n_3\}$:

(48) a. $D_G(m) = \{n_1, n_3\}$ d. $TS_G(m) = \emptyset$
b. $E^p_G(m) = \{<n_1, n_3>, <n_3, n_1>\}$ e. $TS_G^+(m) = \emptyset$
c. $E_G = \{<n_1, n_2>, <n_2, n_1>, <n_2, n_3>, <n_3, n_2>\}$ f. $E^p_G(m) \neq TS_G^+(m)$

$TS_G^+(m)$ is empty because $TS_G(m)$ is empty as well, as no edge in E_G contains both nodes in $D_G(m)$. The connectivity condition, accordingly, does not obtain (cf. 48f).

4.2.3 Remarks on the architecture of semantic maps

Obviously, the predictive power of a connectivity map is a function of the number of edges that it contains. Let us assume that the set N_G of nodes is given at the beginning of the investigation (which is of course not true, as the exact nodes used in any given study is subject to change; in a cyclic research design, however, we start each cycle with a specific set of nodes). The researcher's task is to determine the set of edges E_G.

The fewer edges there are, the stronger the hypothesis will be. It is a condition of well-formedness that every node needs to be connected to some other node. The minimal number of edges in a connectivity map is therefore $2 \times (|N_G| - 1)$ (if edges are bidirectional, as assumed above, and reflexive edges are excluded), the maximal number is $|N_G|^2 - |N_G|$ (under the same condition). While Occam's Razor compels us to build a map coming as close to $2 \times (|N_G| - 1)$ as possible, we should bear in mind that simplicity is not the only criterion for the appropriateness of a semantic map. As has been mentioned, we interpret edges as possible diachronic developments from one node to another. The best piece of evidence in support of individual edges on a connectivity map is thus the observation of historical change in the domain of investigation. Moreover, the nodes need to be defined in terms of feature combinations which mirror the historical developments in question. This takes us back to human impersonal pronouns, and our proposal for a connectivity map predicting their distribution.

5 A connectivity map for human personal pronouns

The first step in building a semantic map of human impersonal pronouns consists in identifying the properties of sentences or utterances which restrict the distribution of such pronouns in some languages while not restricting it in others. In other words, we need to find (distributional) parameters of variation. Candidates for useful parameters of variation are provided by categories that are known to be relevant from research into polarity-sensitive expressions (e.g. indefinites and focus operators). These categories are best identified on the basis of detailed studies of (samples of) individual languages. In our case, the parameters of variation are largely based on the work done by Anna Siewierska and Maria Papastathi (Siewierska 2008, 2010, 2011, Siewierska & Papastathi 2011) as well as the large body of studies on specific, mostly European languages, e.g. Dimowa (1981a), Zifonun (2001) and Linthe (2010) on German *man*, Hoekstra (2010) on Frisian *men*, Cabredo Hofherr (2008) and Creissels (2008) on French *on*, Cabredo Hofherr (2006) on French *ils*, etc. Moreover, there are many comparative or contrastive publications, e.g. Dimowa (1981b) on German/Bulgarian and Weerman (2006) on English/Dutch/German. Of course, we also rely on our own earlier publications, in particular Coussé & van der Auwera (2012) and van der Auwera et al. (2012).

We will distinguish two major sets of parameters of variation:
1. properties of the state of affairs described by the sentence in question
2. properties of the set of human participants

5.1 The state of affairs

We will use three pairs of features for the state of affairs (note that unlike in van der Auwera et al. 2012, we distinguish between modal contexts in a narrow sense and other, non-modal contexts, e.g. conditionals):

1. veridical vs. non-veridical
2. episodic vs. generic
3. modal vs. non-modal

The feature 'veridical vs. non-veridical' (cf. Giannakidou 2011) concerns the proposition denoted by the 'bare clause' containing the human impersonal pronoun.[7] The proposition denoted by a (bare) clause is veridical if it is assumed to be true, in the context in which it is uttered (cf. Note 3 above), with the notion of 'truth' being relativized to an 'individual anchor' in the sense of Farkas (1992). The most typical cases of non-veridical clauses are provided by conditional clauses, modal predications and questions (i.e., contexts typically licensing negative polarity items).

Veridical propositions are further sub-classified into episodic and generic ones (cf. Krifka et al. 1995). Episodic states of affairs are spatio-temporally anchored, i.e., they are thought of has taking place at a specific time and place. Generic states of affairs generalize over time and space.

Non-veridical clauses can be further sub-classified into modal and non-modal ones. Modal clauses contain a (non-veridical) modal operator, i.e., an expression of possibility or necessity. Non-modal clauses do not contain any such (overt) operator.

---

[7] The bare clause contains the predicate plus its arguments and any adjuncts, as well as any internal negation. If the bare clause is non-veridical, this means that it is contained in the scope of some non-veridical operator other than negation. Negation is considered as being part of the bare clause because it does not seem to be a licensing factor in the distribution of human impersonal pronouns.

The classification of states of affairs is hierarchically ordered as shown in (49). Note that the terminal nodes are not mutually exclusive; for instance, generic sentences may be modal as well as non-modal. Such differentiations do not seem to play a role in the distribution of human impersonal pronouns in European languages, however.

(49)
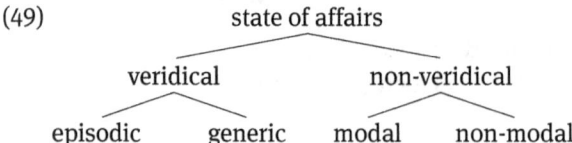

There are, thus, four types of feature combinations (terminal nodes). Examples of each type are given in (50), using German *man* for illustration.

(50) a. veridical/episodic
   Man hat geklopft.
   'They've knocked on the door.'

 b. veridical/generic
   Man lebt nur einmal.
   'You only live once.'

 c. non-veridical/modal
   Man sollte nicht betrunken Auto fahren.
   'You shouldn't drink and drive.'

 d. non-veridical/non-modal (= non-assertive)
   Was passiert, wenn man saure Milch trinkt?
   'What happens if one drinks sour milk?'

5.2 The type of quantification expressed

The second group of parameters of variation concerns the type of quantification expressed. We can distinguish two major types, universal quantification and existential quantification. In the context of human impersonal pronouns, 'universal' is to be understood in the sense of 'quasi-universal' or 'generic', insofar as these pronouns typically allow for exceptions.

Among the universal uses we can make a distinction according to the 'perspective' taken, i.e., 'internal' vs. 'external'. This distinction is largely parallel, but not identical, to the one between 'speaker-inclusive' and 'speaker-exclusive' reference (which we made in van der Auwera et al. 2012).

Speaker- or hearer-inclusive reference can be assumed to be invariably internal, in terms of the perspective taken. But an internal perspective can also be taken if the speaker or hearer is not contained in the set of potential referents. As Moltmann (2010) has argued, impersonal pronouns (of a specific type) are used for 'detached self-reference' – with 'referential shift' in terms of Malamud (2012). This means, roughly speaking, that a 'center of consciousness' (e.g. the speaker or hearer) identifies, or is identified, with the set of referents under discussion in a process of 'generic simulation'. For example, a sentence like (51) could be regarded as an instruction for the addressee to 'put herself into the shoes' of a Royal and consider the consequences of this act of 'generic simulation'.

(51) *As a member of the Royal family you have a lot of duties.*

The parameter 'internal' vs. 'external perspective' can be illustrated with the examples in (52):

(52) a. *I'd love to live in France. They have excellent food there.*
(exclusive/external)

b. *It's great to live in France. You have excellent food here.*
(inclusive/internal)

c. *It's great to live in France. You have excellent food there.*
(exclusive/internal)

They in example (52a) is exclusive and takes an external perspective. Neither the speaker nor the hearer are French or live in France. Example (52b) could be uttered by a Frenchman or someone living in France. In this sense it is inclusive, and the perspective taken is internal. Example (52c) could be thought of as being uttered by someone not (at present) living in France, but taking an internal perspective, inviting the addressee to identify with people living in France.

A similar contrast can be observed between examples (53a) and (53b) below. (53a) suggests that John ate the mushrooms in question (internal perspective), while (53b) suggests that he did not eat them (external perspective).

(53) a. *John found out that one gets sick when one eats these mushrooms.*
(internal)

b. *John found out that people get sick when they eat these mushrooms.*
(external)

(Moltmann 2010: 448)

Among the existential uses of human impersonal pronouns we can make further distinctions according to the categories of definiteness and number. The referents may either be accessible in the discourse environment, i.e., definite, or they may be inaccessible, i.e., indefinite. Existential quantification may either be vague with respect to number, or it may be unambiguously plural (singular reference is not regarded as a case of impersonalization). The 'classification tree' for the parameters classifying the type of referential restriction associated with impersonalization is shown in (54).

(54)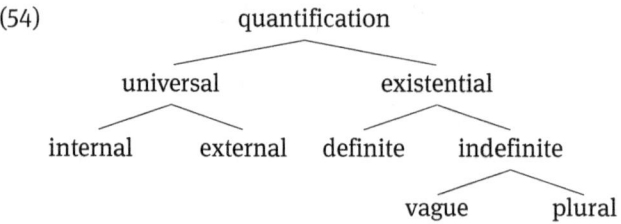

Again, the two sets of features are not fully orthogonal.[8] We will focus on those feature combinations that are often involved in differences between European languages.

As has been mentioned, we will provide (generalized) diagnostic sentences for each feature combination. These diagnostic sentences are given in (55)– (61). The words in bold face represent the slots for impersonalized argument positions ('S' stands for 'sentence', 'HP' for 'human participant').

(55) S: veridical/episodic
HP: existential/indefinite/vague
They're knocking on the door.

(56) S: veridical/episodic
HP: existential/indefinite/plural
They've surrounded us.

(57) S: veridical/episodic
HP: existential/definite
They've raised the taxes again.

---

[8] Cf. van der Auwera et al. (2012) for a more detailed description of possible feature combinations in the domain of impersonalization, and for reasons why specific feature combinations have not been taken into account; the set of features used in van der Auwera et al. (2012) is slightly different from the one used here, however.

(58) S: veridical/generic
HP: universal, external
They *eat dragonflies in Bali.*

(59) S: veridical/generic
HP: universal, internal
One *only lives once.*

(60) S: non-veridical/modal
HP: universal, internal
One *should never give up.*

(61) S: non-veridical/non-modal (=non-assertive)
HP: universal, internal
*What happens if **one** drinks sour milk?*

The nodes corresponding to the generalized utterance meanings can be arranged in a graph as shown in (62). The numbers of the nodes correspond to the order of contexts and diagnostic sentences in (55)–(61), and we will use these numbers for reference to individual nodes in what follows.

(62)

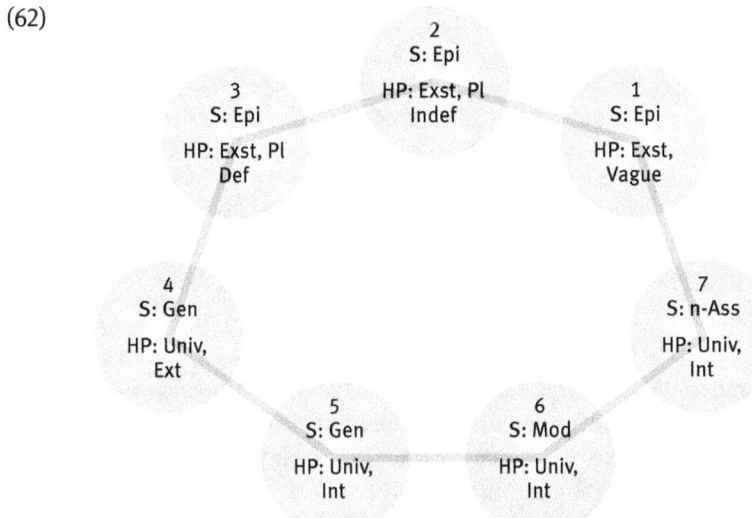

The map has the form of a ring. We will discuss this point in Section 6.3. In this context, we will also consider the 'feature geometry' of the map in some detail. For the time being, suffice it to say that the map is mainly structured by two dimensions. The top row (nodes 1–3) is associated with existential quantification, the bottom row (nodes 4–7) with universal/generic quantification. Moreover, there is an increase in specificity from right to left, with respect to both the states of affairs described and the type of reference made. As will be argued in Section 6.3, each edge connecting two nodes corresponds to a single change in the feature specifications of the relevant nodes (though in specific cases a change in one feature implies a change in another feature; cf. Section 6.3). Our connectivity map of human impersonal pronouns with diagnostic sentences instead of feature combinations is shown in (63). This version will be used in Section 6 to represent the distribution of human impersonal pronouns.

(63)

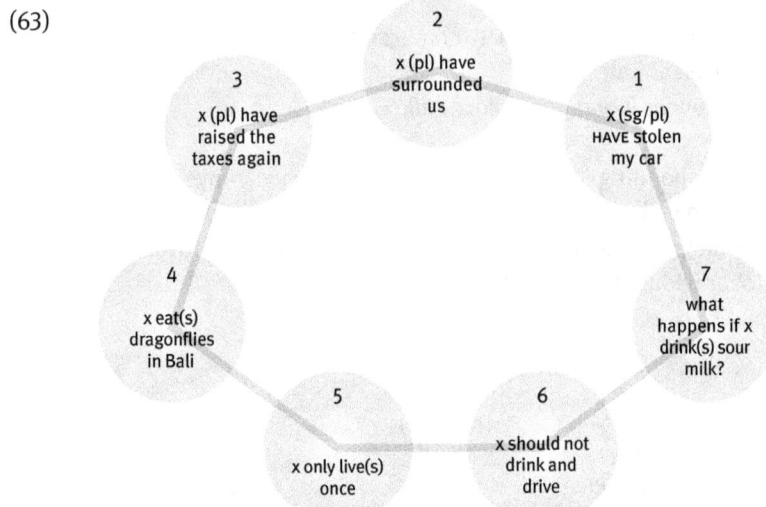

Before considering some types of human impersonal pronouns from European languages, let us briefly consider how our map relates to the 'man'-cline of Giacalone Ramat & Sansò (2007) and to the 3pl-map of Siewierska & Papastathi (2011). A comparison is provided in Table 1.

There are contexts on the 'man'-cline and the 3pl-map which we have not taken into account because they do not imply impersonalization as defined in (16) above, in particular species-generic cases (node (a) of the 'man'-cline) and deictic reference (node (d) on the 'man'-cline).

Node (d) of the 3pl-map has been exempt from consideration because it is not entirely clear to us whether or not it can be subsumed under one of the other nodes. Siewierska & Papastathi (2011) not only assign an independent status to it but even regard it as a more or less independent development, as it is located on a different side of the source node (a) than all the other uses. In our view, this particular use requires more (esp. diachronic) investigation.

Table 1. A comparison of the three maps

HIP-map	'man'-cline	3PL-map
1	(c)	(e), (f), (g)
2	(c)	(e), (f), (g)
–		(d)
3	(c)	(c)
4	–	(b)
5	–	–
6	(b)	–
7	(b)	–
–	(a)	–

We have collapsed the distinction between 'vague', 'inferred', and 'specific' made by Cabredo Hofherr (2006) and adopted by Siewierska & Papastathi (2011) because we lack evidence for it in the languages investigated by us. An additional distinction in comparison to Siewierska & Papastathi (2011) is made with respect to the category of number (vague/node 1 vs. plural/node 2). Given that we have neutralized two distinctions made by Siewierska & Papastathi (2011) while adding another, orthogonal one, our nodes 1 and 2 both correspond to nodes (e), (f), and (g) on the 3pl-map.

6 Human impersonal pronouns on the connectivity map

6.1 Major types of pronouns

The first type of human impersonal pronoun to be discussed covers the entire map. German *man*, Dutch/Frisian *men*, French *on* etc. can be used in all types of contexts. Examples from German are given for each of the diagnostic contexts in (64).

(64) a. Node 1

veridical/episodic, indefinite/vague

Man klopft an der Tür.
'They're knocking on the door.'

b. Node 2

veridical/episodic, indefinite/plural
Man hat uns umstellt.
'They've surrounded us.'

c. Node 3

veridical/episodic, definite
Man hat schon wieder die Steuern erhöht.
'They've raised the taxes again.'

d. Node 4

veridical/generic, universal/external
In Bali isst man Libellen.
'In Bali they eat dragonflies.'

e. Node 5

veridical/generic, universal/internal
Man lebt nur einmal.
'You only live once.'

f. Node 6

non-veridical/modal, universal/internal
Man sollte nie aufgeben.
'You should never give up.'

g. Node 7

non-veridical/non-modal, universal/internal
Was passiert, wenn man saure Milch trinkt?
'What happens if one drinks sour milk?'

Third person plural pronouns like English *they* typically cover nodes 1 to 4 on the map. The distribution of *they* can thus be represented as shown in (65), where only nodes allowing *they* are connected with edges (the other nodes are moreover shaded in dark grey).

Other third person plural pronouns are slightly more restricted than English *they*. For example, German *sie* is not normally used with a vague number specification (i.e., for node 1), as it entails a plurality of referents (see example 66). This is different in English, where *they* can also be used (impersonally) when there is just a single referent, as in example (67) (cf. Siewierska & Papastathi 2011: 581–582).

(65)

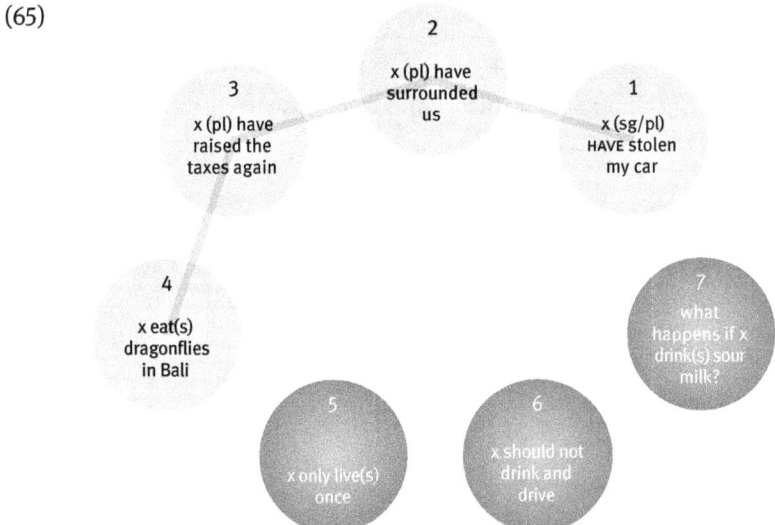

(66) *Jetzt haben sie schon wieder geklopft*
      'They (pl) have knocked once again.' (node 2)

(67) *They're knocking on the door. It's your mother.* (node 1)

We will proceed counter-clockwise in the ring constituting the connectivity map, considering more examples of impersonal pronouns as we go along. Node 4, which constitutes the leftmost node of *they*, provides the 'starting point' of the Italian middle marker *si*, which is used in all types of context where universal quantification is expressed, i.e for nodes 4–7.

(68) Node 4

   In Spagna si   cena   tardi.
   in Spain IMPS eat.3SG late
   'In Spain they eat late.'

(69) Node 5

   Si   vive   solo una volta.
   IMPS live.3SG only one time
   'You only live once.'

(70) Node 6

Non si deve bere alla guida.
NEG IMPS should.3SG drink at.the steering.wheel
'One should not drink and drive.'

(71) Node 7

Cosa succede se si beve del latte scaduto?
what happens if IMPS drinks PREP.DEF.MASC milk sour
'What happens if one drinks sour milk?' (L. Deringer, p.c.)

The map corresponding to It. *si* is shown in (72).

(72)

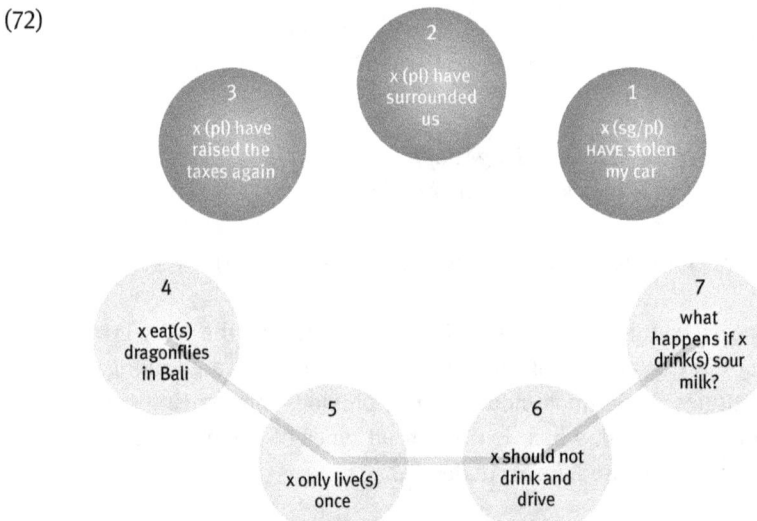

Second person pronouns or verb forms are typically used in contexts 5, 6 and 7 (see the Bulgarian examples in 73). The corresponding map is shown in (74).

(73) a. Node 5

Samo živeeš vednăž.
only live.2SG.PRS once
'You only live once.'

b. Node 6

Ne   biva   da   lăžeš.
not should.3SG.PRS PTCL lie.2SG.PRS
'You shouldn't lie.'

c. Node 7

Tova se   slučva,   kogato pie-š.
this   REFL.ACC   happen.3SG.PRS   when   drink-2SG.PRS
razvaleno   mljako
sour.NEUT   milk
'This happens if you drink sour milk.' (A. Rauhuth, p.c.)

(74)

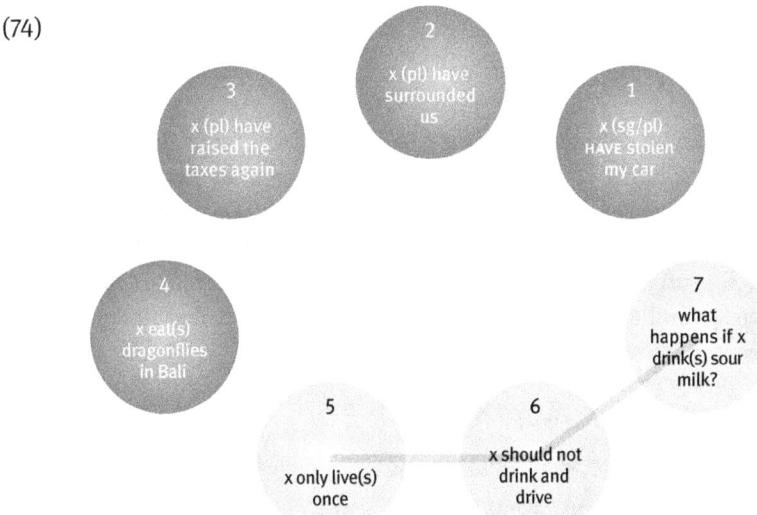

Finally, indefinite pronouns functioning as existential quantifiers like English *someone*, German *jemand*, etc. are used in contexts 7 and 1, thus closing the circle (see examples 75 and 76).

(75) a. Node 7

Wenn jemand liegen blieb, kam immer Hilfe.
'If someone broke down, help always came.'

b. Node 1

Jemand hat mir das Fahrrad gestohlen.
'Someone has stolen my bike.'

(76)

It should be mentioned that existential quantifiers like *jemand* differ systematically from typical human impersonal pronouns like German *man* in at least two respects. First, *man* (as well as French *on*, etc.) always takes narrow scope relative to sentential adverbials such as event quantifiers, independently of the order of elements (cf. example 77). *Jemand*, by contrast, takes wide scope when it precedes event quantifiers (in basic/underlying word order) while it takes narrow scope when it follows such quantifiers (cf. 78).

(77) a. *Man hat zweimal geklopft.*
 'They've knocked twice.' (same person or different person)

  b. *Zweimal hat man geklopft.* (≡ 77a)

(78) a. *Jemand hat zweimal geklopft.*
 'Someone has knocked twice.' (same person knocked twice)

  b. *Zweimal hat jemand geklopft.*
 'They've knocked twice.' (same person or different person)

  c. *Es hat zweimal jemand geklopft.* (≡ 78b)

Another difference between human impersonal pronouns and existential quantifiers was pointed out in Section 1. Unlike human impersonal pronouns, existential quantifiers can introduce discourse referents, and can therefore be taken up by an anaphoric pronoun, (cf. 79a vs. 79b).

(79) a. *Da hat jemand$_i$ geklopft. Er$_i$ ist sehr verärgert.*
 'Someone has knocked on the door. He is very angry.'

 b. **Man$_i$ hat geklopft. Er$_i$ ist sehr verärgert.*

Even though existential quantifiers like *jemand* are not human impersonal pronouns according to the definition given in (16), they lend support to the 'circular' form of our connectivity map. The connection between nodes 7 and 1 is of course also documented independently. As Giacalone Ramat & Sansò (2007) have shown, 'man'-pronouns (tend to) extend their range of distribution from our node 7 (their context b) to our node 1 (their context c). The connection between nodes 1 and 7 is discussed in Section 6.3.

6.2 Summary: Major types of human impersonal pronouns

Even though the semantic map of human impersonal pronouns illustrated in the previous section allows for a great number of patterns of polysemy – there are 43 possible continuous combinations of nodes on a circle of seven nodes – only a few combinations are attested in European languages. This is obviously related to the fact that the degrees of similarity between neighbouring nodes are not identical. We have found eight major types of human impersonal pronoun. Their distributions are shown in Table 2 below. (Row 1 occurs twice, at the top as well as at the bottom, in order to illustrate the circular nature of the table).

Table 2. Major types of human impersonal pronouns

	1	2	3	4	5	6	7	examples
1	✓	✓	✓	✓	✓	✓	✓	Dutch *men*, French *on*, German *man*
2	✓	✓	✓	✓				English *they*, Russian 3PL, Italian 3PL
3		✓	✓	✓				German *sie*, Dutch *ze*
4			✓	✓				German *die*
5				✓	✓	✓	✓	Italian *si*, Spanish *se*
6					✓	✓	✓	Spanish *uno*, 2SG-verbs, Bulgarian *čovek*
7						✓	✓	Russian (modal +) infinitive
8	✓						✓	English *someone*, Dutch *iemand*
9	✓	✓	✓	✓	✓	✓	✓	German *man*, French *on*, Dutch *men*

So far, we have illustrated or at least mentioned types 1, 2, 3, 5, 6 and 8. Type 4 is instantiated by Germ *die*. This pronoun is more or less distributed like *sie*, but there is a difference: *Die* is not normally used for (plural) indefinite impersonalization as represented by node 2. Example (80) below suggests that the referents in question are visible and identifiable. *Die* is only used for corporate or collective cases (as in example 81/node 3) and for universal quantification with an external perspective (as in example 82/node 4).

(80) Definite reference (not impersonal)

Die haben uns umstellt.
'They (def.) have surrounded us.'

(81) Node 3

Die haben schon wieder die Steuern erhöht.
'They've raised the taxes again.'

(82) Node 4

Die essen Libellen in Bali.
'In Bali, they eat dragonflies.'

Another strategy that has not been discussed in detail is the one in row 7. In Table 2, we call it (modal +) infinitive. Russian uses bare infinitives in conditional clauses (as in example 83a), and it has a number of impersonal modals which combine with (bare) infinitives, too (see example 83b). Similar strategies can be found in non-Slavic European languages as well, but they are not as widely distributed as in Russian.

(83) Russian

    a. Node 7

    Vot cto slŭcitsja, esli vypit' kisloe moloko.
    that what happens if drink.INF sour milk
    'That's what happens if one drinks sour milk.'

    b. Node 6

    Ètogo ne sleduet delat'.
    this not should.IMPS.PRS do.INF
    'One shouldn't do that.' (O. Rudolf, p.c.)

Examples like those in (83a) raise the question to what extent the 'covert' arguments associated with infinitives ('PRO', in generative terminology) are comparable to human impersonal pronouns like French *on*. It seems to us that Moltmann (2006: 260) is basically right when she points out that "[a]rbitrary PRO in fact appears to be the manifestation of generic *one* when an overt NP, for syntactic reasons... is not possible", even though we have preferred to speak of 'impersonalization', rather than assuming phonologically empty pronouns.

6.3 Why is the map a ring?

While most semantic maps proposed in typological research (e.g. Haspelmath 1997, van der Auwera & Plungian 1998) are 'open', the map proposed in this study is circular. The question arises why this should be so.

Note first that both the horizontal and the vertical dimension on the map can be interpreted linguistically. From right to left there is an increase in 'referentiality'. In the top row (nodes 1 to 3) there is a gradual change from 'indefinite and vague with respect to number' (node 1) to 'definite' (node 3). In the bottom row (nodes 7 to 4) there is an increase in the specificity of states of affairs, from 'non-veridical' (node 7) to 'veridical/generic' (node 4). The vertical dimension separates the existential readings in the top row (nodes 1–3) from the universal readings in the bottom row (nodes 4–7).

Let us consider the feature specifications of the various nodes in more detail. All nodes in the top row are episodic and existential. There is a one-by-one feature change in the categories of number and definiteness, as is illustrated in Table 3.

Table 3. Feature changes from nodes 1 to 3

Node 1		Node 2		Node 3
episodic		episodic		episodic
existential		existential		existential
indefinite		indefinite	≠	definite
vague	≠	plural		plural

Similarly, the bottom row is arranged in such a way that one feature changes from one node to the next. This is illustrated in Table 4 (empty cells are not specified for the features in question).

Table 4. Feature changes from nodes 4 to 7

Node 4	Node 5		Node 6		Node 7
veridical	veridical		≠ non-veridical		non-veridical
modal				≠	non-modal
generic	generic				
universal	universal		universal		universal
external	≠ internal		internal		internal

In order to understand why the graph is circular we need to look at the 'transition points' between episodic/existential (in the top row) and generic/universal (in the bottom row), i.e., the pairs <3, 4> and <1, 7>. Table 5 compares nodes 3 and 4, with those feature specifications that have not been indicated, but can be inferred from other features, in parentheses:

Table 5. From node 3 to node 4

Node 3		Node 4
episodic	≠	generic
existential plural	≠	universal (plural)
definite		(definite)
(external)		external

The transition from node 3 to 4 appears to imply two changes, i.e., from episodic to generic and from existential to universal. As a matter of fact, these two changes can be regarded as two sides of the same coin. By definition, a generic sentence quantifies (quasi-)universally over both referents and events. In order to see that, let us reconsider the two diagnostic contexts for nodes 3 and 4:

(84) *They've raised the taxes again.* (node 3)

(85) *In Bali, they eat dragonflies.* (node 4)

They in (84) is interpreted existentially, as not everyone has raised the taxes, but only those responsible for tax raising. If the implicit referential restriction of the predicate 'raise the taxes' is taken into account, *they* could also be regarded as referring exhaustively to the set of 'tax raisers'. It can thus be paraphrased as either 'some members of the government have raised the taxes' or 'those responsible for tax raising have raised the taxes'. The latter interpretation is 'exhaustive', in accordance with the definite status of the NP, and this exhaustivity already implies a type of universal quantification.

When the state of affairs described by the relevant sentence is generic, the pronoun necessarily acquires a (quasi-)universal reading. For example, in its generalizing reading example (85) says that 'the people in Bali habitually eat dragonflies', i.e., it expresses generic/habitual quantification over events. This implies generic quantification over Agents. Generic quantification over events and Agents thus goes hand in hand, and a change of one feature conditions a change of another feature. Even though there are two differences in the feature specification, we can thus assume that pronouns may extend their distribution from node 3 to node 4 (and perhaps vice versa) in a single process of reanalysis.

Let us finally turn to the last pair of nodes, i.e., 7 and 1. Their feature specifications are shown in Table 6 (cells with empty feature specifications are irrelevant).

Table 6. From node 7 to node 1

Node 7		Node 1
non-veridical	≠	veridical
		episodic
universal	≠	existential
internal	≠	(external)
(plural)		vague

The features associated with each node are almost diametrically opposed to each other. In particular, the specifications for 'veridicality' and 'type of quantification' have opposite values. Moreover, there is a difference with respect to the perspective ('internal' vs. 'external'). We believe that this type of 'co-variation of features' can be explained in a similar way as the co-variation between the quantification over events and referents in propositions instantiating nodes 3 and 4.

The similarity between node 7 and node 1 is related to the fact that the interpretation of indefinites – as well as that of human impersonal pronouns, according to the analysis proposed by Moltmann (2006) – varies systematically with the type of quantification over events. Such interpretive dependencies have been called 'quantificational variability effects' by Lewis (1975) (cf. also Heim 1982). Given that conditionals imply the expression of necessity, i.e., universal quantification over possible worlds (cf. Kratzer 1986), indefinites often have universal quantificational force in the protasis of a conditional. (86a) is therefore equivalent to (86b).

(86) a. *If a student fails an exam, he is disappointed.*

b. *Every student who fails an exam is disappointed.*

The pair of examples in (86) shows that existential quantification may be equivalent to universal quantification under alternative scope construals. In particular, existential quantification within a conditional is (often) equivalent to universal quantification with the quantifier taking scope over the non-veridical operator. This equivalence is shown in (87).[9]

(87) $\exists x[P(x)] \to \rho \equiv \forall x[P(x) \to \rho]$

The connection between nodes 7 and 1 can thus be explained as follows: Human impersonal pronouns basically behave like indefinites. As such, they receive a universal interpretation in specific contexts, e.g. in the protasis of a conditional. In other contexts – in episodic ones, to be precise – they are interpreted as existential quantifiers. Accordingly, two of the differences shown in Table 6 co-vary and condition each other. While it is *prima facie* surprising to see that node 1 is veridical and existential, whereas node 7 is non-veridical and universal, this fact becomes much less mysterious when we consider that node 7 is universal *because* it is non-veridical.

The third difference, finally – that node 7 is 'internal' while node 1 is 'external' – can be related to the type of quantification expressed by each type of sentence. These values simply represent 'default' settings associated with existential (external) and universal (internal) quantification. Indefinites with an existential interpretation by default take an external perspective. This could be related to matters of informativity. A sentence like *A man came in* is normally interpreted in such a way that *a man* does not refer to the speaker, even though this is not logically excluded. Universal quantification, in turn, is by default 'internal', as reference to all individuals normally includes the speaker. We have assumed that there are instances of universal quantification with an external perspective – in node 4 – but in such cases there is always some constituent explicitly excluding the speaker from the range of reference. We can thus assume that the third difference between node 7 and node 1 – internal vs. external perspective – is not really part of the lexical specification in each case, but rather a matter of conversational pragmatics and default inferencing.

---

9 As Dik Bakker has pointed out to us, there is an important difference between the two formulas. The existential quantifier can only bind a variable in the protasis, while the universal quantifier can also bind a variable in the apodosis. For the present purposes, this difference is not crucial.

7 Conclusions

We have aimed to achieve three things in this article. First, we have proposed a way of combining the semantic maps or grammaticalization clines for 'man'-pronouns and third person plural pronouns, and to formulate a general typology for such means of impersonalization. As a consequence of our onomasiological approach, we have considered a broader range of expressive means for impersonalization than did Anna Siewierska in her pioneering work, e.g. (originally) deictic pronouns (*you*), non-pronominal strategies such as (impersonal modals +) infinitives and middle markers (e.g. Italian *si*). Finally, we have tried to show that the 'geometry' of the semantic map proposed in this study is not fortuitous but reflects the (sets of) features shared by neighbouring nodes, assuming that the edges of the map correspond to 'minimal' steps of reanalysis.

We have proposed a graph-theoretic treatment of connectivity maps, which makes them 'computationally tractable'. It is our intention to develop an 'infrastructure' for the computational treatment of connectivity maps in the near future. First experiments of implementation (in PHP and R) have been quite successful. We intend to be able to generate and test connectivity maps directly from typological database systems such as XLD (cf. Note 4). Such a computational approach will also allow us to combine connectivity maps with proximity maps, and perhaps to develop new methods of representing multi-dimensional variation.

So far, our semantic map is only based on European languages and it remains to be determined to what extent it covers other, non-European languages as well. Given that the features that we have used for the classification of the nodes in our map appear to be more or less universal, we are optimistic that the map will prove to be relatively robust when more data are considered.

Abbreviations

2 second person, 3 third person, ACC accusative, ART article, DEF definite, DYN dynamic, FIN finite, HP human participant, INF infinitive, IMPS impersonal, MASC masculine, MID middle marker, NEUT neuter, PART partitive, PL plural, PRS present tense, PREV preverb, PTCL particle, REFL reflexive, S sentence, SG singular.

References

Blevins, James. 2003. Passives and impersonals. Journal of Linguistics 39. 473–520.
Cabredo Hofherr, Patricia. 2006. "Arbitrary" pro and the theory of pro-drop. In Peter Ackema, Patrick Brandt, Maaike Schoorlemmer & Fred Weerman (eds.), *Agreement and Arguments*, 230–257. Oxford: Oxford University Press.
Cabredo Hofherr, Patricia. 2008. Les pronoms impersonnels humains: Syntaxe et interprétation. *Modèles linguistiques* 29. 35–55.
Coussé, Evie & Johan van der Auwera. 2012. Human impersonal pronouns in Swedish and Dutch – A contrastive study of *man* and *men*. *Languages in Contrast* 12. 121–138.
Creissels, Denis. 2008. Impersonal pronouns and coreference: The case of French *on*. Ms., Université Lumière (Lyon 2).
Cristofaro, Sonia. 2010. Semantic maps and mental representation. *Linguistic Discovery* 8. 35–52.
Croft, William. 2001. *Radical Construction Grammar: Syntactic Theory in Typological Perspective*. Oxford: Oxford University Press.
Croft, William & Keith T. Poole. 2008. Inferring universals from grammatical variation: Multidimensional scaling for typological analysis. *Theoretical Linguistics* 34. 1–37.
Cysouw, Michael, Martin Haspelmath & Andrej Malchukov, ed. 2010. Semantic Maps: Methods and Applications. *Linguistic Discovery* 8. Dartmouth: Dartmouth College.
Diestel, Reinhard. 2006. *Graphentheorie*. Heidelberg: Springer.
Dimowa, A. 1981a. Die Polysemie des Pronomens *man* in der deutschen Gegenwartssprache und die Kontextbedingungen für seine Monosemierung. *Beiträge zur Erforschung der deutschen Sprache* 1. 47–75.
Dimowa, A. 1981b. Die Polysemie des Pronomens *man* unter Berücksichtigung seiner Äquivalente im Bulgarischen. *Deutsch als Fremdsprache* 18. 38–44.
Donellan, Keith. 1966. Reference and definite descriptions. *The Philosophical Review* 77. 281–304.
Farkas, Donka F. 1992. On the semantics of subjunctive complements. In P. Hirschbühler & K. Koerner (eds.), *Romance Languages and Linguistic Theory*, 69–104. Benjamins.
Fröhlich, Jürg. 1951. *Der indefinite Agens im Altenglischen, unter besonderer Berücksichtigung des Wortes 'man'*. Winterthur-Töß: Paul Gehring.
Gast, Volker. 2004. The interpretation of logophoric *self*-forms, and some consequences for a model of reference and denotation. In T. McEnery, A. Branco & R. Mitkov (eds.), *Proceedings of the 5th Discourse Anaphora and Anaphora Resolution Colloquium*, 75–80. Lisbon: Edições Colibri.
Gast, Volker. 2009. A contribution to 'two-dimensional language description': The Typological Database of Intensifiers and Reflexives. In Martin Everaert, Simon Musgrave & Alexis Dimitriadis (eds.), *The Use of Databases in Cross-Linguistic Research*, 209–234. Berlin & New York: De Gruyter Mouton.
Giacalone Ramat, Anna & Andrea Sansò. 2007. The spread and decline of indefinite 'man'-constructions in European languages: An areal perspective. In P. Ramat & E. Roma (eds.), *Europe and the Mediterranean as Linguistic Areas: Convergences from a Historical and Typological Perspective*, 95–131. Amsterdam: Benjamins.
Giannakidou, Anastasia. 2011. Negative and positive polarity items. In K. von Heusinger, C. Maienborn & P. Portner (eds.), *Semantics* (HSK 33.2), 1660–1712. Berlin & New York: De Gruyter Mouton
Haspelmath, Martin. 1997. *Indefinite Pronouns*. Oxford: Oxford University Press.
Heim, Irene. 1982. The semantics of definite and indefinite noun phrases. Doctoral Dissertation, University of Massachusetts at Amherst.

Hewitt, George. 1979. *Abkhaz*. London: Routledge.
Hoekstra, J. 2010. On the impersonal pronoun *men* in Modern West Frisian. *Journal of Comparative Germanic Linguistics* 13. 31–59.
Jud-Schmid, Elisabeth. 1956. *Der indefinite Agens von Chaucer bis Shakespeare. Die Wörter und Wendungen für 'man'*. Meisenheim am Glan: Anton Hain.
Kemmer, Suzanne. 1993. *The Middle Voice*. Amsterdam: Benjamins.
Kleiber, Georges. 1994. *Anaphores et pronomes*. Louvain-la-Neuve: Duculot.
Kratzer, Angelika. 1986. Conditionals. *Proceedings of the Chicago Linguistics Society* 22. 1–15.
Krifka, M., F. J. Pelletier, G. N. Carlson, A. ter Meulen, G. Link & G. Chierchia. 1995. Genericity: An introduction. In G. N. Carlson & F. J. Pelletier (eds.), *The Generic Book*, 1–124. Chicago: University of Chicago Press.
Ladusaw, William A. 1979. Polarity Sensitivity as inherent scope relations. Doctoral Dissertation, University of Texas, Austin.
Lewis, David. 1975. *Counterfactuals*. Oxford: Blackwell.
Linthe, A. 2010. Exploring the function and distribution of generic pronouns. The example of German *man* and *du*. Master's thesis, University of Sheffield.
Löbner, Sebastian. 2002. *Understanding Semantics*. London: Arnold.
Malamud, Sophia. 2012. Impersonal indexicals: *one, you, man* and *du*. *Journal of Comparative Germanic Linguistics* 15. 1–48.
Meyer, Hans Heinrich. 1953. *Der indefinite Agens im Mittelenglischen (1050–1350). Wörter und Verwendungen für 'man'*. Bern: Francke.
Moltmann, Friederike. 2006. Generic *one*, arbitrary PRO, and the first person. *Natural Language Semantics* 14. 257–281.
Moltmann, Friederike. 2010. Generalizing detached self-reference and the semantics of generic 'one'. *Mind and Language* 25. 440–473.
Pesetsky, David. 1996. *Zero Syntax*. Cambridge, MA: MIT Press.
Siewierska, Anna. 2004. *Person*. Cambridge: Cambridge University Press.
Siewierska, Anna. 2008. Introduction: Impersonalization from a subject centred vs. agent-centred perspective. *Transactions of the Philological Society* 106. 115–137.
Siewierska, Anna. 2010. From 3pl to passive: incipient, emergent and established passives. *Diachronica* 27. 73–109.
Siewierska, Anna. 2011. Overlap and complementarity in reference impersonals: 'Man'-constructions vs. third person plural-impersonals in the languages of Europe. In Anna Siewierska & Andrej Malchukov (eds.), *Impersonal Constructions: A Cross-linguistic Perspective*, 57–89. Amsterdam: Benjamins.
Siewierska, Anna & Maria Papastathi. 2011. Third person plurals in the languages of Europe: Typological and methodological issues. *Linguistics* 43. 575–610.
van der Auwera, Johan. 2013. Semantic maps: For synchrony and diachrony. In A. Giacalone Ramat, C. Mauri & P. Molinelli (eds.), *Synchrony and Diachrony: A Dynamic Interface*, 153–176. Amsterdam: Benjamins.
van der Auwera, Johan & Vladimir Plungian. 1998. Modality's semantic map. *Linguistic Typology* 2. 79–124.
van der Auwera, Johan, Volker Gast & Jeroen Vanderbiesen. 2012. Human impersonal pronouns in English, Dutch and German. *Leuvense Bijdragen* 98. 4–26.
Weerman, F. 2006. It's the economy, stupid. Een vergelijkende blik op men en man. In M. Hüning, U. Vogl, T. van der Wouden & A. Verhagen, *Nederlands tussen Engels en Duits*, 19–46. Leiden: Stichting Neerlandistiek Leiden.
Zifonun, Gisela. 2001. Man lebt nur einmal. *Deutsche Sprache* 28. 232–253.

Zwarts, Frans. 1995. Nonveridical contexts. *Linguistic Analysis* 25. 286–312.
Zwarts, Frans. 1998. Three types of polarity. In Fritz Hamm & Erhard Hinrichs, (eds.), *Plurality and Quantification*, 177–238. Dordrecht: Kluwer.

Beate Hampe and Christian Lehmann[1]
Partial coreference

1 Introduction

Let us assume a two-place predicate, such as 'exploit', both of whose arguments may be human. Let us further pursue the question of what constellations of participants are possible in its two argument positions – or, syntactically speaking, what kinds of subjects can be combined with what kinds of direct objects. Selection restrictions or the entire extension of the empathy hierarchy do not matter here, because that parameter is already set to the value 'human'. The most relevant subdivisions inside this subcategory are provided by person and number. The question is thus which person and number values of the subject can be combined with which person and number values of the direct object and, analogously, of other syntactic functions of two- and three-place predicates.

Before we elaborate on the theoretical side of the issue, let us consider Table 1, which provides an illustrative English example in order to clarify the nature and relevance of the issue. Concerning the forms in the second person, we have made visible the number differences for demonstrative purposes by using Early Modern English.

As can be read off from the light grey cells of Table 1, subject-object combinations with identical first or second person and identical number automatically yield coreference between these arguments, which generally makes the use of a reflexive construction obligatory.[2] We have stipulated coreference for the third person, too, so as to complete the picture. However, the light grey cells will not occupy us any further. The white cells of Table 1 display cases with disjoint pronominal references and are thus of no concern to this study either.

---

[1] The names of the authors appear in alphabetical order. We thank Balthasar Bickel, Volker Gast, Martin Haspelmath and Ekkehard König for helpful discussion of the typological data presented at the Leipzig Workshop in memory of Anna Siewierska.
[2] Quirk et al. (1985: 375, 6.2.4, note [c]) remark that the use of personal pronouns in this context is occasionally found, esp. in colloquial American English.

Table 1. Person-number combinations for subject and direct object in English

subject \ object	person	1		2		3	
person	number	SG	PL	SG	PL	SG	PL
1	SG	I exploit myself	I exploit us	I exploit thee	I exploit you	I exploit him	I exploit them
	PL	we exploit me	we exploit ourselves	we exploit thee	we exploit you	we exploit him	we exploit them
2	SG	thou exploitest me	thou exploitest us	thou exploitest thyself	thou exploitest you	thou exploitest him	thou exploitest them
	PL	you exploit me	you exploit us	you exploit thee	you exploit yourselves	you exploit him	you exploit them
3	SG	he exploits me	he exploits us	he exploits thee	he exploits you	he exploits himself	he exploits them
	PL	they exploit me	they exploit us	they exploit thee	they exploit you	they exploit him	they exploit themselves

The problem at issue appears in the dark grey cells, where subject and direct object exhibit the same person, but different number specifications. These examples seem odd, i.e. English speakers are in doubt about whether and to what degree such sentences are acceptable. Note, however, that these sentences are by no means strange in denotational terms. States of affairs designated by them are quite possible, and there is no *prima facie* reason why they should be designated by anything else than these sentences. In that respect, the examples under investigation here differ from such constellations as 'we beget me', which incur a denotational problem.

Analyzing the reference relations between subject and object in the dark grey cells, we see that the plural pronoun appearing in one argument position refers to a set of persons which properly includes the referent of the singular pronoun in the respective other argument position. That is to say, the reference relation includes a coreference, so that this particular aspect of the expression fulfils the condition for reflexivity. Any attempt to try and improve these sentences by the use of a reflexive pronoun in their object position, however, only seems to make matters worse: *I exploit ourselves, we exploit myself*. The oddness of the expressions in the dark grey cells of Table 1 can therefore be ascribed to the fact that the reference relation they exhibit is neither a case of coreference nor a case of disjoint reference, but somehow both and neither.

Though structurally analogous to the dark grey cells, the black ones are quite unobjectionable. On their most natural readings, these sentences are completely inconspicuous and involve disjoint references for subject and object. It is, in fact, not easy to get the readings corresponding to the dark grey cells, where 'he' is an element of the set designated by *they/them*. Forcing that interpretation, the same kind of 'anomaly' as in the dark grey cells arises. Note, however, that these sentences cannot as easily be discarded as ungrammatical or unacceptable as may be the case with the examples in the first and second person (see the examples in (17), section 4.2 below).

In what follows, we shall focus on the existence of constructions which necessarily involve incomplete, or *partial*, coreference, and therefore exclude third-person constructions from further consideration. As a starting point, let us thus define partial coreference in general and precise terms:[3]

Proposition 1. Partial coreference

> Nominal expression A is partially coreferential with nominal expression B iff the sets of referents R_A and R_B designated by the two expressions overlap in such a way that there is a set R_C which is included in both R_A and R_B and properly included in at least one of them (i.e., R_A and R_B are neither identical nor totally disjoint).

Partial coreference between A and B is syntactically relevant if it occurs inside a clause or, more precisely, if nominal expression A functions as or cross-references the subject of a clause and B functions as or cross-references another dependent (complement or adjunct) of the main-clause predicate of the same clause. Under such conditions, the question arises whether A and B can be represented by simple person forms (pronouns, cross-reference or agreement markers). We are interested in simple forms, because any 'deficiency' supposedly or actually associated with a sentence such as (1a) can in principle be avoided by a reformulation along the lines of (1b).

(1)   a. *I exploit us.*
        b. *I exploit myself and you.*

---

[3] As becomes clear from the definition, partial coreference has nothing to do with "split self" sentences of the type *If I were you, I would hate me/myself*. The most recent treatment of the latter is Kamholz (2012), with references to earlier work.

The constellation of syntactic functions described in the syntactic-relevance condition underlies reflexivity in many languages, viz. (counter to Proposition 1) in case A and B are fully coreferential. The clearest case of the type of construction delineated by the syntactic-relevance condition is the transitive-verb construction, illustrated in (1) and (2a), though the BNC examples in (2b–f) suggest that other syntactic contexts should not be excluded from investigation:

(2)   a. *I embarrass us both.* (BNC-CDA)
        b. *I could send us both to prison.* (BNC-HTT)
        c. *I gave us both an enormous gin and tonic.* (BNC-CL2)
        d. *I never cook for us and we don't have dinner parties.* (BNC-CH5)
        e. *I certainly want us all to enjoy this rare journey, my dear.* (BNC-FU8)
        f. *Let me get us some crusty bread.* (BNC-KD7)

The problem to be investigated is an empirical one: To what degree are constructions with partially coreferential pronominal complements of the verb acceptable in languages?[4] As will be shown, the issue takes on typological interest because in some languages, the construction schemata underlying Table 1 are codified in personal agreement paradigms of transitive verbs. The question is thus what the dark grey cells look like in those paradigms. For the time being (and in line with what was said above), it suffices to anticipate that the sort of paradigm gap that we are confronted with in the first and second persons does not occur in the third person. Apart from typological interest, the problem has also stirred some theoretical discussion in generative grammar (Postal 1966, Cooper 1976), esp. binding theory (Rooryck 2006), concerning the grammaticality of expressions with partially coreferential pronouns. Especially examples like those illustrated in (2a,b) were declared ungrammatical in English by generative treatments from Postal (1966) to Lasnik (2011).

Given that language users need to be able to refer to situations with partially overlapping sets of participants (no matter how infrequent these may be), we hypothetically see expressions with partially coreferential pronominal complements of the verb as the language user's response to a very particular communicative need, which grammars usually do not provide a conventionalized means of expressions for. In other words, we assume that expressions with partially core-

---

[4] A few words of explanation seem at place. Apparently, the problem of partial coreference has been attended to once in the preceding literature (Cysouw & Fernández 2012). In fact, we came across that paper only after our own article was half finished. Our paper shares with Cysouw & Fernández's work the major research question, parts of the methods and the results. We have not reacted to that discovery by renouncing our own work, but try to broaden the empirical basis to both validate and get beyond their theoretical insights.

ferential personal pronouns present compromises, or makeshift solutions, as it were, to the verbalization problem posed by such rare scenarios.

From this, a number of further (likewise empirical) questions follow all of which are related to potential asymmetries in the occurrence of the feature values of the categories of the person forms involved, i.e. person, number and case (if applicable)/syntactic function. Several of these questions have been raised as well as tentatively answered in the preceding literature (cf. Cysouw & Fernández 2012, §2). With respect to the values of the category person, it seems that first-person expressions lend themselves more easily to partial coreference contexts than second-person ones. With respect to the category number (i.e. the question of whether it matters which set of referents includes which), expressions with singular subjects seem to adapt to situations with partial coreference more easily than expressions with plural subjects.[5] With respect to syntactic function, it is assumed here that partial-coreference constellations will be the more readily acceptable the lower the syntactic function of the non-subject complement is in the syntactic hierarchy. Finally, and in close conjunction with the previous assumption, we hypothesize that the acceptability of partial-coreference constellations decreases with increasing degrees of the grammaticalization of the person forms involved.

As a large-scale typological investigation is not feasible at this point, we will approach the issue by combining two complementary methodologies to make up for any potential shortcomings of such an abridged procedure. In section 2, we will take a look at the agreement paradigms of a number of languages in order to check whether and how the space corresponding to the dark grey cells of Table 1 may be filled. It goes without saying that other languages have different person/number categories than English, so the structure of the tables to be analyzed in section 2 below will not simply replicate Table 1. Section 3 will present the results of a systematic corpus study of all first-person pronominal expressions with partial coreference in the BNC World Edition (BNC Consortium 2000), backed up by additional German data from the MECOLB archive of COSMAS II (IDS 2012). In section 4, finally, we will discuss our findings with a special view to the asymmetry issues alluded to above. To anticipate one aspect of our argument in section 5 below, it is no coincidence that we rely on grammars for the investigation of clitic or affixal paradigms, while we do corpus research for the study of free pronouns – it could not be the other way round.

---

[5] Asymmetries between the various person- and numbers specifications were first postulated in Rooryck (2006), where the respective dispreferred values were declared ungrammatical in English and French.

Table 2. Person agreement in Mangarayi

object→ subject↓	person	1						2			3		
person	number	SG	EXCL DU	EXCL PL	INCL DU	INCL PL	TRIAL	SG	DUAL	PL	SG	DUAL	PL
1	SG	[refl]	–	–	–	–	–	ñan-	ṇuran-	ṇuyan-	ŋa-	ŋawuran-	ŋawuyan-
1	EXCL DU	–	[refl]	–	–	–	–	ñir-	ṇuran-	ṇuyan-	ŋir-	ŋirwuran-	ŋirwuyan-
1	EXCL PL	–	–	[refl]	–	–	–	ŋila	ṇuran-	ṇuyan-	ŋila-	ŋilawuran-	ŋilawuyan-
1	INCL DU	–	–	–	[refl]	–	–	–	–	–	ŋi-	ŋiwuran-	ŋiwuyan-
1	INCL PL	–	–	–	–	[refl]	–	–	–	–	ŋala-	ŋalawuran-	ŋalawuyan-
1	TRIAL	–	–	–	–	–	[refl]	–	–	–	ŋar-	ŋarwuran-	ŋarwuyan-
2	SG	ŋan-	ŋiran-	ŋiyan-	ŋin-	ŋayan-	ŋaran-	[refl]	–	–	ña-	ñawuran-	ñawuyan-
2	DUAL	ŋanbur-	ŋiranbur-	ŋiyanbur-	ŋinbur-	ŋayanbur-	ŋaranbur-	–	[refl]	–	ṇur-	ḷawuran-	ḷawuyan-
2	PL	ŋanba-	ŋiranba-	ŋiyanba-	ŋinba-	ŋayanba-	ŋaranba-	–	–	[refl]	ḷa-	ḷawuran-	ḷawuyan-
3	SG	ŋan-	ŋiran-	ŋiyan-	ŋin-	ŋayan-	ŋaran-	ñan-	ṇuran-	ṇuyan-	[refl]	wuran-	wuyan-
3	DUAL	ŋanbur-	ŋiranbur-	ŋiyanbur-	ŋinbur-	ŋayanbur-	ŋaranbur-	ñanbur-	ṇuranbur-	ṇuyanbur-	wur-	[refl]	wuyanba-
3	PL	ŋanba-	ŋiranba-	ŋiyanba-	ŋinba-	ŋayanba-	ŋaranba-	ñanba-	ṇuranba-	ṇuyanba-	wuḷa-	wuyanba-	[refl]

2 Typological case study: Defective agreement paradigms

As announced above, we firstly apply our research question to a convenience sample of languages which possess cross-reference or agreement of the verb with both subject and object in person and number. In doing so, we have to allow for different sets of values for both the person and the number parameter. Importantly, our question is aggravated if a language possesses more numbers, e.g. a dual or different first-person non-singular forms (1+2, 1+3 and the like).

The three languages chosen use free pronouns only for emphasis; the linguistic representation of situations of partial co-reference is thus essentially a question of the paradigm of agreement or cross-reference markers on transitive verbs.

Regarding the method employed in this case study, two remarks are at place: On the one hand, text corpora of these languages are either small or unavailable, and since constellations of partial coreference are rare, anyway, they would not be likely to appear in these corpora. On the other hand, adequate grammars are available, and they are sufficiently explicit about the question at issue.

2.1 Mangarayi

Mangarayi (Merlan 1982, esp. ch. 2.1.3.6.2.2) has agreement of the transitive verb with subject and direct object. There are, in principle, two prefix slots for agreement with each of these dependents. These, however, are occupied following complex rules, and several of the morphs are portemanteau, so that Table 2 follows Merlan's (1982) account in showing one (complex) prefix position.

Just as in Table 1, we stipulate coreference for third-person cells lying on the diagonal, and cells in which special reflexive forms are used appear in light grey, while black cells refer to situations in which third persons act on other third persons. Gaps in the paradigm are marked by dark grey. They are constituted by the cases which fulfill the conditions of Proposition 1, i.e. which exhibit less than complete coreference between the two sets of referents involved. Merlan (1982: 162) speaks of "logical and pragmatic incongruities in the subject-object relation". What strikes the eye is the perfect symmetry along the light grey diagonal with respect to filled vs. empty paradigm cells. For the coding of partial coreference in this language, this implies that it does not matter which set of referents includes which; for whenever there is partial coreference, the subject-object relation cannot be coded on the verb at all.

Table 3. Person agreement in Hixkaryana

object → subject ↓		1			2		3	
person	number	SG	EXCL	INCL	SG	COLL	SG	COLL
1	SG	[refl]	–	–	*ki-*	*ki-V-yatxhe*	*i-*	*i-V-yatxhe*
1	EXCL	–	[refl]	–	*amna o-*	*amna o-V-yatxhe*	*amna ni-*	*amna ni-V-yatxhe*
1	INCL	–	–	[refl]	–	–	*ti-*	*ti-V-yatxhe*
2	SG	*uro mi-*	*amna*	–	[refl]	–	*mi-*	*mi-V-yatxhe*
2	COLL	*uro mi-V-yatxhe*	*amna V-yatxhe*	–	–	[refl]	*mi-V-yatxhe*	*mi-V-yatxhe*
3	SG	*ro-*	*amna*	*ki-V(-yatxhe)*	*o-*	*o-V-yatxhe*	[refl]	*ni-V-yatxhe*
3	COLL	*ro-V-yatxhe*	*amna V-yatxhe*	*ki-V-yatxhe*	*o-V-yatxhe*	*o-V-yatxhe*	*ni-V-yatxhe*	[refl]

2.2 Hixkaryana

Just like Mangarayi, Hixkaryana (Derbyshire 1979, esp. ch. 2.1.3.6) has agreement of the transitive verb with subject and direct object. The verb has only one prefix slot for these morphs, which thus largely amalgamate the categories of these two actants. Table 3 provides a survey of the paradigm.

As can be seen, there is no plural as such, but instead a collective feature. It is marked by the suffix *-yatxhe* for either subject or object or both alike. There are three first-person values: singular, including hearer (incl.), including third person while excluding hearer (excl.). The value 'incl.' combines with the collective suffix just like the other person values; but this is not shown in Table 3. For the constellations of the light grey cells, Hixkaryana has a special reflexive prefix which remains out of consideration, too. What matters is the filling of the dark grey paradigm positions. The paradigm in Derbyshire (1979: 146) presents empty cells for these, nor can any pertinent examples be found in the grammar. It is particularly noteworthy that none of the nine logical combinations of first-person forms are morphologically instantiated. Moreover, the paradigm lacks forms for the combination of a first-person inclusive actant with a second-person actant. Derbyshire (1979:148) ascribes these lacunae to Postal's (1966) "universal 'inclusion constraint'".

2.3 Yucatec Maya

Yucatec Maya has two paradigms of cross-reference morphemes. One of these basically takes the form of enclitics that precede their syntactic head (which is not their phonological host) and cross-reference the subject of verbs and the possessor of nouns. They are therefore called 'subject clitics'. The other paradigm takes the form of suffixes on the (nominal or verbal) predicate which cross-reference the subject of nominal and intransitive predicates and the direct object of transitive predicates. They are therefore called 'absolutive suffixes'. This leads to the combination of clitics with suffixes on transitive verbs and possessed nouns, the former cross-referencing the subject or possessor, the latter the direct object or "referential argument" of the noun, resp. The subject indexes are discontinuous in the second and third person plural, where the clitic is supplemented by a suffixal morph identical in shape with the absolutive suffixes for these values. For the respective combinations of subject/possessor with object/referential argument, the transitive verb and the possessed noun then have two suffixal positions. The full paradigm is shown in Table 4. X is either a transitive verb or a possessed noun.

Table 4. Person cross-reference in Yucatec Maya

object → subject ↓ person		1		2		3	
person	number	SG	PL	SG	PL	SG	PL
1	SG	[refl]	*in X-o'n*	*in X-ech*	*in X-e'x*	*in X*	*in X-o'b*
1	PL	*k X-en*	[refl]	*k X-ech*	*k X-e'x*	*k X*	*k X-o'b*
2	SG	*a X-en*	*a X-o'n*	[refl]	*a X-e'x*	*a X*	*a X-o'b*
2	PL	*a X-en-e'x*	*a X-o'n-e'x*	*a X-ech-e'x*	[refl]	*a X-e'x*	*a X-e'x-o'b*
3	SG	*u X-en*	*u X-o'n*	*u X-ech*	*u X-e'x*	[refl]	*u X-o'b*
3	PL	*u X-en-o'b*	*u X-o'n-o'b*	*u X-ech-o'b*	*u X-e'x-o'b*	*u X-o'b*	[refl]

Since the two paradigms are essentially mutually independent morphologically, the combinations are highly regular. It is perfectly predictable how the dark grey cells would have to behave. However, they do not appear in the grammars, and available texts contain no fully pertinent example. The closest hits found involve the hortative construction, as in (3):[6]

(3) Yucatec

Ba'le'   ko'x   a   bo't   a   p'aax !
however go.HORT SBJ.2 pay   POSS.2 debt
'However, come on, pay your debt!'

The auxiliary *ko'x* is hortative for the speaker and one hearer. It is normally followed by a full verb in first person plural. Instead, (3) features the second person singular as the subject of the full verb. (4) is unique in showing the two subsets of referents addressed by the hortative distributed over subject and direct-object function of the full verb.

(4) Yucatec

Ko'x   a   láak'int-en!
go.HORT SBJ.2 accompany-ABS.1.SG
'Come on, accompany me!'

---

6 Abbreviations in the glosses are found at the end.

As it is probably no coincidence that the only examples from the available texts which exhibit partial coreference involve a hortative construction, it will be checked whether hortative constructions facilitate partial coreference in the two European languages investigated, too. Apart from such cases, the dark grey cells of Table 4 might as well be marked by a hyphen, as in the preceding tables.

While we cannot hope to enumerate here the languages exhibiting the same type of gap in the personal agreement or cross-reference paradigms of their transitive verbs, there are certainly more such languages. Another one that we came across is Tapirapé (Tupí-Guaraní; Leite 1987).

3 Corpus study: Partial coreference in the BNC and Cosmas

As initially announced, the principal goal of the corpus-based part of this investigation is to study expressions like the ones appearing in the dark grey cells of Table 1 in actual usage in a systematic way and thus to accumulate evidence to complement insights from the typological approach. Data displaying partial coreference of pronouns mainly come from English, viz. the World Edition of the British National Corpus (BNC Consortium 2000), which contains about 100 million words and is tagged for word-class. Additional evidence is brought in from German, viz. the MECOLB archive of the Cosmas II corpora (IDS 2012), which contains about 30 million words, which are morpho-syntactically annotated. For obvious reasons (recall the use of Early Modern English forms in Table 1), the BNC study is restricted to first-person expressions. Cosmas II, however, was searched for both first- and second-person expressions.[7]

3.1 Hypotheses

Following from the preceding literature as well as an initial investigation of our own data, we hypothesize that expressions with partial coreference (i) do not generally tend to exhibit reflexive pronouns, which mark full referential identity, making expressions with partial identity, like *I made ourselves a cup of coffee*, generally unacceptable (cf. Introduction). It is furthermore assumed that (ii) expressions with partially coreferential pronouns prefer singular subjects, i.e. occur with singular subjects more frequently than other clauses do, and (iii)

---

[7] A few examples of third-person partial coreference are briefly discussed in section 4.2.

become more acceptable the lower the post-verbal NP is located in the syntactic hierarchy, such that expressions with direct objects are least frequent (and also least acceptable or most doubtful) and expressions with raised objects most frequent. It is furthermore tentatively assumed that (iv) hortative constructions facilitate the use of partially coreferential pronouns.

A few remarks are at place concerning a number of corollaries of hypothesis (iii), which responds in part to the sort of observations that originally inspired principle A of the binding theory in GB-style generative grammar, stating that a post-verbal non-reflexive pronoun (serving as the direct object in a mono-transitive structure) may not be coreferential with the subject-NP. As indirect objects were treated differently in those models (showing lexical as opposed to structural case) and as they do not refer to entities directly affected by the situation, but typically to entities with recipient, beneficiary or source roles, they are expected to be more frequent and acceptable than direct objects when partially coreferential with the subject-NP. The same goes for prepositional objects. Under the assumption that, semantically, the objects of raising constructions are not the complements of the matrix verb at all and not necessarily a part of the matrix at that, such structures should be most readily acceptable with partially coreferential NPs. In this context, it would be interesting to see whether expressions with direct objects from "complex-transitive" structures of the sort of *they drove him out of town, they consider him a genius* or *they call him Fred* (cf., e.g., Quirk et al. 1985: 56) occur more frequently than expressions with direct objects from mono-transitive argument structures. This hypothesis rests on the well-known fact that, analogously to raising constructions, these expressions exhibit instances of what has been called "secondary predication", i.e. their direct objects are often not the arguments of their matrix verbs, but so-called "fake objects" (note the change of meaning incurred in the deletion of the predicative complement: *they drove him/ they consider him/they call him*) and simultaneously serve as the subject of a secondary predication ('he is out of town', 'he is a genius', 'he is Fred'), which is why they have received "small-clause" analyses (cf. e.g., Aarts 1992).

3.2 Methods

Concerning the English data, an exhaustive sample of non-negated first-person expressions exhibiting partial coreference was retrieved from the BNC World Edition, i.e. all instances of the constellation *I*-VERB-*us* and *we*-VERB-*me* were retrieved from the entire BNC. All possible morpho-syntactic contexts were included in the investigation, i.e. the queries asked for all expressions with up to two auxiliary or modal verbs, both with and without intervening adverbials.

The expressions were retrieved from the tagged files of the BNC by using the regular-expression (REGEX) option of the free-ware concordancer ANTCONC 3.2.1. The most complex REGEX employed in the query for expressions with 2 modal/auxiliary verbs and an intervening adverbial (see Appendix Ia) was progressively reduced to retrieve expressions with one or no modal/auxiliary verb and without intervening adverbial.[8] Expressions with prepositional objects were retrieved separately, but along the same lines (see Appendix Ib).[9] In addition, the corpus was searched for non-negated hortative constructions of the forms *let's/let us* VERB *me* and *let me* VERB *us*, including again both intervening adverbials and prepositional objects (see Appendix Ic). By means of a set of queries analogous to those employed for the target expressions with personal pronouns, the corpus was finally also checked for any non-negated clauses showing the constellations *I*-VERB-*ourselves* or *we*-VERB-*myself* (see Appendix Id/e). It goes without saying that the output of all queries was manually checked for false hits.

In order to provide baselines which the corpus results for expressions with partial coreference can be measured against, three data sets were retrieved as controls. The first presents a random sample of 200 non-negated first-person expressions with regular reflexive pronouns. This sample consists of the first 200 true hits of the randomized output of the query to the entire BNC, from which clauses with emphatic/appositive uses of these pronouns had been manually weeded out (for the REGEX of the most complex string, see Appendix If). The sample was coded for singular vs. plural subjects. The second sample consists of 200 non-negated third-person expressions with personal pronouns, again created from the first 200 true hits of the randomized output of the query to the entire BNC. Here, clauses with generic uses of *they*, non-referential uses of *it* and expressions with partial coreference had to be manually discarded (for the REGEX of the most complex string, see Appendix Ig). The sample was again coded for singular vs. plural subjects. Finally, a second, larger third-person sample was created from the same query output and coded for syntactic function, finally comprising 510 expressions with disjoint pronominal references. For reasons of feasibility, expressions with prepositional objects were not included in any of the control samples, such that these needed to be excluded from some parts of the quantitative analyses below.

---

8 Importantly, these strings are also able to detect any occurrences of coreferential expressions without reflexive pronouns: *I* VERB *me* and *we* VERB *us*.

9 Not all prepositional objects occur adjacent to the matrix verb, the queries thus searched for *I*-VERB-PREP-*us* and *we*-VERB-PREP-*me* as well as *I*-VERB-X-PREP-*us* and *we*-VERB-X-PREP-*me*, with X being an intervening phrase that can take on a number of forms.

The study of the German web-based MECOLB archive of Cosmas II is meant to complement our investigations of the BNC, rather than present a full-blown corpus study in its own right, for two main reasons. The first lies in the limitations of the Cosmas archives themselves. Unlike the BNC, the MECOLB archive is not a general, balanced corpus, but provides newspaper material only. The second reason concerns sheer feasibility. The query syntax, determined by the options offered at the user interface of the Cosmas website, retrieved all sentences (unfortunately not clauses!) that contained *ich* ('I': subject case: nominative) and *uns* ('us': object cases: dative and accusative) with 1–5 intervening words as well as a lexical or auxiliary/modal verb in concordance with the former.[10] Analogical queries were carried out for the following pairs of pronouns: *wir* ('we': nominative, pl.) – *mich/mir* ('me': accusative/dative, sg.), *du* ('you': nominative, sg.) – *euch* ('you': dative/accusative, pl.), *ihr* ('you': nominative, pl.) – *dich/dir* ('you': accusative/dative, sg.). While it was possible to inspect the entire output for the second persons, first-person examples with partially coreferential pronouns were not retrieved from the two query outputs exhaustively, as the corpus output was not only huge for these queries, but also consisted largely of false hits (e.g. from complex sentences where the target pronouns belong to different clauses). Instead, the first 1.000 hits of the randomized corpus output were inspected for true hits, thus creating representative samples of the target expressions. In one respect, the query went beyond what was done in the BNC study: not depending on the sequence of the elements in the sentence, the query syntax also retrieved adjuncts containing the dative/accusative pronouns: *mich/mir, uns, dich/dir, euch*.

3.3 Results and discussion of the BNC study

The queries for non-negated first-person expressions with partial coreference resulted in 167 true hits. Given the corpus frequencies of *I* and *we* (about 850.000 and 350.000, respectively), the referential constellation under investigation is a very rare one, indeed: Even under the assumption that about a third of these occurrences of the pronouns do not actually serve as clausal subjects (due to repeats, sentence fragments, non-clausal utterances, etc., in the spoken part of the corpus) – so that 750.000 would be taken as an extremely rough estimation of the number of clauses with these two pronouns – 167 expressions amount to no more than 0.02% of these.

---

[10] The following query syntax was employed: ((ich /w1-5 uns)#OV (ich /s0 uns))#OV (ich /s0 (MORPH(VRB sg P1) oder MORPH(AUX sg P1))). We thank Christian Lehmann's research assistant, Tina König, for retrieving the German raw data from the MECOLB archive.

To anticipate the general tendencies of the corpus results: With the possible exception of hypothesis (iv), the BNC study confirms all of the above hypotheses. The details will be presented for each of these in turn.

3.3.1 Reflexive vs. personal pronouns

As remarked in section 1, partial coreference might provide the grammatical precondition for both a reflexive and a non-reflexive construction. Given that partial coreference expressions present a kind of makeshift response to a highly specific communicative need, speakers' solutions to this problem must be expected to vary to some degree, both within single languages and across them.[11]

However, our corpus results show that English strongly prefers non-reflexive constructions. In view of the size of the BNC (100 million words), the facts that the queries did not return a single valid instance with a reflexive pronoun, but a sizeable number of pertinent expressions with personal pronouns provide evidence beyond any doubt. The handful or even dozen of expressions with reflexive pronouns that can be found on the web (cf. Appendix II, a–d), do for a number of reasons not constitute counter-evidence to this finding: (i) the relative frequency of such examples cannot be assessed, but is incredibly low – given the nearly infinite size of the web as a corpus; (ii) there is no guarantee that these examples were produced by or would at all be acceptable to native speakers, and (iii) instances tend to show similar lexical realizations (esp. ditransitive and complex-transitive uses of the verb to *save*) so that it is not even entirely absurd to assume the existence of isolated lexical chunks/formulae.

3.3.2 Singular versus plural subjects

Despite the fact that expressions with plural subjects, especially with the verbs *elect* and *save*, can occasionally be found on the web (ex 5, see also Appendix II, l–r), the BNC results clearly confirm hypothesis (ii) in that they show an overwhelming tendency of clausal expressions with partially coreferential pronouns towards singular subjects (cf. Figure 1).

(5)   *Wait! I know who we forgot. We forgot me!* (cf. Appendix II.l)

---

[11] In fact, Cysouw & Fernández (2012, §3) adduce an example each from Tungusic and Lezgian to show that the constellation in question may be coded as reflexive in some languages.

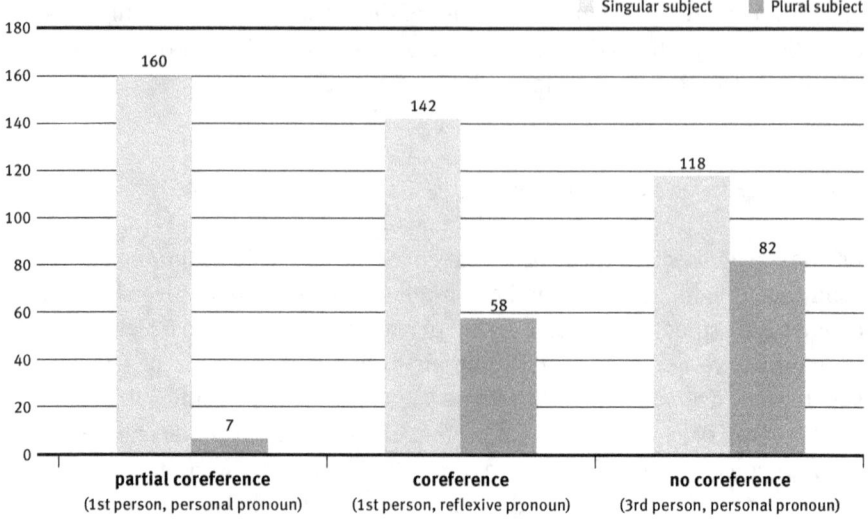

Figure 1a. Sg. vs. pl. subjects in expressions with partial coreference and two control samples (absolute frequencies)

The basis of this assessment, as an approximation of what would generally be expected "elsewhere" in the grammar, was provided by the proportions of singular and plural subjects in the third-person control sample with disjoint references of the pronouns involved (see the right-most column of Figures 1a,b). From this baseline, the distribution of singular and plural subjects in expressions with partial coreference in the BNC diverges significantly ($p_{(Chi2)}$= 3.99E-22***).

On the basis of a further comparison with the other control sample (see the middle column of Figures 1a,b), it can furthermore be excluded that the element of semantic reflexivity found in partial-coreference examples is in any way responsible for this, as the number of singular subjects is still significantly higher than in first-person expressions with reflexive pronouns ($p_{(Chi2)}$= 1.60E-12***).

As indicated at the beginning of section 3, the corpus frequencies of *I* and *we* provide an alternative, but very rough way to assess the frequencies of expressions with singular vs. plural objects, which additionally confirms the assessment reached by means of the comparison with the two control samples. Taking two thirds of all of the occurrences of the two pronouns as a (conservative) approximation of the number of clauses with first-person subjects (*I* = 530.000, *we* = 230.000), the 160 expressions with singular subjects account for less than 0.05% of all clauses exhibiting *I* as a subject, while the 7 expressions with plural subjects present less than 0.005% of all clauses exhibiting *we* as a subject.

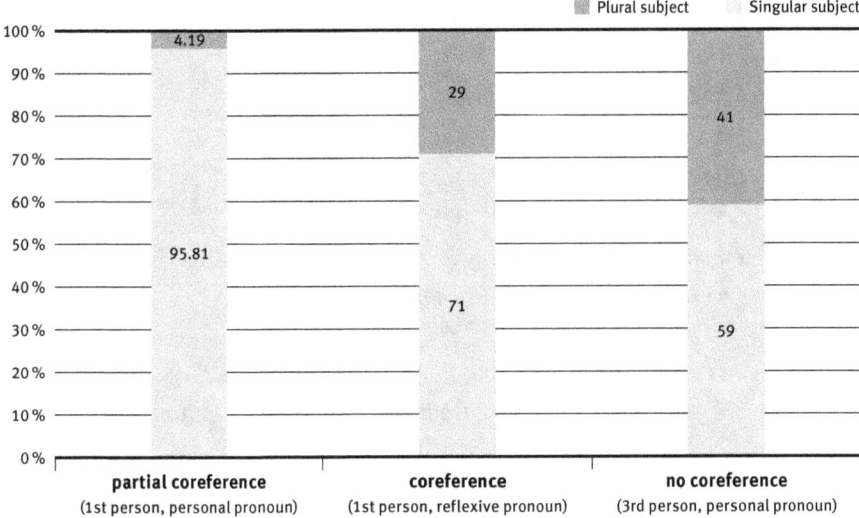

Figure 1b. Sg. vs. pl. subjects in expressions with partial coreference and two control samples (relative frequencies)

3.3.3 Syntactic functions of partially coreferential pronouns

The corpus results strongly confirm hypothesis (iii), too. Firstly, it can be read off directly from Table 5 and Figure 2a that syntactic functions that are lower in the syntactic hierarchy account for dramatically larger portions of our data set. All syntactic functions included in this part of the investigation are illustrated with pertinent corpus examples below: ex (6): direct objects in mono-transitive argument structures,[12] ex (7): direct objects in complex-transitive argument structures, ex (8): indirect objects in ditransitive structures, ex (9): prepositional objects, ex (10): "raised" objects in ACI-constructions.[13]

(6) a. *I embarrass us both.* (BNC-CDA)
 b. *But thinking I could orchestrate us like that was pretty high-handed.* (BNC-JY9)

---

[12] Note that several of the verbs appearing in (7), esp. #b and c, would hardly be used reflexively.
[13] Examples of the type illustrated in (8.b-d) are treated as proper instances of the English "Ditransitive Construction" (cf. Goldberg 1995), in which an indirect object precedes a direct one. In this respect, these examples contrast with their alternations, which exhibit benefactive adjuncts in the form of prepositional phrases: *I will get some tea for us. I could buy a house for us.*

(7) a. *I got us out of the alleyway.* (BNC-HTU)
 b. *I drove us there.* (BNC-B1Y)
 c. *I could send us both to prison.* (BNC-HTT)
 d. *I propel us straight to a Vintage Horror All-Nighter.* (BNC-HGN)
 e. *I shall book us into a lodge for 2 nights.* (BNC, HPP)
 f. *I called us Murphy.* (BNC, HTS)
 g. *I remind us that it was only ... a few months ago.* (BNC-JJ9)
 h. *Can I ask us to move the amendment ... ?* (BNC-KGX)

(8) a. *I gave us both an enormous gin and tonic.* (BNC-CL2)
 b. *We gave him a drink, we gave him some chocolate buttons, we gave me a big [unintelligible item].* (BNC-KC2)
 c. *I will get us some tea.* (BNC-AD1)
 d. *I could buy us a house.* (BNC-FPM)

(9) a. *I was listening to us* (BNC-KCE)
 b. *I shall tell Donna about us today, said Juliet.* (BNC-JY0)

(10) a. *Now what I want us to do is to look at these questions.* (BNC-JSU)
 b. *I would envisage us looking critically at what we`re doing.* (BNC-FUL)
 c. *If we wish to progress up the football ladder, I can only see us doing so by winning promotion.* (BNC-FR9)
 d. *... and we always plan for me to run a personal best every season.* (BNC-BMM)

Table 5. Kinds of post-verbal arguments in first-person expressions with partial coreference

type of post-verbal argument	*I* VERB *us*	*we* VERB *me*	ALL
mono-trans.: direct object (ex 6)	5 (3.12%)	0	5 (2.99%)
complex-trans.: direct object (ex 7)	26 (16.25%)	0	26 (15.57%)
ditrans.: indirect object (ex 8)	16 (10%)	2 (28.57%)	18 (10.78%)
prepositional object (ex 9)	9 (5.6%)	2 (28.57%)	11 (6.59%)
ACI: raised object (ex 10)	104 (65%)	3 (42.86%)	107 (64.07%)
TOTAL	160	7	167

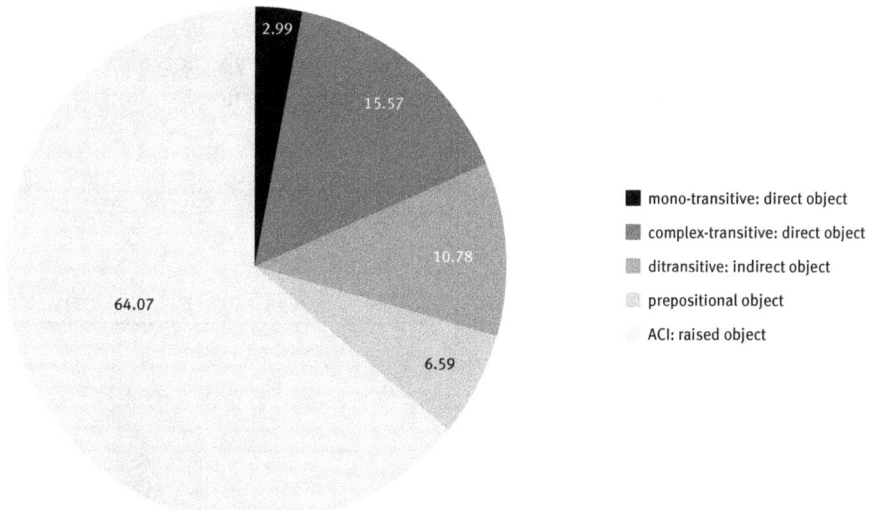

Figure 2 a. Relative frequencies (per cent) of post-verbal arguments in first-person expressions with partial coreference

To further corroborate this finding, the distribution of the syntactic functions in 156 expressions with partially coreferential pronouns was again compared with what happens "elsewhere in the grammar".[14] The baseline was provided by the proportions in the second third-person control sample of 510 expressions with disjoint pronominal references. While the two data sets contrast sharply – the difference being highly significant ($p_{(Chi2)} = 4.12\text{E-}134$***), it is worth noting in which respects the distribution of syntactic functions in the data set with partial coreference diverges from that in the control sample (cf. Figure 2b):

(i) With the exception of raised objects, all kinds of objects occur less frequently than would be expected on the basis of the control sample (though not significantly so for indirect objects).

(ii) Raised objects (ex 10) are by far more frequent than all other kinds of objects together and about 6 times more frequent than in the control sample, while expressions with direct objects in mono-transitive argument structures (ex 6) are excessively rare, with the control sample showing more than ten times as many of these structures.

---

14 Recall that prepositional objects were excluded from this part of the analysis, due to their exclusion from the control sample, thus the reduction of the data set to 156 expressions.

(iii) As expected, indirect objects (ex 8) are more frequent than direct ones in mono-transitive argument structures (but, interestingly, not more frequent than direct objects in complex-transitive argument structures).

(iv) Expressions with direct objects in complex-transitive argument structures (ex 7), finally, are by far more frequent than those with direct objects in mono-transitive argument structures.

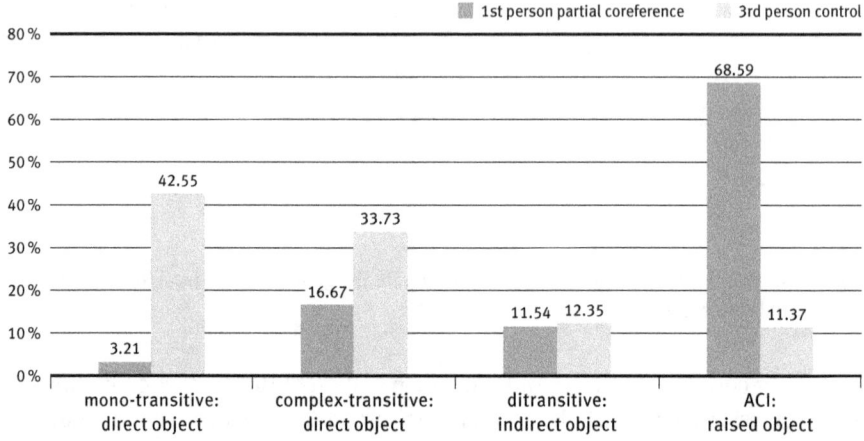

Figure 2 b. Relative frequencies of syntactic functions in 156 first-person expressions with partially coreferential pronominal arguments (vs. in the third-person control sample)

3.3.4 Hortative constructions

The BNC search for non-negated first-person hortative constructions with *let* exhibiting partial coreference yielded only a single true hit (ex 2e, here repeated as ex 11), although hortative constructions are not particularly rare, otherwise:

(11) *Let me get us some crusty bread.* (BNC-KD7)

While this does not rule out that expressions with partial coreference are facilitated by hortative constructions (the single example accounting for 0.6% of the entire set of 167+1 true hits), the issue cannot be followed up any further for reasons of data sparsity.

It should not go entirely unmentioned, however, that hortative constructions in English do, in fact, provide a type of expression with partially coreferential pronouns. As the pronouns involved here diverge in both number and person, however, these expressions remain beyond the scope of the present investigation. It must thus suffice to remark that they can be found with some frequency in the BNC (17 non-negated instances) and would certainly not be considered as odd or anomalous in any way (in that respect, they resemble third-person expressions with partial coreference). Note that, as with other partially coreferential constructions, post-verbal arguments realizing lower syntactic functions dominate (in fact, none of the partially coreferential pronouns involved is a direct object from a mono-transitive argument structure).

(12) a. *Let's just show you something.* (BNC-F8S)
 b. *Let us talk about you.* (BNC-JYF)
 c. *Let's put to you the three questions.* (BNC-KS7)
 d. *Let us just reinforce that for you.* (BNC-F8D)
 e. *Let's just remind you what second messengers are.* (BNC-J8K)
 f. *Then let us see you pass a spell.* (BNC-HA3)

3.4 Results of the Cosmas study

The query to the MECOLB archive of Cosmas II for partial-coreference examples with first-person pronouns did yield true hits. In particular, the query for the constellation with singular subjects (*ich*-VERB-*uns*) produced 54 true hits in the first 1,000 lines of the query output. While these contained only one example with a direct object from a mono-transitive structure (ex 13a) as well as one with a direct object from a complex-transitive one (ex 13b) and one with an indirect object (ex 13c), 36 of them were adjuncts (ex 13d,e):

(13) a. *Als ich uns anmeldete...* (Cosmas II: Mecolb, SOZ07)
 'When I registered us...'

 b. *Ich habe uns sofort zur Fortbildung geschickt.* (Cosmas II: Mecolb BRZ05)
 'I sent us to further training immediately...'

 c. *Während Katharina ihren Kaffee trank, machte ich uns ein gediegenes Frühstück.* (Cosmas II: Mecolb BRZ09)
 'While Katharina had her coffee, I made us a solid breakfast.'

 d. *Für uns rechne ich mit etwa fünf Prozent.* (Cosmas II: Mecolb NUN08)
 'For us, I expect about 5 per cent.'

 e. *Bei uns habe ich schon viel erreicht.* (Cosmas II: Mecolb NON09)
 'For [literally: at] us, I have achieved quite a lot.'

Additional examples can of course be found elsewhere, amongst which there are also more mono-transitive expressions, even such involving verbs that cannot be used reflexively at all (ex 14a), as well as ditransitive ones (ex 14b):

(14) a. *In diesem Sinne möchte ich uns ermutigen.* (Cosmas II: A99/APR.28690)
'I that sense, I wish to encourage us.'

b. *Ich wünsche uns allen ein friedvolles neues Jahr!* (cf. Appendix II.u)
'I wish us all a peaceful new year!'

In contrast, the first 1,000 lines of the MECOLB query for examples with plural subjects (*wir*-VERB-*mich/mir*) did not yield a single true hit. While relevant examples can of course be found elsewhere in the Cosmas archives (ex 15), this result suffices to support the claim that in German, like in English, partial-coreference examples with singular subjects are by far more frequent than those with plural subjects. Note, by the way, that some of our chance findings with plural subjects appear in the hortative construction:

(15) a. *Wir haben den typischen Macho, wir haben den Alleswisser, wir haben mich.* (Cosmas II: RHZ11/AUG.31135)
'We have the typical macho, we have the know-it-all, we have me.'

b. *Meinen Namen kann ich nicht offenbaren, nennen wir mich Nummer vier.* (Cosmas II: BRZ11/APR.06316)
'I cannot reveal my name, let us call me Number 4.'

c. *Nehmen wir nur mich.* (Cosmas II: E98/OKT.25822)
'Let us take only me.'

d. *Nehmen wir mich als Beispiel.* (Cosmas II: NUN04/AUG.02960)
'Let us take me as an example.'

Furthermore, the search for clauses containing the second-person constellations *du*-VERB-*euch* and *ihr*-VERB-*dich/dir* did not produce a single true hit in the entire (much smaller) output from the MECOLB archive, though the web again yields very few pertinent examples (ex 16):[15]

(16) *Er hat deinen Freund geschlagen und du hast euch verteidigt.*
(cf. Appendix II v)
'He beat your friend and you [sg.] defended you both.'

---

15 Cysouw & Fernández (2012, §2) also quote one example from the web.

So far, the (somewhat preliminary) German results support hypotheses (i) and (ii) relating to the preference of first-person over second-person constructions and to the preference of singular over plural subjects. The German data also support hypothesis (iii), concerning the tendency towards lower syntactic functions (cf. Table 6). The large majority of our examples exhibit adjuncts rather than complements. Within the group of examples with coreferential pronouns that are elements of the verb complementation, indirect objects as well as objects from complex-transitive argument structures are by far more frequent than direct objects from mono-transitive argument structures. Raised objects are missing, which does not come as a surprise, as many English raising structures do not have a direct German equivalent.

Table 6. Distribution of syntactic functions in German first-person expressions with singular subjects exhibiting partial-coreference constellations

type of post-verbal argument	*ich* VERB *uns*
mono-transitive: direct object (ex 13a)	1
complex-transitive: direct object (ex 13b)	8
ditransitive: indirect object (ex 13c)	9
prepositional object	0
adjunct (ex 13 d,e)	36
ACI: raised object	0
TOTAL	**54**

In addition, the corpus results can also be roughly assessed in the following way: Given that the MECOLB archive is about a third of the size of the BNC and considering that only about a third of the randomized corpus output for expressions with first-person subjects was inspected, it can be stated that first-person expressions with partial coreference in German are about as frequent as those in English, namely just below 2 expressions per million words. Factoring in that the German dataset also contains a majority of examples where the partially coreferential pronoun is part of an adjunct, while the English data set does not, we can furthermore tentatively assume that German is less open than English to partially coreferential pronouns that are arguments of the verb.

4 Discussion: Asymmetries in expressions with partial coreference

Though most of our findings do in fact confirm the claims made by Cysouw & Fernández (2012, §2), the combination of complementary methods employed in our study has clearly managed to put these claims on a much firmer empirical footing.

While clauses involving partially coreferential pronouns are possible in principle in both English and German, the results have demonstrated that pertinent examples may be classified by a variety of parameters such that partial coreference becomes more acceptable with certain parameter settings. Such asymmetries are formulated below in terms of implicational hierarchies. In language use, these hierarchies manifest themselves in the form of the relative frequencies and corresponding degrees of acceptability of their subtypes. In the extreme and most clear-cut case, they can surface in the impossibility of the *implicans* as opposed to the possibility of the *implicatum*.[16]

4.1 Asymmetry in the values of the number parameter

In accordance with previous claims (cf. Cooper 1976: 213, Cysouw & Fernández 2012, §2), both of our corpus studies show that partial coreference expressions prefer constellations where singular acts on plural over the reverse case.[17] This asymmetry may be represented by the implicational hierarchy of numbers, where '>' is to be read as 'acting on', combined with Proposition 2. In this hierarchy and the following ones, left-right order symbolizes top-down order, and the arrow is the replication arrow, i.e. given element implies the element to its left.

---

16 Recall that Rooryck (2006) postulated the asymmetries between the various person and number values, declaring the respective implicantia ungrammatical in English and French, which most likely they are not.

17 Concerning the possible reasons for the direction of this asymmetry, it could be tentatively argued that, in terms of their respective distances to situations in which either a personal or a reflexive pronoun would be adequately used, the two constellations are not the exact mirror images of one another, as reflexivity needs to be marked on a verbal complement that is not the subject. Loosely speaking, constellations with singular subjects are somewhat closer to contexts allowing for the use of personal pronouns than those with plural subjects, for in the former case the action of the single referent of the subject NP affects a set of other participants, of which at least half are actually *not* referentially identical with it. In contrast, constellations with plural subjects are more akin to contexts requiring a reflexive pronoun, as the single referent of the object-NP is always identical with a member of the set of referents specified by the subject-NP. On the basis of such considerations, expressions with singular subjects should be expected to lend themselves more easily to partial-coreference contexts than expressions with plural subjects.

Proposition 2. Partial coreference and the hierarchy of numbers

singular > plural ← plural > singular
If partial coreference between arguments occurs at the lower position of the above hierarchy, then it occurs at its higher position.

It must be emphasized here that the BNC study provides quantitative evidence that this hierarchy cannot be reduced to a consequence of the fact that singular subjects act on plural objects more frequently than plural subjects do on singular objects (cf. Figures 1a,b), as the differences in frequency observed for expressions with partial coreference go far beyond this general number difference.

4.2 Asymmetry in the values of the person parameter

The data presently available to us also suffice to put forward an implicational hierarchy for the person parameter. While both English and German clearly allow for partial-coreference constellations in the first person, these are technically impossible with second-person expressions in present-day English (due to the loss of the number distinction), and are obviously also extremely rare with second-person expressions in German. The implicational hierarchy is formulated as Proposition 3.

Proposition 3. Partial coreference and the hierarchy of persons

first person ← second person
If partial coreference between arguments occurs at the lower position of the hierarchy, then it occurs at its higher position.

Note that, despite the argument put forward by Cysouw and Fernández (2012, §2), we think it highly unlikely that the lower frequency of partial coreference in the second person as opposed to the first person presents a logical consequence of the overall lower text frequency of the second as against the first person. Analogously to what was said concerning the number parameter, the absence of second-person expressions with partial coreference from a corpus of 30 million words indicates that they are rare to an extent that goes well beyond the differences in the text frequencies of first- and second-person pronouns in German. At the same time, the presence of very few isolated examples on the web (as a corpus of nearly unlimited size) only serves to demonstrate that such expressions do in principle exist (though that does not necessarily say anything about their acceptability). We thus do not expect the hierarchy postulated here to merely reflect the frequency effect generally found for first- vs. second-person pronouns.

Finally, a few remarks on third-person expressions with partial coreference are also at place. Although it is practically unfeasible to retrieve expressions with partial coreference exhaustively from a large sample of third-person expressions (as these can only be identified by studying in close detail the larger textual environment of each single case), the few expressions identified during the creation of the third-person control samples suffice to ascertain the existence as well as indisputable well-formedness of these expressions in English (ex 17).

(17) a. *She embraced him with her eyes, pleased, and as she poured them both more wine, rewarded him with a view of her leg.* (BNC-H84)

b. *As much as I can, she laughed as she poured them both a cup of coffee.* (BNC-JYF)

c. *She... called Rachel to come ... while she found them both some clothes.* (BNC-A6J)

d. *Taking care not to panic her, he persuaded [the leopardess] to carry her cub into the boat. Then he ferried them across.* (BNC-CK2)

e. *And what things did he want them both to forget?* (BNC-JXU)

f. *She wanted them to go on being friends.*(BNC-JXU)

As mentioned above, third-person expressions with partial coreference are inconspicuous, as the respective constellations of pronouns (*he/she/it*-VERB-*them*, *they*-VERB-*him/her/it*) are in no way formally different from expressions where these pronouns are used with disjoint reference. It can thus be assumed that, if the implicational hierarchy presented above were extended to include third person, it would be highly likely to figure at the left-hand pole of the hierarchy.

4.3 Asymmetry in the values for the syntactic-function parameter

The results of both corpus studies provide clear evidence that functions that are lower in the syntactic hierarchy (Proposition 4 below) occur more frequently in expressions with partial coreference than higher ones. In addition, the BNC study shows that this distribution contrasts sharply with the distribution of syntactic functions in expressions with disjoint reference. In this section, the results of the corpus studies will be discussed in the broader context of the entire syntactic hierarchy. In the following, we will move down this hierarchy, illustrating and discussing each of the constellations with partial coreference between the subject and another dependent lower in the hierarchy, with a special focus on those parts of the hierarchy that (one of) the corpus studies did not cover. Although strictly speaking outside the scope of the clause, the lowest level of the hierarchy has to be included, not just to complete the picture, but also for the reasons discussed below.

While direct objects do not need much further comment, except to emphasize their near-absence from expressions with partially coreferential pronouns, a number of remarks about the lower categories in the hierarchy are certainly at place. "Other complements" are mainly constituted by prepositional objects in both English and German (cf. ex 11), whereby the border between these and some kinds of adjuncts is not always entirely clear-cut. Consider (18), for example: the adverbial of direction is sometimes treated as a complement of the verb denoting goal-oriented movement:

(18)   *Then we come back to me in the studio.* (BNC-G12)

Concerning indirect objects and adjuncts, it needs to be stated that, for the purposes of the corpus studies and in line with much work in construction grammar on the Ditransitive Construction (cf. Goldberg 1995), the first NP of a "ditransitive" pattern in English, and the dative NP from a double-object pattern in German are treated here as proper instances of indirect objects, rather than as benefactive adjuncts, even if carrying the semantic role of beneficiary (ex 8c,d; 13c). If formally realized as prepositional phrases, however, benefactive adjuncts that are partly coreferential with the subject, are rather frequent in the BNC. The corpus search for prepositional objects also uprooted 7 benefactive adjuncts (which were not included in the English data set, which was restricted to pronouns serving as verbal complements). Four of these examples are presented in (19).[18]

(19)   a.   *I never cook for us and we don't have dinner parties.* (BNC-CH5)
       b.   *I get those little ones for us.* (BNC-KB2)
       c.   *Tremayne vaguely suggested coffee, and I made a mug of instant for us each.* (BNC-ADY)
       d.   *I prayed for us both before the altar.* (BNC-AC6)

---

18 A re-categorisation of (the sizeable number of) indirect objects with beneficiary roles in our data sets as "benefactive adjuncts" would only increase the number of adjuncts, thus lending additional support to the hypothesis presented here.

The study of the MECOLB archive of Cosmas II also brought to light the strongly increased frequency of benefactive and other adjuncts in German expressions exhibiting partially coreferential pronouns (ex 13d,e), which made up nearly two thirds of the data.

When talking about the subjects of dependent clauses, as the lowest syntactic function in the hierarchy, two kinds of constructions deserve further discussion, as they show an exceptionally high degree of clausal integration, where the formal object of the matrix verb simultaneously serves as the logical subject of a second(ary) proposition. The first construction exhibits a complex-transitive argument structure and involves what has been called a "small clause" (ex 20, 21).

(20) a. *I shall book us into a lodge for 2 nights.* (BNC-HPP)
 b. *I called us Murphy.* (BNC-HTS)
 c. *We elected me captain once the lieutenants had been decided on.* (cf. Appendix II.n)

(21) a. *Uns sehe ich ganz vorne.* (Cosmas II: Mecolb M08)
 'I see us right in front'
 b. *Denn ich halte uns nach wie vor nicht für eine Riesenmannschaft.* (Cosmas II: A98/OKT.61837)
 'For I still don't consider us a huge team.'

Both our English and our German data have confirmed that expressions with direct objects in mono-transitive structures are extremely rare (or near-unacceptable) in these languages, while expressions with objects from complex-transitive frames, which can be said to function as the logical subjects of a secondary predication, are not.

The other construction is syntactically more complex in that it involves an ACI-construction, i.e. some kind of non-finite subordinate clause whose subject is coded like a direct object of the main predicate, thus "raised" (ex 22, cf. also ex 10).

(22) *I should like us to be friends.* (BNC-BNT)

Partially coreferential pronouns can freely appear in these constructions, whose high acceptability is mirrored by their extremely high relative frequency in the BNC data. Their absence from the German data is mainly due to the fact that German prefers control structures and generally exhibits fewer raising constructions than English.

Concerning adnominal functions (and thus moving entirely beyond the corpus studies), finally, the two cross-linguistically most important subclasses of relational nouns, viz. body-part and kinship terms, might appear to be good candidates for nominal constructions involving partial coreference at face value, but drop out upon closer inspection. The former do not take persons as their first (i.e. their referential) argument (at least in their literal reading), and the latter do not naturally allow for reflexivity. While some constellations like *I am our knee* or *I am our daughter* are obviously impossible on denotational grounds (with sentences such as *I am our youngest sibling* seeming extremely far-fetched at best), there are certainly relevant examples with certain suitable relational nouns. (23) is one of more than a dozen independent occurrences of *I am our leader* on the web.[19]

(23)   *I am teaching the people I work with how to get things done. Which is something I barely know about myself, yet I am our leader in figuring it out.*
(cf. Appendix II s)

There are also a few suitable relational adjectives, such as *proud*. (24a) is attested a couple of times on the web. Though (24b) is not, it does not sound implausible. The construction can be found in the Cosmas II corpus and also seems quite natural with comparatives and superlatives, although no authentic English data were uncovered (ex 25, 26). Note, again, that these examples, too, are in no way unacceptable or odd.

(24)   a.   *I am proud of us.* (cf. Appendix II t)
      b.   *We should be proud of me.*

(25)   *I am the richest of us all.*

(26)   a.   *Ich bin der Bessere von uns.* (Cosmas 2, M99/DEZ.84498)
        'I am the better one of us.'

      b.   *Ich bin der Jüngste von uns.* (Cosmas 2, HMP07/JAN.00851)
        'I am the youngest of us.'

      c.   *Du bist der Erste von euch fünf!* (Cosmas 2, DIV/APR.00001)
        'You are the first one of the five of you.'

---

19 We thank the editors for making us aware of examples like *We cut my hair. I cut our hair. We visited my aunt, I visited our daughter.* We wish to stress that these do not fall under the scope of Proposition 1 because the partially coreferential elements involved are not the arguments of one verb or noun. It is thus not surprising that these examples are entirely acceptable.

In sum, it is safe to say that the hierarchy of syntactic functions, which underlies so many laws of syntax, appears to play its role in expressions with partially coreferential pronouns, too. In our context, its effect is the one specified by Proposition 4.

Proposition 4. Partial coreference and the hierarchy of syntactic functions

subject ← direct object ← indirect object ~ adnominal complement ← other complement ← adjunct ← subject of dependent clause
If partial coreference with the subject occurs for a pronominal dependent at a given position of the hierarchy, then it occurs for all dependents lower on the hierarchy.

Note, by the way, that this implicational hierarchy is the exact mirror image of the principle underlying reflexivization, which roughly states: If coreference between the subject and a dependent at a given position of the syntactic-function hierarchy is coded as reflexive, then coreference between the subject and all dependents higher up on it is coded as reflexive (cf. Siewierska 2004, ch. 5.3.2).

4.4 Asymmetry in the degree of grammaticalization

We found that partial coreference does not exist in Hixkaryana and Mangarayi, the two languages where it would have to be coded by affixal person forms. It is barely existent in Yucatec, where it would partly be coded by clitics, partly by affixes. Though subject to the constraints discussed above, it does exist in English and German, two languages which code partial coreference by free pronouns. These findings thus confirm Cysouw & Fernández's (2012, §4) hypothesis that partial-coreference constructions are sometimes possible with free pronouns, but are not grammaticalized into verb forms exhibiting bivalent personal agreement or morphological cross-reference marking.

The relevant parts of the grammaticalization scale of person forms (Lehmann 2002: 49) are reproduced below. This scale is, of course, independently motivated. The role played by it in partial coreference is expressed as Proposition 5.

While a number of languages have been found whose paradigm of person indexes on transitive verbs is defective (see section 2), no language has been found with a paradigm which would be complete to the level of partial coreference. It is clear, however, that Proposition 5 has not been demonstrated. For the time being, it remains a hypothesis, but a hypothesis that is entirely compatible with the data available to us and with the theoretical framework of grammaticalization.

Proposition 5. Partial coreference and grammaticalization

degree of grammati- calization	weak ←――――――――――――――――――→ strong						
person form	independent personal pronoun	>	clitic personal pronoun	>	separate cross-reference marker	>	separate agreement affix	>	amalgamated agreement affix

If partial coreference is possible for a person form at a given position of the scale, then it is possible for person forms at all positions to the left of it.

4.5 Underlying motivations

We have identified four implicational hierarchies that are operative in the coding of a partial coreference relationship by person forms: the person hierarchy, the number hierarchy, the hierarchy of syntactic functions and the grammaticalization scale of person forms. The associated Propositions relate to the cross-linguistic level, where they are to be taken as typological hypotheses. Moreover, they relate to the intralingual level in that they predict the relative frequencies of constructions that are admissible in the language.

The hierarchy of syntactic functions and the grammaticalization scale operate in parallel: constructions higher up on the hierarchy of syntactic functions are syntactically tighter, and tighter constructions tend to display symptoms of heightened grammaticalization. Consequently, the locus of person forms occupying positions near the right pole of Proposition 5 is in constructions at the higher levels of the hierarchy of proposition 4. We have seen that the constraints on partial coreference are tighter both for constructions at the top of the syntactic-functions hierarchy and at the right pole of Proposition 5.[20] If we rephrase the question of codability as one of accessibility of certain functions to certain pronominal expressions, then these results are fully compatible with the assertion that "the syntactic constraints on the distribution of anaphors and pronominals are indeed grammaticalized accessibility preferences" (Siewierska 2004: 192).

---

20 This correlation is explicitly recognized for Mangarayi: "Of course, it is possible to express other types of relations (e.g. benefactive) between such categories [i.e. the person-number values of subject and object which represent partial coreference in Table 2] by using the system of independent pronouns to express the indirect object relation." (Merlan 1982: 162)

The question remains why partial coreference should be subject to any constraints at all, i.e., why, even granting all those grammatical constraints, (some of) the English and German sentences feel odd. As emphasized from the start, the situations designated by them do occur in principle, and the respective sentences seem to be the 'regular' (though somewhat provisional) way of coding them. Taking recourse to the rarity of the situations in question (Cysouw & Fernández 2012) as the only explanation will probably not suffice, given the nature of many of our corpus examples. A few more precise remarks are thus at place. For instance, the situations described by the English examples (7b), (8b,c), (10) and the German examples (13a,c), (14a,b) or (16), to single out but a few, represent recurring types of every-day situations. As speakers do not regularly encounter different situations that naturally give rise to partial-coreference expressions, they may be doubtful about the acceptability of any constructed and de-contextualized example that does not clearly relate to such a situation (see Table 1).

Apart from this, it seems that there is a conspiracy of semantic and grammatical factors working in the same direction which render such sentences unusual or odd.

The semantic irregularity results from the way in which a relation coded by a transitive verb is made concrete, if its argument positions are filled by different kinds of participants. It is well-known that verbs can change their meaning considerably if combined with noun phrases of different categories; and this effect is made use of in the rhetorical figure of syllepsis, illustrated by example (27).

(27) *Here Thou, great Anna! whom three Realms obey, Dost sometimes Counsel take – and sometimes Tea.* (Alexander Pope, *The Rape of the Lock*)

The effect is less dramatic, but still perceptible if a reflexive and a non-reflexive NP are conjoined to form the direct object of one verb, as in (28).

(28) *I sacrificed myself and all the others.*

The point is that the action designated is not quite the same if applied to any person or to oneself. In constructions of partial coreference, this generates a sylleptic effect, which may render them semantically incoherent (example 29), though that does not always need to be the case.

(29) *I sacrificed us.*

The semantic difference alluded to is reflected in grammar in the form of reflexive constructions: In many languages, the reflexive counterpart to a certain two-argument construction is not just the construction in question plus a mark of reflexivity, but a special one-argument construction. Thus, instead of converting *he shaved him* into *he shaved himself* in cases of coreference, many languages would have a closer counterpart to *he shaved*, possibly with some reflexive mark on the verb. That is the case, for instance, for Mangarayi and Hixkaryana, where the verb form to be inserted in the light grey cells of Tables 2 and 3 would be a special reflexive form of the intransitive verb. In such a language, the constructions for disjoint reference and coreference would differ syntactically. Consequently, in situations of partial coreference, the general (transitive) construction would not fit the coreferential part of the constellation, while the reflexive construction would not fit its non-coreferential part. At lower levels of grammaticalization, this may lead to variation between the two types of construction. With advanced grammaticalization, however, either alternative is just ungrammatical.

5 Conclusion

By way of coming to a close, we will briefly survey the results of this study. We hope to have provided abundant evidence to show that constructions of partial coreference are not in general ungrammatical. Instead, their possibility in language systems and in texts is conditioned by four implicational hierarchies:

(i) *the person hierarchy*, by which partial coreference is easier for first person than for second person;

(ii) *the number hierarchy*, by which singular acting on plural is easier than plural acting on singular;

(iii) *the hierarchy of syntactic functions*, by which partial coreference with the subject is the easier for a pronominal form the lower its position on that hierarchy; as well as

(iv) *the grammaticalization scale of person forms*, by which partial coreference is easier for a person form the less grammaticalized it is.

While (iii) and (iv) are clearly grammatical constraints, the results of the corpus studies can with some certainty be taken to suggest that the former two of these are not mere frequency effects, but deserve further research into their motivations.

As emphasized from the beginning, partial coreference is a constellation not foreseen, in general, by grammatical systems. Partial-coreference expressions thus present makeshift responses to a very specific communicative need. If coreference is coded in areas of the grammatical system where rules are less strict – viz. if either person forms of low grammaticality or syntactic functions low on the hierarchy are involved – solving the referential problem by those means normally used for constellations of clear-cut reference does not attract much attention. It is when person forms are highly grammaticalized or syntactic functions high on the hierarchy are involved that rules of grammar are stricter, and constructions incompatible with them become less acceptable or entirely unacceptable, i.e. downright ungrammatical.

Given a bivalent predicate, the coreference of the dependent argument with its prime argument – as opposed to disjoint reference – often affects the interpretation of the predicate itself. Grammars reflect this semantic difference in the distinction between reflexive and non-reflexive constructions. Our claim is that constraints (iii) and (iv) become more active, the further advanced the degree of the grammaticalization of this contrast is. In the extreme, this may lead to the ungrammaticality of constructions exhibiting partial coreference no matter whether they follow the reflexive or the non-reflexive model.

To end on a methodological note, the corpus studies have doubtlessly demonstrated that partial-coreference constructions are exceptionally rare in both English and German. However, these studies have also uncovered highly systematic usage patterns which cannot be considered a chance finding and which diverge dramatically from what occurs "elsewhere" in the grammar of the languages investigated. In particular, there is clear evidence that not all partial-coreference constructions are "on a par" – with some being a lot more frequent (hence: acceptable) than others. Though we have related the frequency of particular types of partial-coreference constructions to their degree of acceptability when postulating four implicational hierarchies, we must stress again that the overall scarcity of relevant data is not due to any predetermined "unacceptability" of these constructions in the first place; they are just as frequent as the need for denoting such situations actually arises.

Abbreviations

1 first person, 2 second person, 3 third person, ABS absoluttive, COLL collective, DU dual, EXCL exclusive, HORT hortative, INCL inclusive, PL plural, POSS possessive, REFL reflexive, SBJ subject, SG singular.

Appendix I

Regular Expressions (REGEX) employed in the BNC corpus study:

a. <w PNP>(I|(W|w)e)\s<w (V(B|M|H)>[a-z|A-Z]*\s<w A..>[a-z]*\s <w V(B|M|H)>[a-z|A-Z]*\s<w (VV.|VV.-...)>[a-z|A-Z|-]*\s<w PNP>(me|us)\s

b. Identical string, but instead of the last element "<w PNP>(me|us)\s" the following sequences were employed: "(<w ([^V]..|[^V]..-...)>[a-z|A-Z|-]*\s){1,5}<w PRP>[a-z|-|\s]*\s<w PNP>(me|us)\s" and "<w PRP>[a-z|-|\s]*\s<w PNP>(me|us)\s"

c. <w VM0>(L|l)et's\s<w AV0>[a-z|A-Z|-]{2,10}\s(<w VV.>|<w VV.-...>)[a-z|A-Z|-]*\s<w PNP>me\s

Instead of the initial element "<w VM0>(L|l)et's\s" the alternative beginnings "<w VV.>(L|l)et\s<w PNP>us\s" and "<w VV.>(L|l)et\s<w PNP>me\s" were used, the latter with the final pronoun in the search string specified as "us\s". For constructions with prepositional objects, the end of the string was manipulated analogously to b. above.

d. <w PNP>I\s<w V(B|M|H)>[a-z|A-Z]*\s<w A..>[a-z]*\s<w V(B|M|H)>[a-z|A-Z]*\s<w (VV.|VV.-...)>[a-z|A-Z|-]*\s<w PNX>ourselves\s

e. <w PNP>(w|W)e\s<w V(B|M|H)>[a-z|A-Z]*\s<w A..>[a-z]*\s<w V(B|M|H)>[a-z|A-Z]*\s<w (VV.|VV.-...)>[a-z|A-Z|-]*\s<w PNX>myself\s

f. <w PNP>(I|(w|W)e)\s<w V(B|M|H)>[a-z|A-Z]*\s<w A..>[a-z]*\s<w V(B|M|H)>[a-z|A-Z]*\s<w (VV.|VV.-...)>[a-z|A-Z|-]*\s<w PNX>(myself|ourselves)\s

g. <w PNP>((H|h)e|(S|s)he|(I|i)t|(T|t)hey)\s<w V(B|M|H)>[a-z|A-Z]*\s<w A..>[a-z]*\s<w V(B|M|H)>[a-z|A-Z]*\s<w (VV.|VV.-...)>[a-z|A-Z|-]*\s<w PNP>(him|her|it|them)\s

Appendix II

Collection of examples with partially coreferential pronouns taken from the world-wide web:

a. Thanks to a *Pinterest* idea, *I saved ourselves* from buying a crazy number of stocking holders <http://missingolivia.blogspot.de/2012/01/best-christmas-ever.html>, consulted 25/04/2012

b. I am proud to say that *I saved ourselves* from the hassle of waiting in a long queue. <http://kaloka.livejournal.com/87139.html>, consulted 25/04/2012.
c. *I saved ourselves* 1000 Rs. <http://www.bmcindia.org/travelogue/scuba-diving.htm>
d. *We saved myself* a lot of money by not using a lawyer. <http://www.immigration.ca/discussion2/topic.asp?TOPIC_ID=25007>; consulted 25/04/2012.
e. Oh, yeah, *I forgot us*, wow, that's terrible. <http://www.accenture.com/SiteCollectionDocuments/PDF/Accenture_Case_in_Point_US_Department_of_Health_and_Human_Services_Transcript.pdf>; accessed 25/04/2012.
f. how can *I defend us* in the matter? <http://www.avvo.com/legal-answers/how-can-i-get-a-lawsuit-against-my-wife-transferre-100024.html>; accessed 22/04/2012.
g. *I wish us* good luck. <http://www.tumblr.com/tagged/i-wish-us-good-luck-lol>; consulted 24/07/2012.
h. *I can get us* out of here tonight. title of a song, <http://lucerotabs.blogspot.de/2008/05/i-can-get-us-out-of-here-tonight.html>; accessed 22/04/2012.
i. *I vote for Us*! Halston and Casey <http://www.wedoweddingphotography-blog.com/best-of-2011-canvas-contest/>; consulted 25/04/2012.
j. It wasn't an easy start for us in terms of games this season, ... but *I fancied us* to get something. <http://au.fourfourtwo.com/news/112427,ref-sent-scholes-off-on-reputation-ferguson.aspx>; accessed 22/04/2012.
k. *I vote for us* doing the same <http://lauramappin.com/TPD/pages/bhutanizeUs.php>; consulted 25/04/2012.
l. Wait! I know who we forgot. *We forgot me*! <http://www.census.gov/schools/pdf/materials/cis_lesson_k4US.pdf>; accessed 25/04/2012.
m. It was never going to be done just because *we elected me*. <http://www.freerepublic.com/focus/f-news/2412777/posts>; accessed 20/04/2012; attributed to B. Obama.
n. *We elected me* captain once the lieutenants had been decided on. <http:// www.litmir.net/br/?b=127970&p=46>
o. I fell in love with my brother when *we saved me* for some school bullies. <http://www.fanfiction.net/s/7942053/2/the_copy_twins_naruto_and_naruko_namikaze, consulted 25/04/2012>
p. *we saved me* from picking pine needles out of the carpet in March. <http://www.myblogisboring.com/2011/12/christmas-you-say-okay-fine.html>; consulted 25/04/2012.

q. *In me we trust* <www.kullin.net/2006/01/in-me-we-trust/>; accessed 22/04/2012.
r. either we vote for a career politician ... or *we vote for me,* a hard-working student officer activist.
<http://www.nusconnect.or asset event 6001 bsc_2012_cd8_manifestos.pdf>
s. I am teaching the people I work with how to get things done. Which is something I barely know about myself, yet *I am our leader* in figuring it out. <http://peacecorpsjournals.com/?Journal&journal_id=11164>; consulted 21/02/2013.
t. *I am proud of us.* <http://simplyhorse-crazy.blogspot.de/2011/11/ i-am-proud-of-us.html>; accessed 22/04/2012.
u. *Ich wünsche uns allen* ein friedvolles neues Jahr!
<https://nohoearmy.wordpress.com/ 2012/01/01/ich-wuensche-uns-allen-ein-friedvolles-neues-jahr/>
v. Er hat deinen Freund geschlagen und *du* hast *euch verteidigt.*
<http://archiv.raid-rush.ws/t-328896.html>; accessed 22/04/2012.

References

Aarts, Bas. 1992. *Small clauses in English*. Berlin & New York: De Gruyter Mouton.
Cooper, William E. 1976. Inclusions. *Lingua* 40. 203–222.
Cysouw, Michael & Javies Fernández Landaluce. 2012. On the (im)possibility of partial argument coreference. *Linguistics* 50. 765–782.
Derbyshire, Desmond C. 1979. *Hixkaryana*. Amsterdam: North-Holland (Lingua Descriptive Studies, 1).
Goldberg, Adele. 1995. *Constructions. A Construction-Grammar Approach to Argument Structure*. Chicago: The University of Chicago Press.
Kamholz, David. 2012. How do languages keep their selves straight?. Unpublished manuscript at the Max-Planck-Institute of Evolutionary Anthropology, Leipzig, June 15, 2012. (Available from http://linguistics.berkeley.edu/~kamholz/research)
Lasnik, Howard. 2011. The syntax of pronoun interpretation: some recurrent themes. Paper presented at the UMD MayFest, May 6, 2011. (http://ling.umd.edu/~lasnik/Handouts/Lasnik Pronouns MayFest HO.pdf; accessed 22/04/2012.)
Lehmann, Christian. 2002. *Thoughts on grammaticalization*. Erfurt: Seminar für Sprachwissenschaft der Universität (ASSidUE, 9) (2nd revised edition).
Leite, Yonne. 1987. As cisões no sistema referencial de pessoa em Tapirapé. Paper presented at the Working Conference on Amazonian Languages, Eugene, Oregon. Rio de Janeiro: [s.ed.].
Merlan, Francesca. 1982. *Mangarayi*. Amsterdam: North-Holland (Lingua Descriptive Studies, 4).
Postal, Paul M. 1966. A note on 'understood transitively'. *International Journal of American Linguistics* 32. 90–93.
Quirk, Randolph, S. Greenbaum, G. Leech, & J. Svartvik. 1985. *A comprehensive grammar of the English language*. London: Longman.
Rooryck, Johan. 2006. Binding into pronouns. *Lingua* 10(116). 1561–1579.
Siewierska, Anna. 2004. *Person*. Cambridge: Cambridge University Press.

Corpora

BNC Consortium 2000, *British National Corpus. World Edition*. Humanities Computing Unit of Oxford University. (http://www.hcu.ox.ac.uk/BNC)

IDS (Institut für Deutsche Sprache)) 2012, *Cosmas II, Version 1.8*. (https://cosmas2.ids-mannheim.de/cosmas2-web)

Martin Haspelmath
Argument indexing: a conceptual framework for the syntactic status of bound person forms

1 Introduction

In this article, I propose that the concept of **(argument) indexing** is more useful in typology (and typically also in language description) than the commonly used concepts of **pronoun** and **agreement** for situations like those in (1)–(2), where we find bound person-marking forms on the verb.

(1) Georgian (Boeder 2002: 98–99)

    a. *V-Ø-č'am.*
        1.SUBJ-3.OBJ-eat
        'I eat it.'

    b. *Me v-Ø-č'am ma-s.*
        I   1.SUBJ-3.OBJ-eat it-DAT
        'I eat it.'

(2) Mam (Mayan; England 1983: 156)

    a. *Ma tz'-ookx t-uj jaa.*
        PST 3SG.ABS-go.in 3SG-in house
        'She went in the house.'

    b. *Ma tz'-ookx Mal t-uj jaa.*
        PST 3SG.ABS-go.in María 3SG-in house
        'María went in the house.'

The basic observation is that it is not primarily the phenomena observed in the world's languages, but apparently the descriptive tradition of some well-known European languages (especially German, English and French) that has led many linguists to describe bound person forms as "pronouns" or as "agreement markers". Instead, I will argue that bound person forms are best seen as phenomena sui generis that in most cases neither fall under a coherent concept of pronoun nor under a coherent concept of agreement.

There is an enormous literature on bound pronouns and their syntactic status (e.g. Jelinek 1984, Mithun 1986, Bresnan & Mchombo 1987, Marácz & Muysken (eds.) 1989, Launey 1994, Baker 1996, Evans & Sasse (eds.) 2002, Corbett 2003, Siewierska 2004: 120–127, Kibrik 2011: ch. 6, Schultze-Berndt 2011, Hengeveld 2012), so I will not say anything that is completely new here. But since most of this literature seems to debate the same old question, namely whether bound person forms are agreement markers or pronouns, I feel it may be helpful to propose a reframing of the issues by adopting a terminology that makes no reference to agreement or pronouns at all (argument indexing).

Grammatical terminology is often thought of as arbitrary and trivial, irrelevant to matters of substance. However, there are good reasons to think that there are strong Whorfian effects, in the sense that familiar and entrenched terminology shapes the thinking of linguists. For example, since linguists have long been used to describing grammatical structures in terms of "words" (word combinations and word parts), many linguists have looked for the syntax–morphology boundary, often without asking what linguistic phenomena (beyond orthographic conventions) justify such a distinction in the first place (cf. Haspelmath 2011a). Conferences and edited volumes have been organized around traditional terms such as "finiteness" (Nikolaeva 2007) and "impersonals" (Malchukov & Siewierska 2011), even though it is far from clear that any coherent concepts of general linguistics can be associated with these terms. Most of the concepts of general linguistics derive from concepts originally created for the description of particular languages. Often such concepts can usefully be extended from the descriptive (language-particular) level to the general level, but in many cases, this does not work because languages are too different. It seems that the terms *pronoun* and *agreement*, while useful for languages like German and English, cannot be readily extended to languages of different types without confusion arising.

The concepts that I will be concerned with are comparative concepts, i.e. concepts of general linguistics that are needed for making cross-linguistic generalizations, or for contrastive statements of any sort (cf. Haspelmath 2010). A selection of significant cross-linguistic generalizations that can be easily stated in terms of the concepts developed here is given in Appendix A. But in addition, for the sake of comprehensibility of language descriptions, it is helpful if the descriptive terms do not diverge too strongly from the corresponding comparative terms, especially if the descriptive categories are close to the corresponding comparative concepts. Thus, my terminological proposals here will also be useful for language description.

It seems to me that in the discussions of bound person forms, a number of empirical observations have often been ignored, and that by taking these seriously, we are naturally led to the proposals of this article:

(3) a. Person forms have heterogenous functions: Speech-role forms refer deictically to speech-act participants, while 3rd person forms refer to other entities that do not necessarily need a full NP to point to them.

b. Anaphoric pronouns often agree with their antecedent in number (and sometimes in gender), but deictic personal pronouns (1st and 2nd person) never agree with anything, and personal pronouns never agree in person.

c. Bound person forms that require the presence of a coreferential nominal (a conominal) are very unusual in the world's languages (cf. Siewierska 1999).

d. Meaning is often expressed in a distributed way, i.e. there is nothing anomalous about a situation in which a single meaning element is expressed by two form elements (or vice versa, for that matter).

e. Affixal and clitic person forms are not distinguishable in general, as there are no good general criteria for distinguishing between affixes and clitics (see Haspelmath 2011a).

2 Bound person forms: indexes

The basic phenomenon addressed in this article is **bound person forms**, for which the shorter term **indexes** can conveniently be used (following Lazard 1998: 6).[1] Bound person forms are relatively straightforward to delimit from other phenomena. Let us begin with the definition of *person form*.

Person form is a cover term for speech-role (or locuphoric) forms and allophoric forms (the term *allophoric* is from Dahl 2000).[2] A speech-role form is a form that refers to one of the speech-roles speaker(s) and addressee(s). An allophoric form is a form that is used as a reduced referential device (cf. Kibrik 2011: 39) for a non-speech-role referent occurring in the shared context, the previous discourse, or in the same clause. The term *person* as a cover term for locuphoric and allophoric forms is decidedly odd, but linguists have used the term for many

---

[1] The term *(actant) index (indice actanciel* in French, Lazard 1994: 7, Bossong 1998) has been used in French linguistics for some time, especially the form *indice personnel* (e.g. Dumézil & Esenç 1975: 11). It seems to have its origin in Tesnière (1959: § 41.22, p. 85).
[2] For speech-role forms, Dahl (2000) uses *egophoric*, but this sounds odd for 2nd person forms. The term *locuphoric* (cf. *locution* 'speech') is more transparent (and is clearer than the alternative term "local person" that is sometimes used as a cover term for 1st and 2nd person).

centuries, so I am not proposing that it should be abandoned. It would be difficult to come up with an alternative term, because person as defined in this way is not a unified semantic domain (see observation 3a). What unifies speech-role forms and non-speech-role forms is exclusively the fact that they tend to be expressed in parallel ways across languages. These parallel forms are conveniently called *first person*, *second person*, and *third person* (as well as perhaps others, see Cysouw 2003). Consider paradigms such as those in (4), which are familiar from practically all languages.

(4)

	Somali			Armenian			French			Lavukaleve	
SG	1	*anigu*	SG	1	*es*	SG	1	*moi*			
	2	*adigu*		2	*du*		2	*toi*			
	3F	*iyadu*		3	*na*		3M	*lui*	SG	1	*a-*
	3M	*isagu*	PL	1	*menk'*		3F	*elle*		2	*ngo-/ne-*
PL	1EX	*annagu*		2	*duk'*	PL	1	*nous*		3	*o-*
	1IN	*innagu*		3	*nrank'*		2	*vous*	DU	1EX	*le-*
	2	*idinku*	(Dum-Tragut 2009)				3	*eux*		1IN	*me-*
	3	*iyagu*								2	*mele-*
(Berchem 1991: 76)										3	*lo-*
									PL	1EX	*e-*
										1IN	*me-*
										2	*me-*
										3	*ma-*
									(Terrill 2003: 243)		

Person forms in this sense can be identified in all languages. Siewierska (2004) extensively discusses person forms and deals with a small number of phenomena that may not be readily classifiable as either a person form or something else. Overall, there is not much room for controversy here.

Somewhat more problematic is the distinction between **bound** and **free** person forms (or dependent and independent person forms). Contemporary authors typically make a three-way distinction "affix – clitic – nonclitic word", which can be mapped onto the binary distinction "bound" (= affix and clitic) vs. "free" (= nonclitic word) (e.g. Zwicky & Pullum 1983, Haspelmath 2002, Aronoff & Fudeman 2005).[3] For cross-linguistic purposes, the bound vs. free distinction is much more useful than the tripartition. Distinguishing in a general way between affixes and clitics seems to be impossible (observation 3e), because there is no

---

[3] In contrast to this quasi-standard terminology, Kibrik (2011) only regards affixes as "bound", while both clitics and nonclitic words are "free". But no clear criteria for distinguishing affixes and clitics are given (Kibrik 2011: 86–89).

single criterion and the various criteria do not converge to a sufficient extent (Haspelmath 2011a, 2011b). But distinguishing in a general way between bound elements and free elements is quite straightforward, because there is a single criterion: Free forms are forms that can occur on their own, i.e. in a complete (possibly elliptical) utterance (Bloomfield 1933: 160). This criterion correlates very highly with the criterion of contrastive use: Only free forms can be used contrastively. Thus, we can say that if a person form cannot be used on its own or contrastively, it is a **bound person form**.

Bound person forms most often occur on verbs (expressing verbal arguments), but they may also be used on nouns (expressing possessors) or adpositions (expressing the adpositional complement), and languages often use similar forms for the three host types (e.g. Siewierska 1998, Bakker 2005). In this article, I mostly talk about verbal person forms, but this is only to simplify the exposition. Everything I say applies to nominal and adpositional person forms as well.

When a person form is free, calling it a **pro-noun** is justified in the etymological sense, because it usually behaves like a noun (or rather an entire noun phrase, or **nominal**). It can occur as an argument or adjunct of a clause or as a referential modifier of a nominal. Nouns (or nominals), too, are free forms and can occur in these roles. Free person forms are thus "pro-nouns" in that they occur in syntactic contexts where a noun (or nominal) could occur, substituting for a noun, so to speak (*pro nomine*).

When person forms are bound, as in (1)–(2) above and the Lavukaleve forms in (4), it is much less clear that they are pronouns in the same sense. They behave differently in two respects: (i) They seem to be part of the verb (or noun or adposition), rather than being separate nominal expressions; (ii) in most cases, they can cooccur with a nominal (a *conominal*) with the same reference and role in the same clause.

As a result of these differences, it is not very helpful to call them "pronouns" ("bound pronouns", "pronominal affixes", or "pronominal markers") (see further in section 8). Alternatively, linguists often talk about them in terms of "agreement". But agreement is generally thought of as an asymmetrical kind of category-form covariation (the form of the target depends on the category of the controller), and in most uses of most person forms, there is no controller (at least no controller of the person category) present (see further in section 9).

Instead of describing bound person forms in terms of the 'pronoun' concept or the 'agreement' concept, I propose to regard them as phenomena sui generis and to call them **argument indexes** (or person indexes, or simply indexes), as in Lazard (1998). The grammatical process of providing verbs, nouns and adpositions with argument indexes can be called **indexing** (or indexation). Argument indexes on verbs are often called subject and object indexes after their argument-class,[4] indexes on nouns are called possessive indexes, and indexes on adpositions can be called adpositional indexes.

In addition to the noun *index*, we can make use of the verb *to index*, and this verb is in fact widely used in the literature, as seen in (5).[5] In this respect, the terminology proposed here is already fairly established.

(5) a. "Core participants (subjects and objects) can be indexed on the verb by proclitics and enclitics" (Klaiman 1988: 63)

b. "(In Kanuri) the recipient phrase is indexed on the verb in the same way as direct objects of ordinary transitive verbs are" (Newman 1996: 31)

c. "In many languages subjects and/or objects are indexed on verbs by means of affixes or clitics." (Lichtenberk 1997: 301)

d. "the referent of an involuntary state predicate, which *is indexed on the verb* with dative suffixes, may appear in nominative case" (Donohue & San Roque 2004: §4.1.2, on I'saka)

Since this usage is quite familiar, there should be no obstacle to using *index* also as a noun, in the sense of 'bound person form, which indexes arguments on verbs, nouns and adpositions'.[6]

---

4 *Argument-class* is my term for categories like subject and object (often called syntactic functions or grammatical relations).
5 This use of *be indexed* is semantically identical to *be cross-referenced*. The latter is perhaps more widespread:
(i) „Direct agents, patients, and subjects are cross-referenced on verbs" (England 1983: 155)
(ii) „The following sentences illustrate clitic pronouns which cross-reference S. Note that in general a cross-referenced NP need not itself be present in the surface string." (Smith 1985: 102)
Note that the transitive verb also has the advantage over the prepositional verb *to agree with* that it can easily be used in the active or the passive:
(iii) The verb indexes the object. (Cf. The verb agrees with the object.)
(iv) The object is indexed on/by the verb. (Cf. ??The object is agreed with by the verb.)
(v) Indexed objects have freer word order than unindexed objects.
(Cf. ??Agreed-with objects have freer word order than unagreed-with objects.)
6 The term *index* is of course used in other ways, e.g. for referential indices (e.g. Chomsky 1980) or quotative indexes (Güldemann 2008). Context should generally make it clear which sense is intended, so the longer forms *argument index* or *person index* can generally be abbreviated to *index*. Note that the plural form is *indexes*, not *indices* (cf. Lazard 1998: 6). (And quite recently, the term "indexing" has been used in a rather different new typological sense by Evans & Fenwick to appear).

3 Index-sets

If one thinks of bound person forms in terms of the person suffixes of the older and conservative Indo-European languages, one may be inclined to think of them as a single set, and to say that the verb marks person and number in the same way as it marks tense, mood and voice.[7]

In fact, however, person and number are not categories of the verb properly speaking, but categories of the verb's argument(s), and since a verb may have more than one argument, it may have more than one person form attached to it, or (putting it more abstractly) it may inflect for more than one person(-number) category. For example, in Yimas (Papua New Guinea), a verb may have up to three different person-number affixes:

(6) Uraŋ   k-mpu-ŋa-tkam-t.
     coconut(G6.SG) G6.SG.ABS-3PL.ERG-show-PERF-3DU.DAT
     'They showed them two the coconut.'   (Foley 1991: 208)

In other languages, the person-number affixes are not different for the different arguments but are only distinguished by their position, e.g. in Bantu languages such as Tswana:

(7) Kí-ló-χờ-fílè.
     1SG.SUBJ-3SG.G11.OBJ-2SG.OBJ-give
     'I've given it to you.'   (Creissels 2005: 63)

Here the subject and object indexes are different, but the theme and recipient suffixes are not different.

Thus, indexes are like nominals in that with different argument-classes they may have the same form, or different forms – this is analogous to subject and object nominals having different forms (nominative and accusative markers, adpositions) or the same form, distinguished only by linear order or context.

The different forms of nominals are usually called **case** forms. For indexes that have different forms for different argument-classes, this terminology is not normally used, but no other established terminology exists. I propose to call such different forms of indexes simply **index-sets**. The "set" terminology is familiar

---

[7] Cf. quotations such as the following from an influential grammar of German: „Eine Kategorie des Verbs ist die der Person (im grammatischen Sinne). Sie ist in jeder konjugierten Form des Verbs enthalten. Es sind drei Personen zu unterscheiden..." (Helbig & Buscha 1988: § 1.3.3). The authors just say that person is „a category of the verb".

from Mayan linguistics, for example, where traditionally two index-sets are distinguished, Set A (ergative/possessive) and Set B (absolutive), e.g.

(8) Tzutujil (Mayan; Dayley 1985: 62–64)

		Set A	Set B
SG	1	nuu-/in-/w-	in-
	2	aa(w)-	at-
	3	r(uu)-	Ø
PL	1	q(aa)-	oq-
	2	ee(w)-	ix-
	3	k(ee)-	ee-

One might alternatively extend the term *case* to index-sets, so we could say that a subject index bears nominative case, or that an object index bears accusative case. This has been done occasionally (e.g. Wichmann 2009 for Tlapanec), but it does not seem advisable as a general solution, because this would lead to very odd consequences (e.g. saying that 3rd singlar -*s* in English verbs bears nominative case). Other reasons why *case* is rarely used for indexes are (i) that most languages with different index-sets do not have case-marking on nouns at all, and (ii) that indexes of different index-sets are rarely segmentable into "index stems" and "index-set markers".

But it is important to recognize that index-sets and cases/adpositions are functionally quite parallel and can make quite similar distinctions (see Kibrik 2012). Thus, it is not far-feteched to label them with similar labels, such as "nominative index-set", "accusative index-set", and so on (as was done in (6) above; see also Haspelmath 2009: 510). Moreover, different index-sets may be diachronically derived from pronouns inflected for different cases. For example, the French nominative, accusative and dative indexes in (9) are derived from the Latin nominative, accusative and dative cases, respectively.

(9)

	Nominative	Accusative	Dative
1SG	je	me	
2SG	tu	te	
3SG.M	il	le	lui
3SG.F	elle	la	lui

In the terminology proposed here, one would not call these index-sets cases because the term case is reserved for nominals, and the person forms in (9) are bound forms and not independent personal pronouns (i.e. indexes and not nominals; Miller 1992 regards them as affixes). But since diachronically they derive from independent personal pronouns, it would of course not be completely wrong to talk about them in this way.

4 Conominating bound person forms

4.1 Conominals

Argument indexes can cooccur, in the same narrow clause, with nominals that have the same role and reference. We saw examples of such nominals above in (1)–(2). More examples are in (10)–(11), with the index alone in the (a) examples and the index together with the nominal in the (b) examples.

(10) Jaminjung (Mirndi; Schultze-Berndt 2000: 154)

    a. *Gan-angu warrag.*
       3SG>3SG-handle catfish
       '(S)he caught a catfish.'

    b. *Nalyarri-ni gan-angu warrag.*
       Nalyarri-ERG 3SG>3SG-handle catfish
       'Nalyarri caught a catfish.'

(11) Latin/Italian

    a. *Veni-t*   *Vien-e*
       come.PRS-3SG   come.PRS-3SG
       'he comes'

    b. *Marcus veni-t*   *Marco vien-e*
       Marcus come.PRS-3SG   Marco come.PRS-3SG
       'Marcus/Marco comes'

I propose to call such a nominal a **conominal**. In addition, it is useful to have a verb expressing the presence of a conominal of an index: We can say that an index is **conominated** when a coreferential nominal in the same clause is present. An index may be conominated by a full nominal (as in 10–11) or by a free pronoun (as in 1).[8]

---

[8] Note that conominals only seem to occur with person indexes, not with independent personal pronouns (see Universal A in Appendix A). Croft (2001: 198, 2003: 16) and Siewierska (2004: §2.1.2.3) cite examples of conominated non-bound pronouns, but I believe that these person forms are actually bound forms. There is no space here to justify this claim.

By saying that the conominal must be in the same narrow clause, I am excluding dislocated nominals, as in (12) from French.

(12) Ma grande-mère, elle=l'=aimait,   mon grand-père.
      my grandmother 3SG.F.NOM=3SG.M.ACC=loved   my grandfather
      'My grandmother, she loved him, my grandfather.'

Here the nominals *ma grande-mère* and *mon grand-père* are not conominals, but dislocated nominals that are outside the narrow clause, detached from it by an intonation break. Sentence (12) from French is thus similar to its English translation, where the dislocated nominals cooccur with free pronouns.

Now crucially, not all indexes can be conominated (i.e. cooccur with conominals) to the same extent. Broadly speaking, we can distinguish three different situations: A conominal may be **obligatory** (section 4.2), it may be **optional** (section 4.3), or it may be **impossible** (section 4.4) (cf. Siewierska 1999, Hengeveld 2012: Table 1).

4.2 Indexes with obligatory conominal: gramm-indexes

When the conominal is obligatory, the index tends to be highly grammaticalized and is usually called *(grammatical) agreement marker*. A possible short label for an index of this kind is therefore **gramm-index**. Well-known examples of gramm-indexes are the subject indexes in German and Russian, and also the 3rd person singular index *-s* in English. For 3rd person gramm-indexes, the conominal (agreement controller) can be a full nominal or a free pronoun, while for deictic-person gramm-indexes, it must be a free pronoun.

(13) a. German

         ich komm-e 'I come'   (*komme)
         du komm-st 'you come'   (*kommst)
         sie komm-t 'she comes'   (*kommt)
         Elli komm-t 'Elli comes'

      b. English

         she come-s   (*come-s)
         Mary come-s

Gramm-indexes are very rare in the world's languages (cf. observation 3c),⁹ but since they occur prominently in the well-known European languages German and Russian (and marginally also in the even better-known language English), they have been very influential for the way linguists have been thinking about indexes in general. Gramm-indexing can be regarded as a canonical form of agreement, and indeed the term *agreement* or *concord* has been used since the 16th century for the relationship between the pronoun and the person marker in languages like German and English.¹⁰ But (grammatical) agreement is not a suitable concept for the next two cases (as discussed in section 9).

4.3 Indexes with optional conominal: cross-indexes

When the conominal is optional, indexing is often referred to as *cross-referencing*.¹¹ A convenient short label for an index of this kind is therefore **cross-index**, and instead of cross-referencing, we can also say *cross-indexing*. We saw cross-indexes in (1–2) and (10–11) above, where the index was conominated in (a) but not conominated in (b). In fact, most of the examples of indexes in this article are cross-indexes, as cross-indexes seem to be the most frequent kind of verbal index in the world's languages. Siewierska (1999) reports that among object indexes, gramm-indexes do not occur at all.

Siewierska uses the term *ambiguous agreement marker* for cross-indexes, but as this is based on a dual-nature view of cross-indexes for which there is no evidence (see section 5.3 below), this is not a good term. Kibrik (2011: 96) uses the term *tenacious pronoun* for cross-indexes, as opposed to *alternating pronoun* for

---

9 It seems that they almost exclusively occur with verbs, not with nouns, and quite marginally with adpositions (the only example I know of is Modern Welsh). The other two types of indexes occur widely with nouns and adpositions.
10 Palsgrave (1530) writes in the first grammar of the French language: "Adjectyves agre onely in gendre and nombre, but theyr verbes agre with theyr nominatyve cases in nombre and parsone." (OED, s.v. *agree*)
11 It seems that this term goes back to Bloomfield (1933: § 12.9, p. 193–194) (see also Hockett 1958: § 25.5, p. 217–218). Bloomfield and Hockett did not adopt the German and English situation as a model for their primary distinctions, and did not simply subsume indexing/cross-referencing under agreement (which is another example of the limited influence of Eurocentrism on the thinking of American structuralists). Cross-reference is described by Bloomfield as involving an "actual mention" of the participant "in the shape of a substitute-form, resembling our pronouns" (= an index), which are "in cross-reference with a substantive expression that makes specific mention" of the participant (= a conominal). Examples are Latin *puella canta-t* '(the) girl she-sings', and non-standard English *John his knife*, as well as Cree forms with "substitutive (pronominal) mention of both an actor and an undergoer".

person forms that cannot cooccur with conominals (pro-indexes, as seen in the next subsection).

4.4 Indexes with impossible conominal: pro-indexes

When a conominal is impossible, the index stands "instead of" a nominal and in this sense is truly "pro-nominal". A possible short label for an index of this kind is therefore **pro-index**.[12] Like free pronouns, pro-indexes occur in complementary distribution with full nominals, and they cannot be conominated by free pronouns either. In the (a) examples in (14)–(15), we see a full nominal, which alternates with a pro-index in the (b) examples.

(14) Oko (Benue-Congo, Nigeria; Atoyebi 2010: 87, 187)

    a. *Àde cìna óbín.*
        Ade become king
        'Ade has become a king.'

    b. *È-cìna óbín.*   (*Àde ècìna óbín)
        3SG.SUBJ-become king
        'He has become a king.'

(15) Standard Arabic

    a. *Ra'ay-tu l-kalb-a.*
        see.PRF-1SG.SUBJ DEF-dog-ACC
        'I saw the dog.'

    b. *Ra'ay-tu-hu.*   (*Ra'aytuhu lkalba)
        see.PRF-1SG.SUBJ-3SG.M.OBJ
        'I saw it.'

Since full nominals have to be dislocated in standard French (cf. example 12 above), the subject and object indexes in French are pro-indexes, too (though in the colloquial language, they increasingly come to resemble cross-indexes, cf. section 6).

---

[12] Since pro-indexes are closer to cross-indexes than to gramm-indexes, it may be useful to have a cover term for pro-indexes and cross-indexes. One could use **solo-index** for such indexes that can occur alone without a conominal. By contrast, indexes that can occur together with a conominal can be called **con-indexes** (i.e. conominatable indexes, a cover term for gramm-indexes and cross-indexes).

Siewierska (1999, 2004: 126) uses the term *anaphoric agreement marker* for pro-indexes, but as noted by Hengeveld (2012: n. 4), *anaphoric* is not appropriate for locuphoric person forms, and agreement is not involved either (cf. section 9).

5 Four ways of conceptualizing bound person forms

Now that I have laid out my favoured way of thinking about person indexes and talking about them, let us look at four ways in which the relevant phenomena have been conceptualized in the literature. Especially the most common type of indexing (cross-indexing) has been treated quite differently by linguists, even though the facts are undisputed.

The first three ways of conceptualizing bound person forms (i.e. indexes) have in common that they try to reduce all of them to the concepts of "pronoun" and "agreement" in one way or another. On the virtual-agreement view (section 5.1), cross-indexes are treated as if they were gramm-indexes (agreement). On the bound-argument view (section 5.2), they are treated as if they were pro-indexes (pronouns). On the dual-nature view (section 5.3), they are treated as if they were both, depending on the circumstances. The fourth view, which I will endorse here, treats indexes as a phenomenon sui generis, and thus does not try to subsume cross-indexing under either of the two less common types (agreement and pronouns).

5.1 The virtual-agreement view

In the virtual-agreement view, indexes are uniformly regarded as agreement markers, even when there is no conominal. In such situations, this approach claims that there is a virtual controller, which is not pronounced, but is still present in some way. Thus, Caesar's *veni, vidi, vici* 'I came, I saw, I conquered' is represented as in (16). The empty pronoun, not the index, is the subject argument of the verb that controls its agreement.

(16)   [ ]$_{PRO,1SG}$ *ven-i*, [ ]$_{PRO,1SG}$ *vid-i*, [ ]$_{PRO,1SG}$ *vic-i*

This approach has been adopted implicitly by many linguists over the last two centuries, and explicitly especially by most generative grammarians (at least before Jelinek (1984) and Baker (1996), but also after these publications). In generative grammar, argument indexing with no conominal as in (16) is said to involve "pro-drop" (since Chomsky 1981) or "null subjects" (if the cross-indexing is restricted to subject indexing, as in most Romance languages; Rizzi 1982).

The problem with this approach is that it is abstract and Eurocentric. It assumes an inaudible virtual agreement controller that is justified only by the analogy with 3rd person indexes that are often conominated by full nominals giving more descriptive information about the referent than the index. In sentences like (11b) (Latin: *Marcus venit* 'Marcus comes'), one may want to say that the subject is expressed only by the nominal *Marcus*, perhaps invoking a principle of uniqueness that does not allow an argument to be expressed twice. If one does this, one is then forced to assume an abstract zero pronoun for the case of (11a) (*venit* 'he comes'), too.

It is very likely that this degree of abstractness was widely accepted only because of the influence of well-known European languages like German, English and (somewhat less clearly) Russian,[13] which have gramm-indexing of the subject on the verb, where the conominal is obligatory (Dryer 2005: 411). From the perspective of these languages, it looks as if something is missing in unconominated cross-indexing patterns, so the notion of "pro-drop" may seem natural. However, we now know that the great majority of languages with bound person forms do not require a conominal (observation 3c),[14] so if the possibility of conomination is recognized as normal, then the virtual-agreement view loses its attractiveness.

Moreover, in a number of languages, argument indexes make more person and number distinctions than independent personal pronouns. In these languages, the virtual-agreement view is particularly inappropriate (see Mithun 2013, in this volume, on Mohawk).

5.2 The bound-argument view

In the bound-argument view, cross-indexes are regarded as something radically different from gramm-indexes. While the latter are agreement markers, cross-indexes are nominal-like participants, pronouns of some sort, that happen to be bound. When a cross-index coccurs with a conominal, it is still the index that is the argument of the verb, while the conominal is characterized vaguely as having "appositive" or "adjunct" status.

---

[13] For conomination in Russian, see Kibrik (2013) in this volume.
[14] Matthew Dryer (p.c.) informs me that in his database, only 26 languages (about 3% of the entire set of languages in the database) have subject affixes but require conominating pronouns. Of these, 10 are European languages.

This approach has been explicitly proposed in generative grammar by Jelinek (1984) and Baker (1996), but it has been favoured much more widely. In fact, it is well-known that it goes back to Boas (1911) or even earlier.

The problem with this approach is that it is quite unclear what it means that the conominals are not arguments. Authors typically hedge on this matter and rarely say precisely what they mean by "adjunct" or "apposition". Often they say that the bound person forms are the "true arguments" of the verb (as if the conominals were also arguments of some kind, "pseudo-arguments"). Sometimes proponents of the bound-argument view claim that certain properties typical of arguments are lacking in the conominals in cross-indexing constructions, so that in these constructions we observe free word order, discontinuous constituents, and no flagging of the conominals. These latter claims are particularly characteristic of the so-called Pronominal Argument Hypothesis (cf. Jelinek 1984, and Baker 2001 for a good overview). However, the claims of this hypothesis have been disconfirmed rather thoroughly (e.g. Austin & Bresnan 1996, LeSourd 2006). Cross-indexing is more widespread than suspected by Jelinek and is found also in many languages that are not like Warlpiri, and free word order is not dependent on cross-indexing. Siewierska (2001) discusses the potential "apposition" status of cross-indexed conominals in great detail and finds no support for the claim that they systematically behave in a special way.

Thus, in many or most languages with cross-indexing, the conominals are indistinguishable from nominal arguments of languages without cross-indexing, and it seems ill-advised to say that they are not arguments.

5.3 The dual-nature view

In the dual-nature view, cross-indexes are regarded as being both agreement markers and pronouns (nominal-like participants) depending on the circumstances: When a conominal is present, they are agreement markers, and when no conominal is present, they are pronouns.

This approach has been adopted by Bresnan & Mchombo (1987) and by Van Valin & LaPolla (1997), Van Valin (2005).[15] Siewierska (1999), (2004) adopts the term "ambiguous agreement" for cross-indexing, explicitly under the influence of Bresnan & Mchombo (1987).

---

[15] This view has an ancient pedigree as well. Paul (1920: § 217, p. 311) writes about a „zweifache Funktion" (dual function) of the suffixed pronoun in Latin: „In einigen Fällen dient es noch als Subjekt (lat. *lego, legi*), in anderen zeigt es nur durch die Kongruenz die Beziehung auf das Subjekt (*pater legit, ego scribo*)."

The problem with this approach is that no independent evidence is normally adduced in favour of the dual nature of cross-indexes. Rather, the dual nature of the forms seems to be imposed exclusively from outside, by linguists who start out with a concept of agreement and a concept of pronoun and who try to accommodate the phenomenon of cross-indexing in this conceptual framework. But cross-indexing is an extremely common and robust phenomenon in the world's languages, so if a conceptual framework is available that does not force a dual nature on these elements, it would be preferable. The virtual-agreement view and the bound-argument view attribute a single nature to cross-indexes, but we saw that they have their own serious problems. In the next subsection, we will see an approach that avoids all of these problems.

5.4 The double-expression view

In the double-expression view, cross-indexes are regarded neither as agreement markers nor as pronouns, but as elements providing person information that are compatible with further information in the same clause provided by conominals. In other words, they are regarded as phenomena sui generis, not as special cases of something else. This is the simplest view: We simply say that in a clause like Latin *venit* 'he comes', the index *-t* is the verb's subject argument (providing the information that the argument is a 3rd person referent available in the context), while in a clause like *Marcus venit* 'Marcus comes', the index and its conominal jointly constitute the subject argument. Thus, arguments may be doubly expressed in this view, which is clearly articulated in Kibrik (2011) and Schultze-Berndt (2011) (see also Steele 1989, Dixon 2010: 40).

The only possible disadvantage of this approach is that it goes against the expectation that arguments should not be expressed twice, but only by a single element. But there is no reason why this expectation should be made absolute. Uniqueness of argument expression has sometimes been elevated to a theoretical principle, but the primary motivation of this principle has been to exclude the possibility of different referential expressions expressing the same argument, not to exclude combined and distributed referential expressions such as index + conominal combinations. In general, distributed expression of meaning is not unusual in languages (observation 3d).

6 The continuum between gramm-indexes, cross-indexes and pro-indexes

Using the simple criteria of obligatoriness and possibility of a conominal, we can identify many indexes clearly as gramm-indexes, cross-indexes or pro-indexes. But there are also many cases where this criterion does not give clear results. As Corbett (2006: 100) notes, "most of the intervening territory [between the extreme cases of canonical agreement and pronominal affixes] can be filled". This has been noted by Siewierska (1999) and emphasized by Siewierska & Bakker (2005), and it will be briefly illustrated in this section. The continuum-like nature of the three subtypes of indexing is the primary justification for giving a single name (indexing) to all of them. In the following subsections, I will briefly illustrate the "intervening territory" between the three cardinal types.

6.1 Between cross-indexing and pro-indexing

As noted by Siewierska (1999), the complementarity between index and conominal may depend on a variety of factors, e.g. on the contrast between independent pronoun and full nominal, as in Welsh, where the subject index looks like a cross-index in (17a–b) but like a pro-index in (17c–d).

(17) Welsh (cited after Siewierska 1999: 228–229)

    a. *Gwel-sant   y   ferch.*
       see-3PL.PST the girl
       'They saw the girl.'

    b. *Gwel-sant hwy y   ferch.*
       see-3PL.PST they the girl
       'They saw the girl.'

    c. **Gwel-sant y   bechgyn y   ferch.*
       see-3PL.PST the boys   the girl
       'The boys saw the girl.'

    d. *Gwel-odd   y   bechgyn y   ferch.*
       see-PST   the boys   the girl
       'The boys saw the girl.'

In Yagua, the possibility of a conominal depends on word order. In (18a–b) the index looks like a cross-index, but in (18c) it looks like a pro-index.

(18) Yagua (Peru; Payne 1990: 30)

    a. *Sa-juuy.*
       3SG-fall
       'She falls.'

    b. *Sa-juuy Anita.*   (*sa-*: cross-index)
       3SG-fall Anita
       'Anita falls.'

    c. *Anita juuy.*   (*sa-*: pro-index)
       'Anita falls.'

But of course the indexes are the same in each case. These languages require more complex statements to characterize them typologically than the simple distinction between cross-indexing and pro-indexing.

6.2 Between cross-indexing and gramm-indexing

Like the presence of the index, the presence of the conominal may depend on a variety of factors. In several Swiss German dialects, for instance, the second person singular pronoun is obligatory in preverbal position, but it is optional (and usually absent) when it would come in postverbal position, as in questions:

(19) Zurich German

    a. *Du gaasch.*   (**Gaasch*)
       you go.2SG
       'You are going.'

    b. *Woane gaasch?*
       whither go.2SG
       'Where are you going?'

Thus, in (19a) the 2SG suffix *-sch* looks like a gramm-index, while in (19b) it looks like a cross-index.

Moreover, conominating pronouns may not be simply obligatory or optional (and rarely present), but they may be more or less frequent in closely related languages or different stages of a language. For example, for Brazilian Portuguese of the last 150 years, Duarte (2000) cites the data in Figure 1, where we see that the frequency of conominating pronouns as a percentage of their total potential presence rose quite gradually. It is difficult to say where the cross-indexing ends and the gramm-indexing begins.

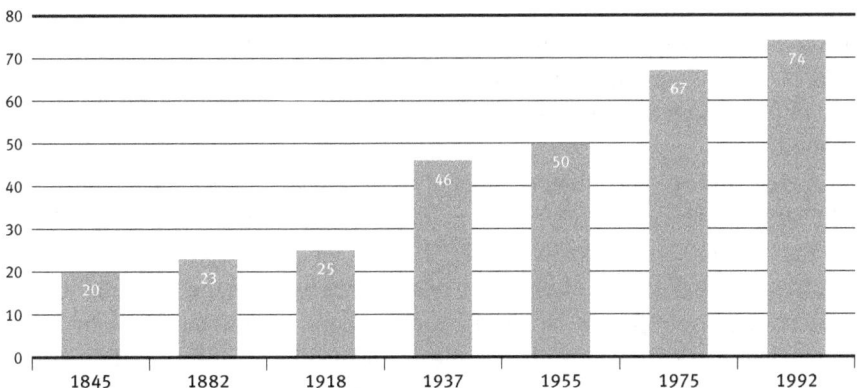

Figure 1. Lexical subject pronouns in Brazilian Portuguese theatre plays (Duarte 2000, cited after Kaiser 2009)

Or consider the Slavic languages, where generally Russian is regarded as a gramm-indexing language and the others are regarded as cross-indexing, but the data in Table 1 show that different languages show different frequencies, and conominating pronouns are far from obligatory in Russian (see also Kibrik 2013, in this volume).

Table 1. Conominating subject pronouns in various Slavic languages (Seo 2001, cited after Corbett 2006: 106)

	no pronoun	pronoun	% pronoun
Russian	443	1557	77.9%
Bulgarian	1556	444	22.2%
Serbo-Croatian	1683	317	15.9%
Czech	1829	171	8.6%
Polish	1859	141	7.1%

7 Coding syntactic relationships: the non-symmetry of "dependent marking" and "head marking"

The conceptualization of argument indexes is also relevant to the well-known head vs. dependent marking distinction. Here I will briefly point out that in the light of the argument-indexing perspective, this typological contrast looks somewhat different.

A view that one encounters commonly, especially after Nichols's (1986) influential article on head and dependent marking (but see already Lehmann 1983), is that the two marking loci are symmetrical, in the sense that both loci can perform the same function, that of marking the relationship between the head and the dependent, more specifically the role of the dependent. In head marking, the marking element marks the dependent's role on the head and references the dependent (by reflecting its person, number and/or gender features), while in dependent marking, the marking element occurs directly on the dependent. Both head and dependent marking may include role information, as we saw in section 3.

Schematically, this can be shown as in (20)–(21), which are schematic renderings of a sentence such as 'The mother helped the sons'.

(20) head marking
mother(F.SG) – 3SG.F.NOM-help-3PL.M.ACC – sons(M.PL)

(21) dependent marking
mother-NOM – help – sons-ACC

But crucially, this symmetry exists only for full nominal dependents. When the arguments are person forms (as in the majority of cases in most types of discourse), a language with a dependent-marking construction of the type (21) usually still shows dependent marking, as schematized in (22) below. But a language with a head-marking construction as in (20) normally shows the corresponding pattern in (23), where we cannot say that the arguments are "marked" by marking elements on the verb – the marking elements themselves ARE the arguments.

(22) dependent marking
she-NOM – help – them-ACC

(23) "head marking"
3SG.F.NOM-help-3PL.M.ACC

Maintaining that the contrast in (22)–(23) is of the same general type as the contrast in (20)–(21) thus presupposes that the virtual-agreement view is adopted, as is made explicit by Nichols (1992: 59).[16] This leads to curious formulations, such as Nichols's statement that in Indo-European languages, verbal person marking "indexes certain features of one word on another" (1992: 48), as in Latin *am-o* 'I love', *ama-s* 'you love', etc. But in these examples, there is just one word, so saying that Latin *-o* indexes features of a word on another word makes sense only if one assumes an abstract analysis with an empty free pronoun whose features are indexed on the verb (as in section 5.1 above). But as we saw earlier, such empty free pronouns are primarily motivated by a Eurocentric perspective.

Thus, "head-marking" is a problematic concept that cannot be used instead of indexing to avoid the problems associated with the distinctions between gramm-indexing, cross-indexing and pro-indexing (cf. Witzlack-Makarevich 2011). As formulated by Nichols (1986, 1992), the head/dependent marking distinction is too broad anyway, as head-marking encompasses not only person marking on the head, but also construct marking on the head, and dependent-marking also includes gender and number agreement of modifiers (as in Italian *nuovo libro* 'new book' (masculine) vs. *nuova casa* 'new house' (feminine)) (see also Croft 2001: section 5.4.1 for critical comments on the head/dependent marking distinction).

Of course, the contrast between (21)/(22) and (20)/(23) is a striking one, but it is probably best characterized by simply saying that the languages with (21)/(22) rely on **argument flagging** (case or adpositional marking), while languages with (20)/(23) rely on **argument indexing**.

8 A coherent concept of pronoun

Bound person forms (or indexes) are often called "bound pronouns" (Kibrik 2011: 92–104), "pronominal affixes" (e.g. Mithun 2003, Corbett 2006: 99–112), "incorporated pronouns" (e.g. Jones 1911, Bresnan & Mchombo 1987) or simply "pronouns".[17]

---

[16] "Languages with rich verbal agreement generally omit independent overt pronouns except in emphatic or contrastive contexts (i.e., these are pro-drop languages)."

[17] Especially in the widely used (but rather odd) term "pronominal argument language/hypothesis" (Jelinek 1984), the term "pronoun/pronominal" is clearly used in the sense of '*bound* person form'. Nobody has ever suggested that free pronouns play a role in this context, so a term such as "index-argument language/hypothesis" would be much more appropriate.

Of course, bound person forms share salient properties with free personal pronouns, especially the translation into languages like German and English, which employ the same forms for contrastive and non-contrastive use. But calling them "pronouns" leads us to an incoherent notion of "pronoun". Note that originally, the term *pronoun* was used for free forms that can *constitute a referential phrase on their own without a noun*, or in other words, occur instead of a noun in a referential phrase.[18] Thus, the forms in the right-hand column in (24) are pronouns, as opposed to the modifier (or determiner) forms in the left-hand column.

(24)

	modifier	pronoun
demonstrative	*this*	*this one*
possessive	*my, your, ...*	*mine, yours, ...*
interrogative	*which*	*which one, what, who*
anaphoric	*the*	*he/she/it*
deictic		*I/you/we*

In older grammars, one often reads about possessive adjectives *my, your*, etc., contrasting with possessive pronouns *mine, yours*, etc.

This use of the term "pronoun" may not be highly salient anymore, but it has not disappeared, so we still talk about "personal pronouns", because there are also other kinds of pronouns. But since personal pronouns are the most frequent type of pronoun in languages like German and English, it is easy to forget that there are non-personal pronouns, and to use "pronoun" in a narrower sense to refer just to personal pronouns. From there it is a small step to extending the use of "pronoun" to person forms which are not free forms (i.e. to pro-indexes), and next to person forms which do not stand instead of nouns, but cooccur with them as conominals (i.e. to cross-indexes). This type of semantic change of a grammatical term is not unusual: Grammatical terms originally denoting a formal category are commonly changed to denote semantic categories (cf. Lehmann 2007).

Semantic change is a fact of life and is not too damaging in everyday speech, but in technical scholarly discourse, ambiguity must be avoided if we want to be taken seriously as scientists. Either one uses "pronoun" only in the sense "person

---

18 Lyons (1977: 637) notes that if taken etymologically, pro-*nouns* should always substitute for *nouns*, though in fact they mostly stand in positions of nominals. However, since every noun can serve as a nominal, I do not find the distinction so significant. Moreover, Lyons thinks that the „substitution" metaphor implies that the anaphoric function of pronouns is more basic than the deictic function, whereas the opposite is the case. However, if we just say that a pronoun stands in a position in which a noun could occur, this applies equally to deictic and anaphoric nouns and nominals.

form", or only in the sense "noun substitute". Since the former is the innovative use and the alternative term *person form* is readily available and well-established (cf. Siewierska 2004), it seems best to restrict *pronoun* to the sense of "noun substitute".

9 A coherent concept of agreement

Agreement can be defined as "the phenomenon by which a word carries morphological features that originate somewhere else" (Bickel & Nichols 2007), i.e. a situation in which a target form has grammatical marking that is controlled by another element. The most typical situation of agreement is gender agreement, as in Italian *il nuov-o libro* [the.M new-M book(M)] vs. *la nuov-a casa* [the.F new-F house(F)].

However, in cross-indexing constructions, there is usually no "other element" that could be said to control the person feature of the verb. In the majority of actual cases, the person form on its own suffices to express the argument, and it is only in a minority of cases that we find a conominal. Linguists who still want to view this situation in terms of agreement have resorted to one of two strategies:

(i) Some have said that there is a controller in the clause after all, but it is not pronounced (this is the virtual-agreement view that we saw in section 5.1 above);

(ii) Others have said that there is a controller, but it does not occur in the same clause: Just as independent personal pronouns often agree (in number and gender) with an antecedent in a preceding clause, cross-indexes can be said to agree with an earlier antecedent (Corbett 2006: 21–23, 110–111).

The problem with the latter view is that while independent personal pronouns do indeed show gender and number agreement in many cases, they never show *person agreement* (see observation 3b above). Deictic forms like *I* and *you* refer to speech-act participants directly and never show person agreement, i.e. the second occurrence of *I* in an expression like *I think that I must go* refers to the same entity independently, rather than agreeing with the first *I* (cf. Lehmann 1982: 211). For allophoric forms like *she* and *he*, a description in terms of person agreement (agreement with an antecedent full nominal that has a third person feature) might seem more promising, but it does not work well for such forms either. First, third person forms can often be used without any overt antecedent that could control agreement (as in *Who is he?*, pointing to a person). Second, it is not clear that full nominals need to have a third person feature (after all, they can normally be used with other persons as well, as in *I, Claudius*, or *you idiot*).

With English independent pronouns, cooccurrence of deictic person forms and full nominals is possible only in appositional constructions, but in cross-indexing constructions, it is quite common for languages to allow full nominals to conominate deictic person forms, as in (25)–(27) (Mithun 1985 referred to such cases as showing "disagreement").

(25) Spanish (Moravcsik 1978: 351, cf. also Jelinek 1984: 48)

La gente de aquí no comemos eso.
'We people from here don't eat that.'

(26) Lai (Chin, Tibeto-Burman, Bickel 2000: 587)

Tsó:npiaktu: ni? làw ka-thlo? vé:.
teacher   ERG field 1SG.A-work even
'Even as a teacher I can work in the field.'

(27) Georgian (Boeder 2002: 88)

Did-i   tevz-i   mo-m-it'an-a   babua-m   Tamaz-s.
big-NOM fish-NOM PREV-1SG.OBJ-carry-3SG.SUBJ grandfather-ERG Tamaz-DAT
'Grandfather brought me, Tamaz, a big fish.'

Moreover, many languages allow nonsingular indexes to occur with singular conominals to express an inclusory construction, as in example (28). Here the verb *rlini* 'go' has the cross-indexing 1st person dual prefix *rnirri-*, which is conominated by the singular noun 'man'.

(28) Marra (Heath 1981: 302)

Rna-na   gariyi-marr   rnirri-rlini.
M.SG-ART.NOM man(NOM)-NON.PL 1DU.EX-go.PST.CONT
'The man and I went.'

One could try to subsume all these cases under agreement in some way, but I am not aware of a definition of agreement that characterizes this notion as comprising a coherent set of phenomena and that includes (25)–(28). Lehmann's (1982: 203) definition of agreement excludes them, as noted explicitly by Lehmann (1982: 218). (Corbett's (2006) "canonical agreement" is explicitly intended only to account for the least controversial cases of agreement, i.e. it does not attempt to define a coherent concept of agreement.)

Thus, since there is no coherent concept of agreement that would comprise the most widespread cases of bound person forms (cross-indexes), reference to "(person) agreement" is not necessarily helpful when discussing bound person forms.

10 Conclusion

By shifting the attention from "pronouns" to **person forms** in her 2004 book and related work, Anna Siewierska has drawn attention to the striking similarities between all kinds of person forms, whether they are bound or free, and whether they are noun substitutes (pronouns) or may/must cooccur with conominals. Here I have focused on bound person forms, which are conveniently called person indexes, and I have argued that one should not try to conceptualize person indexes uniformly as either "pronouns" of a special kind or as "agreement markers" of a special kind. As shown by Siewierska, bound person markers are most commonly cross-indexes (optionally cooccurring with a conominal), and these are best regarded as phenomena sui generis. The model of some well-known (but quite unusual) European languages should not be imposed on the majority of the world's languages.

Acknowledgements

I am grateful to Matthew Dryer, Michael Cysouw, Dik Bakker, David Erschler, and Alena Witzlack-Makarevich for useful comments on an earlier version of this article. I also thank audiences in Zurich and Leipzig for discussing these issues with me. This article ultimately grew out of an e-mail discussion I had with Anna Siewierska after reading and reviewing her 2004 book *Person*, which inspired me to think in these directions. Thank you, Anna, for everything!

Abbreviations

1 first person, 2 second person, 3 third person, A agentive, ABS absolutive, ACC accusative, ART article, CONT continuative, DAT dative, DEF definite, DU dual, ERG ergative, EX exclusive, F feminine, G6 gender class 6, G11 gender class 11, IN inclusive, M masculine, N neuter, NOM nominative, OBJ object, PERF perfect, PL plural, PREV preverb, PRS present, PST past, SG singular, SUBJ subject.

Appendix A:
Some universals involving argument indexes

The following are hypothesized universals which I lack the space to justify here. The primary purpose of this list is to show that we need a comparative concept of *argument index*, without which the universals cannot be formulated.

A. Bound person forms (= indexes), but not independent personal pronouns, may occur with a conominal.

B. Bound pronouns always index arguments, never non-arguments (though of course not all arguments need to be indexed by bound pronouns).

C. If a language has both cross-indexes and independent pronouns, the independent pronouns cannot be used as bound variables (Siewierska 2004: 11).

D. The scale "gramm-index > cross-index > pro-index" is aligned with the scale "affix > clitic". In fact, gramm-indexes are always affixes (Siewierska 1999: 231).

E. Gramm-indexing is always with the A argument (agent of typical transitive verb) and with no other argument (Siewierska 1999: 238).

F. If a language cross-indexes the P argument, it also cross-indexes the A argument (Siewierska 1999: 238).

G. If in a language indexing is possible in some contexts but not in others, and if independent personal pronouns are obligatory in some contexts but optional in others, then they are obligatory when indexing is impossible.

H. In languages with index paradigms that do not make all person distinctions, obligatory conomination (= gramm-indexing) is more likely than in languages with fully distinctive index paradigms.

I. Bound person forms (= indexes), but not independent personal pronouns, may show syncretism of 1st person singular and 2nd person singular.

References

Aronoff, Mark & Kirsten Anne Fudeman. 2005. *What is morphology?* Malden, MA: Blackwell.
Atoyebi, Joseph Dele. 2010. *A reference grammar of Oko*. Cologne: Rüdiger Köppe Verlag.
Austin, Peter & Joan Bresnan. 1996. Non-configurationality in Australian Aboriginal languages. *Natural Language & Linguistic Theory* 14(2). 215–268.

Baker, Mark C. 1996. *The Polysynthesis Parameter*. New York: Oxford University Press.
Baker, Mark C. 2001. Configurationality and polysynthesis. In Martin Haspelmath, Ekkehard König, Wulf Oesterreicher & Wolfgang Raible (eds.), *Language typology and language universals*, vol. 2, 1433–1441. Berlin & New York: De Gruyter Mouton.
Bakker, Dik. 2005. Person marking on adpositions. In Martin Haspelmath, Matthew S. Dryer, David Gil, & Bernard Comrie (eds.), *The world atlas of language structures*, 198–201. Oxford: Oxford University Press.
Berchem, Jörg. 1991. *Referenzgrammatik des Somali*. Köln: Omimee.
Bickel, Balthasar & Johanna Nichols. 2007. Inflectional morphology. In Timothy Shopen (ed.), *Language typology and syntactic description*, vol. III: Grammatical categories and the lexicon, 169–240. Cambridge: Cambridge University Press.
Bickel, Balthasar. 2000. On the syntax of agreement in Tibeto-Burman. *Studies in Language* 24(3). 583–610.
Bloomfield, Leonard. 1933. *Language*. New York: H. Holt and Company.
Boas, Franz. 1911. Introduction. In Franz Boas (ed.), *Handbook of American Indian Languages*, 1–83. Washington, DC: Bureau of American Ethnology.
Boeder, Winfried. 2002. Syntax and morphology of polysynthesis in the Georgian verb. In Nicholas Evans & Hans-Jürgen Sasse (eds.), *Problems of polysynthesis*, 87–111. (Studia Typologica 4). Berlin: Akademie Verlag.
Bossong, Georg. 1998. Vers une typologie des indices actanciels: Les clitiques romans dans une perspective comparative. In Paolo Ramat & Elisa Roma (eds.), *Sintassi storica*, 9–43. Roma: Bulzoni.
Bresnan, Joan & Sam A. Mchombo. 1987. Topic, pronoun, and agreement in Chicheŵa. *Language*. 741–782.
Chomsky, Noam A. 1980. On binding. *Linguistic Inquiry* 11(1). 1–46.
Chomsky, Noam A. 1981. *Lectures on government and binding*. Dordrecht: Foris.
Corbett, Greville G. 2003. Agreement: the range of the phenomenon and the principles of the Surrey Database of Agreement. *Transactions of the Philological Society* 101(2). 155–202.
Corbett, Greville G. 2006. *Agreement*. Cambridge: Cambridge University Press.
Creissels, Denis. 2005. A typology of subject and object markers in African languages. In F. K. Erhard Voeltz (ed.), *Studies in African linguistic typology*, 43–70. Amsterdam: Benjamins.
Croft, William. 2001. *Radical construction grammar: syntactic theory in typological perspective*. Oxford: Oxford University Press.
Cysouw, Michael. 2003. *The paradigmatic structure of person marking*. Oxford: Oxford University Press.
Dahl, Östen. 2000. Egophoricity in discourse and syntax. *Functions of Language* 7(1). 37–77.
Dayley, Jon P. 1985. *Tzutujil grammar*. Berkeley: University of California Press.
Dixon, Robert M. W. 2010. *Basic linguistic theory, vol. 1: Methodology*. Oxford: Oxford University Press.
Donohue, Mark & Lila San Roque. 2004. *I'saka: a sketch grammar of a language of north-central New Guinea*. (Pacific Linguistics). Canberra: Australian National University.
Dryer, Matthew S. 2005. Expression of pronominal subjects. In Martin Haspelmath, Matthew S. Dryer, David Gil, & Bernard Comrie (eds.), *The world atlas of language structures*, 410–413. Oxford: Oxford University Press.
Duarte, Maria Eugênia Lamoglia. 2000. The loss of the 'avoid pronoun' principle in Brazilian Portuguese. In Mary A. Kato & Esmeralda Vailati Negrão (eds.), *Brazilian Portuguese and the Null Subject Parameter*, 17–36. Frankfurt am Main: Vervuert.

Dum-Tragut, Jasmine. 2009. *Armenian*. Amsterdam: John Benjamins.
Dumézil, Georges & Tevfik Esenç. 1975. *Le verbe oubykh: études descriptives et comparatives*. Paris: Klincksieck.
England, Nora C. 1983. *A Grammar of Mam, a Mayan Language*. Austin: University of Texas Press.
Evans, Nicholas & Eva Fenwick. To appear. Marking vs. indexing: revisiting the Nichols marking-locus typology. To appear in: Balthasar Bickel, Lenore A. Grenoble, David A. Peterson, & Alan Timberlake (eds.), What's where why? Language typology and historical contingency. A festschrift to honor Johanna Nichols. Amsterdam: Benjamins.
Evans, Nicholas, & Hans-Jürgen Sasse (eds.). 2002. *Problems of polysynthesis*. Berlin: Akademie Verlag.
Foley, William. 1991. *The Yimas language of New Guinea*. Stanford: Stanford University Press.
Güldemann, Tom. 2008. *Quotative indexes in African languages: a synchronic and diachronic survey*. Berlin & New York: De Gruyter Mouton.
Haspelmath, Martin. 2002. *Understanding Morphology*. London: Arnold.
Haspelmath, Martin. 2009. Terminology of case. In Andrej L. Malchukov & Andrew Spencer (eds.), *The Oxford handbook of case*, 505–517. Oxford: Oxford University Press.
Haspelmath, Martin. 2010. Comparative concepts and descriptive categories in cross-linguistic studies. *Language* 86(3). 663–687.
Haspelmath, Martin. 2011a. The indeterminacy of word segmentation and the nature of morphology and syntax. *Folia Linguistica* 45(2). 31–80.
Haspelmath, Martin. 2011b. The gradual coalescence into "words" in grammaticalization. In Heiko Narrog & Bernd Heine (eds.), *The Oxford handbook of grammaticalization*, 342–355. Oxford: Oxford University Press.
Helbig, Gerhard & Buscha, Joachim. 1988. *Deutsche Grammatik: ein Handbuch für den Ausländerunterricht*. Leipzig: Enzyklopädie.
Hengeveld, Kees. 2012. Referential markers and agreement markers in Functional Discourse Grammar. *Language Sciences* 34(4). 468–479.
Hockett, Charles F. 1958. *A course in modern linguistics*. New York: MacMillan.
Jelinek, Eloise. 1984. Empty categories and non-configurational languages. *Natural Language and Linguistic Theory* 2. 39–76.
Jones, William. 1911. Algonquian (Fox). In Franz Boas (ed.), *Handbook of American Indian languages* (Bureau of American Ethnology bulletin 40), part 1, 735–873. Washington, DC: Government Printing Office.
Kaiser, Georg A. 2009. Losing the null subject. A contrastive study of (Brazilian) Portuguese and (Medieval) French. In Georg A. Kaiser & Eva-Maria Remberger (eds.), *Proceedings of the Workshop on Null-subjects, expletives, and locatives in Romance*, 131–157. Konstanz: University of Konstanz. <http://inlist.uni-konstanz.de/pages/publ/arbeitspapiere.html>
Kibrik, Andrej A. 2011. *Reference in discourse*. Oxford: Oxford University Press.
Kibrik, Andrej A. 2012. What's in the head of head-marking languages, or is there case in head-marking languages? In Pirkko Suihkonen, Bernard Comrie & Valery Solovyev (eds.), *Argument structure and grammatical relations: a cross-linguistic typology*, 211–240. Amsterdam: Benjamins.
Kibrik, Andrej A. 2013. Peculiarities and origins of the Russian referential system. This volume.
Klaiman, M. H. 1988. Affectedness and control: a typology of voice systems. In Masayoshi Shibatani (ed.), *Passive and voice*, 25–83. Amsterdam: Benjamins.
Launey, Michel. 1994. *Une grammaire omniprédicative: Essai sur la morphosyntaxe du nahuatl classique*. CNRS Editions.

Lazard, Gilbert. 1994. *L'actance*. Paris: Presses universitaires de France.
Lazard, Gilbert. 1998. *Actancy*. Berlin & New York: De Gruyter Mouton.
Lehmann, Christian. 1982. Universal and typological aspects of agreement. In Hansjakob Seiler & Franz Josef Stachowiak (eds.), *Apprehension: Das sprachliche Erfassen von Gegenständen*, 201–267. Tübingen: Narr.
Lehmann, Christian. 1983. Rektion und syntaktische Relationen. *Folia Linguistica* 17(1–4). 339–378.
Lehmann, Christian. 2007. On the upgrading of grammatical concepts. In Fons Moerdijk, Ariane Santen & Rob Tempelaars (eds.), *Leven met woorden: Opstellen aangeboden aan Piet van Sterkenburg*, 409–422. Leiden: Brill.
LeSourd, Philip S. 2006. Problems for the pronominal argument hypothesis in Maliseet-Passamaquoddy. *Language* 82(3). 486–514.
Lichtenberk, František. 1997. Head-marking and objecthood. In Joan L. Bybee, John Haiman & Sandra A. Thompson (eds.), *Essays on language function and language type, dedicated to T. Givón*, 301–322. Amsterdam: Benjamins.
Lyons, John. 1977. *Semantics*. Cambridge: Cambridge University Press.
Malchukov, Andrej & Anna Siewierska (eds.). 2011. *Impersonal Constructions a cross-linguistic perspective*. Amsterdam: Benjamins.
Marácz, László & Pieter Muysken (eds.). 1989. *Configurationality: the typology of asymmetries*. Dordrecht: Foris.
Miller, Philip H. 1992. *Clitics and constituents in phrase structure grammar*. New York: Garland.
Mithun, Marianne. 1985. Disagreement: the case of pronominal affixes and nouns. *Georgetown University Round Table on Language and Linguistics* 1985. 50–66.
Mithun, Marianne. 1986. When zero isn't there. *Berkeley Linguistics Society* 12. 195–211.
Mithun, Marianne. 2003. Pronouns and agreement: the information status of pronominal affixes. *Transactions of the Philological Society* 101(2). 235–278.
Mithun, Marianne. 2013. Prosody and Independence: Free and Bound Person Marking. This volume.
Moravcsik, Edith A. 1978. Agreement. In Joseph H. Greenberg, Charles A. Ferguson & Edith A. Moravcsik (eds.), *Universals of human language*, vol. 4, 331–374. Stanford: Stanford University Press.
Newman, John. 1996. *Give: A cognitive linguistic study*. Berlin & New York: De Gruyter Mouton.
Nichols, Johanna. 1986. Head-marking and dependent-marking grammar. *Language* 66. 56–119.
Nichols, Johanna. 1992. *Linguistic diversity in space and time*. Chicago: University of Chicago Press.
Nikolaeva, Irina (ed.). 2007. *Finiteness: theoretical and empirical foundations*. Oxford: Oxford University Press.
Palsgrave, John. 1530. *L'esclarcissement de la langue francoyse*.
Paul, Hermann. 1920. *Prinzipien der Sprachgeschichte*. 5th ed. Halle: Max Niemeyer.
Payne, Doris L. 1990. *The pragmatics of word order: typological dimensions of verb initial languages*. Berlin & New York: De Gruyter Mouton.
Rizzi, Luigi. 1982. *Issues in Italian syntax*. Dordrecht: Foris.
Schultze-Berndt, Eva. 2000. Simple and Complex Verbs in Jaminjung: A Study of Event Categorization in an Australian Language. Ph.D. dissertation, Katholieke Universiteit Nijmegen.
Schultze-Berndt, Eva. 2011. Looking for the governor, or the problem of argument status in double-marking languages: A Construction Grammar perspective. Presentation at the conference Explorations in Syntactic Government and Subcategorisation, University of Cambridge, UK.

Seo, Seunghyun. 2001. *The frequency of null subject in Russian, Polish, Czech, Bulgarian and Serbo-Croatian: an analysis according to morphosyntactic environments*. Ph.D. dissertation, Indiana University.
Siewierska, Anna. 1998. Nominal and verbal person marking. *Linguistic Typology* 2. 1–53.
Siewierska, Anna. 1999. From anaphoric pronoun to grammatical agreement marker: why objects don't make it. *Folia Linguistica* 33(1–2). 225–252.
Siewierska, Anna. 2001. On the argument status of cross-referencing forms: some problems. *Revista Canaria de Estudios Ingleses* 42. 215–236.
Siewierska, Anna. 2004. *Person*. Cambridge: Cambridge University Press.
Siewierska, Anna & Dik Bakker. 2005. The agreement cross-reference continuum: person marking in Functional Grammar. In Casper de Groot & Kees Hengeveld (eds.) *Morphosyntactic expression in Functional Grammar*, 203–248. (Functional Grammar Series 27). Berlin & New York: De Gruyter Mouton.
Smith, Ian. 1985. The syntax of clitic cross-referencing pronouns in Kugu Nganhcara. *Anthropological Linguistics* 27(1). 102–111.
Steele, Susan. 1989. Subject values. *Language* 65(3). 537–578.
Terrill, Angela. 2003. *A Grammar of Lavukaleve*. (Mouton Grammar Library). Berlin & New York: De Gruyter Mouton.
Tesnière, Lucien. 1959. *Éléments de syntaxe structurale*. Paris: Klincksieck.
Van Valin, Robert D., Jr. & Randy J. LaPolla. 1997. *Syntax: structure, meaning, and function*. Cambridge: Cambridge University Press.
Van Valin, Robert D., Jr. 2005. *Exploring the syntax-semantics interface*. Cambridge: Cambridge University Press.
Wichmann, Søren. 2009. Case relations in a head-marking language: verb-marked cases in Tlapanec. In Andrej L. Malchukov & Andrew Spencer (eds.), *The Oxford Handbook of Case*, 797–807. Oxford: Oxford University Press.
Witzlack-Makarevich, Alena. 2011. *Typological variation in grammatical relations*. Leipzig: University of Leipzig dissertation.
Zwicky, Arnold M. & Geoffrey K. Pullum. 1983. Cliticization vs. inflection: English n't. *Language* 59(3). 502–513.

Andrej A. Kibrik
Peculiarities and origins of the Russian referential system[1]

1 Introduction

Reference to entities is performed in languages by two major types of expressions: full referential devices, such as proper names and common nouns (with or without modifiers), and reduced referential devices, such as pronouns (both free and bound) and zero forms. Most generally, reduced referential devices are employed when a referent in question is activated in the speaker's cognitive system (Kibrik 2011, inter alia). Reduced referential devices, particularly pronouns, are intimately interwoven with a language's grammar, so their properties are important to a language's general typological profile. In this article I limit my attention to the functions and use of reduced referential devices. The expression "reference to activated referents by means of reduced referential devices" is often abbreviated below to "reduced reference". The term "referential system" is taken to mean the system of reduced referential devices and the principles of their discourse use in a certain language. In this study I will only discuss referential devices in the subject position[2].

Compared to other European languages of the Indo-European language family, the East Slavic languages, and in particular Russian, have a very different referential system, with respect to the reduced reference in the subject position. In Russian, a free pronoun is most commonly used in this function, but in about one third of instances a free pronoun is missing and subject reference is performed only by the inflection on the verb (categories of person, number, and gender), functioning as bound pronouns. Furthermore, verbal inflection differs depending on tense. The Russian system has thus departed strongly from the original Slavic (and Indo-European) type, still largely preserved in West and South Slavic and many Romance languages, but has not quite reached the situation of Germanic

---

[1] This study was supported by grant #11-04-00153 from the Russian Foundation for the Humanities.
[2] As is well known (Keenan 1976, Van Valin 1993: 50–65, A. E. Kibrik 1997), the notion of "subject" is problematic and non-universal. However, in the context of this paper it is relatively straightforward, as I will only be discussing the grammatical phenomena of European languages. Probably each use of the term "subject" could be replaced with the more typologically valid term "Principal" (A. E. Kibrik 1997) referring to the cluster of semantic roles characteristic of languages inclined to accusative alignment.

where verb inflection has almost lost the capacity for independent reference and subject pronouns have become obligatory in most contexts. The East Slavic referential system is among the typologically most convoluted ones and a number of various diachronic factors may have led to its formation. In this article I describe the details of the East Slavic system, and inquire into the possible factors responsible for its development.

These factors fall into two main groups, internal and external. On the one hand, it appears that the East Slavic development is related to the restructuring of the past tenses in Old Russian: numerous old past tenses with person inflection were replaced by the new generalized past tense, former perfect, based on the participle in -*l* and a copular verb, and after the loss of the person-marked copulas subject personal pronouns were drafted as main carriers of referential function. On the other hand, the East Slavic system resembles the Germanic one, and it is unlikely that two similar and rather unusual systems, Germanic and East Slavic, emerged completely independently in geographical proximity. So external factors contributing to the formation of the Russian referential system must also be considered. The possibility and potential timing of Germanic influence upon East Slavic need to be explored, as well as alternative potential external influences, such as Turkic and Finno-Ugric.

This article is structured as follows. Section 2 presents the basics of the typology of referential systems. Section 3 formulates the main puzzle associated with the Russian referential system. Sections 4 and 5 provide a characterization of this system. Sections 6 and 7 consider internal and external factors, respectively, which are responsible for the formation of the Russian system. In section 8 I discuss possible counterarguments to the proposed treatment, and in section 9 I present conclusions and directions for further studies.

2 Referential systems world-wide and the Germanic system

The three basic types of reduced referential devices employed in languages are: free (including clitic) pronouns, bound (affixal) pronouns, and zero forms (Kibrik 2011). Let me begin with a simple example illustrating what is meant by reduced referential devices and a language's referential system. Table 1 shows simple clauses from several major and widely known languages, all meaning 'he plays' or 'he played'[3].

---

[3] I have to use various tenses for different languages because of certain idiosyncrasies associated with a language's referential system, such as the presence of third person singular inflection in English simple present, despite the fact that English is generally devoid of person inflection.

Table 1. Reduced referential devices in several of the world's major languages

Zero	Japanese	Ø *asonda*
Free pronoun	English	*he played*
Free pronoun ~ zero	Mandarin	*tā* ~ Ø *zà wánshuǎ ne*
Inflection (bound pronoun)	Latin	*lūd-it*
Bound pronoun	Spoken French	*i-žu* (written *il joue*)
Free pronoun plus inflection (agreement)	German	*er spiel-t*

Japanese uses the simplest system, regularly employing zero forms to mention activated referents. English is also relatively simple (but see fn. 3), systematically using free pronouns. Mandarin Chinese employs both free pronouns and zeroes in a certain discourse-based distribution that is not at issue here. Latin, as well as other conservative Indo-European languages, uses referential person inflection on the verb, or, in other words, bound pronouns (see Kibrik 2011: 210–213)[4]. Spoken French, having gone through a complex evolutionary path, has almost got rid of the old personal suffixal inflections but developed what can probably be considered new personal prefixal inflection (Kibrik 2011: 248–260). German displays the most complex system of all, relying primarily on free pronouns as carriers of the referential function, but still using the old Latin-style person inflection.

These facts alone suffice to demonstrate that the referential system, as understood in this article, is among the basic grammatical properties of a language. It has an important bearing upon many other grammatical features and domains, including:

- categories of person, number, gender
- use of finite and non-finite verb forms
- pronouns as a lexical class
- clause-internal syntax
- argumenthood
- syntax of complex sentences

Many languages of the world are quite consistent in using one of the above mentioned types of reduced devices. A general picture of the relative frequency of three kinds of such consistent languages can be obtained by composing the studies of Dryer (2011) and Siewierska (2011)[5]. This general picture is shown on Figure 1.

---

[4] Of course, Latin and other conservative Indo-European languages do use free subject pronouns, but only in special semantic or pragmatic circumstances, such as contrastiveness.
[5] See Kibrik (2011: 115–116) for details of this composing procedure.

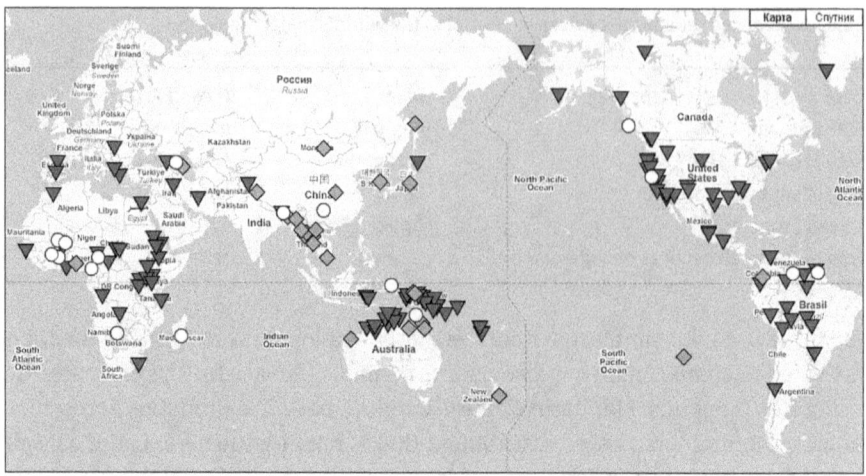

○ free pronoun languages, ▼ bound pronoun languages, ◇ zero reference languages

Figure 1. Referentially consistent languages, as derived from the studies Dryer 2011 and Siewierska 2011.

Languages using affixal pronouns in the subject position clearly dominate worldwide, zero reference prevails in one area (Southeast Asia), and free pronoun languages are scattered as a rather rare type in various parts of the world.

Many other languages, however, are internally inconsistent and display variation with respect to the use of reduced devices. (I discuss a typology of such inconstistencies, or sensitivities, in Kibrik 2011: Chapter 5). For example, a language may use a bound pronoun in the subject position and a free pronoun in the non-subject positions, or a zero form under particularly strong referent activation and a pronoun in the case of intermediate-level activation. Other languages are still more complex in simultaneously using more than one reduced referential device; an example is provided by the Germanic languages. The Germanic referential system, often conceived of as a typological point of departure, is in fact a rather complicated one.

As has already been mentioned above, the German system, illustrated in Table 1, uses two person forms at a time, on every single act of reduced subject reference: a free pronoun and a person inflection. Person inflection is less than fully referential, but still must be considered an ancillary referential device (Kibrik 2011: 221–228). This system is very much alive in German and is vestigially present in English. The rise of this system is generally attributed to the so-called verb-second (V2) pattern that spread at a certain point throughout the Germanic languages (see e.g. Faarlund 2001: 1708; Braunmüller 2005): independent pronouns "came to be used obligatorily to avoid declarative sentences with initial verbs" (Siewierska 2004: 272). Anna Siewierska proposed the term "syntactic agreement" to capture the peculiar character of this system of person inflection, not occurring without a free referential form. This system is "extremely well represented among the languages of Western Europe" (Siewierska 2004: 268), including a number of Germanic languages, French and Rhaeto-Romance (syntactic borrowing from Germanic, along with the verb-second pattern), and also Russian[6]. The reason why I discuss the Germanic system in some detail is exactly because of its similarity to Russian, see section 4 below.

Relying on her extensive sample-based study, Siewierska (2004) reported only a handful of languages with syntactic agreement outside of Europe, specifically in Oceania (three Austronesian and four non-Austronesian languages)[7]. The Germanic system thus must be judged a typological outlier, and it is no surprise that a number of Germanic languages, including Scandinavian and, largely, English, have eventually got rid of person inflection on the verb, thus joining or approaching the group of consistent free pronoun languages.

3 The Russian referential system: the conundrum

Old Slavic languages, including Old Church Slavonic and early Old Russian, used the same referential system as other conservative Indo-European languages, such as Latin: reduced subject reference is performed by means of person inflection. (An Old Church Slavonic example will be provided below in section 5.) Modern Slavic languages of the Western and Southern branches (such as Polish, Czech, Bulgarian, Serbian, etc.) have kept the system of subject reference[8] fundamentally intact, even though the material shape of the actual forms may have changed (a Polish example is provided in Table 2 below; on other Slavic languages see Kibrik 2011: 260–263).

In contrast, the Russian (and generally the East Slavic) referential system has departed from this conservative pattern strongly. Unlike Old Slavic, West Slavic, and South Slavic, East Slavic languages do use free subject pronouns extensively. They have also kept the fully-fledged system of verbal inflection (but modified it, see section 4). In a first approximation, the Russian system is similar to the

---

[6] Anna actually listed Russian among West European languages. No matter whether that was intentional or accidental, it is certainly a generous thing to do on the part of a person with a Polish last name.
[7] A few more languages appear to belong to this group, if one combines the WALS features described in Siewierska (2011) and Dryer (2011).
[8] In contrast to the system of object reference.

Germanic one. In order to appreciate the degree of similarity, as well as the difference from "general Slavic", consider Table 2 containing translations of a discourse excerpt into four languages: English, German, Polish, and Russian.

Table 2. Excerpt from Hans Christian Andersen's tale "The tinder box" in four languages (from the web site www.logoslibrary.eu)

	English	German	Polish	Russian
1.	"I should like very much to see her,"	"Ich möchte sie wohl sehen!"	"Chciałbym ją zobaczyć"	"Éx, kak by na nee pogljadet' ",
2.	thought the soldier [...]	dachte-ø der Soldat [...]	– pomyślał-ø żołnierz [...]	– dumal-ø soldat [...]
3.	However, <u>he</u> passed a very pleasant time;	Nun lebte-ø <u>er</u> recht lustig,	Tymczasem więc pędził-<u>ø</u> wesołe życie,	Žil-ø <u>on</u> teper' kuda kak veselo:
4.	went to the theatre,	besuchte-ø das Theater,	chadzał-ø do teatru,	xodil-ø v teatry,
5.	drove in the king's garden,	fuhr-ø in des Königs Garten	zwiedzał-ø ogród królewski,	vyezžal-ø na progulki v korolevskij sad
6.	and gave a great deal of money to the poor,	und gab-ø den Armen viel Geld,	a biednym dawał-ø zawsze dużo pieniędzy,	i mnogo deneg razdaval-ø bednjakam,
7.	which was very good of him;	und das war hübsch von ihm;	co było bardzo ładnie z jego strony:	i xorošo delal-ø!
8.	<u>he</u> remembered what it had been in olden times to be without a shilling.	<u>er</u> wusste-ø noch von früheren Zeiten her, wie schlimm es ist, nicht einen Groschen zu besitzen!	pamiętał-<u>ø</u> bowiem z dawnych czasów, jak to niedobrze być bez grosza!	Ved' <u>on</u> po sebe znal-ø, kakovo sidet' bez groša v karmane.

Let us focus only on mentions of the protagonist (the soldier) in Table 2, and among these on lines 3 and 8[9]. In these two lines references to the soldier are underlined. In English, these are free personal pronouns. German uses free personal pronouns plus ancillary person inflection on the verbs. Polish uses person

---

[9] It is specifically these two lines that are of interest to us here because they contain such references to the soldier that are, first, reduced and, second, not determined by the syntactic environment. Reference to the soldier in line 2 is full, not reduced. Lines 4–6 are non-first coordinate clauses, in which all of the included languages normally do not employ subject NPs, so in all of the given languages no subject pronoun is observed and the desired contrast cannot be demonstrated. Finally, in line 7 translators employed different clause constructions for different languages, and line 1 is quoted speech that is beyond our concern here.

inflection alone as the reduced referential device. The Russian pattern appears parallel to the German one. (Note that despite the apparent morphological similarity between Polish and Russian verb forms, Polish zero inflection in the past tense is restricted to third person singular masculine, whereas in Russian it conveys only singular masculine, no person; see section 4.)

Here we approach the main conundrum associated with the Russian referential system. The pattern found in this system is very similar to the Germanic one. We have already seen that the Germanic system is highly unusual, but its historical roots are understood: the verb-second syntactic pattern. Also quite clear appears the emergence of a similar system in northern Romance that borrowed the verb-second pattern and, as a consequence, the unrestricted use of subject pronouns. Now, what about the Russian (East Slavic) system? It is very different from Old, West, and South Slavic and relatively recent (see section 6 below). Given the typologically unusual character of the Germanic system, how likely is it that the Russian system emerged indepedently in a rather close geographical area? In my view, such independent emergence would count almost as a areal-typological miracle. But if the Russian system is related to Germanic, can it be that the Germanic system was borrowed into East Slavic failing to affect West and South Slavic, with which Germanic was in more intense contact? Could such borrowing have happened, somehow leaping over Polish that is located geographically between East Slavic and Germanic? If yes, through what particular sociogeographic scenario? If all that must be judged impossible, then, again, why is the Russian system so similar to the Germanic one?

In the subsequent sections of this article I address this set of questions, attempt to come closer to possible answers, and propose certain hypotheses on the rise of the Russian referential system.

4 Further details of the Russian referential system

On closer examination, it turns out that the Russian referential system is not quite identical to the Germanic one. The most common way to convey the clause 'He plays' (cf. Table 1 above) in Russian is as follows:

(1) *On igra-et.*
 he play-PRES.3SG
 'He plays.'

However, quite frequently one can observe the following shape of such a clause:

(2)　　Igra-et.
　　　　play-PRES.3SG
　　　　'He/she/it plays.'

Consider a natural discourse example, consisting of three consecutive clauses (from Pavlova 2010):

(3)　　a.　A　　on　sejčas　ne　u　neë　živ-ët …
　　　　　　but　he　now　not　at　her　live-PRES.3SG
　　　　　　'But he does not live at hers now…'

　　　　b.　S"exa-l-ø …
　　　　　　move-PAST-M.SG
　　　　　　'He has moved.'

　　　　c.　Dom　snima-et.
　　　　　　house　rent-PRES.3SG
　　　　　　'He is renting a house.'

According to a number of quantitative studies (Kibrik 1996, Grenoble 2001, Seo 2001, Zdorenko 2009), the pattern "free pronoun + inflection", as in (1) and (3a), is responsible for the majority of discourse occurrences, between 2/3 and 3/4 of all. Correspondingly, the pattern "inflection alone", as in (2) and (3b, c) accounts for 1/4 to 1/3 of all occurrences.

Apparently, Russian, unlike Germanic, still preserves the conservative Slavic (and Indo-European) pattern "inflection alone", in which inflectional morphemes are the only overt carriers of the referential function. So, unlike Germanic, Russian inflectional endings are fully-fledged referential devices, or bound pronouns. However, this pattern is minor, whereas the pattern "free pronoun + inflection" has become the dominant one. Overall, this system can be characterized as the Germanic pattern with a strong imprint of old Indo-European.

A further complication of the Russian referential system can be dubbed "tense split". The non-past tense inflection follows the familiar old Indo-European pattern, according to which person-number inflection is fused with the grammatical meaning of tense; cf. the ending -et in (2) that indicates, simultaneously, non-past, third person, and singular. In contrast, the past tense morphology is quite different. Consider examples (4) and (5), counterparts of (1) and (2) in the past tense:

(4)　　On　igra-l-ø.
　　　　he　play-PAST-M.SG
　　　　'He played.'

(5) Igra-l-ø.
     play-PAST-M.SG
     'I/you/he played.'

The grammatical meaning of past tense is conveyed by the suffix -*l*, followed by gender-number inflection. More examples of past tense clauses appeared in Table 2 and example (3b) above. Past tense forms are marked for gender and not for person, while non-past forms for person but not gender. Both are marked for number. (4) and (5) occur in about the same discourse contexts as (1) and (2), respectively. As will be seen in section 6, the tense split may be relevant for determining the origins of the Russian referential system.

To recapitulate, Table 3 provides a comparison of three referential systems – German, Polish, and Russian, including the information on referential devices, typological peculiarities, and assessment of cross-linguistic typicality.

Table 3. German, Polish, and Russian referential systems: typological assessment

	German	**Polish**	**Russian**
Referential device	free pronoun	referential inflection (= bound pronoun)	(free pronoun +) referential inflection
Peculiarities	non-referential inflection		split: – non-past: person-number – past: gender-number
Typicality	unusual	very common	highly unusual

5 Flexibility of Russian

What governs the choice between the two Russian patterns in discourse use? This question is a complex one, is not sufficiently researched, and will not be pursued in detail in this study. Just a couple of comments are in order, to give the reader a feeling of how subtle the choice is.

The study of Fougeron & Breillard (2004), focusing specifically on the presence/absence of the first person singular subject pronoun, lists a wide spectrum of relevant factors. One factor to mention is that the particle/conjunction *a*, appearing clause-initially and indicating a certain kind of discourse discontinuity, seems to be incompatible with the "inflection alone" pattern. McShane (2009: 118–128) presents a range of factors favoring the absence of subject pronouns, such as series of same-subject sentences (cf. (3) above) or clauses functioning as elaborations to mainline material.

It is quite clear that the choice between the two patterns is sensitive to discourse register/genre/style distinctions. To illustrate this point, consider Table 4, which contains an excerpt from the Gospel according to Luke (with certain omissions), provided in Old Church Slavonic (OCS) and in two Russian translations (all in Cyrillic), as well as in English.

Table 4. Comparison of two Russian translations from Luke (19, 12–15) with those in Old Church Slavonic and in English

1.	OCS	ЧЕЛОВЕКЪ ЕДИНЪ ДОБРА РОДА ИДЕ НА СТРАНѪ ДАЛЕЧЕ
	Russian Synodal	Некоторый человек высокого рода отправлялся в дальнюю страну
	Russian Averintsev	Некий человек высокого рода отправился в дальнюю страну
	English	A certain nobleman went into a far country
2.	OCS	[...] И БЫС<u>ТЪ</u> ЕГДА СѦ ВЪZВРАТИ
	Russian Synodal	[...] И когда возвратил-ø-ся
	Russian Averintsev	[...] И вот когда <u>он</u> возвратил-ø-ся
	English	[...] When <u>he</u> was returned
3.	OCS	[...] И РЕЧ<u>Е</u> А ПРИГЛАСѦТЪ ЕМОУ РАБЫ ТЫ
	Russian Synodal	[...] велел-ø призвать к себе рабов тех
	Russian Averintsev	[...] велел-ø <u>он</u> вызвать к себе тех слуг
	English	[...] then <u>he</u> commanded these servants to be called unto him,
4.	OCS	ИМЪ ЖЕ ДАС<u>ТЪ</u> СЪРЕБРО
	Russian Synodal	которым дал-ø серебро
	Russian Averintsev	которым дал-ø деньги
	English	to whom <u>he</u> had given the money.

The excerpt in Table 4 includes four clauses. Clause 1 is irrelevant for our discussion, as it contains a full nominal subject. Clauses 2–4 all contain anaphoric subjects. In all of these three clauses Old Church Slavonic follows the conservative Indo-European pattern of subject reference, similar to Latin, Spanish, or Polish: referential person inflection on the verb. All relevant referential elements are underscored. English, obviously, follows the familiar pattern: free pronoun *he* in all of the clauses 2–4. The first Russian translation, so called Synodal, was created and approved by the Holy Synod of the Russian Orthodox Church in the 19th century and still is the most widely used Russian version of the Bible. As is generally recognized, even though the language of the Synodal translation is Russian (East Slavic), its grammar, especially syntax, is strongly influenced by Old Church Slavonic (South Slavic). We readily see a confirmation of this generalization in the excerpt: in all of the clauses 2–4 no free subject pronoun is used, just verb inflection is used to perform reference, mimicking the OCS pattern. For a native speaker of Russian, this usage clearly has overtones of archaism and a certain sacrality of the text. This suggests that the use of the pattern "inflection alone" in this particular context goes against the complex (but existing) rules of subject reference in modern Russian. However, the absence of pronouns does not render the text obscure or grammatically incorrect. It is just sociolinguistically marked as belonging to the religious register/genre/style. In contrast, the second Russian translation was recently created by the renowned Russian philologist Sergey Averintsev, specifically in order to make the Bible sound more contemporary and closer to lay readers. This translator's intention is readily displayed by the presence of subject pronouns in clauses 2 and 3, which indeed makes them sound much closer to neutral modern Russian[10]. However, in clause 4 even Averintsev's translation does not contain a free pronoun, but in this case the absence does not make the text sound archaic; this is one of those instances in which modern Russian favors or at least admits the "inflection alone" pattern[11].

This analysis suggests that the Russian system is not fixed and straightforward. In fact, it is not just a syntactic phenomenon, it is a phenomenon on the verge between syntax and sociolinguistics. The stylistic aspects of subject pronouns use were referred to more than once by Fedor Dostoevsky. In particular, in the story "The village of Stepanchikovo and its inhabitants" the main character Foma Opiskin is mocked by the storyteller as follows: ' "Went up to the looking-glass and looked into it today", Foma continued, pompously omitting the pronoun *I*.'[12] Apparently, for Dostoevsky the excessive use of the "inflection alone" pattern sounds too pretentious and too high-style for colloquial usage.

---

10 Numerous lexical and syntactic choices employed by Averintsev demonstrate the same point: addition of the colloquial discourse marker *vot* in clause 2; *vyzvat'* instead of more archaic *prizvat'* 'summon' in clause 3; modern word order *tex slug* instead of *rabov tex* 'those servants' in clause 3; *den'gi* 'money' instead of *serebro* 'silver', etc.
11 Probably this instance of pronoun absence can be accounted for with the help of McShane's (2009: 120) notion of same-subject subordinate structure.
12 English translation from: The friend of the family, or Stepantchikovo and its inhabitants. From the Russian by Constance Garnett. The novels of Fyodor Dostoevsky. Volume XII. New York: The Macmillan company. 1920. P. 78.

The fluid character of the Russian system may even suggest that it is still in transition from the conservative Indo-European pattern to the Germanic-style pattern. In the following sections I proceed with suggestions on the rise of the Russian system.

6 Possible internal factors

Two kinds of factors could be responsible for the rise of the convoluted Russian referential system: language-internal structural changes and external linguistic influences. I will consider these two kinds of factors in turn, beginning with the language-internal ones. A scenario of internally-driven evolution was proposed in Kibrik (2004, 2011: §7.4.4); its main tenets are reproduced here with some additional comments.

Early Old Russian, just as Old Church Slavonic, had a set of past tenses, including the synthetic forms of aorist and imperfect[13], as well as the analytic perfect and pluperfect (a rare form). Perfect forms originally consisted of the *l*-participle of the content verb, inflected for gender and number, and the copular verb 'be' in an appropriate tense-person-number form, for example[14]:

(6) a. *Da-l-ъ   jes-mь.*
       give-PTC-M.SG be.PRES-1SG
       'I (masc.) have given.'

   b. *Da-l-ъ   jes-tь.*
       give-PTC-M.SG be.PRES-3SG
       'he has given.'

Beginning from the early Old Russian period, perfect forms started becoming a generalized past tense form (meaning 'I (masc.) gave' and 'he gave' for (6a, b), respectively), supplanting the old past tenses of aorist and imperfect (Borkovskij & Kuznecov 2006 [1963]: 282–283; Gorškova & Xaburgaev 1981: 306–312; Lindseth 1998: 60–64). This process was also shared by Old Polish (Xaburgaev 1991). In the third person, both in Old Russian and in Old Polish the person-marked copula started disappearing, the new third person of the past often appearing simply as

---

13 There is a controversy on whether imperfect actually existed as an East Slavic form (Borkovskij & Kuznecov 2006: 257–260) or rather was transported from Old Church Slavonic (Gorškova & Xaburgaev 1981: 332).
14 Both orders "participle + copula" and "copula + participle" were attested in Old Russian texts. In (6) I randomly choose the first of these orders to illustrate the structure of the perfect.

dalъ 'he gave'. Forms of this kind, however, were still bearing the grammatical meaning 'third person', because the copulas were present in the first and second persons, and thus third person forms remained semiotically opposed to them, being negatively marked for person. This kind of morphological system is still retained in modern Polish, be it with some phonological simplification and morphological consolidation (see e.g. Migdalski 2009).

The next evolutionary step taken by Old Russian (but not Polish) was the gradual loss of copulas in all past tense (former perfect) forms (Borkovskij & Kuznecov 2006: 323, Gorškova & Xaburgaev 1981: 311, Ivanov 1990: 333–337), leading to the elimination of the category of person from the past tense clauses. In this emerging morphological system, *dalъ* became a synthetic form, new past, ambiguous for person, meaning either 'he gave' or 'I (masc.) gave' or 'you (masc.) gave' (note that these forms remain marked for gender and number; *dala* meant 'she gave' or 'I (fem.) gave' or 'you (fem.) gave'). It is likely that this disappearance of the marking for person in past tense clauses paved the way to the increase of use of personal subject pronouns: forms such as *dalъ*, no longer marked for person, could not perform subject reference efficiently enough, and personal pronouns were drafted to compensate for this function. This was happening gradually over the centuries. The spread of subject pronouns speeded up in the 15th century and landslided in the 16th century (see references above and also Eckhoff & Meyer 2011). The usage of subject pronouns became the default pattern, beginning from the 17th century and into modern Russian. Table 5 summarizes this development.

Table 5. Development of the referential system in the history of Russian: a summary[15]

	Early Old Russian	Middle-Late Old Russian (12th – 15th century)[16]	Modern Russian (from the 17th century)
Perfect/Past 1Sg.M 3Sg.M	Perfect *dalъ jesmь* *dalъ jestь*	New past *dalъ [jesmь]* (~ *ja dalъ*) *dalъ* — (~ *onъ dalъ*)	Past *ja dal* (~ *dal*) *on dal* (~ *dal*)
Present, 3Sg	*daetь*	*daetь* (~ *onъ daetь*)	*on daët* (~ *daët*)

The pattern dominating in the middle Old Russian past tense (*dalъ jesmь* 'I (masc.) gave', *dalъ* 'he gave') is materially different from the earlier system (with

---

15 There is no single established periodization of Old Russian, compare Borkovskij & Kuznecov (2006: 32) and Gorškova & Xaburgaev (1981: 27–29). The periodization in Table 5 is tentative and adapted to the issue under investigation.
16 Note that the Middle-Late Old Russian column indicates the use outside of contrastive subject contexts and other specialized contexts (Borkovskij & Kuznecov 2006: 380–381; Zaliznjak 2008: 248 ff.). In such contexts the use of subject pronouns was required, irrespective of other factors.

old synthetic past tenses aorist and imperfect), but systemically it is equivalent: verb inflection distinguishes subject persons. In contrast, the modern Russian pattern has changed: verb forms do not mark subject person anymore, that can only be performed by means of subject pronouns.

The connection between the loss of person marking in past tense verb forms and the expansion of subject pronoun use has been discussed in the previous literature on the history of Russian. However, the proposed causal relation was usually the reverse of what is claimed here[17]. As was suggested by a number of authors (Borkovskij & Kuznecov 2006: 324, 378; Gorškova & Xaburgaev 1981: 310; Ivanov 1982: 100 ff.; Zaliznjak 1995: 153; Zaliznjak 2008: 246ff., inter alia), what happened was the following. Subject pronouns expanded the domain of their use[18], which made the person-marked copulas redundant and eventually led to their fall. From my perspective, this hypothesis on the causal relation between the restructuring of the past tense and the pattern of subject pronouns use is problematic. Unmotivated expansion of subject pronouns appears a typologically unlikely process, whereas the simplification of verb paradigms is cross-linguistically common. Moreover, as was demonstrated above, there was a substantial pressure for such simplification and restructuring in Old Russian.

In order to further test the direction of the causal connection, i.e. what caused what, the following logic can be applied. One can look at a corpus of Old Russian documents and compare the frequency of the emergent new pattern in the past tense and present tense clauses. If it is more common in the past tense, that would be an indication that this pattern first emerged as a response to the trend of dropping person-marked copulas. In Kibrik (2011: 271–272), the earliest Novgorod birchbark letters (Zaliznjak 1995: 223ff.), belonging to the 11th century and the first half of the 12th century, were analyzed (for non-contrastive contexts only), with the following results. In the past tense clauses, the proportion of the

---

[17] As I found out during the preparation of the present article, the same causal direction as in my hypothesis was previously proposed by Jakobson (1971 [1935]), Franks & King (2000: 187), and Lindseth (1998: 63). To quote from Jakobson, "La perte des formes du présent du verbe auxiliaire et du verbe-copule exigeait qu'on introduisît dans des propositions telles que *dal* (< *dal esi*), *mal* (< *mal est'*) un pronom personnel pour exprimer le sujet (*ty dal* – tu as donné, *on mal* – il est petit). Cette construction a été généralisée. D'après le type *ty dal* on a normalisé le type *ty daëš'* (tu donnes)." (1971: 21). Also, similar appears the suggestion by Ivanov (1990: 374) (but cf. p. 333–334 in the same publication).

[18] Zaliznjak (2008) points out that the expansion of subject pronouns and the loss of copulas happened, in the first place, in nominal clauses (schematically, the pattern *am not your sister* was replaced by *I not your sister*), and was only later extended to verbal clauses, including the perfect/past and present tense clauses; on nominal clauses also see Jakobson (1971), Xaburgaev (1978), and Kopotev (2011).

patterns *dalъ jesmь* and *ja dalъ* is 18 to 5 [19], whereas in the present tense clauses the proportion of *daetъ* and *onъ daetъ* is 21 to 1[20]. In other words, in accordance with these quantitative data, at the incipient stage the new pattern was used in Old Russian around six times as frequently in the past tense as in present tense clauses.

On the other hand, Sidorova (2012) studied a large set of Old Russian documents between the 11th and the 15th centuries and compared these data for relative frequency of the old and the new referential patterns in the past and present tense clauses. Her results turned out to be opposite to what is reported above: the use of subject pronouns is generally more frequent in the present tense compared to the past tense. If that is true, then the expansion of subject pronouns could not be due to the restructuring of the past tense morphology. However, in Sidorova's study special semantic and syntactic contexts, such as contrastiveness and clause coordination, were not filtered out, so a more detailed assessment of these data is in order. For the purposes of the present study I continue to assume that the formation of the new referential pattern started in past tense clauses.

Borkovskij & Kuznecov (2006: 379–380) observe that the difference in the frequency of subject pronouns depending on tense remained visible in the 17th century: free subject pronouns were used primarily in past tense clauses and rarely in the present tense (except for specialized semantic contexts). Pavlova (2010) undertook a corpus study aimed at testing whether such a quantitative difference might have survived in modern Russian as well. Since in the present tense (or, more accurately, non-past tense[21]) person is marked on the verb, it is reasonable to hypothesize that subject personal pronouns are used more rarely in present-

---

19 In these counts another kind of forms based on the *l*-participle was also included, namely the conjunctives.
20 In this study no difference was made between various persons. As was pointed out by Mikhail Kopotev (p.c.), it might be more illuminating to look into the differential timing of changes in the first/second persons vs. the third person. We have seen above that the fall of copulas in the third person started earlier. In addition, old Slavic languages, such as Old Church Slavonic and early Old Russian, did not have dedicated third person pronouns (Borkovskij & Kuznecov 2006: 321–322; Gorškova & Xaburgaev 1981: 262). So the details of the story of the first/second persons and the third person are indeed somewhat different. Eckhoff & Meyer (2011) provide separate quantitative results for the first/second persons and the third person and conclude that the expansion of pronouns was developing much slower in the third person; also cf. Borkovskij & Kuznecov (2006: 379). If that is correct, that is another argument for the proposed direction of the causal connection: it is especially clear in the third person that the fall of the copulas and the rise of subject pronouns were separated by several centuries.
21 Morphologically identical forms are distributed in Russian over present and future tenses in accordance with aspect, for example, the first person singular non-past form from *pisat'* 'write' (imperfective) is *pišu* 'I write', and from *napisat'* 'write (perfective)' it is *napišu* 'I will write'.

tense clauses than in past tense clauses. Indeed, Pavlova discovered significantly more clauses without a pronominal subject in non-past tenses, see Table 6.

Table 6. Frequencies of clauses with and without subject pronouns in modern Russian, based on Pavlova 2010

	With subject pronoun	Without subject pronoun	Total
Non-past	147 (56%)	117 (44%)	264 (100%)
Past	91 (67%)	45 (33%)	136 (100%)

Levshina (2012) performed a statistical analysis (multiple regression) on Pavlova's (2010) data and concluded that the past tense does significantly increase the chance of using a subject pronoun (only in main clauses) and the future tense creates a strong no-subject effect.

Fedorova (2012) undertook a pilot experimental study, in which stimulus material in the form of series of pictures was used to elicit spoken stories about a single character. A statistically significant difference between tenses was obtained for the use vs. non-use of subject pronouns: in the past tense, 55% of the clauses contained a subject pronoun, while in the non-past tense, only 42%. (It seems that the stimulus material generally encouraged the use of the "inflection alone" referential pattern above average.) So there is converging evidence that modern Russian still bears some traces of the predominant use of subject pronouns in past tense clauses.

To conclude the discussion of the internal factors of the Russian referential system, an important difference between the structurally similar processes in Germanic and in East Slavic must be observed. The old Germanic system with the double representation of subject person once emerged as a response to the verb-second syntactic pattern. Some Germanic languages, such as German, get along with the redundancy, having downgraded person inflection to the status of less than referential "agreement". Some other Germanic languages made a step towards simplification and got rid of this redundancy, letting person inflection gradually decay. That is, a transition happened from one person form to two person forms and then, in some of the Germanic languages, back to one (of a different nature).

In contrast, the unrestricted use of subject pronouns emerged in Old Russian as a response to the beginning disappearance of person marking on the verb. This has led to partial redundancy as well, particularly in the non-past tense clauses. But, unlike Germanic, there are no signs of Russian inflection on the verb losing its referential potential, as is attested by the substantial share of clauses without subject pronouns.

7 Possible external influence

In this section I address potential external factors that might have contributed to the formation of the modern Russian referential system, whose rudiments appeared already in the middle Old Russian period. Old Russian had substantial contact with several groups of neighboring languages, including Finno-Ugric, Turkic, Baltic, and West Slavic. After considering the possible contributions of these languages (7.1), I discuss the potential influence of the more distant Germanic languages (7.2).

7.1 Neighboring languages

The map in Figure 2, produced by Yuri Koryakov, shows the geographical relationship between Old Russian and neighboring languages in the late Old Russian period. During several previous centuries, relevant for the present discussion, the areal distribution of languages was similar, with minor exceptions.

First and foremost, since the arrival of the Slavs in the eastern European territory, Old Russian was in intense contact with Finno-Ugric. Essentially, Russian

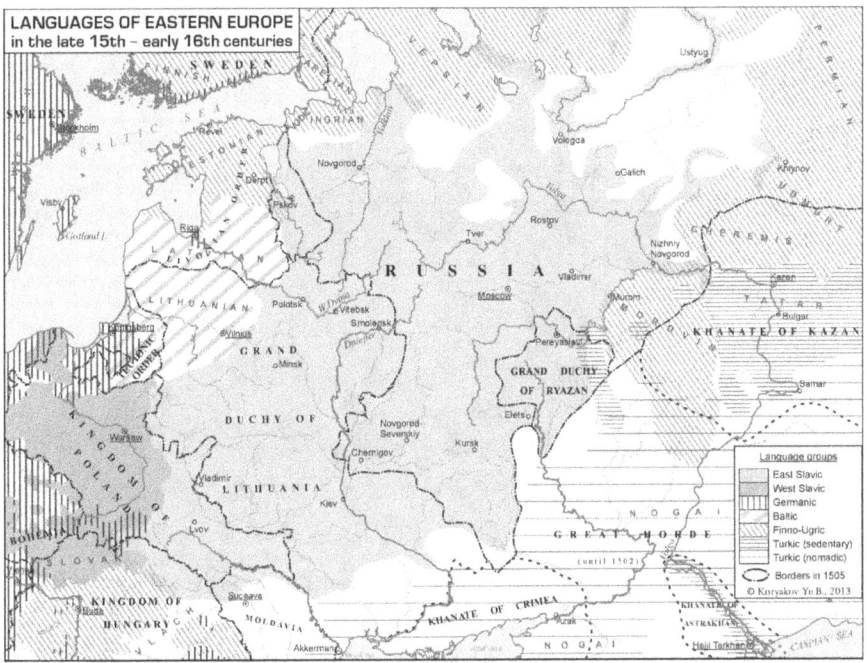

Figure 2. Languages of Eastern Europe at the turn of the 15th and 16th centuries

replaced Finno-Ugric on this territory (see e.g. Sedov 2002; Puškina 2006: 427–438), leaving Finno-Ugric languages on its periphery (e.g. Karelian and Ingrian in the North-West, Mordvin in the East, etc.). Opinions vary on how much Finno-Ugric affected East Slavic. On the one hand, there is a tradition of listing potential influences on all levels of linguistic structure; cf. Veenker (1967), Künnap (1997), Čekmonas (2001b). On the other hand, many of these suggestions are not sufficiently conclusive, cf. Dahl & Koptjevskaja-Tamm (1992), Kopotev (2007, 2011)[22].

Could the Russian referential system be influenced by the Finno-Ugric substratum? Let us consult the situation in modern Finno-Ugric. Extensive evidence on more eastern Finno-Ugric is provided by the recent publication Kuznecova (ed.) (2012). The analysis of data of Mordvin-Erzya (Shoksha dialect), Meadow Mari (Old Toryal dialect), Udmurt (Besermyan dialect), and Komi-Zyrian (Pechora dialect) in that volume provides a bulk of evidence that these languages generally follow the Russian pattern. Both reference by means of inflection alone and the additional use of subject pronouns are observed, the latter slightly outnumbering the former[23]. For example, consider both kinds of clauses in a Mordvin discourse excerpt:

(7) Mordvin-Erzya, Shoksha dialect (Kuznecova ed. 2012: 826)

    a. *Er'e-st'*   *jon-sta* […]
       live-PAST.3PL good-EL
       'They lived good.'

    b. *L'ad-st*   *syn'* *er'a-ma*   *t'et'e-t'*   *mar^hta*.
       remain-PAST.3PL they live-NMZR father-DEF.GEN together
       'They remained to live with the father.'

    c. *I*   *vot* *er'e-t'*.
       and here live-PRES.3PL
       'And so they live.'

    d. *Ivaga syn' vanu-sy-z'* …
       and now they   see-PRES-3O.3PL.S
       'And now they see…'

---

[22] Kopotev (2007, 2011) provides a critical analysis of the idea of the Russian copula-free nominal clauses resulting from Finnish influence, which is related to the research question of the present article.
[23] An impressionistic evaluation of the data in Kuznecova (ed.) (2012) suggests that the share of clauses with subject reference by inflection alone is larger in Finno-Ugric than in Russian.

In (7a,c) we see the use of verbal inflection alone, whereas in (7b,d) subject pronouns are also found.

Generally, a similar picture is observed in those western (Baltic) Finno-Ugric languages that for centuries were in most intense contact with Russian, as well as with Germanic, such as Vodic (Markus & Rožanskij 2011) and Ingrian (Rožanskij & Markus 2012). Consider an Ingrian example, intentionally taken from the earliest available source – the 1885 publication by Volmari Porkka:

(8) Ingrian (Rožanskij & Markus 2012: 490)

a. *Kuin mȫö nüD mā̈-mmää kottī?*
how we now go.PRES-1PL home
'How do we go home now?'

b. *NüD taba-mma tämä-n veljä-n.*
now kill.PRES-1PL this-GEN brother-GEN
'Now we kill this brother.'

This example, quite typical of the Ingrian text in general, shows a pronoun in (8a) and lack thereof in (8b).

Theoretically, this situation, which is quite similar to Russian, could be the original Finno-Ugric pattern. However, such a hypothesis is disproved by other considerations. Although we have no direct evidence on the ancient Finno-Ugric referential system at the time of Old Russian, Finno-Ugric experts generally believe that the original system of these languages is of the conservative Indo-European style: reduced subject reference by means of verbal inflection (Tatiana Agranat, p.c.). Analysis of Finno-Ugric grammars indicates that the "inflection alone" pattern is dominant, including some of the languages cited above. For example, for Mordvin Koljadenkov (1954: 64) states that "the absence of a personal subject pronoun with a first or second person predicate is the norm in Mordvin, whereas its presence is exceptional"; the same appears to be true for the third person (p. 109–110). Koljadenkov even says that "subject is expressed by the personal endings of the verb in the first and second persons [...]. They carry no other function apart from expressing the subject" (1954: 176). Note that Mordvin is a language that has been in contact with Russian for centuries. Probably all modern speakers are bilingual, and the pattern we observed in (7b, d) most likely is the result of Russian syntactic influence. Note that the above mentioned modern Finno-Ugric texts abound with calques and borrowings from Russian and display frequent code switching, so syntactic borrowing from Russian is quite possible.

If we move to more peripheral Finno-Ugric or (related) Samoyedic languages, that have not been exposed to a prolonged and intensive Russian (or Germanic) influence a still clearer picture emerges. For Khanty (West Siberia), Filchenko (2007: 327, 362) remarks that subject (in his terms, Agent) is usually expressed by verbal agreement: "whenever the Agent is overt, it is seen to be emphasized (pragmatically marked)". For Saami languages (northern Scandinavia) Sammalahti (1998: 95–96) states that "the subject is not an obligatory constituent: first and second person verb forms do not require the subject pronoun, and third person pronouns are optional in subordinations". As for Samoyedic, Tereščenko (1973: 131–133) describes the common Samoyedic system of subject reference as avoiding the use of subject pronouns. She points out though the growing tendency of certain dialects to use pronouns increasingly, and suggests that this tendency may be the result of contact with Russian. According to the judgement of the consulted Samoyedic experts (Anna Urmanchieva, Valentin Gusev, Andrey Shluinsky, p.c.), Samoyedic languages follow the "inflection alone" pattern and do not use subject pronouns in neutral contexts[24].

To conclude the Finno-Ugric theme, it is most likely that the modern Finno-Ugric languages, which underwent massive Russian influence in recent centuries, have copied the Russian pattern to their discourse use. (It could also be Germanic influence in the case of the Finnic languages.) The original Finno-Ugric (and, more generally, Uralic) type of referential system is "inflection alone". It appears improbable that Finno-Ugric could have contributed to the formation of the modern Russian referential system, with its extensive use of subject pronouns.

As for the Turkic languages, bordering Old Russian in the East and South, the situation is still clearer. Turkic generally performs reduced subject reference by means of verbal inflection. This can be seen throughout many centuries, beginning from the earliest written documents to modern vernacular forms. Consider an example from Old Turkic:

(9) Runic Turkic, 8th century (Kononov 1980: 228)

   Arqïš   id-maz   tejin   sülä-di-m.
   caravan send-FUT.NEG.3SG because campaign-PAST-1SG
   'Since he would not send caravans (with tribute), I campaigned against him.'

In this typical example both clause subjects are only expressed by verb inflection.

To see the modern pattern, let us consider a couple of examples from a dialect of Tatar. Tatar is used because it is geographically the closest to the traditional Russian territory among the Turkic languages. And I use dialectal evidence because literary Tatar might have undergone Russian syntactic influence.

---

24 Multiple texts in the Samoyedic languages Nganasan and Enets attesting to this generalization can be consulted at the repository http://languedoc.philol.msu.ru/ds/imdi_browser/.

(10) Mishar Tatar (Lyutikova & Tatevosov eds. 2000 ms., text "Letter to the daughter")

    a. *Mɤnča-nɤ   tübän ɤčtagɤ*
       steambath-ACC lower end
       kɤrmaj   rinat-lar-ɤ-n-da   ker-ä-m
       Nickname Rinat-PL-3-OBL-LOC enter-ST.IPFV-1SG
       'I go to the Rinat's steambath at the lower end.'

    b. *Niček jäš-i-sen?*
       how   live-ST-2.SG
       'How are you?'

Apparently, Turkic has been consistent in using the "inflection alone" pattern throughout the centuries, and it must be concluded that Turkic is ruled out as a possible factor in the development of the Russian referential system.

Likewise ruled out is Polish (West Slavic). As was discussed above, it has preserved the traditional Slavic (and Indo-European) system, with some minor formal changes; some additional remarks on Polish will be made below in section 8.

As for the Baltic languages, there is little or no information on ancient stages of these. A number of Baltic groups (and languages) existed much to the east and south of the modern Baltic area (Toporov 2006a, Koryakov 2006); these groups were later absorbed by the East Slavs during their eastward and northward expansion, just like some Finno-Ugric tribes. The best documented of the old Baltic languages, Prussian, was spoken on the Baltic coast between the Vistula and Neman rivers. Prussian has reached us only in the form of written documents, mostly of the 16th century, with massive syntactic calquing from German (Toporov 2006b). So the original referential system of the Baltic languages is obscure[25]. Among the two surviving Baltic languages, the Latvian pattern is close to that of Russian, whereas the Lithuanian pattern is close to that of Polish. Dryer (2011) classified these two languages as using personal subject pronouns and inflection alone, respectively. However, some experts believe that Lithuanian uses more subject pronouns than Polish and is not that different from Latvian (Aleksey Andronov and Axel Holvoet, p.c.). With respect to Latvian, which appears a clearer case, it is likely that the common use of pronouns may be related to the extensive contact with German over the centuries. Balode & Holvoet (2001: 10) call German syntactic influence upon Latvian "pervasive". Wiemer & Hansen (2012: 72–73) remark

---

[25] Toporov (2006a: 41) remarks in his brief summary of the Baltic syntax that "the noun phrase may be absent altogether", which may be interpreted as the possibility or even widespread occurrence of clauses without subject pronouns.

on moderate to null attestation of contact-induced borrowing of grammatical patterns into Slavic from Baltic (as well as from Turkic and Finno-Ugric). Overall, it is unlikely that Latvian or other Baltic languages could have contributed to the formation of the Russian referential system.

To conclude the discussion of possible geographically adjacent sources of the Russian referential system, we are not finding any probable candidates. Quite the opposite, Russian seems to have affected Finno-Ugric, and languages of the Baltic area (both Finnic and Baltic) were probably influenced by Germanic and Russian.

7.2 Germanic

Structurally, Germanic is a possible influence upon Russian. Typologically, it is a likely influence because of the extreme rarity of subject personal pronouns combined with person inflection on the verb. But is there a plausible sociogeographic scenario that is compatible with this hypothesis?

Before considering this question, let me first mention a couple of Slavic parallels indicating that Germanic influence of this kind is possible in principle. It has been pointed out above that West and South Slavic languages were in extensive contact with German over the centuries, have many lexical and grammatical borrowings (see e.g. Dickey 2011 and Wiemer & Hansen 2012 on the latter) but failed to change their referential system. On the other hand, the westernmost West Slavic languages, which used to be under very intensive German influence, did change it, resulting in a situation similar to that of Russian. Sorbian and Kashubian have both developed the extensive use of subject pronouns, also keeping referential verb inflection (Stone 1993a, b). In Kashubian the similarity to Russian is enhanced due to the disappearance of copulas in the past tense forms. Consider the following example:

(11)   Kashubian (Duličenko 2005: 392–393)

   Jô   jem   chodzy-ł.   ~   Jô   chodzy-ł.
   I   COP.1SG walk-PAST   I   walk-PAST
   'I walked.'

Duličenko reports that the first form with the copula is literary and archaic, while the second form is vernacular.

Lindseth (1998: ch. 4) provides an interesting account of Sorbian that acquired extensive use of subject pronouns, along with person inflection, probably on the German model. This kind of referential system is amply registered in older Sorbian texts, but beginning from the 1840s in the case of Upper Sorbian (and beginning from the end of the 19th century in the case of Lower Sorbian) the "puristic" trend prevailed in written language (pp. 97–113). According to this trend, Sorbian texts were supposed to be freed from German-like patterns and, in particular, the frequent use of subject pronouns has been strongly discouraged in prescriptive grammars and the actual practice of writing, following the model of Czech and Polish. Still, despite these prescriptive requirements, the usage in less formal modern Sorbian discourse is such that subject pronouns are typically used (pp. 84–90).

Another possible instance of Germanic influence upon Slavic is provided by a study of heritage Russian speakers in Toronto (Hollett 2011). In that study, heritage Russian speakers used the "inflection alone" pattern of subject reference much more rarely than first generation speakers (24% as opposed to 38%). Hollett attributes this difference to the intensive contact with English in the case of the Russian variety spoken by heritage speakers[26].

Now turning to the feasibility of the Germanic influence upon the Russian referential system, the question arises on whether the Germanic languages acquired the extensive use of subject pronouns early enough to possibly affect East Slavic. There is a certain controversy on when the Germanic languages acquired the verb-second pattern and the obligatoriness of subject pronouns (see discussion in Axel 2007: 295–298; Axel & Weiß 2010: 25). Given the wide distribution of these features, they might have been present already at the Proto-Germanic stage. According to Nielsen (2000), early Runic Germanic was a verb-second language from a very early stage, beginning from the 6th century (see Dahl 2001: 222 on the problematic affiliation of early Runic as Norse or West Germanic). On the other hand, Braunmüller (2005) suggests that early Runic did have free word order and "null subject"[27]; Gothic (Guxman 1958: 214–215) and early Old High German (8–9th centuries, Axel 2007: 293; Axel & Weiß 2010: 22–24) did use many clauses in which subject reference was performed by verb inflection alone. This is sometimes attributed to possible Greek or Latin influence, but overall it is more likely that the verb-second pattern and the ensuing expansion of subject pronouns emerged after the individual Germanic languages were already formed, probably at the end of the first millennium, and spread as a wave throughout the whole language group. Later attested forms of Germanic (beginning from the 10th

---

26 However, Nagy et al. (2011) argue against this latter point.
27 Braunmüller also discusses the Germanic-Latin bilingualism of the early Runic writers who vacillated between the traditional patterns (pragmatic word order, inflection alone), as in Latin, and the innovative patterns (verb-second, subject pronouns). One can conclude from this that Latin functioned as a conserving force in Old Germanic, impeding the development of the new patterns, at least in writing.

or 11th century) were all verb-second languages with the common use of subject pronouns; see Faarlund (2001: 1708, 1710) on Germanic in general and Faarlund (2008: 191, 221) on Old Norse. So we can conclude that, in any case, the Germanic referential system was formed early enough to be a possible source of the later Russian expansion of subject pronouns.

The earliest contact of Old Russian with Germanic was with Old Norse. There is vast historical literature on the Scandinavian presence in Eastern Europe during the early Russian statehood; see e.g. Mel'nikova (ed.) (1986); Džakson (2001); Klejn (2009). As is well known, vikings, or varangians, explored the Russian territory beginning from the 8th century and crucially participated in the foundation of the Russian state in the late 9th century. During the 10th century the Scandinavian element among the Kievan nobility and merchants was very noticeable; varangians were also hired by the Russian princes as mercenaries. Varangians were accommodating in terms of language: for example, the 911 treaty between Kiev and Byzantium was written in Old Church Slavonic, even though it was signed almost exclusively by persons with Scandinavian names (Jakubinskij 1953: 91). Many varangians were assimilated into the Russian society during the 10th century. Contacts between Russians and Scandinavians existed throughout the subsequent centuries as well (see e.g. Vernadsky 1973: XI.3). Scandinavians had extensive economic connections with Novgorod, and had significant representation among the town's elite, including in the 11th and 12th centuries (Gippius 2006). Linguistic contacts between Swedish and Russian, also involving other languages of the Baltic area, continued later on, cf. Koptjevskaja-Tamm & Wälchli (2001: 619). Specialized studies of Scandinavian influence upon the eastern neighbors barely discuss any Russian evidence and address lexical borrowings at most (Koivulehto 2002, Panzer 2002). In principle, some grammatical influence cannot be ruled out, but it appears that the socially restricted character of contact could have hardly led to substantial bilingualism and grammatical borrowing. No instances of such influence are noted in Dahl & Koptjevskaja-Tamm (eds.) (2001: Appendix 2).

Much more extensive and numerous contacts between the speakers of Old Russian and Germanic are associated with the later period of commercial, rather than political, interactions in the Northwest of the Old Russian area. The account below is largely based on the fundamental study Squires & Ferdinand (2002) on the linguistic situation in Novgorod and other Northwestern and Baltic towns during the late Middle Ages.

Trade between the Germanic-speaking world and Novgorod was started in the 12th century by Scandinavians from Gotland and, a bit later, by Germans[28]

---

[28] Andreevskij (1855: 1-2) reported that Germans were present in the Novgorod area beginning from the 11th century, and Scandinavians were colonizing this territory much earlier.

from Gotland and mainland German towns, primarily Lübeck. Germanic-speaking merchants were accessing Novgorod via the rivers Neva and Volkhov. Beginning from the 13th century the Baltic German towns of Riga, Dorpat (Tartu) and Reval (Tallinn) also played an important role in the Novgorod trade. Germans had a permanent settlement in Novgorod from the late 12th century. German and Scandinavian trade further developed with the establishment of the Hanseatic league that included all the aforementioned towns[29]. Speakers of Low German in Novgorod did not have a natural means of communication with Russians as the languages were too different. There is no evidence of any kind of Russian-German pidgin; rather translators were used for communication, and those translators were native German speakers who acquired Russian. In the 13th and 14th centuries the role of translators was fulfilled by young men (so-called *Sprakelerere*), usually sons of senior merchants, who were lodged in the Russian Novgorod homes. Somewhat later professional interpreters appeared, some of which were of Baltic or Finno-Ugric origin, but the language of interethnic communication invariably remained Russian. There is no evidence of Russians acquiring German in Novgorod until the end of the 15th century. Hanseatic merchants used their knowledge of Russian as a way to monopolize the commercial relations between Russians and the West. "The Hanseatic League and Novgorod created a point in which important interests came together and in which both sides were maximally committed to establishing mutual understanding and favorable contact" (Squires & Ferdinand 2002: 70; also see Squires 2009: 28).

Relying on this background information, the following sociolinguistic scenario can be proposed. During several centuries, native German speakers were acquiring Russian for the purposes of business communication and using their non-native language in interaction with native Russians. It is a well-known fact that speakers of languages with extensive use of subject pronouns tend to transfer this property of their native language when speaking a second language in which the "inflection only" pattern prevails. For example: "Russian speakers learning Czech or Serbo-Croatian find the regular lack of pronominal subjects very striking and must make a conscious effort to avoid the overuse of overt pronouns." (Lindseth 1998: 48). Or, to take another example, "Overuse of subject pronouns – the equivalent of words such as "he," "she" and "they" – is common among English speakers learning Spanish".[30] Assuming that the German *Sprakelerere* and interpreters did overuse subject pronouns, it is quite possible that the

---

[29] Note that the Hanseatic network involved speakers of Swedish and Norwegian as well, and Hanseatic Low German was influenced by Norse.
[30] From: http://spanish.about.com/od/pronouns/a/subject_pronoun.htm. I, a native speaker of Russian, can report the same experience while learning to speak Spanish.

Russian inhabitants of Novgorod, exposed to the foreigners' Russian speech for many generations, were picking up and copying this property, possibly perceiving it as educated, prestigious or fashionable. This scenario is inevitably hypothetical; but cf. the positive evidence of about 100 Low German lexical borrowings in Russian (Thomas 1976). Also cf. the somewhat parallel account by Trudgill (2011: 56–58) of German-Scandinavian linguistic interaction in the Hanseatic towns of Bergen and Stockholm.

Apart from the Novgorod trade route, another Hanseatic-related network included the towns of Riga, Polotsk, and Vitebsk along the Western Dvina (Daugava) river, as well as Smolensk. Riga, an originally German town located at the mouth of Western Dvina, served as the major trade interface for the inhabitants of Polotsk and other Russian towns of the area. There were extensive commercial contacts between the Russian towns and Riga from the 13th century on (Berežkov 1877). Riga, both a Hanseatic town and (later) the capital of the Livonian order had substantial Russian population. There was a whole street in Riga populated by Russians, primarily from Polotsk (Berežkov 1877: 346). Russians constituted a noteceable minority in Riga between the 13th and the 17th century (Semenova 1977: 197, cited in Čekmonas 2001a: 90). Russian merchants in Riga often had joint businesses with the people of Baltic (Latvian) and Finno-Ugric (Liv) origin (Berežkov 1877: 353). Russians from Riga served as important suppliers of Western goods for the whole of Russia.

The Riga situation suggests an alternative (or, rather, complementary) sociolinguistic scenario that could have also brought about the borrowing of the subject pronoun pattern into Russian. From the above account of the social situation in Riga, it is clear that, unlike Novgorod, in this case it was Russians who were bilingual in German, German being the dominant language of the place. Non-native speakers of German could have transferred the manner of the extensive use of subject pronoun from their second language into their first language.

It remains for further study to identify which scenario, the Novgorod one or the Riga one or, perhaps, both in conjunction, is more realistic. The difference between the scenarios is that in the Novgorod setting Russian was the dominant language, whereas in Riga the dominant language was Low German. According to the reasoning in Sakel (2007), the borrowing of matter usually goes from a dominant language to a dominated language. But the borrowing of patterns can go either way.

The spread of the subject pronoun pattern in the Northwestern corner of the East Slavic area only explains the incipient point; we still need an account of this trend covering all of the East Slavic varieties. The hypothesis of the Northwestern Germanic contact is corroborated by the results of the study Sidorova (2012). Among the groups of local Old Russian documents analyzed in that study, the predominance of the subject pronoun pattern is first attested in Polotsk letters in the 13th and 14th century, followed by Tver and Pskov, Novgorod[31] (15th century), and finally Moscow (16th century). Note that the Polotsk letters (Xoroškevič 1977–1978) attest to massive contact with Baltic Germans, and some of them are actually written in German. So it appears likely that a phenomenon originating in one specific location later spread like a wave through the whole of the East Slavic area.

If the hypothesis developed in this section is correct, this study contributes to the area of Circum-Baltic language contact, forcefully started in Dahl & Koptjevskaja-Tamm (eds.) (2001). I find it very possible that the process of transfer of the subject pronoun pattern from German was a rather general phenomenon of the late medieval East Baltic area affecting Russian, Latvian, and the Finnic languages. That is, the formation of the modern East Slavic, Baltic, and Finnic referential systems, all resembling each other and Germanic, may be not several independent processes but rather facets of a single historical process of the Baltic zone.

In section 9 I provide a unified scenario combining the internal and external factors that contributed to the formation of the modern Russian referential system. But before that, in section 8, I will discuss a number of possible objections.

8 Polish and other objections

Before proceeding with the conclusions of this study, some comments are in order regarding possible objections to my theory of the "Germanic trace" in Russian. The main puzzle is associated with the fact that the other Slavic languages, in spite of the even closer contact with German over the centuries, remained faithful to the original Indo-European referential system. Particularly worrying is the case of Polish, located geographically right in between the main German-speaking area and the East Slavic languages. There are at least two lines of argumentation helping to reconcile this geographical fact with the proposed account, and I will briefly discuss them in turn.

Reasoning about the probability of contact-induced change sometimes relies on a covert assumption that can be roughly formulated as follows: we expect that the likelihood and extent of structural transfer from one language to another is invariably and universally proportional to geographical proximity between the languages. But is this assumption necessarily correct? First, there is hardly

---

31 Eckhoff & Meyer (2011) characterize the referential pattern of the northern part of Russia (particularly, Novgorod) as the "progressive" one.

anything in contact-induced changes that is fully determined; we can explain observed facts by factors such as proximity, but we cannot predict a change on the basis of proximity. Second, what matters for language contact is not the relative locations of the languages' demographic "centers of gravity" in the physical space, but rather the communicative channels that connect people over extended periods of time (see Squires 2009: sections 8.3, 8.4 for an argument supporting the latter point). As has been demonstrated in section 7, the contact between the Russian and German speakers was rather persistent in terms of both time and intensity. Third, there is a dependency of the kind of change on the sociolinguistic situation. There is an emerging field of sociolinguistic typology (see e.g. Trudgill 2011, Nichols 2012, Matras and Sakel 2007), from which we learn that rather subtle sociolinguistic parameters, such as the age of language acquisition, size of a community, intensity of contact, extent of contact, relative social importance of languages, the amount of bilingualism, et cetera, can affect the type, pace, and likelihood of linguistic influence. Wiemer & Hansen (2012) document multiple examples of German influence upon Slavic languages, differing in accordance with the sociolinguistic type of contact. They also point out (pp. 135–137) that some kinds of structural borrowing happen more easily under less intense language contact and less general bilingualism, illustrating this point with a number of cases from German-to-Slavic borrowings.

As for Polish itself, the situation in this language is not as unequivocal as it is usually pictured, including in the present article. According to Seo's quantitative study (2001: 92), Polish only uses subject pronouns 7% of the time (compared to 78% in Russian). However, McShane (2009: 107) reports that non-standard, colloquial Polish demonstrates substantial use of subject pronouns. McShane (2009: 109) also quotes Nilsson who actually says that "in colloquially colored Polish texts [...] the pattern is similar to the Russian one" (1982: 58). If this kind of account has truth to it, it may also echo the situation in Old Polish. As is reported by Eckhoff & Meyer (2011), in the Polish texts of the 15th century there was a substantial variation in the share of subject pronouns according to genre: from 1% in religious texts up to 26% in sermon. So we may hypothesize that the process of the subject pronoun expansion, characterstic of Russian, also did affect Polish at a certain point in time, but was not entrenched in the norm. In the case of Polish, Latin could have functioned as a conserving factor, as it functioned once in the case of old Germanic (see note 27 above).

Another possible objection against the hypothesis of the Germanic contribution to the Russian referential system could be that we are not finding other syntactic influences of the kind in Russian. However, the use of subject pronouns does not have to be a hard-core syntactic issue, once we are outside the Germanic domain per se. The plus or minus subject pronoun variation in Russian is not a purely syntactic phenomenon, it is largely a subtler stylistic or discourse issue. During the Old Russian period, much of the variation was dependent on the influence of Old Church Slavonic, functioning as a factor conserving the traditional referential system and impeding innovations. This is an issue even now, cf. the discussion of Bible translations in section 5 above. The presence or absence of a pronoun may be a matter of ideology, identity, fashion, etc. It is even partly available to a language user's conscious awareness. Cf. the discussion of Sorbian in section 7.2 above; as was demonstrated by Lindseth (1998), language users' decisions on using subject pronouns are sensitive to the intentional imitation of either the German or the Czech model. Similar phenomena are observed in other languages allowing variation in their referential system. For example, in the Samoyedic languages, as pointed out by Tereščenko (1973: 132), folklore discourse exhibits excessive use of subject pronouns and such use is perceived as a way of "ornamentation of speech". In the languages allowing both the "inflection alone" and the "pronoun plus inflection" patterns the variation is on the verge between syntax and rather soft stylistics, and it can play the role of a social marker. Once again, it appears that this kind of transfer could have happened in the situation of partial language contact, not involving massive bilingualism.

So, overall, I believe that the conservative referential systems of Polish and other major West and South Slavic languages in no way disprove the possibility of the German influence upon East Slavic. Moreover, it seems possible that superficial syntactic features such as the frequency of use of subject pronouns can well be borrowed even under the conditions of rather geographically restricted contact. Also, partly jokingly, I can say that the idea of the Russian partial and inconsistent mimicking of the Germanic referential system reminds one of the general trend of how Russians deal with cultural and social patterns imported from the West: imitate them up to a point but keep a share of original distinctiveness.

9 Conclusions and directions for further studies

Having considered the possible internal and external factors contributing to the rather serious change of the Russian referential system, a combined scenario explaining this change can now be formulated. The tentative scenario that I propose can be summarized as follows.

The change of the system of past tenses was clearly a Slavic-internal process, shared by East and West Slavic, including the former perfect taking over as a generalized past tense and the loss of copulas in the third person and, later, in other persons. This restructuring of the past tense morphology created the prerequisites for the expansion of free subject pronouns, beginning with the past tense clauses and then extending to all clauses. Later the influence of languages exerting a contact influence, using the free pronoun pattern, enhanced the use of free pronouns. Most likely this influence came from the Germanic languages, in particular Low German in the areas of contact between Russians and the Hanseatic league, such as Novgorod and Riga. It appears that the fashion of using subject pronouns in Russian speech first developed in the north-west of Russia and/or in the neighboring Baltic German towns, and later spread to other areas. This process of spread took several centuries and reached its present condition by the 17th century. So the modern Russian referential system, with its hybrid character, probably resulted from a combination of internal and external factors. The evolutionary stages of the process are captured quite well by the triad suggested by Wiemer & Hansen (2012): innovation – propagation – entrenchment.

The scenario of the emergence of the Russian referential system described above recalls the notion of "narrowing" proposed by Heine (2008: 40):

> Such examples appear to be fairly common in situations of language contact: Speakers of the replica language select among the structural options that are available in their language the one that corresponds most closely to a structure they find in their model language. What "selection" means is that the option is used more frequently and acquires a wider range of contexts. In the end – that is, in extreme cases – this may turn out the only structure used, eliminating all the other options that used to be available.

Apparently, the Russian referential system has not reached the extreme case described in the last sentence of the quotation.

Directions for further studies inquiring into the essence and origins of the Russian referential system include at least the following:

- Historical geography of the spread of the quasi-Germanic pattern in East Slavic: fine-grained chronology and areality of the new pattern in Old Russian and early modern Russian, Ukrainian, and Belorussian;
- Further analysis of Old Russian documents, with special attention to vernacular style;
- Analysis of bilingual Russian-German documents created during the Hanseatic period;
- Analysis of early Russian texts written by Germans, in contrast to native Russian texts;
- Analysis of historical literature on Russian-Germanic contacts, as well as multiethnic contacts in the Baltic area;

- Implementation of experimental studies of the kind briefly mentioned in section 6.

I will conclude with a thoughtful quotation from Anna Siewierska's book devoted to the topics very close to the ones addressed in this article (Siewierska 2004: 273–274):

> The type of sociolinguistic situations which may lead to sporadic instances of borrowing are too numerous to contemplate [...] It is not always easy to determine whether a particular change in person marking is due to the influence of another language or to language-internal factors. [...] Consequently, some of the instances attributed to language contact [...] are necessarily of a speculative nature.

Acknowledgements

I am very grateful to the editors Dik Bakker and Martin Haspelmath who read through this article carefully and provided dozens of important comments. I also thank numerous colleagues who provided useful input on this study, including Tatiana Agranat, Aleksey Andronov, Kurt Braunmüller, Bernard Comrie, Stephen Dickey, Olga Fedorova, Pavel Graschenkov, Valentin Gusev, Axel Holvoet, Mikhail Kopotev, Yuri Koryakov, Natalia Levshina, Ekaterina Lyutikova, Anna Pichxadze, Fedor Rozhanskij, Natalia Serdobolskaya, Andrey Shluinsky, Ekaterina Squires, Anna Urmanchieva, and Björn Wiemer.

Abbreviations

1 first person, 2 second person, 3 third person, ACC accusative, COP copula, DEF definite, EL elative, FUT future, GEN genitive, IPFV imperfective, LOC locative, M masculine, NEG negative, NMZR nominalizer, O object marker, OBL oblique, PAST past, PL plural, PRES present, PTC participle, S subject marker, SG singular, ST stative.

References

Andreevskij, Ivan. 1855. *O dogovore Novagoroda s nemeckimi gorodami i Gotlandom, zaključennom v 1270 godu* [On the treaty concluded by Novgorod with the German cities and Gotland in 1270]. Master of Law thesis, St. Petersburg Emperor's University. St. Petersburg: Jakov Trei's printing house.

Axel, Katrin. 2007. *Studies in Old High German syntax. Left sentence periphery, verb placement and verb-second.* Amsterdam: Benjamins.
Axel, Katrin & Helmut Weiß. 2010. What changed where? A plea for reevaluation of dialectal evidence. In Anne Breitbarth, Christopher Lucas, Sheila Watts & David Willis (eds.), *Continuity and change in grammar*, 13–34. Amsterdam: Benjamins.
Balode, Laimute & Axel Holvoet. 2001. The Latvian language and its dialects. In Östen Dahl & Maria Koptjevskaja-Tamm (eds.), Vol. 1, 3–40.
Berežkov, M. 1877. O torgovle russkix s Rigoju v XIII-m i XIV-m vekax [On the Russians' trade with Riga in the 13th and 14th centuries]. *Žurnal ministerstva narodnogo prosveščenija, fevral'* 1877. 330–357.
Borkovskij, Viktor I. & Petr S. Kuznecov 2006 [1963]. *Istoričeskaja grammatika russkogo jazyka [A Historical grammar of Russian].* Moscow: URSS.
Braunmüller, Kurt. 2005. Variation in Word Order in the Oldest Germanic Runic Inscriptions: A Case for Bilingualism? In *Papers on Scandinavian and Germanic Language and Culture.* 15–30. (NOWELE 46/47).
Čekmonas, Valeriy. 2001a. Russian varieties in the southeastern Baltic area: Urban Russian of the 19th century. In Östen Dahl & Maria Koptjevskaja-Tamm (eds.), 81–100.
Čekmonas, Valeriy. 2001b. On Some Circum-Baltic Features of the Pskov-Novgorod (Northwestern Central Russian) Dialect. In Östen Dahl & Maria Koptjevskaja-Tamm (eds.), 339–359.
Dahl, Östen & Maria Koptjevskaja-Tamm. 1992. Language typology around the Baltic Sea. *Papers from the Institute of Linguistics, University of Stockholm, Publication* 61.
Dahl, Östen. 2001. The origin of the Scandinavian languages. In Östen Dahl & Maria Koptjevskaja-Tamm (eds.), 215–236.
Dahl, Östen & Maria Koptjevskaja-Tamm (eds.). 2001. *The Circum-Baltic languages. Typology and contact.* Vol. 1, 2. Amsterdam: Benjamins.
Dickey, Stephen M. 2011. The Varying Role of *po-* in the Grammaticalization of Slavic Aspectual Systems: Sequences of Events, Delimitatives, and German Language Contact. *Journal of Slavic Linguistics* 19(2). 175–230.
Dryer, Matthew S. 2011. Expression of Pronominal Subjects. In Matthew S. Dryer & Martin Haspelmath (eds.), *The World Atlas of Language Structures Online.* Munich: Max Planck Digital Library, chapter 101. Available online at http://wals.info/chapter/101.
Duličenko, Aleksandr D. 2005. Kašubskij jazyk [Kashubian]. In Aleksandr M. Moldovan, Sergej S. Skorvid, Andrej A. Kibrik, Natal'ja V. Rogova, Ekaterina I. Jakuškina, Aleksej F. Žuravlev & Svetlana M. Tolstaja (eds.), *Jazyki mira: slavjanskie jazyki*, 383–403. Moscow: Academia.
Džakson, Tat'jana N. 2001. Varjažskij vopros [The Varangian issue]. *Rodina* 2001.
Eckhoff, Hanne & Roland Meyer. 2011. Conditions on Null Subjects in Old Church Slavonic, a Contrastive View. Paper presented at the 20th International Conference on Historical Linguistics. Osaka, July 25, 2011.
Faarlund, Jan Terje. 2001. From ancient Germanic to modern Germanic languages. In Martin Haspelmath, Ekkehard König, Wulf Oesterreicher & Wolfgang Raible (eds.), *Language typology and language universals. An international handbook*, 1706–1719. Berlin & New York: De Gruyter Mouton.
Faarlund, Jan Terje. 2008. *The syntax of Old Norse.* Oxford: Oxford University Press.
Fedorova, Olga V. 2012. Working materials on subject omission. Moscow State University. Ms.
Filchenko, Andrey Yury. 2007. A grammar of Eastern Hanty. Ph.D. diss. Houston, University of Texas.

Fougeron, Irina & Jean Breillard [Irina Fuženon & Žan Brejar]. 2004. Mestoimenie "ja" i postroenie diskursivnyx svjazej v sovremennom russkom jazyke [The pronoun "ja" and construction of discourse links in modern Russian]. In Tatyana M. Nikolaeva (ed.), *Verbal'naja i neverbal'naja opory prostranstva mežfrazovyx svjazej*, 147–166. Moscow: Jazyki slavjanskoj kul'tury.

Franks, Steven & Tracy Holloway King. 2000. *A handbook of Russian clitics*. Oxford: Oxford University Press.

Gippius, A. A. 2006. Skandinavskij sled v istorii novgorodskogo bojarstva (v razvitie gipotezy A. A. Molčanova o proisxoždenii posadnič'ego roda Gjurjatiničej-Rogovičej) [The Scandinavian trace in the history of the Novgorod nobility (developing the A. A. Molčanov's hypothesis on the origin of the mayor family Gjurjatinič-Rogovič)]. In Juhani Nuorluoto (ed.) *The Slavicization of the Russian North. Mechanisms and Chronology. Slavica Helsingiensia* 27, 93–108. Helsinki: Yliopistopaino.

Gorškova, Klavdija V. & Georgij A. Xaburgaev. 1981. *Istoričeskaja grammatika russkogo jazyka [A Historical grammar of Russian]*. Moscow: Vysšaja škola.

Grenoble, Lenore. 2001. Conceptual reference points, pronouns and conversational structure in Russian. *Glossos* 1. (http://www.seelrc.org/glossos/issues/1/grenoble.pdf)

Guxman, M. M. 1958. *Gotskij jazyk [Gothic]*. Moskva: Izdatel'stvo literatury na inostrannyx jazykax.

Heine, Bernd. 2008. Contact-induced word order change without word order change. In Peter Siemund & Noemi Kintana (eds.), *Language contact and contact languages*, 33–60. Amsterdam: Benjamins.

Hollett, Meghan. 2011. Null Subject Variation in Heritage Russian in Toronto. Master's thesis, University of Toronto.

Ivanov, Valerij V. 1982. Istorija vremennyx form glagola [History of verbal tense forms]. In Ruben I. Avanesov & Valerij V. Ivanov (eds.), *Istoričeskaja grammatika russkogo jazyka. Morfologija. Glagol*, 25–131. Moscow: Nauka.

Ivanov, Valerij V. 1990. Istoričeskaja grammatika russkogo jazyka [A Historical grammar of Russian]. Moscow: Prosveščenie.

Jakobson, Roman. 1971 [1935]. Les enclitiques slaves. In Roman Jakobson, *Selected Writings*, Vol. II, 16–22. The Hague: Mouton. (Original publication: Atti del Congresso di Linguistica tenuto in Roma il 19–26 Settembre 1933. Firenze, 1935).

Jakubinskij, L. P. 1953. *Istorija drevnerusskogo jazyka [A history of Old Russian]*. Moscow.

Keenan, Edward. 1976. Towards a universal definition of "Subject". In Charles N. Li (ed.), *Subject and topic*, 303–334. New York: Academic Press.

Kibrik, Aleksandr E. 1997. Beyond subject and object: Toward a comprehensive relational typology. *Linguistic Typology* 1(3). 279–346.

Kibrik, Andrej A. 1996. Anaphora in Russian narrative discourse: A cognitive calculative account. In Barbara A. Fox (ed.), *Studies in anaphora*, 255–304. Amsterdam: Benjamins.

Kibrik, Andrej A. 2004. Zero anaphora vs. zero person marking in Slavic: A chicken/egg dilemma? In António Branco, Ruslan Mitkov & Tony McEnery (eds.), *Proceedings of the 5th Discourse Anaphora and Anaphor Resolution Colloquium (DAARC 2004)*, 87–90. Lisbon: Edições Colibri.

Kibrik, Andrej A. 2011. *Reference in discourse*. Oxford: Oxford University Press.

Klejn, Lev S. 2009. *Spor o varjagax [The debate on Varangians]*. Saint-Petersburg: Evrazija.

Koivulehto, Jorma. 2002. Contact with non-Germanic languages II: Relations to the East. In Oskar Bandle, Lennart Elmevik & Gun Widmark (eds.), *The Nordic languages: An International handbook of the history of the North Germanic languages*, 583–594. Berlin & New York: De Gruyter Mouton.

Koljadenkov, M. N. 1954. *Grammatika mordovskix (ėrzjanskogo i mokšanskogo) jazykov. II. Sintaksis [A grammar or Erzya and Moksha Mordvin. II. Syntax]*. Saransk: Mordovskoe knižnoe izdatel'stvo.

Kononov, Andrej N. 1980. *Grammatika jazyka tjurkskix runicheskix pamjatnikov VII–IX vv. [A grammar of the language of the Turkic Runic documents of the 7th – 9th centuries]*. Leningrad: Nauka.

Kopotev, Mikhail V. 2007. Where Russian syntactic zeros start: Approaching Finnish? In Juhani Nuorluoto (ed.) *Topics on the Ethnic, Linguistic and Cultural Making of the Russian North*, (Slavica Helsingiensia 32), 116–137. Helsinki: Yliopistopaino.

Kopotev, Mikhail V. 2011. Reconstruction and idiomacity: The origin of Russian verbless clauses reconsidered. Paper presented at the 20th International Conference on Historical Linguistics, Osaka, 2011. Available at: www.helsinki.fi/~kopotev/kopotev_reconstruction_and_idiomacity.pdf.

Koptjevskaja-Tamm, Maria & Bernhard Wälchli. 2001. The Circum-Baltic languages: An areal-typological approach. In Östen Dahl & Maria Koptjevskaja-Tamm (eds.), 615–750.

Koryakov, Yuri B. 2006. Arxeologičeskie kul'tury III-IV vv. n.ė. i baltijskie gidronimy [The archaeological cultures of the 3–4th centuries AD and the Baltic hydronyms]. In V. N. Toporov, M. V. Zav'jalova, A. A. Kibrik, N. V. Rogova, A. V. Andronov & Yu. B. Koryakov (eds.), *Jazyki mira: baltijskie jazyki*, first end-leaf. Moscow: Academia.

Künnap, Ago. 1997. Potential Finno-Ugric Substratum in Slavic. *Linguistica Uralica* 33(4). 253–257.

Kuznecova, Ariadna I. (ed.) 2012. *Finno-ugorskie jazyki: fragmenty grammaticheskogo opisanija. [Finno-Ugric languages: Fragments of grammatical description]*. Moscow: JaSL.

Levshina, Natalia. 2012. Results of statistical analysis of the data in Pavova 2010. University of Jena. Ms.

Lindseth, Martina. 1998. *Null-subject properties of Slavic languages: with special reference to Russian, Czech and Sorbian*. München: Otto Sanger.

Lyutikova, Ekaterina A. & Sergey G. Tatevosov (eds.). 2000. *Mishar Tatar texts*. Moscow State University. Ms.

Markus, Elena B. & Fedor I. Rožanskij. 2011. *Sovremennyj vodskij jazyk. Teksty i grammatičeskij očerk*. Vol. 1, 2. Saint-Petersburg: Nestor-Istorija.

Matras, Yaron & Jeanette Sakel. 2007. Investigating the mechanisms of pattern replication in language convergence. *Studies in Language* 31(4). 829–865.

McShane, Marjorie. 2009. Subject Ellipsis in Russian and Polish. *Studia Linguistica* 63(1). 98–132.

Mel'nikova, Elena A. (ed.). 1986. *Slavjane i skandinavy [Slavs and Scandinavians]*. Moscow: Progress.

Migdalski, Krzysztof. 2009. The Diachronic Syntax of Perfective Auxiliaries in Polish. In B. Hansen & J. Grković-Major (eds.), *Diachronic Slavonic Syntax: Gradual Changes in Focus* (Wiener Slawistischer Almanach, Sonderband 74). 143–153.

Nagy, Naomi G., Nina Aghdasi, Derek Denis & Alexandra Motut. 2011. Null Subjects in Heritage Languages: Contact Effects in a Cross-linguistic Context. *University of Pennsylvania Working Papers in Linguistics* 17(2). 134–144.

Nichols, Johanna. 2012. Geolinguistics: Contact and language areas. Lecture presented at HSE, Moscow, Russia, in April 2012.

Nielsen, Hans Frede. 2000. *The early Runic language of Scandinavia: Studies in Germanic dialect geography*. Heidelberg: Winter.

Nilsson, B. 1982. *Personal Pronouns in Russian and Polish: A study of their communicative function and placement in the sentence* (translated from Swedish by Charles Rougle). Stockholm: Almqvist & Wiksell International.
Panzer, Baldur. 2002. Language contact during the Old Nordic period II: with Eastern Europe. In Oskar Bandle, Lennart Elmevik & Gun Widmark (eds.), *The Nordic languages: An International handbook of the history of the North Germanic languages*, 583–594. Berlin & New York: De Gruyter Mouton.
Pavlova, Elizaveta. 2010. Vzaimosvjaz' meždu markirovaniem lica v glagole i v podležaščnom mestoimenii v russkom jazyke [Relationship between person marking on the verb and on subject pronoun in Russian]. Year paper. Dept. of Theoretical and Applied Linguistics, Moscow State University.
Puškina, T. A. 2006. Vostočnaja Evropa v rannem Srednevekov'e [Eastern Europe in early Middle Age]. In V. L. Janin (ed.) *Arxeologija: Učebnik [Archaeology: A textbook]*, 398–462. Moscow: Izdatel'stvo Moskovskogo universiteta.
Rožanskij, Fedor I. & Elena B. Markus. 2012. Zolotaja ptica (publikacija ižorskoj skazki, zapisannoj v XIX veke). [The golden bird. A publication of an Ingrian tale recorded in the 19th century]. In *Acta Linguistica Petropolitana* VIII(1), 447–502. Saint-Petersburg: Nauka.
Sakel, Jeanette. 2007. Types of loan: matter and pattern. In Y. Matras & J. Sakel (eds.), *Grammatical borrowing in cross-linguistic perspective*, 5–29. Berlin & New York: De Gruyter Mouton.
Sammalahti, Pekka. 1998. *The Saami languages. An introduction*. Kárášjohka: Davvi Girji.
Sedov, V. V. 2002. Osvoenie slavjanami Vostočnoevropejskoj ravniny [Slavs' settlement of the Eastern European Plain]. In T. I. Alekseeva (ed.) *Vostočnye slavjane. Antropologija i etničeskaja istorija*, chapter 8. Moscow: Naučnyj mir.
Semenova, M. F. 1977. Iz istorii jazykovyx otnošenij v gorode Rige [From the history of linguistic relationships in Riga]. In *Kontakty latyšskogo jazyka*, 192–215. Riga: Zinatne.
Seo, Seunghyun. 2001. The frequency of null subjects in Russian, Polish, Bulgarian and Serbo-Croatian: An analysis according morphosyntactic environments. Ph.D. thesis. Dept. of Slavic languages and literatures, Indiana University.
Sidorova, Evgenija. 2012. Xronologija formirovanija russkoj referencial'noj sistemy [A chronology of the formation of the Russian referential system]. Year paper. Dept. of Theoretical and Applied Linguistics, Lomonosov Moscow State University.
Siewierska, Anna. 2004. *Person*. Cambridge: Cambridge University Press.
Siewierska, Anna. 2011. Verbal Person Marking. In Matthew S. Dryer & Martin Haspelmath (eds.), *The World Atlas of Language Structures Online*. Munich: Max Planck Digital Library, chapter 102. Available online at http://wals.info/chapter/102.
Squires, Catherine [Skvajrs, Ekaterina R.] & S. N. Ferdinand. 2002. *Hansa i Novgorod: Jazykovye aspekty istoričeskix kontakov. [Hanseatic League and Novgorod: Linguistic aspects of historical contacts]*. Moscow: Indrik.
Squires, Catherine. 2009. *Die Hanse in Novgorod: Sprachkontakte des Mittelniederdeutschen mit dem Russischen, mit einer Vergleichsstudie über die Hanse in England*. Köln: Böhlau.
Stone, Gerald. 1993a. Cassubian. In Bernard Comrie & Greville G. Corbett (eds.), *The Slavonic languages*, 759–794. London: Routledge.
Stone, Gerald. 1993b. Sorbian. In Bernard Comrie & Greville G. Corbett (eds.), *The Slavonic languages*, 593–685. London: Routledge.
Tereščenko, Natal'ja M. 1973. *Sintaksis samodijskix jazykov. Prostoe predloženie [Syntax of the Samoyedic languages. Simple sentence]*. Leningrad: Nauka.

Thomas, George. 1976. Srednenižnenemeckie zaimstvovanija v russkom jazyke [Middle Low German loanwords in Russian]. *Russian Linguistics* 3(1). 55-62.
Toporov, Vladimir N. 2006a. Baltijskie jazyki [Baltic languages]. In V. N. Toporov, M. V. Zav'jalova, A. A. Kibrik, N. V. Rogova, A. V. Andronov & Yu. B. Koryakov (eds.), *Jazyki mira: baltijskie jazyki*, 10-50. Moscow: Academia.
Toporov, Vladimir N. 2006b. Prusskij jazyk [Prussian]. In V. N. Toporov, M. V. Zav'jalova, A. A. Kibrik, N. V. Rogova, A. V. Andronov & Yu. B. Koryakov (eds.), *Jazyki mira: baltijskie jazyki*, 50-93. Moscow: Academia.
Trudgill, Peter. 2011. *Sociolinguistic typology: Social determinants of linguistic complexity*. Oxford: Oxford University Press.
Van Valin Jr., Robert D. 1993. A synopsis of Role and Reference Grammar. In Robert D. Van Valin Jr. (ed.), *Advances in Role and Reference Grammar*, 1-164. Amsterdam: Benjamins.
Veenker, Wolfgang. 1967. *Die Frage des finnougrischen Substrats in der russischen Sprache*. Bloomington: Indiana University.
Vernadsky, George. 1973. *Kievan Russia*. New Haven: Yale University Press.
Wiemer, Björn & Björn Hansen. 2012. Assessing the range of contact-induced grammaticalization in Slavonic. In Björn Wiemer, Bernhard Wälchli & Björn Hansen (eds.), *Grammatical replication and borrowability in language contact*, 67-158. Berlin & Boston: De Gruyter Mouton.
Xaburgaev, Georgij A. 1978. Sud'ba vspomogatel'nogo glagola drevnix slavjanskix analitičeskix form v russkom jazyke [The destiny of the auxiliary verbs in the Old Slavic analytic forms in Russian]. *Vestnik Moskovskogo universiteta. Philologija* 1978(4). 42-53.
Xaburgaev, Georgij A. 1991. Drevnerusskij i drevnepol'skij glagol v sopostavlenii so staroslavjanskim [Old Russian and Old Polish verb in contrast to Old Church Slavonic verb]. In G. A. Xaburgaev & A. Bartoševič (eds.), *Issledovanija po glagolu v slavjanskix jazykax. Istorija slavjanskogo glagola*, 42-54. Moscow: Izdatel'stvo Moskovskogo universiteta.
Xoroškevič, A. L. 1977-1978. *Polockie gramoty XIII – nachala XVI veka. [Polotsk letters of the 13th – early 16th century]*. Vol. 1, 2. Moscow: Institut istorii SSSR AN SSSR.
Zaliznjak, Andrej A. 1995. *Drevnenovgorodskij dialekt [Old Novgorod dialect]*. Moscow: Jazyki russkoj kul'tury.
Zaliznjak, Andrej A. 2008. *Drevnerusskie ènklitiki [Old Russian enclitics]*. Moscow: Jazyki slavjanskoj kul'tury.
Zdorenko, Tatiana. 2009. Subject omission in Russian: a study of the Russian National Corpus. *Language and Computers* 71(1). 119-133.'

Andrej L. Malchukov
Alignment preferences in basic and derived ditransitives[1]

1 Introduction

The term ditransitive has been used in the linguistic literature in two distinct senses. In the English studies (e.g., Mukherjee 2005), the term is used to refer to the double object constructions (e.g., *I gave Mary flowers*) as opposed to the prepositional construction (e.g., *I gave flowers to Mary*). In more recent typological use (Haspelmath 2004, 2005a, 2005b; Siewierska 2003, 2004; Siewierska & Bakker 2007; Malchukov, Haspelmath & Comrie 2010), the term is used in the semantic rather than syntactic sense, referring to verbs taking an agent argument (A), a recipient-like argument (R), and a theme argument (T). In what follows we will see that these two uses are related rather than orthogonal (semantic ditransitives showing a preference for a double object construction), but here I follow the typological tradition and use the term ditransitive in the semantic sense. Indeed, it is a common assumption in typology that the categories to be compared are given a semantic definition, which allows the identification of these categories across structurally different languages.

---

[1] I had the privilege of getting to know Anna Siewierska better over the last years when we collaborated on an editorial project concerning typology of impersonal constructions (Malchukov & Siewierska 2011), yet I learned of and from Anna's work much earlier. Our typological interests overlapped considerably, as we were both interested in the typology of voice, valency, alignment, and also ditransitive constructions (the topic of the present paper). I recall an enjoyable trip to Saxony's castles some time in the spring of 2008 with Anna and Dik, and my wife Larissa, when we had an opportunity to discuss many scientific and non-scientific matters. Although I had met Anna also on earlier and later occasions, it is probably this sunny spring day I would recall first when I think about Anna...

  This article is an outgrowth of the DFG-funded project based at Max Planck Institute for Evolutionary Anthropology on the typology of ditransitive constructions. The results of this project are partially published (Malchukov, Haspelmath & Comrie (eds.) 2010), but partially in preparation (Malchukov & Haspelmath, in preparation). The introductory part of the paper draws on the coauthored position paper (a version of which appeared as Malchukov, Haspelmath & Comrie 2010) and owes much to the insights of Martin Haspelmath and Bernard Comrie. Finally, I am indebted to the editors of the volume, Dik Bakker and Martin Haspelmath for insightful comments on the draft of this paper. The usual disclaimers apply.

Thus, the most typical ditransitive constructions contain a verb of physical transfer such as 'give', 'lend', 'hand', 'sell', 'return', describing a scene in which an agent participant causes an object to pass into the possession of an animate receiver (= recipient). It appears that in most languages, some verbs denoting a mental transfer (such as 'show' or 'tell') behave in a very similar way, which leads us to include these verbs in our definition of *ditransitive* as well. The animate argument of 'show' and 'tell' is not a recipient in the narrow sense, but we also regard it as an R-argument (i.e. a recipient-like argument). Likewise, we include less central transfer verbs such as 'offer', 'bequeath' and 'promise' into the ditransitive class.

A closely related construction type is the **benefactive construction**, which in many languages is expressed like the ditransitive construction. In some cases, it is not even clear whether we are dealing with a transfer situation (i.e. a ditransitive) or a benefactive situation (e.g. *She brought me a coffee*, which can be paraphrased as *She brought a coffee to me* or *She brought a coffee for me*). The key difference between benefactives and ditransitives is that beneficiaries may also occur with intransitive verbs (as in *She sang for me*). So, while noting that benefactives and ditransitives are often similar, we do not subsume the former under the latter.

Another way in which the term *ditransitive* is sometimes extended is by including **derived ditransitives** such as **causatives** and **applicatives**. In causative constructions, the causee often behaves like an R of ditransitive constructions, and the applicative object is often a beneficiary. The argument configuration of both causatives (of transitive verbs) and applicatives (of transitive verbs) is often very similar to that of ditransitive verbs. This is of course not an accident, because the meanings of transfer verbs contain a 'cause' element: 'Give' can be paraphrased as 'cause to have'. This paper will address the question how basic and derived constructions differ with respect to syntactic preferences.

The paper is organized as follows. In section 2 I discuss the main alignment types of ditransitive constructions. In section 3 I argue that ditransitive verbs show a preference for the double object construction, as well as discuss a motivation behind this preference. Section 4 compares alignment preferences of basic and derived ditransitives, concluding that the preference for neutral alignment (double object construction) is still more pronounced for derived ditransitives. In the discussion in section 5, this finding is explained by the higher complexity of derived (morphological) ditransitives, which fall into the mid-range on the complexity scale between lexical (basic) and syntactic ditransitives. The final section 6 provides a brief summary of the main findings of the article.

2 Basic alignment types

The notion of (syntactic) alignment has been traditionally applied in linguistic typology to the classification of monotransitive constructions, as compared to intransitive ones. Monotransitive constructions (with an agent or agent-like argument A and a patient or patient-like argument P) are usually compared to intransitive constructions (with a single argument S), and in this way one arrives at the classification into three major alignment types: accusative alignment (A = S ≠ P), ergative alignment (A ≠ S = P), and neutral alignment (A = S = P).

However, in the work of Haspelmath (2005a, 2005b) and Siewierska (2003, 2004) (following up on the earlier work by Comrie 1982, Blansitt 1984, and, especially, Dryer 1986) the notion of alignment has been extended to the study of ditransitive constructions. Martin Haspelmath and Anna Siewierska suggested that one can identify different ditransitive alignment types by comparing ditransitive constructions to monotransitives, in the same way as monotransitive alignment was identified by comparing monotransitive construction to intransitives. In this work the following three basic alignment types of ditransitive constructions are distinguished in terms of the encoding of T (theme) and R (recipient) compared to the monotransitive P (patient):

(i) Indirect object alignment, or **indirective alignment**: The R is treated differently from the P and the T (T = P ≠ R). Such constructions are also called 'dative constructions', or 'indirect object constructions'. An example comes from German, which has Dative case on the R and Accusative case on the P and the T.

(1) German

    a. (monotransitive)
    Ich   aß   den   Apfel.
    I.NOM ate the.ACC apple
    'I ate the apple.'

    b. (ditransitive)
    Ich   gab   dem   Kind   den   Apfel.
    I.NOM gave the.DAT child the.ACC apple
    'I gave the child the apple.'

(ii) Secondary object alignment, or **secundative alignment**: The T is treated differently from the P and the R (T ≠ P = R). Such constructions are also called 'primary object constructions'. This type is illustrated by West Greenlandic, which has Instrumental case on the T, and Absolutive case on the R and the P.

(2) West Greenlandic (Fortescue 1984: 193, 88)

    a. (monotransitive)
    Piita-p takurnarta-q tuqup-paa?
    Peter-ERG.SG stranger-ABS.SG kill-INT.3SG>3SG
    'Did Peter kill the stranger?'

    b. (ditransitive)
    (Uuma) Niisi aningaasa-nik tuni-vaa.
    (that.ERG) Nisi.ABS money-INSTR.PL give-IND.3SG>3SG
    'He gave Nisi money.'

(iii) **Neutral alignment:** The P, the R and the T are encoded in the same way (T = P = R). Such constructions are also often called 'double object constructions'. An example comes from Dagaare (Gur; Ghana), and of course the English translations of (1b), (2b) and (3b) also exemplify this type.

(3) Dagaare (Bodomo 1997: 41–42)

    a. (monotransitive)
    O na ngmɛ ma la.
    He FUT beat me FACT
    'He will beat me.'

    b. (ditransitive)
    O ko ma la a gane.
    he give.PERF me FACT DEF book
    'He gave me the book.'

A schematic representation of these alignment types is given in Figure 1 (from Malchukov, Haspelmath & Comrie 2010; cf. Croft 2003; Siewierska 2004; Haspelmath 2005b; and Dryer 2007):

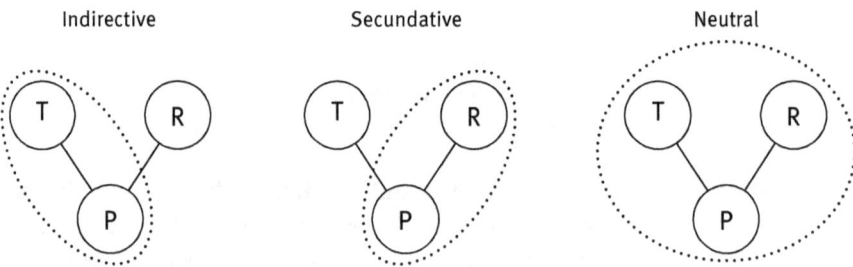

Figure 1. Ditransitive alignment maps

These three patterns are predicted to be the most frequent types as they comply with the functional principles of economy and distinguishability which apply to case marking in general. The indirective and secundative patterns are both economical in that they have at most two markers but still satisfy distinguishability between the R and T arguments. The neutral pattern is most economical because it needs no marker, and it is possible because distinguishability can also be ensured by other clues such as word order. There are other conceivable alignment types (tripartite, horizontal), but these are more rare and will not be discussed here (see Malchukov et al. 2010 for some discussion). There are further complications in determining ditransitive alignment (echoing similar problems for monotransitive alignment). In particular, one must distinguish between alignment in 'flagging' (case or adposition marking) and 'indexing' (agreement and cross-referencing). In many cases, 'flagging' and 'indexing' (the terms suggested by Haspelmath; see also Haspelmath, this volume) show the same alignment pattern (e.g., in Eskimo, ditransitive alignment is secundative both with respect to flagging – note the instrumental flagging on the T – and to indexing – R like P is indexed through object person marking), but in other cases they need not match (see Malchukov, Haspelmath & Comrie 2010 for a discussion of complexities in this domain). In this article ditransitive alignment will be identified on the basis of flagging, if not indicated otherwise.

In the next section, the alignment preferences for ditransitive verbs will be evaluated in comparison to other related verb types.

3 Alignment variation and lexical splits in ditransitive constructions

Intralinguistic variation in ditransitive constructions may be due to different factors. On the one hand, we find ditransitive alternations (such as the dative alternation) and splits, conditioned by the semantics of the construction, intrinsic properties of arguments, or their discourse characteristics. The dative alternation has been discussed from a typological perspective by Siewierska (1998, 2003), Haspelmath (2005b), and Malchukov et al. (2010), and will not be addressed here. Of more relevance to the present discussion is the issue of **lexical splits**, where the choice of a ditransitive pattern depends on a verbal lexeme. Such lexical splits are very common cross-linguistically, if not universal, at least on a broad view of the ditransitive domain. Thus, in English, *give* is either indirective (*give sth to sb*), or neutral (*give sb sth*), *say* is indirective only, and *present* can also be secundative (*present sb with sth*). In German *geben* 'give' is indirective (taking a dative R), while *lehren* 'teach' is neutral (occurring in a double object construction). In Russian, *(po-)darit'* 'give as a gift' is indirective, taking a dative R, but *o-darit'* (with a different perfectivizing prefix) is secundative, taking R as a direct object and T as an instrumental. Similar examples can be provided for many other languages. Lexical splits have not been studied systematically partly because much of the research has focused on the properties of canonical ditransitives, such as 'give' (e.g. Haspelmath 2005a,b). Yet, it has long been noted that 'give' may be an atypical ditransitive verb, with exceptional properties, and not representative for its class (Borg & Comrie 1984, Kittilä 2006). This also suggests that when one looks beyond prototypical ditransitives, such splits may be pervasive cross-linguistically.

Recent typological work on ditransitive constructions (Kittilä 2006, Conti 2008, Malchukov et al. 2010) has revealed that ditransitives show a preference for a double object construction. Although this preference cannot be stated in absolute terms (in fact, Haspelmath 2005a,b finds for a sample of languages represented in WALS that 'give' verbs show a preference for indirective alignment in flagging[2]), this preference can be detected by comparing ditransitive verbs to other, related, verb types (see Margetts & Austin 2007 for discussing typology of three-argument verbs from a cross-linguistic perspective). Malchukov et al. (2010), show that while caused motion verbs (like 'throw') and verbs with beneficiaries (e.g., 'build for smb') show a preference for indirective alignment and verbs of impact (e.g., 'hit') have a preference for secundative alignment, canonical ditransitives (as well as verbs of dispossession like 'steal') show a preference for neutral alignment, unless they align themselves with the neighboring semantic types. On different grounds, a similar conclusion has been reached by Kittilä (2006), who noted that in languages with closed class of verbs appearing in a double object construction, 'give'-verbs almost invariably belong to this class.

What can account for this predisposition of 'give' verbs for a double object construction (DOC), and what can account for counterexamples? Kittilä (2006) attributes this predilection to the fact that 'give' counts as "highly transitive" on a number of semantic transitivity parameters (identified by Hopper & Thompson 1980): In particular, it takes three arguments (unlike verbs with external beneficiaries), and depicts a situation with an R participant that is affected (unlike caused motion verbs like 'send' which do not carry this implication). Indeed, both features seem to be relevant. In particular, the role of affectedness is most obvious in the case of languages like English or Zulu (Taylor 1998), where the dative alter-

---

[2] Actually, Haspelmath (2005b) finds a strong indirective preference for flagging with ditransitives, but this preference holds if one compares indirective alignment to secundative alignment (58 cases vs. 6 cases in a 100-language sample), not if one compares indirective alignment to neutral (58 cases vs. 45).

nation is related to affectedness. The role of this factor can also be appreciated by looking at languages which go against the general tendency to assign 'give' to the class of double object verbs. For example, in Mandarin Chinese, verbs like 'steal' appear invariably in the DOC, while one of the 'give' verbs (*song*) allows variation between a DOC and a prepositional construction. Actually, it seems to be common that a DOC includes some of the verbs like 'steal', 'take away, snatch' and the like. Arguably, these verbs score higher on the scale of affectedness than 'give', which would account for their frequent use in a double-object construction.

As argued in Malchukov et al. (2010), another factor contributing to the preferential use of the 'give' verbs in a double object construction is an asymmetry between the two object arguments in prominence (animacy/ referentiality). This asymmetry has long been noticed for 'give' verbs, which normally have an animate R and inanimate T (Sedlak 1975), and definitely contributes to the use of unmarked patterns with ditransitives. Indeed, in a situation where the respective roles of the two objects are disambiguated through animacy, case marking becomes dispensable. Note that those ditransitive verbs which necessarily involve two animate objects do not show a predisposition for a double object construction (cf. *He introduced John Mary*; see Siewierska & van Lier 2012 for a typological study of such verbs). And a language may shift from a neutral to an indirective pattern in a situation when T is animate (as in Chinantec), or when T is pronominal (as in some varieties of English, see Haspelmath 2004 for other languages showing the Ditransitive Person-Role Constraint). For some verbs like 'teach', this asymmetry is even more pronounced, hence they can appear in a double object pattern even in languages where 'give' cannot (cf. the discussion of German *lehren* 'teach' in Plank 1987).

4 Alignment in basic vs. derived ditransitives: the data

Above we have seen that there are functional factors like affectedness and prominence-asymmetry which can explain the predisposition of 'give' verbs for a double object construction, but also account for counterexamples: These counterexamples involve verbs which outrank 'give' on one of the parameters: 'steal/snatch' verbs score better on affectedness, while 'call/teach' verbs do so on the asymmetry dimension. There is, however, another class of counterexamples, which has a structural rather than functional explanation. In what follows it will be shown that derived ditransitives show an even stronger preference for neutral alignment as compared to basic ditransitives.

Consider a case of Malayalam, mentioned by Kittilä 2006 as a counterexample to a stronger claim that in any language that has a closed class of verbs appearing in a double object construction 'give' will belong to this class. Thus, in Malayalam, 'give' takes a dative construction, while "less canonical ditransitives" (Asher & Kumari 1997: 205) like 'entrust' and 'feed' take a DOC:

(4)   Malayalam (Asher & Kumari 1997: 205)

    a. *kuṭṭi enikkə peena tannu.*
       child I.DAT pen give.PST
       'The child gave me the pen.'

    b. *ɲaan puuccakkə paal koṭuttu*
       I COW.PL.ACC grass eat.CAUS.PST
       'I fed the cows grass.'

Importantly, the verbs in the construction of (4b) are (lexicalized) causatives, and causatives of transitives in Malayalam regularly take a double object construction. This is not an isolated case. In a number of other languages, derived ditransitives (causatives and applicatives) appear in a DOC, while basic ditransitives do not. This is true, for example, for Imbabura Quechua; compare the dative construction with basic ditransitives in (5a) and the double object construction with derived ditransitives in (5b):

(5)   Imbabura Quechua (Cole 1982: 70, 136)

    a. *Juzi Marya-man muti-ta kara-rka.*
       José María-to mote-ACC give-PST.3
       'José gave/served mote to María.'

    b. *Juzi-ka Marya-ta-mi Juan-ta riku-chi-rka.*
       José-TOP María-ACC-VAL Juan-ACC see-CAUS-PST.3
       'José caused María to see Juan.'

In North Tungusic (Even and Evenki; Malchukov & Nedjalkov 2010), basic ditransitives take a dative construction (as in (6a) below), while causatives of transitives appear either in a dative (as in (6b)) or a double object construction (as in (6c)). In the latter case they have exclusively the 'factitive-coercive' reading:

(6)   Even (Malchukov 1995: 14)

    a. *Ewe-sel Kad'd'ak-tu miine-w böö-r.*
       Even-PL K.-DAT wine-ACC gave-NONFUT.3PL
       'Evens gave the wine to Kad'd'ak'

b. *Ewe-sel Kad'd'ak-tu miine-w kool-ukan.*
   Even-PL K.-DAT wine-ACC drink-CAUS.NONFUT.3PL
   'Evens made/let Kad'd'ak drink the wine.'

c. *Ewe-sel Kad'd'ak-u miine-w kool-ukan.*
   Even-PL K.-ACC wine-ACC drink-CAUS.NONFUT.3PL
   'Evens made Kad'd'ak drink the wine.'

Similarly, in some other languages, the DOC is either more restricted or optional for basic ditransitives, as compared with derived ones. In Udihe (East Tungusic; Nikolaeva & Tolskaya 2001), the DOC is restricted to a few lexical ditransitives, but is productive with derived ones (causatives of transitives). In Koyra Chiini (Heath 1998), only two basic ditransitives can appear in the double object construction, but derived ditransitives (causatives) regularly do so.

(7) Koyra Chiini (Heath 1998: 247, 135)

   a. *Ay noo ga i se.*
      1SG.SUBJ give 3SG.OBJ 3PL DAT
      'I gave it to them.'

   b. *Ay noo ni ga.*
      1SG.SUBJ give 2SG.OBJ 3SG.OBJ
      'I gave it to you.'

   c. *Ay ŋaa-ndi gi bita.*
      1SG.SUBJ eat-CAUS 3PL.OBJ porridge
      'I fed them some porridge.'

In Tümpisa Shoshone (Dayley 1989), there are few basic ditransitives, appearing in a double object construction, while most ditransitives are derived:

(8) Tümpisa Shoshone (Dayley 1989: 40)

   a. *Tuinuppü tammi eti uttuppühantü.*
      boy 1PL.INCL.ACC gun.ACC give.PST
      'The boy gave us a gun.'

   b. *Antsia tümüüngküppühantü nüü kwasu'unna.*
      Angie.ACC bought.APPL I dress.ACC
      'I bought Angie a dress.'

In Meithei (also called Manipuri; Bhat & Ningomba 1997, Chelliah 1997), basic ditransitives normally follow a dative-locative pattern (the DOC pattern is marginal, and not mentioned by Chelliah 1997 for basic ditransitives).

(9) Meithei (Bhat & Ningomba 1997: 113)

  əy-nə   maŋon-də   sən-du-bu   pi.
  1SG-AG   he-LOC   COW-DEF-PAT   give.PST
  'I gave that cow to him.'

The usual pattern for causatives, by contrast, is a DOC. (Chelliah 1997 notes, however, an alternative indirective pattern with the causee in the locative case, a pattern not reported by Bhat & Ningomba 1997).

(10) Meithei (Chelliah 1997: 111)

  əy-nə   Tombə-pu   səgol   tóŋ-hən-ləm-í.
  1sg-AC Tomba-PAT horse   ride-CAUS-EVD-NHYP
  'I made Tomba ride the horse.'

In Yaqui (Guerrero & Van Valin 2004), a few basic ditransitives occur in the DOC, while the majority take the "postpositional construction" with the 'dative' marker *-tau* (actually a combination of the accusative and the directional postposition):

(11) Yaqui (Guerrero & Van Valin 2004: 291)

  a. *Aurelia   Karmen-ta   toto'i-ta   miika-k.*
     Aurelia[NOM]   Carmen-ACC   hen-ACC   give-PSTP
     'Aurelia gave Carmen the hen.'

  b. *Aurelia   Karmen-ta-u   toto'i-ta   nenka-k.*
     Aurelia[NOM]   Carmen-ACC-DIR   hen-ACC   sell-PSPT
     'Aurelia sold the hen to Carmen.'

With derived ditransitives the double-accusative construction is the only option. This is illustrated below for the benefactive applicative:

(12) Yaqui (Guerrero & Van Valin 2004: 291)

  Aurelia   Goyo-ta   u-ka   wakabak-ta   joa-ria-k.
  Aurelia[NOM]   Goyo-ACC   the-ACC   wakabaki-ACC   cook-APPL-PSTP
  'Aurelia cooked Goyo the wakabaki.'

The same is true of the causative construction (with the suffix *-tua*) when it is built on transitives:

(13) Yaqui (Guerrero & Van Valin 2004: 312)

Goyo   im   chu'u-ta   nee   me'e-tua-k.
Goyo[NOM] 1SG.POSS dog-ACC 1SG.ACC kill-CAUS-PSPT
'Goyo made me kill my dog.'

Similarly, in Saliba (Oceanic; Margetts 2002), 'give' alternates between an allative pattern and a DOC, while for causatives only the DOC is possible. In Kashmiri (Wali & Koul 1997), R is dative with the basic ditransitives, but may be either dative or accusative with derived ones. Dixon (2000: 52) mentions some other languages where only derived ditransitives form a DOC.

Some further data from the ditransitive database (Malchukov & Haspelmath, in preparation; see Appendix for a list of languages in the database) providing evidence for the predisposition of derived ditransitives for a double object construction are summarized in the table below with numbers appended (variable patterns are ignored here)[3]:

Table 1. Alignment preferences in basic vs. derived ditransitives

BASIC	DERIVED	NUMBER	TOTAL
neutral	**neutral**	33 (100%)	
neutral	indirective	—	33 (44.6%)
neutral	secundative	—	
indirective	neutral	10 (30.3%)	
indirective	**indirective**	**21 (63.6%)**	33 (44.6%)
indirective	secundative	2 (6.1%)	
secundative	neutral	—	
secundative	indirective	—	8 (10.8%)
secundative	**secundative**	**8 (100%)**	
TOTAL		74	74

---

[3] The numbers in Table 1 refer to languages represented in the database that have morphological causatives and applicatives. Further excluded from the count are languages (like Kambera and Koasati) where causatives are not built productively on transitives, or where all ditransitives are derived (like Ainu and Tzotzil; see example (23) below).

Table 1 clearly shows a tendency for the matching relation between the basic and derived patterns (boldfaced), on the one hand, and, on the other hand, direction of possible mismatches which systematically associates indirective alignment with the basic pattern and neutral alignment (less commonly secundative alignment) with the derived pattern. In what follows we will refer to the first tendency as **Matching**, and to the second as a neutral **Bias** of derived ditransitives.

Thus we find the following possible patterns (illustrated below with representative language examples):

A. Consistent patterns

1) Basic neutral – Derived neutral

In Lai (Peterson 1998), both basic and derived ditransitives feature a double object construction (alignment of indexing is secundative, though). The basic construction is illustrated in (14a), the causative construction in (14b) and the benefactive applicative in (14c) (Lai features a large array of other applicative verbal suffixes, which behave similarly syntactically):

(14) Lai (Peterson 1998: 91, 94, 97)

    a. *Paŋpaar ʔan-rak-ka-peek.*
       flowers 3PL.SUBJ-PST-1SG.OBJ-give
       'They gave me flowers.'

    b. *Niihuu=niʔ boom kha   ʔa-ka-hmuʔ-sak.*
       Ni Hu=ERG basket DEICT 3PL.SUBJ-1SG.OBJ-see-CAUS
       'Ni Hu showed me the basket.'

    c. *Tsewmaŋ=niʔ   rool   ʔa-ka-tsuan-piak.*
       Tsewmang=ERG meal 3PL.SUBJ-1SG.OBJ-prepare-APPL
       'Tsewmang made a meal for me.'

2) Basic indirective – Derived indirective

In Kazakh (a Turkic language), both basic and derived (causatives) feature a dative construction:

(15) Kazakh (Talant Mawkanuli, p.c)

    a. *Men oquwšï-ğa kitap ber-di-m.*
       I student-DAT book give-PST-1SG
       'I gave the student a book.'

    b. *Men oğan kitap kör-set-ti-m.*
       I he.DAT book see-CAUS-PST-1SG
       'I showed him a book.'

3) Basic secundative – Derived secundative

In Movima (Haude 2006), both basic and derived ditransitives show secundative alignment in case marking. The R is the core argument, while the T is introduced by an oblique. Movima shows a further complication insofar as the expression of R in ditransitive construction depends on whether the verb is in the direct or inverse form: yet in both cases the R behaves like P by all relevant diagnostics, so the alignment remains secundative. The following example shows the direct version of the ditransitive construction (with the A argument indexed on the verb, the R in the object slot, and T as an oblique).

(16) Movima (Haude 2006: 276)

    Kayałe=us os pa:ko n-os charke.
    give.DIR=3SG.M ART dog obl-ART meat
    'He gave the dried meat to the dog.'

Similarly for causatives (of transitives) the causee is the core argument, while the original Patient is demoted to an oblique; likewise in applicatives the applied object is the core argument, and the original Patient surfaces as an oblique:

(17) Movima (Haude 2006: 397)

    Rim-eł-na-kwa-na=us nono' n-os ma:kina='nes
    trade-APPL-DIR-BEN-DIR=ART.M grandfather OBL-ART.N machine=ART.F
    majniwa=us.
    child_of=M
    'My grandfather bought the sewing machine for his daughter.'

Thus, in all the above cases the coding (alignment) of the basic ditransitives and derived ditransitives is identical, in accordance with the Matching principle.

B. Inconsistent patterns

Now let us turn to **inconsistent patterns,** where there is a discrepancy between alignment in basic and derived ditransitives.

4) Basic indirective – Derived neutral

In Wappo (Thompson et al. 2006), basic ditransitives appear in the dative construction; causatives, by contrast, form a double object construction ("with two unmarked nominals"):

(18) Wappo (Thompson et al. 2006: 12, 128)

    a. *Ce k'ew-i chica-thu ew ma-hes-taʔ.*
       DEM man-NOM bear-DAT fish DIR-give-PST
       'The man gave the fish to the bear.'

    b. *Cephi i oyaʔ keʔ- tis - taʔ.*
       3SG.NOM 1SG pot break-CAUS-PST
       'S/he made me break the pot.'

5) Basic indirective – Derived secundative

In Semelai (Kruspe 2004: 102), R is introduced by LOC preposition *ʔen* (or by a "deictic" locative marker indicating orientation towards the speaker); in both cases the alignment is indirective:

(19) Semelai (Kruspe 2004: 250)

    De=jon kweh ʔen smaʔ driʔ.
    3AG=give biscuit.PL LOC people 1.self
    'They gave biscuits to my people.'

The causative construction, by contrast, shows secundative alignment, with the causee appearing unmarked as the main object, and the original P in the locative form:

(20) Semelai (Kruspe 2004: 250)

    Ki=par-yəŋ la=ciʔgu hɛʔ bapaʔ.
    3AG=CAUS-hear AG=teacher LOC.above father
    'The teacher informed the father (of it).'

Note, however, that the following pattern is not attested in our data and presumably impossible or rare (hence marked by *):

- *Basic neutral – Derived indirective

The reviewed data suggest that derived ditransitives show a stronger preference for neutral (or sometimes secundative) alignment than basic ditransitives. This impression is strengthened when we take alternating patterns into consideration.[4] Thus, we find cases where the basic construction has indirective alignment, while the derived ditransitive allows for an alternation between indirective and neutral construction (Basic neutral – Derived indirective~neutral). This is the case in Even, where causatives of transitives may either take the regular dative construction attested for basic ditransitives, or, in case of a forceful factitive causative, also a double object construction (see (6) above). On the other hand, some languages may allow a variation with the basic ditransitives between the indirective and neutral construction, but use the double object construction exclusively with the derived ditransitives (thus: Basic indirective~ neutral – Derived neutral). This is a case in Koyra Chiini (see (7) above), where a few basic ditransitives ('give', 'show', marginally 'send'), apart from the canonical postpositional indirective construction, allow a double object construction (most other ditransitives allow for a 'dative shift' of a topical R, but the dative postposition is retained). However, we do not readily find languages where neutral alignment is found with basic ditransitives, while the derived ones allow for an indirective pattern as an option (*Basic neutral – Derived indirective ~ neutral), or where the basic ditransitives alternate between indirective and neutral alignment, but derived ditransitives show indirective alignment exclusively (*Basic indirective~neutral – Derived indirective).

Thus, on the basis of the preceding discussion we conclude that there are both consistent and inconsistent patterns with respect to alignment of basic vs. derived ditransitives. Moreover, in case of inconsistencies, derived ditransitives show a stronger preference for neutral alignment (double object construction) as compared to basic ditransitives. The possible explanations behind both these tendencies are discussed in the next section.

---

[4] As is clear from Table 1, there are also other unattested patterns involving secundative alignment (Basic secundative – Derived indirective; Basic secundative – Derived neutral; Basic neutral – Derived secundative), but these patterns will be ignored here. Given that secundative alignment (in flagging) is generally infrequent, our data do not warrant any generalizations in that respect.

5 Alignment in basic vs. derived ditransitives: discussion

Above we concluded that there are two basic generalizations emerging from our data (to the extent they are representative):

- **Matching**: alignment of basic and derived ditransitives tends to be identical
- **Bias**: derived ditransitives show a stronger preference to neutral alignment as compared to basic ditransitives.

In what follows we will discuss the possible explanations behind these cross-linguistic tendencies. Let's start with the Matching principle, as it has been debated already in the literature. In a way, the matching relation is expected, given semantic similarity of basic and derived ditransitives. Thus, as observed earlier, the connection to causatives is plausible because the meanings of transfer verbs contain a 'cause' element, and a connection to benefactive applicatives is expected given similarities between recipients and beneficiaries. Yet, in the literature a more specific explanation of this parallelism has been proposed. In particular, a number of authors working in a cognitive tradition such as Kemmer & Verhagen (1994), Song (1996)[5], and Shibatani (1996), have claimed that derived ditransitives (causatives) are modeled on basic ditransitives, in particular on verbs of giving. This seems an attractive solution, also given that the tendency to conceptualize less basic events in terms of a more salient basic event carries over to other constructions. Thus, Haspelmath & Müller-Bardey (2004) propose a general constraint on valency changes to the effect that derived valency patterns must be identical to valency patterns that occur with at least some non-derived verbs (see also Dik's 1997: 158 Principle of Formal Adjustment to the same effect). This explanation seems most appropriate for cases when the cognitive explanation is supported by structural considerations and can be given a straightforward diachronic interpretation. Shibatani's (1996) discussion of the applicative periphrasis of the type observed in Japanese and Korean provides a good example. Shibatani observed that in both Japanese and Korean 'give'-based applicatives follow the pattern of

---

5 Song (1996), following Gerdts (1988), proposes a somewhat different explanation to the matching relation which he attributes to general constraints on the number of core argument positions available for different languages ("NP-density"). On that approach, the possibility of a double object construction is dependent on the number of object slots available for a particular language. If a language admits two core object slots, it is expected that it would admit a double object construction both for basic and derived ditransitives.

'give'-verbs, leading to subtle differences between the two languages (the applicative construction in Japanese allows only the dative case on the applied object, while Korean allows for a variation – in the form of the beneficiary):

(21) Japanese (Shibatani 1996)

 a. *Hahaoya-ga kodomo-ni/*-o hon-o yat-ta.*
  mother-NOM child-DAT/-ACC book-ACC give-PST
  'Mother gave a book to the child.'

 b. *Hahaoya-ga kodomo-ni/*-o hon-o kat-te yat-ta.*
  mother-NOM child-DAT/-ACC book-ACC buy-CONV give-PST
  'Mother bought the child a book.'

(22) Korean (Shibatani 1996)

 a. *Emeni-ka ai-eykey/-lul chaek-ul cwu-ess-ta.*
  mother-NOM child-DAT/-ACC book-ACC give-PST-IND
  'Mother gave a book to the child.'

 b. *Emeni-ka ai-eykey/-lul chaek-ul sa-cwu-ess-ta.*
  mother-NOM child-DAT/-ACC book-ACC buy-give-PST-IND
  'Mother bought the child a book.'

Shibatani (1996) comments:

> In languages that make a distinction between the accusative and the dative case, the beneficiary nominal of a benefactive applicative generally takes the dative case. Korean and Japanese, however, differ in this respect. Korean allows accusative marking on the applied beneficiary, while Japanese does not. This is apparently connected to the fact that while Korean allows double accusative constructions with the basic ditransitive verb 'give' (*cwuta*), Japanese does not.

For cases where causatives or applicatives are based on the verb 'give' (see Newman 1996; Creissels 2010 for further discussion and exemplification of the grammaticalization of the verb 'give' to a causative or an applicative marker), the conclusion that derived ditransitives are modeled on basic ditransitives is uncontroversial. Yet, contrary to the claims in the literature (Kemmer & Verhagen 1994), it turns out that in addition to derived ditransitives being modeled on basic ditransitives, basic ditransitives can be modeled on derived ditransitives as well. This is especially clear in languages with a small class of ditransitives (such as Koyra Chiini in (7) or Tümpisa Shoshone in (8) above; see Malchukov et al. 2010, Kittilä 2006, Conti 2008 for other languages). Bottom line cases constitute languages where all ditransitives including 'give' are derived, as in the case of Tzotzil:

(23) Tzotzil (Aissen 1983: 280)

> Ti mi č-av-ak'-b-on ʔep tak'ine.
> if Q ASP-2ERG-give-BEN-ABS.1 much money
> 'If you will give me a lot of money.'

The same is true of Ainu (Bugaeva 2010), where all ditransitive verbs are derived, either as causatives (e.g., kor-e have-CAUS 'give'), or as applicatives (ko-itak APPL-speak 'tell'). For such languages, the question of derived ditransitives being modeled on basic ones does not arise. But also for languages with a small closed class of ditransitives following the pattern of the derived ditransitives it stands more to reason to say that basic ditransitives are modeled on derived ones and through analogy assimilated to the latter syntactically.

Yet, the observation of a matching relation between basic and derived ditransitives made by Comrie (1981: 171), Kemmer & Verhagen (1994), Song (1996) and Shibatani (1996) generally holds, as is also obvious from the table above. This tendency is especially clear for cases where there is a parallel split (or alternation) attested for both basic and derived verbs. This is observed in Sahaptin (Rude 1997), where a neutral/indirective alternation is conditioned by the animacy hierarchy. Ditransitive verbs feature a double object construction if T is inanimate, but an indirective construction when T is pronominal. When T is animate but non-pronominal both neutral (as in (24a) and indirective alignment (as in (24b)) is possible. (Rude 1997 describes these options in terms of a dative shift being a) obligatory, b) optional or c) impossible).

(24) Sahaptin (Rude 1997: 335)

> a. Pa-ní-ya tílaaki miyúux-na.
> PL.NOM-give-PST woman chief-OBJ
> 'They gave the woman to the chief.'

> b. Pa-ní-ya tílaaki-na muyuux-mí-yaw.
> 3PL.NOM-give-PST woman-OBJ chief-GEN-ALL
> 'They gave the woman to the chief.'

Importantly, in the present context, this alternation is equally observed for basic and derived ditransitives. Sahaptin shows a variety of valency increasing categories, but this conclusion pertains to all of them: below the ditransitive alternation is illustrated for desideratives (formed periphrastically), which can be regarded as a subvariety of causatives (an A-adding operation):

(25) Sahaptin (Rude 1997: 344)

a. *I-tq'íx-ša=aš   kíʔlawi-t   núsux.*
   3NOM-want-IPFV=1SG taste-NZR salmon
   'He wants me to taste the salmon.'

b. *I-tq'íx-ša   in-mí-yaw   kíʔlawi-t   núsux-na.*
   3NOM-want-IPFV 1SG-GEN-ALL taste-NZR salmon-OBJ
   'He wants the salmon to be tasted by me.'

To conclude, there is a cross-linguistic preference for a matching relation between alignment patterns of basic and derived ditransitives. This matching preference is motivated by semantic and cognitive similarities, but also strengthened by particular diachronic developments where either the applicative and causative constructions are based on 'give'-verbs, or 'give'-verbs themselves are derived through causative or applicative marking. Yet, as with other functionally motivated preferences, this matching relation should be seen as a typological preference, not as an absolute universal (as suggested, e.g., by Song 1996). As is also clear from our data, another, potentially interfering, factor is the tendency for derived ditransitives to have neutral alignment (Bias). This results in a consistent pattern of mismatches, where derived ditransitives show a double object pattern in contrast to basic ditransitives (Dixon 2000: 52 also mentions a number of languages such as Hebrew, Quechua, Amharic, Oromo, Gano, where only causatives show a double object pattern).

It seems that this preference for neutral alignment of derived ditransitives can be explained by structural considerations. That is, derived ditransitives often allow two objects because they are more complex formally and thus can have more arguments. Indeed, derived ditransitives (causatives and applicatives) can be placed in the mid-range on the scale, with basic (non-derived) ditransitives, at one pole, and the syntactic (periphrastic) applicatives and causatives at another pole of the scale (cf. Comrie's 1981: 164 complexity continuum for causative formation ranging from lexical to analytic causatives).

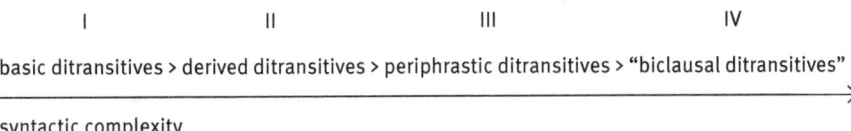

basic ditransitives > derived ditransitives > periphrastic ditransitives > "biclausal ditransitives"

syntactic complexity

Figure 2. Complexity scale for basic vs. derived ditransitives

The term 'basic ditransitive' refers here to non-derived ditransitives (with monomorphemic stems); the derived ditransitives conventionally refer to (productive) morphological causatives and applicatives; periphrastic ditransitives refer to multi-verb constructions with auxiliaries and serial verbs with applicative and causative functions, and "biclausal ditransitives" refer to complex multiclausal patterns synonymous to one of the aforementioned constructions (see Nedjalkov & Sil'nickij 1969, Song 1996, Dixon 2000 for discussion of structural varieties of causatives, and Peterson 2007 and Creissels 2010 on applicatives). "Biclausal ditransitives" ranking highest on the complexity scale appear in quotation marks as they lie beyond the definition of the ditransitive constructions in the sense of Haspelmath (2005b) and Malchukov et al. (2010). Here, a causative (or benefactive, malefactive, etc) event is expressed by a separate lexical verb, and in that case it is trivially true that both verbs introduce their own objects. But also with periphrastic ditransitives involving auxiliaries or serial verbs having two (direct) objects is a predominant pattern. This is most obvious for serial verb constructions, which introduce R and T as core arguments of two separate verbs. This can be illustrated for Yorùbá, where the theme is introduced by the serial verb *fi* 'take, use' (which is rather grammaticalized and glossed as a secundative marker) and the recipient is introduced by the verb *fún* 'give':

(26) Yorùbá (Atoyebi et al. 2010: 150)

mo fi ayéè mi fún ẹ
1SG.SUBJ SEC life.POSS 1SG.POSS give 2SG.OBJ
'I give my life to you.'

Judging from the data represented in the ditransitive database (Malchukov & Haspelmath, in preparation), cases such as Supyire, where a serial verb may also take an adpositional object, such as the beneficiary in (27), seem to be exceptional.

(27) Supyire (Carlson 1994: 297)

Kà pi í shwɔ? ´ha à kan pi à.
and they NARR cook SC give them to
'They cooked for them.'

The same holds for other types of periphrastic constructions, which may, however, allow more variation. A well-known case involves the periphrastic *faire*-causative in French, showing more syntactic integration ("clause union", in terms of Relational Grammar) and aligning itself with (lexical) ditransitives (introducing the causee through the preposition *à* used for recipients). At the other side of the complexity cline we find basic ditransitives, which, by definition count as single predicates and may be subject to restrictions on the expression of (core) arguments found in individual languages. Note that some languages impose strict constraints on the number of argument slots, especially with respect to the number of direct (unmarked) objects that can be accommodated (Gerdts 1988; Song 1996). Finally, derived ditransitives fall in the mid-range of the complexity scale, and may align themselves either with basic ditransitives (which overall show a predisposition for indirective alignment in flagging, at least in Haspelmath's 2005a/b data, though not so much in our database), or else may align themselves with periphrastic causatives and applicatives which show a neutral preference. Therefore if a language disallows a double object construction with derived ditransitives (morphological causatives and applicatives), the same restrictions will be found with basic ditransitives (lexical causatives and applicatives), which show a tighter syntactic integration.

Thus, my prediction is:

(28) a. if a language has indirective alignment of derived ditransitives, it will also have indirective alignment with basic ditransitives; and

b. if a language has neutral alignment with basic ditransitives, it will also have neutral alignment with derived ditransitives.

As can be seen from Table 1 above, this generalization is corroborated by our data; yet it needs one qualification. The qualification is needed for a variety of applicatives, which might challenge the implicational generalization above. While the benefactive applicatives (promoting beneficiaries or, possibly, recipient and animate goals) generally support the generalization above, instrumental applicatives used to promote instruments to a primary object might be problematic. Indeed, if an instrumental applicative applies both to Instruments and Themes of ditransitives, it can promote a Theme to the primary object at the expense of demoting a Recipient to the oblique. This would result in the indirective alignment in languages featuring secundative or neutral alignment of basic ditransitives. Consider the case of West Greenlandic (Fortescue 1984), where basic ditransitives mostly follow the secundative pattern (there are a few ditransitive verbs with an indirective pattern as well). As illustrated in (29), in the basic secundative pattern R appears in the absolutive case, while T appears in the instrumental case.

(29)   West Greenlandic (Fortescue 1984: 88)

Niisi aningaasa-nik tuni-vaa.
Niisi money-instr.PL give-IND.3SG>3SG
'He gave Nisi money.'

Now, West Greenlandic features an applicative marker -*uT*-, which performs a wide range of functions. When applied to secundative ditransitives (as in (29)), it performs a function similar to instrumental applicatives. The base theme appears in the absolutive case and R is "demoted" to an allative oblique, resulting in the overall indirective pattern.

(30) West Greenlandic (Fortescue 1984: 88)

Aningaasa-t   Niisi-mut tunni-up-pai.
money-PL.ABS Nisi-ALL   give-APPL-IND.3SG>3PL
'He gave money to Nisi.'

Thus, when applied to secundative ditransitives the applicative marker changes alignment from secundative to indirective. Yet, elsewhere (when applied to monotransitive verbs and also less typically, to some indirective ditransitives), the same applicative marker -*uT*- performs a seemingly opposite function, promoting the beneficiary to the absolutive status. Note that the base object is in the instrumental, while the beneficiary is indexed through object agreement in (31):

(31) West Greenlandic (Fortescue 1984: 325)

Qaanna-mik sana-ap-paa.
boat-INSTR   make-APPL-IND.3SG>3SG
'He made a kayak for him.'

In the latter case the applicative formation yields a secundative pattern matching the secundative pattern of basic ditransitives. This pattern of markedness reversal, with the same applicative marker used to promote a recipient/beneficiary with one class of verbs, and to demote it with another class, reminds us that applicative formation is designed to change rather than maintain basic alignment. As we saw above, in languages with a basic secundative alignment, this dependency of an applicative on the basic alignment can produce patterns inconsistent with our generalization in (28a), and, more generally, with the Matching principle.

Yet, it should be noted that the effect of this factor seems generally negligible. First, an instrumental applicative (of the type illustrated above for West Greenlandic) may be restricted to instruments of verbs of impact and not extend to themes of ditransitive verbs (as is, e.g., the case in Dyirbal; Dixon 1972: 95). Second, the applicative formation (also of the instrumental type) may result in a double object construction, conforming to the suggested generalization. And, most importantly, the cases of pattern reversal as observed in West Greenlandic, may be argued to be irrelevant for the proposed generalization, given that elsewhere we compare the behavior of basic ditransitives to causatives and applicatives based on monotransitives rather than on ditransitives.

6 Conclusions

In the present article I have discussed the alignment patterns of basic and derived ditransitives. I concluded that ditransitives show a certain preference for neutral alignment (double object construction), even though this preference can be detected through comparison with other verb types rather than stated in absolute terms. A comparison of alignment types of basic and derived ditransitives (causatives and applicatives of monotransitives) has further revealed two generalizations. On the one hand, our data confirm a tendency for a matching relation between coding of basic and derived ditransitives, as already observed in the functional-typological literature. In some cases this matching relation can be attributed to a general tendency to model derived constructions on basic ones. In other cases, where basic ditransitives constitute a closed class, it arguably stands more to reason to regard basic ditransitives as aligning themselves to derived ditransitives used productively in a double object construction. Moreover, it has been shown that derived ditransitives show a still stronger preference to neutral alignment, as compared to basic ditransitives. This finding has been attributed to the fact that derived ditransitives show less syntactic integration than the basic ones, falling into a mid-range between basic ditransitives and biclausal constructions.

Of course, there may be further differences between basic and derived ditransitives across languages, which remain unexplored here. Thus, in a number of languages (including Malayalam, Hindi and Hungarian, to name a few), the causee of derived ditransitives can be marked by the instrumental case, while instrumental marking of Rs is virtually unattested. Yet, this difference does not affect alignment as such and therefore falls beyond the scope of this article (but see Comrie 1976, Kemmer & Verhagen 1994; Dixon 2000 for discussion of cross-linguistic variation in coding of causees and their motivations). Also some other questions such as systematic comparison of causatives and applicatives with respect to alignment preferences are left unaddressed here and are left for future research.

Abbreviations

1 first person, 2 second person, 3 third person, 1 ABS absolutive, ACC accusative, AG agent, ALL allative, AOR aorist, APPL applicative, ART article, ASP aspect, BEN benefactive, CAUS causative, CONV converb, DAT dative, DEF definitive, DEICT deictic, DIR direct (voice), DOC double object construction, ERG ergative, EVD evidential, F feminine, FACT factual, FUT future, GEN genitive, INCL inclusive, IND indicative, INSTR instrumental, INT interrogative (mood), IPFV imperfective, LOC locative, M masculine, N neuter, NARR narrative, NOM nominative, NHYP non-hypothetical, NONFUT nonfuture, NZR nominalizer, OBJ object, OBL oblique, PAT patient, PERF perfect, PL plural, POSS possessive, PST past, PSTP past perfective, Q question, SC serial verb connective, SEC secundative, SG singular, SUBJ subject, TOP topic, VAL validator.

Appendix

List of languages represented in the ditransitive database (Malchukov & Haspelmath, forthcoming)

This list includes languages that feature morphological applicatives and/or causatives. Those languages, which either lack basic ditransitives (indicated by *), or lack causatives and applicatives based on monotransitives are in brackets.

Abkhaz, (Ainu*), Alamblak, Amele, Amharic, Bajau, Basque, Cashinahua, Chamorro, Chinantec, Chintang, Crow, Diyari, Djingili, Dyirbal, Even, Evenki, Garo, Georgian, Greenlandic, Halkomolem, Hixkaryana, Hungarian, Hupa, Ika, Indonesian, Itonama, (Jacaltec), Jamul Tiipay, Japanese, (Kambera), Kashmiri, Kazakh, Ket, (Khanty), Khwarshi, (Koasati), Korean, Koyra Chiini, Kwaza, Lai, Lakhota, Lango, (Lavukaleve), Laz, Malayalam, Manam, Maricopa, Mapudungun, Martuthunira, Meithei, Movima, Newari, Ojibwa, Olutec, Oriya, Paiute, Panjabi, Pomo, Passamaquoddy, Qiang, Quechua, Sahaptin, Saliba, Semelai, Shipibo, Shoshone, Supyire, Swahili, Tariana, Teop, Tiriyo, Totonac, Tukang Besi, (Tzotzil*), Vafsi, Wappo, Yaqui, (Yoruba), Yuracare, Zulu, !Xun.

References

Aissen, Judith L. 1987. *Tzotzil Clause Structure*. Studies in Natural Language and Linguistic Theory, 7. Dordrecht: Reidel.
Asher, Ronald E. & Kumari, T. C. 1997. *Malayalam*. London: Routledge.
Atoyebi, Joseph, Martin Haspelmath & Andrej Malchukov. 2010. Ditransitive constructions in Yorùbá. In Andrej Malchukov, Martin Haspelmath & Bernard Comrie (eds.), *Studies in ditransitive constructions*, 145–166. Berlin & New York: De Gruyter Mouton.
Bhat, D. N. S. & Ningomba, M. S., 1997. *Manipuri Grammar*. München: Lincom.
Blansitt, Edward L. Jr. 1984. Dechticaetiative and dative. In Frans Plank (ed.), *Objects: Towards a Theory of Grammatical Relations*, 127–150. London: Academic Press.
Bodomo, Adams. 1997. *The Structure of Dagaare*. Stanford: CSLI Publications.
Borg, Albert, & Bernard Comrie. 1984. Object diffuseness in Maltese. In Frans Plank (ed.), *Objects: Towards a Theory of Grammatical Relations*, 109–126. London: Academic Press.

Bugaeva, Anna. 2010. Ainu applicatives in typological perspective. *Studies in Language* 34(4). 749–801.
Carlson, Robert. 1994. *Grammar of Supyire*. Berlin & New York: De Gruyter Mouton.
Chelliah, S. L. 1997. *A Grammar of Meithei*. Berlin & New York: De Gruyter Mouton.
Cole, Peter. 1982. *Imbabura Quechua*. [Lingua Descriptive Studies, Vol 5]. Amsterdam: North-Holland Publishing Company.
Comrie, Bernard. 1981. *Language Universals and Linguistic Typology*. Chicago: University of Chicago Press.
Comrie, Bernard. 1982. Grammatical relations in Huichol. In Paul J. Hopper & Sandra A. Thompson (eds.), *Studies in Transitivity*, 95–115. [Syntax and Semantics 15]. New York: Academic Press.
Conti, Carmen. 2008. *Receptores y beneficiarios: estudio tipológico de la ditransitividad*. Munich: Lincom.
Creissels, Denis. 2010. Benefactive-applicative periphrasis: a typological approach. In Fernando Zúñiga & Seppo Kittilä (eds.), *Benefactives and malefactives: typological perspectives and case studies*, 28–66. Amsterdam: Benjamins.
Croft, William. 2003. *Typology and Universals*. Second edition. Cambridge: Cambridge University Press.
Dayley, Jon P. 1989. *Tümpisa (Panamint) Shoshone Grammar*. Berkeley. University of California Press.
Dik, Simon. 1997. *The theory of Functional Grammar*. Vol. 2. *Complex and derived constructions*. Berlin & New York: De Gruyter Mouton.
Dixon, Robert Malcolm Ward. 1972. *The Dyirbal Language of North Queensland*. Cambridge. Cambridge University Press.
Dixon, Robert Malcolm Ward. 2000. A typology of causatives: form, syntax, and meaning. In Dixon, R. M. W. & A. Y. Aikhenvald (eds.), *Changing valency: case studies in transitivity*, 30–83. Cambridge: Cambridge University Press.
Dryer, Matthew S. 1986. Primary objects, secondary objects, and antidative. *Language* 62. 808–845.
Dryer, Matthew S. 2007. Clause types. In Timothy Shopen (ed.), *Language Typology and Syntactic Description*, vol. II, 2nd ed., 224–275. Cambridge: Cambridge University Press.
Fortescue, Michael D. 1984. *West Greenlandic*. London. Croom Helm.
Gerdts, Donna B. 1988. *Object and Absolutive in Halkomelem Salish*. New York: Garland Publishing.
Guerrero, Lilián & Van Valin Jr., Robert D. 2004. Yaqui and the Analysis of Primary Object Languages. *International Journal of American Linguistics* 70(3). 290–319.
Haspelmath, Martin. 2004. Explaining the Ditransitive Person-Role Constraint: a usage based account. *Constructions* 2/2004, 49 pp. (free online journal, University of Düsseldorf; http://www.constructions-online.de/articles/35)
Haspelmath, Martin. 2005a. Ditransitive Constructions: The Verb 'Give'. In Martin Haspelmath, Matthew S. Dryer, David Gil & Bernard Comrie (eds.), *The World Atlas of Language Structures*, 426–429. Oxford: Oxford University Press.
Haspelmath, Martin. 2005b. Argument marking in ditransitive alignment types. *Linguistic Discovery* 3(1). 1–21.
Haspelmath, Martin & Thomas Müller-Bardey. 2004. Valency change. In Geert Booij, Christian Lehmann & Joachim Mugdan (eds.), *Morphology: A Handbook on Inflection and Word Formation*. Vol. 2, 1130–1145. Berlin & New York: De Gruyter Mouton.
Haude, Katharina. 2006. A Grammar of Movima. Ph. Diss. Universiteit Nijmegen.

Heath, Jeffrey. 1998. *A grammar of Koyra Chiini, the Songhay of Timbuktu*. Berlin & New York: De Gruyter Mouton.
Hopper, Paul J. & Sandra Thompson. 1980. Transitivity in Grammar and Discourse. *Language* 56. 251–299.
Kemmer, Susan & Arie Verhagen 1994. The grammar of causatives and the conceptual structure of events. *Cognitive Linguistics* 5. 115–156.
Kittilä, Seppo. 2006. The anomaly of the verb 'give' explained by its high (formal and semantic) transitivity. *Linguistics* 44(3). 569–612.
Kruspe, Nicole. 2004. *A Grammar of Semelai*. Cambridge: Cambridge University Press.
Malchukov, Andrej L. 1995. *Even*. Munich: LINCOM.
Malchukov, Andrej & Igor' Nedjalkov. 2010. Ditransitive constructions in Tungusic languages. In Andrej Malchukov, Martin Haspelmath & Bernard Comrie (eds.) *Studies in ditransitive constructions*. Berlin & New York: De Gruyter Mouton, 316–352. Berlin & New York: De Gruyter Mouton.
Malchukov, Andrej, Martin Haspelmath & Bernard Comrie. 2010. Ditransitive constructions: a typological overview. In Andrej Malchukov, Martin Haspelmath & Bernard Comrie (eds.), *Studies in ditransitive constructions*, 1–65. Berlin & New York: De Gruyter Mouton.
Malchukov, Andrej & Martin Haspelmath. In preparation. *Ditransitive constructions*.
Margetts, Anna. 2002. The linguistic encoding of three-participant events in Saliba. *Studies in Language* 26. 613–637.
Margetts, Anna, & Peter K. Austin. 2007. Three participant events in the languages of the world: towards a crosslinguistic typology. *Linguistics* 45(3). 393–451.
Mukherjee, Joybrato. 2005. *English Ditransitive Verbs: Aspects of Theory, Description and a Usage-based Model*. Amsterdam/New York: Rodopi.
Nedjalkov, Vladimir P. & G. G. Sil'nickij. 1969. Tipologija morfologičeskogo i leksičeskogo kauzativov. In Aleksandr A. Xolodovič (ed.), *Tipologija kauzativnyx konstrukcij: Morfologičeskij kauzativ*, 20–50. Leningrad: Nauka.
Nikolaeva, Irina & Tolskaya, Maria. 2001. *A grammar of Udihe*. Berlin & New York: De Gruyter Mouton.
Newman, John. 1996. *Give: A Cognitive Linguistic Study*. Berlin & New York: De Gruyter Mouton.
Peterson, David A. 1998. The morphosyntax of transitivization in Lai (Haka Chin). *Linguistics of the Tibeto-Burman Area* 21(1). 87–153.
Peterson, David A. 2007. *Applicative constructions: a study of their convergent typologies*. Oxford: Oxford University Press.
Plank, Frans. 1987. Direkte indirekte Objekte: Was uns *lehren* lehrt. *Leuvense Bijdragen* 76. 37–61.
Rude, Noel. 1997. Dative shifting and double objects in Sahaptin. In Talmy Givón (ed.), *Grammatical Relations: A Functionalist Perspective*, 323–349. Amsterdam. Benjamins.
Sedlak, Philip A. S. 1975. Direct/indirect object word order: a cross-linguistic analysis. *Stanford Working Papers on Language Universals* 18. 117–164.
Shibatani, Masayoshi. 1996. Applicatives and benefactives: A cognitive account. In Masayoshi Shibatani & Sandra A. Thompson (eds.), *Grammatical constructions. Their form and meaning*, 157–194. Oxford: Clarendon Press.
Siewierska, Anna. 1998. Languages with and without objects. *Languages in Contrast* 1(2). 173–190.
Siewierska, Anna. 2003. Person agreement and the determination of alignment. *Transactions of the Philological Society* 101(2). 339–370.

Siewierska, Anna. 2004. *Person*. Cambridge: Cambridge University Press.
Siewierska, Anna & Dik Bakker. 2007. Bound person forms in ditransitive clauses revisited. *Functions of Language* 14(1). 103–125.
Siewierska, Anna & Eva van Lier. 2012. Ditransitive constructions with two human non-agentive arguments. *Faits de Langues* 39. 140–156.
Song, Jae Jung. 1996. *Causatives and causation: a universal-typological perspective*. Longman: London.
Taylor, John R. 1998. Double object constructions in Zulu. In John Newman (ed.), *The Linguistics of Giving*, 67–96. Amsterdam. Benjamins.
Thompson, Sandra A., Joseph Sung-Yul Park & Charles N. Lee. 2006. *A reference grammar of Wappo*. Berkeley: University of California Press.
(Available online at http://repositories.cdlib.org/ucpress/)
Wali, K. & O. Koul. 1997. *Kashmiri: a cognitive-descriptive grammar*. London: Routledge.

Marianne Mithun
Prosody and independence: free and bound person marking

1 Introduction

In her major work on Person, Anna Siewierska opens her discussion of their typology with the statement 'the major parameter responsible for the cross-linguistic variation in person markers is morphophonological form' (2004:16). She draws a primary division between free and bound markers. Free forms, also called independent, full, self-standing, cardinal, focal, or strong, constitute separate words and may take primary word stress. Bound forms, also referred to as dependent or reduced, typically cannot be stressed, are often phonologically reduced relative to the free forms, and are morphologically dependent on another element in the utterance. As she observes, languages with bound forms always contain free forms as well, but the reverse is not necessarily true.

The presence of two or more sets of person markers within a language immediately raises questions about possible differences in their functions. Answers that have been proposed reflect both a variety of approaches and the diversity of language structures to be understood. On some accounts, the free forms are viewed as the only true arguments. On others, the free forms are described as 'emphatic'. Here one common type of system is described, with examples from Mohawk, an Iroquoian language indigenous to northeastern North America. An examination of the markers in spontaneous use, complete with their discourse contexts and prosodic patterns, shows that taking the free forms as the point of departure is actually the wrong approach. It is the bound forms which constitute a unified system, explicable in terms of the mechanisms by which person markers can evolve over time. Fundamental to these mechanisms are the positions in which the forms occur and the prosodic structures over which they operate. The free forms simply constitute the residue of markers not subject to these developments.

2 Free and bound forms in Mohawk

Mohawk contains both free pronouns and pronominal prefixes on verbs. Both types can be seen in (1), the free second person pronoun *í:se'* 'you' and the second person prefix *sa-*.

(1) Mohawk free and bound forms: Kaia'titáhkhe' Jacobs, speaker[1]

Í:se'	*tóka'*	*wà:kehre'*		*tóka'*	*thé:nen'*
íse'	toka'	wa'-k-ehr-e'		toka'	thenen'
you	maybe	FACT-1SG.AGT-think-PFV		maybe	something
you	maybe	I thought		maybe	something

sarì:waien'		*ne*	*ahsheri'wanón:tonhse'*.
sa-rihw-a-ien-'		ne	a-hshe-ri'wanonton-hs-e'
2SG.PAT-matter-have-STAT		the	IRR-2SG/FI-ask-BEN.APPL-PFV
you issue have		the	you would ask her

'I thought that you might have some questions to ask her.'

The free pronoun *í:se'* 'you' constitutes a separate word which can bear stress, while the prefix *sa-* cannot stand alone as a word, it is shorter segmentally, and it cannot bear stress of its own (though word stress, which is determined primarily by syllable count, may land on it).

Person prefixes occur on all verbs whether or not there is also a coreferential lexical argument in the clause, as can be seen in (2).

(2) With and without lexical argument

    a. With: Josephine Kaieríthon Horne, speaker

Iawe'tatshà:ni	***kà:sere***	*wa'katóhetste'*.
iaw-e'tatshahni	**ka-'sere**	wa'-**ka**-tohetste-e'
N.PAT-be.frightful	**N.AGT-drag**	FACT-**N.AGT**-pass-PFV
it is frightful	**it/they drag**	it/they passed by
extremely	**car**	**they** passed by

'A lot of cars passed by.'

    b. Without

       *Wa'**ka**tóhetste'*.
       '**They** passed by.'

---

[1] The abbreviations used in the examples are given at the end of the article. Four genders are distinguished in third person in Mohawk: Masculine for male persons and certain male animals, Neuter for inanimates, Feminine-Zoic for animals and certain female persons, and Feminine-Indefinite for generic persons and certain female persons. Neuter and Feminine-Zoic forms are largely the same. Examples are given here in the standard orthography. Most symbols approximate their IPA values. Nasal vowels are written with digraphs <en> for nasal [ʌ] and <on> for nasal [u]; the letter <i> represents a palatal glide [j] before a vowel; the apostrophe <'> represents glottal stop; and the colon <:> represents vowel length. The acute accent represents stress with high or rising tone, and the grave accent stress with a rising-falling pitch contour.

The sentence in (2b) is fully grammatical on its own, comparable to the translation. Speakers do not feel that anything has been left out, any more than English speakers feel that a noun is missing from *They passed by*. (The neuter prefix does not distinguish number.)

One approach to patterns like those in (2a) has been to consider lexical nominals (like *kà:sere* 'car' here) the true arguments, and verbal affixes (like *ka-* here) simply agreement. The lexical nominal would be seen as the controller. But that would leave clauses like that in (2b) with no controller. Siewierska (2004) and Siewierska & Bakker (2005) discuss this pattern with similar examples from Gumawana, an Oceanic language spoken in New Guinea.

(3) (Olson 1992: 326, cited in Siewierska 2004: 23)

   a. *Kalitoni i-paisewa.*
      Kalitoni **3SG**-work
      'Kalitoni worked.'

   b. (Ø) *i-situ   vada sinae-na.*
      3SG **3SG**-enter house inside-3SG.INAL
      'He entered the inside of the house.'

They describe several possible analyses. On one, the subject of (3a) is considered to be *Kalitoni*, and the subject of (3b) is considered to be null, or 'pro'. On another, the subject of both sentences is considered to be the prefix *i-*, the option they prefer. Identification of the verbal prefixes as actual arguments, in apposition with any lexical arguments, makes the most sense for Mohawk as well, for a number of reasons outlined in detail in Mithun (2003). It is also in keeping with the frequent correlation observed in Siewierska & Bakker (2006: 16) between general head-marking typology and bound pronouns.

The full paradigms of Mohawk free and bound markers can be seen in (4) below. The grammatical roles distinguished by the bound markers are semantically based, though now fully grammaticalized: they follow an agent/patient pattern rather than subject/object or ergative/absolutive. Essentially, participants who are in control and instigate events ('I jumped', 'I cut it) are represented by agent forms, and those who are not in control but are affected ('I fell', 'he cut me') are represented by patient forms. Choices between grammatical agent and patient forms are now lexicalized with each verb, however; speakers do not select prefixes as they speak according to degrees of control or affectedness.

(4) Mohawk core arguments

	Free	Bound
1 SG AGENT	ì:'i	k-
1 SG PATIENT	ì:'i	wak-
1 DU INCLUSIVE AGENT	ì:'i	teni-
1 DU EXCLUSIVE AGENT	ì:'i	iakeni-
1 PL INCLUSIVE AGENT	ì:'i	tewa-
1 PL EXCLUSIVE AGENT	ì:'i	iakwa-
1 DU PATIENT	ì:'i	ionkeni-
1 PL PATIENT	ì:'i	ionkwa-
2 SG AGENT	í:se'	hs-
2 SG PATIENT	í:se'	sa-
2 DU	í:se'	seni-
2 PL	í:se'	sewa-
M SG AGENT	raónha	ra-
M SG PATIENT	raónha	ro-
M DU AGENT	ronónha	ni-
M PL AGENT	ronónha	rati-
M DU/PL PATIENT	ronónha	roti-
FI SG AGENT	akaónha	ie-
FI SG PATIENT	akaónha	iako-
FZ SG AGENT	aónha	ka-
FZ SG PATIENT	aónha	io-
FZ DU AGENT	onónha	keni-
FZ PL AGENT	onónha	konti-
FZ DU/PL PATIENT	onónha	ioti-

The prefixes show considerable allomorphy, not detailed here. Agent/patient combinations on transitive verbs are represented by a separate set of portmanteau prefixes. Alienable and inalienable possessive prefixes on nouns show similar but not identical forms.

As can be seen by comparing the columns above, the free forms make many fewer distinctions than the prefixes. The word *ì:'i*, for example, is translatable variously as 'I', 'me', 'we two' (exclusive dual), 'we two' (inclusive dual), 'us two', 'we all' (exclusive plural), 'we all' (inclusive plural), and 'us all', as well as 'my' (inalienable), 'my' (alienable), 'our' (exclusive dual inalienable), 'our' (inclusive dual inalienable), 'our' (exclusive plural inalienable), and 'our' (inclusive plural inalienable), 'our' (dual alienable) and 'our' (plural alienable). The corresponding prefixes distinguish all of these, with three numbers (singular, dual, plural), inclusive and exclusive duals and plurals, two grammatical roles on verbs (agents, patients), and alienable and inalienable possession on nominals.

Free forms in Mohawk not only mark fewer distinctions than prefixes, they are also relatively rare in speech. The proportion of first and second person free forms in a 4000-clause sample of unscripted speech can be seen in (5).

(5) Free pronouns

1. Clauses with 1st person participants, any role   1086
   1st person free pronouns   95
   Percentage   8.9%

2. Clauses with 2nd person participants, any role   414
   2nd person free pronouns   14
   Percentage   3.4%

The proportion of third person free pronouns is even smaller. The figures 1086 and 414 above include both intransitive and transitive clauses. The vast majority of the transitive clauses also contain a third person argument. In this sample of 4000 clauses, nearly all of which contain at least one third person argument and many of which contain two, there were just 14 third person free pronouns: 2 instances of *akaónha* 'she', 7 of *raónha* 'he', and 5 of *ronónha* 'they'.

For some languages, it has been hypothesized that free forms are basic but omitted or 'dropped' when reference is clear. Such a hypothesis is at odds with their distribution in languages like Mohawk, as can be seen from example (1) 'you might have some questions'. Reference to the second person was clear from the obligatory prefix *sa-* on the verb, but the free form *í:se'* still appeared. Furthermore, the free form did little to clarify reference: it indicated only that a second person was involved in some way. The prefix specified not only that the argument was second person, but also that it was singular and a grammatical patient. An analysis of the free forms as the only true arguments of their clauses under such circumstances would be difficult to maintain.

Free forms like these are often labeled 'emphatic' or 'contrastive' in grammars. These terms are rarely defined explicitly, but grammar writers and readers usually feel they have some sense of what is meant by them, generally some functions related to information structure. The next sections examine the uses of these forms in Mohawk constructions conveying marked information structure in unscripted speech.

3 Basic focus constructions

The term 'emphatic' might suggest that the free forms are used to mark focus. Of course the term 'focus' itself is used in a variety of ways. One basic use, as Siewierska notes, is as 'the most important or salient piece of information in the utterance, as perceived by the speaker' (2004:159). Basic focus is often illustrated with lexical gap questions, where the focus is the material requested. The Mohawk free pronouns are indeed used in questions requesting the identity of a referent.

(6)   Focus of question: Watshenní:nen' Sawyer, speaker

    Í:se' ken sá:wen   kí:ken thrák?
    i:se' ken sa-awen   kí:ken thrak
    2   Q   2SG.AL-possession this   truck
    you Q your possession   this   truck
    'Is this **your** truck?'

Mohawk focus constructions are characterized by two principal features. The focused element appears at the beginning of the sentence or clause (sometimes after orienting and/or modal particles) and is pronounced with extra high pitch, as can be seen in Figure 1.

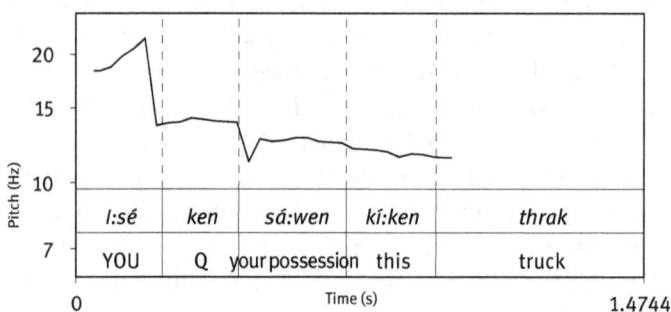

Figure 1. Focus construction in question

This pitch pattern can be contrasted with that of the pragmatically unmarked sentence seen in Figure 2: 'He sold some truck.'

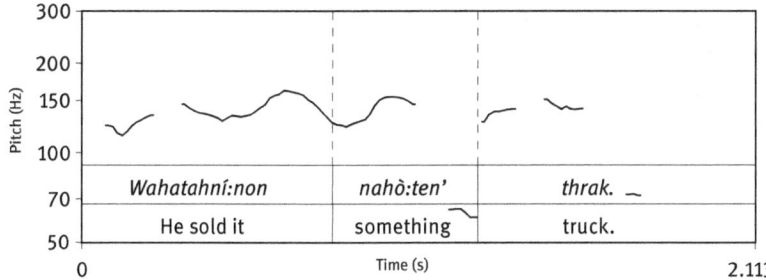

Figure 2. Basic pitch trace: 'He sold some truck.'

Other frequently-cited examples of a basic focus construction are the answers to lexical gap questions. The material that fills the gap, the questioned information, is the focused element. Mohawk free pronouns are also used in this function. The response to the question in (6) was the sentence in (7).

(7)   Focus of response: Watshenní:nen' Sawyer, speaker

    Í: *wahèn:ron'*   *akwá:wen.*
    i:'i wa-ha-ihron-'   akw-awen
    1   FACT-M.SG.AG-say-PRF 1SG.AL-possession
    me he said   my possession
    '"**Mine**," he said, "it's mine."'

The focused free pronoun in this answer was also pronounced with extra high pitch.

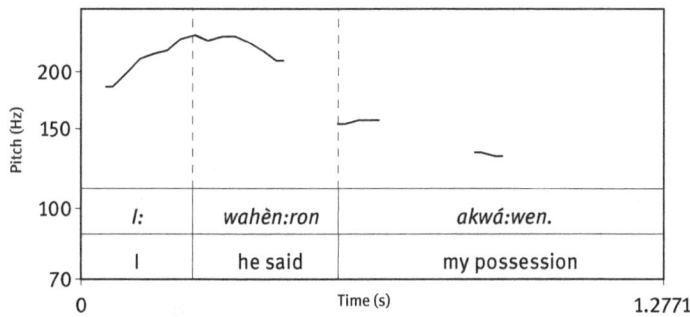

Figure 3. Basic focus construction in answer

Focus constructions are of course not restricted to questions and answers. The statement in (8) contains a focused possessor.

(8) Focused possessor: Wilfred Jaimison, speaker
Í:se' *sarì:wa'* ...
2   your fault
'It's **your** fault [that I am in such misery and want].'

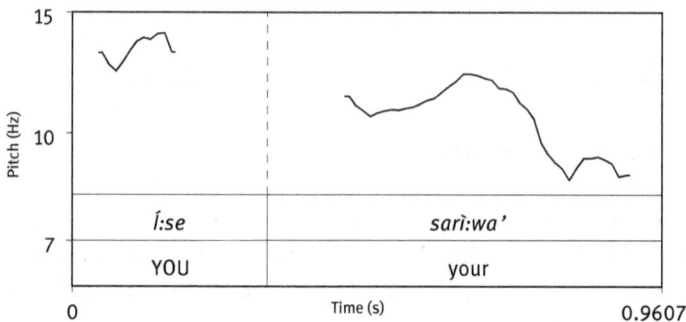

Figure 4. Focused possessor

The significant prosodic feature of the Mohawk focus construction is indeed pitch rather than intensity. The intensity, represented by the continuous, relatively level line in Figure 5, remains essentially stable across the sentence.

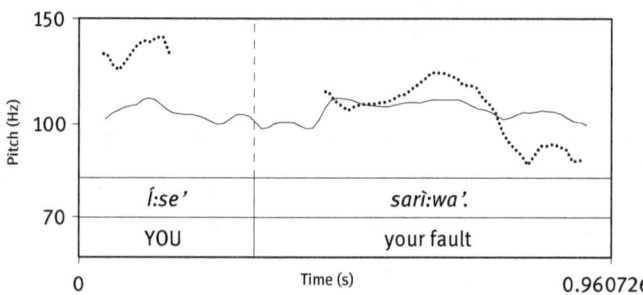

Figure 5. Pitch and intensity.

(Mohawk has contrasting tone on stressed syllables. The tone marked with an acute accent on the vowel, as in *í:se'* 'you', is basically rising. The tone marked with a grave accent, as in *sarì:wa'* 'your fault' rises sharply to a point usually higher than that of the rising tone, then plunges below the baseline pitch. The two contrasting tones can be seen in the pitch trace in Figures 4 and 5).

A focused grammatical patient can be seen in (9) below. The speaker was recounting a conversation between Mary Magdalene and Jesus Christ from a Bible story. The significant new information was expressed in the free pronoun *i:'i* 'me'. The information in the remainder of the clause, 'they were discussing', had already been established.

(9) Focused transitive patient: Harry Miller, preacher
MM 'They used to tell us that one day Jesus Christ would be coming.'

    JC   *Ì:'i ionkwathró:ri.*
          1 one discusses me
          'They were talking about **me**.'

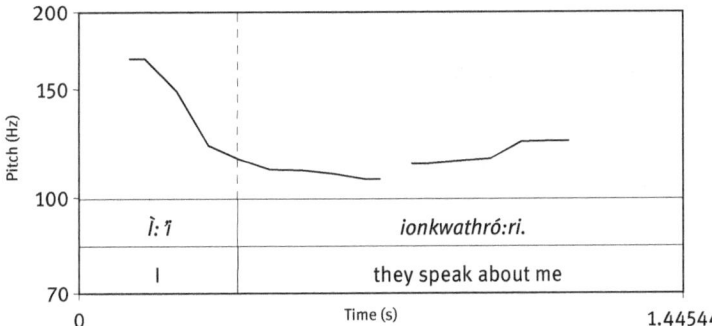

Figure 6. Focused grammatical patient

The focused element need not be a core argument. In (10), part of the same story, the free pronoun *ì:'i* 'me' is not a core argument and is not represented in the verb 'he must enter'.

(10) Focused free pronoun: Harry Miller, preacher
'No man can enter my Father's place directly.'

    Tká:konte'   *í:'   nen   nonká:ti   enthaiénhtahkwe'.*
    it is necessary   **1**   now   side   will he begin from here
    'He must enter through **me**.'

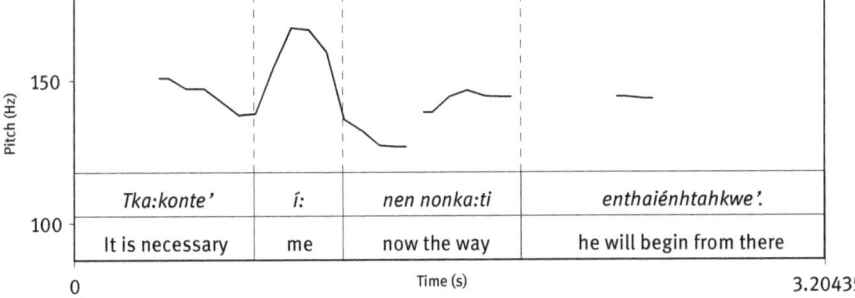

Figure 7. Non-core-argument focused element

Again the focused element appears at the beginning of the clause, pronounced with extra-high pitch.

There are other, more specific types of focus constructions. One is contrastive, where the element in focus is specifically contrasted with another possibility or defined set of possibilities. In Mohawk, the same basic focus construction can be used for this function, with the focused element initial (perhaps after various orienting and/or modal elements) and pronounced with extra high pitch. The article *ne*, which fuses with a following vowel-initial word – *ne ì:'i* > *nì:i, ní:, ni* – marks a referent that has been mentioned previously.

(11) Contrastive focus: Lazarus Jacob, speaker

   Tóka' **ní:se'** *enhsatè:ko',*   *iah ki'*   **nì:'i** *tha:katé:ko'.*
   maybe **the 2** you will escape not in fact **the 1** would I escape
   'Maybe **you** would run away, but **I** wouldn't run away.'

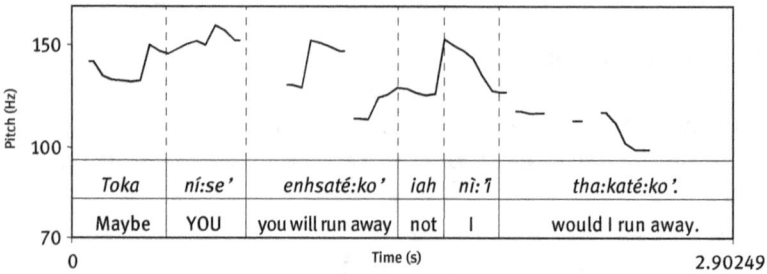

Figure 8. Contrastive focus

4 Cleft constructions

Mohawk also contains a cleft construction, in which a focused element occurs initially and is set off from the following nuclear clause by the particle *nè:'e* or *ne:'*.

(12) Focus of cleft: Sonny Edwards, speaker

   Í: *nè:'*   *enkaten'nikonhraráhseke'*   *nawèn:ke.*
   I   it is   I will always put my mind on it   the water
   '**I** will watch over the water.'

The pitch pattern matches those seen in the previous section, where the focused element is pronounced with extra high pitch.

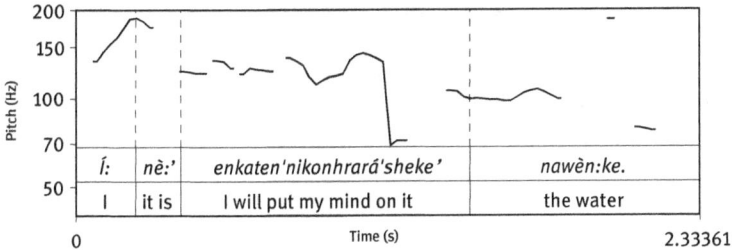

Figure 9. Cleft construction

The cleft construction is not necessarily contrastive, but it may be used for contrastive focus. In (13), the pronoun *í:'* explicitly contrasts the speaker with all others.

(13)   Contrastive cleft: Sonny Edwards, speaker

    í:'   nek   *nè:'e*   *aonhà:'a*   *enkatshennaháwa.*
    1   the only   it is   alone   I will name carry
    'I alone will bear that name.'

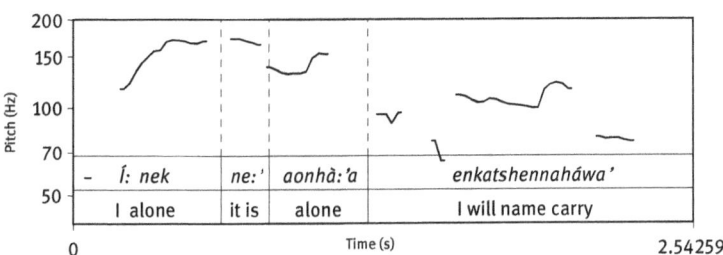

Figure 10. Contrastive focus

5 Contrast without focus

The same free pronouns are used to indicate contrast without focus. In these constructions, the pronoun does not normally appear at the beginning of the sentence, and it is not pronounced with high pitch. An example can be seen in (14). (The entire conversation was in Mohawk, but only the free translation is provided in material showing the context).

(14) Speaker contrast: Josephine Kaieríthon Horne, speaker

CB 'This [translation] work we're doing, what would you call it,
tetewawennanetáhkwahs [we word unlayer]
or: *tetewawennaténie's* [we word change]?'

JH *A:kéhre:'---*
I would think
'I'd think--

*a:kehre'   ki'   **nì:'i**,*
I would think actually **the 1**
I **myself** would think,

tetewawennanetáhkwahs.
we word unlayer
we are translating the words.'

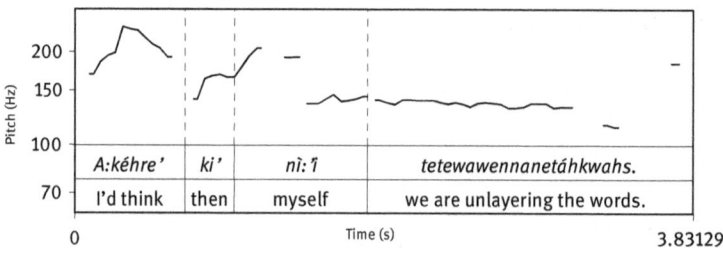

Figure 11. Contrast without focus

The first person free pronoun is much more frequent in this construction, because it often serves a politeness function: 'This is just my opinion or experience or feeling, not necessarily shared by you or others'. In (15) the speaker was contrasting her own experience with that of others, but this was not the focus of her comment.

(15) Speaker contrast: Dorris Kawennanó:ron Montour, speaker

*Akwé:kon   ki'   kí:ken-televísion ki'   **ni'**   wa'katerò:roke'.*
everything actually this   actually **the 1** I watched
'All of this I actually saw on television, **myself**.'

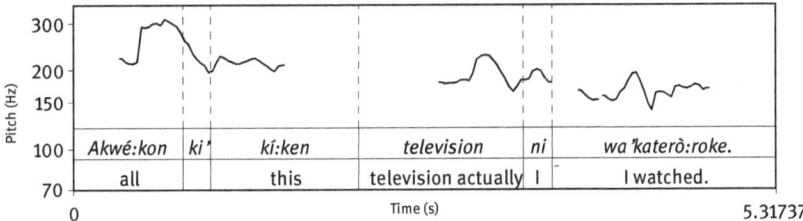

Figure 12. Contrast without focus

6 Topicalization constructions

The free pronouns also occur in another kind of marked information structure. A special topicalization construction is used to indicate a shift in topic. The shift is usually to a topic that is not brand new to the discourse, but one that was previously mentioned or associated with a previously mentioned referent. The topicalized element may be a full lexical nominal or larger phrase, or simply a free pronoun. In (16), the speaker was shifting the discussion from her children and husband to herself.

(16)   Topic shift: Dorris Kawennanó:ron Montour, speaker
'Some of my children worked there, and our husbands, you know.'

Í:'   ò:ni   tho   tewatió'tehkwe',   kwáh   ki:.
1   also   there   I used to work there   even   this
'I **myself** used to work there as well.'

'That is why I felt so bad about what I saw.'

The shifted topics are also pronounced with higher pitch, but they are generally detached prosodically from the nuclear clause, which often, though not always, begins with a pitch reset.

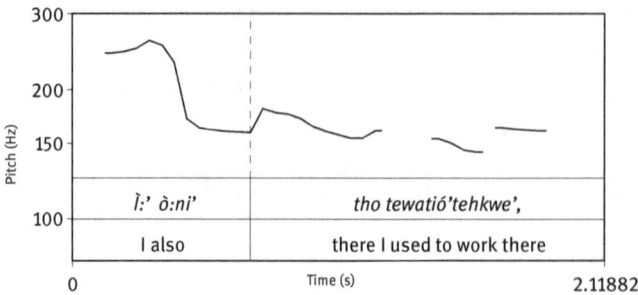

Figure 13. Topic shift

In (17) the speaker had been talking about her little brother, then shifted to discussing herself with the free pronoun *ni'* (short form of *ne ì:'i* 'the I'). She subsequently continued talking about herself, but with only prefixes.

(17)   Topic shift: Cecelia Peters, speaker
'And so she laid him (my little brother) there.'

   *Thó   ki   n   **ni'**   wa'kanitskó:ten'   wahiiaten'nikòn:raren'.*
   there this too **the I** I sat   I set my mind on him
   'And **me**, I sat there too and minded him.

   Iáh   tewakaterièn:tare'   to: sha'tewakohseriià:kon.
   not   do I know   how many   when I had winter crossed
   I don't know how old I was.

   Ken'   shikà:'a.
   small   when I was sized
   I was little.'

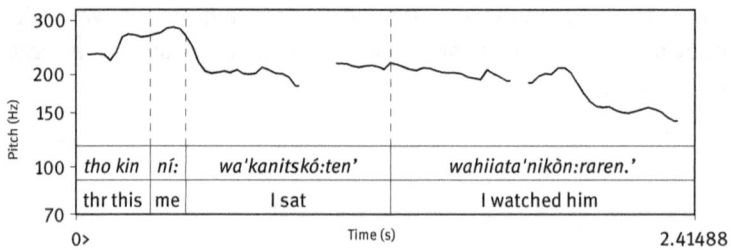

Figure 14. Topic shift

Free pronouns are not used every time there is a shift in what would be expressed with a subject in English. This can be seen in the excerpt from a conversation cited in (17) below. (The conversation was in Mohawk, but only the free translation is provided here for reasons of space). The conversation was about a certain man T., who was already under discussion when this passage begins. What is translated as the subject of many of the sentences differs from that of the previous sentence: lines 2, 3, 4, 5, 6, 7, 9, 10, 11, 18, 19, and 20. Many of these switched subjects are pronominal: lines 3, 4, 5, 9, 10, 18, and 20. But none of these sentences contains a free pronoun: all of those referents are identified uniquely by pronominal prefixes on the verbs. This is because the overall topic remained the same: the man referred to as T. In line 11, another man, J., was introduced with a topicalization construction. His full name was topicalized. Each time J. was referred to in subsequent sentences, it was only with a prefix on the verb. When another speaker asked whether she could pour herself some coffee, she did not use the free pronoun *ì:'i*, because her query was not intended to change the topic of discussion. And it did not, as can be seen in line 20, where no free pronoun was necessary to reintroduce the man under discussion.

(18)   No free pronouns

CB	'That T. was a bad man, wasn't he. [laughter]		1
	Over there there's a school.		2
	That's where **I** started to teach, you know.	NO FREE PRO	3
	He was always chasing the children	NO FREE PRO	4
	They couldn't play near the fence.	NO FREE PRO	5
	His house was right here [gesturing], on this side of the school.		6
	The school was on this side.		7
	Nowadays it's called Step by Step [School].		8
	And **they** would throw their ball there	NO FREE PRO	9
	and **he**'d keep it.	NO FREE PRO	10
	On the other hand, J. used to give it back.		11
	He was bad too.' [laughter].		12
JD	'Yes.'		13
CB	'Yes.		14
	And he planted a nice garden.'		15
JH,WS	'Yes.		16
CB	'J.'		17
KJ	'May **I** have a cup of coffee?'	NO FREE PRO	18
CB	'Nowadays there's a road there.		19
	What would **he** say if he came back and saw it?'	NO FREE PRO	20

The passage in (19) below, by contrast, provides a good example of the use of a free pronoun to shift the topic. The speaker shifted the topic of discussion from stories with monsters to herself with the free pronoun *ni:* (*ne ì:'i* 'the me'): 'As for **me**, I would tremble'. She then continued talking about herself, but with prefixes alone.

(19) Free pronoun with topic shift: Watshenní:ne' Sawyer, speaker

'And at night they would tell stories, scary stories about the skeleton, the monster with just lower limbs, all kinds of things, all kinds of dead things would come and scare you.'

Ó:nen	*ki'*	***ni:***	*watia'tishónhkhwa'*,	FREE PRONOUN
then	in fact	**the 1**	I bodily shake	

So then **as for me**, I would tremble,

I was really scared. So they'd say, "Go to bed!" I would never sleep when I was so scared. I would climb upstairs and sit there at the top of the stairs, waiting for the visitors to leave.'

7 Antitopic constructions

Free pronouns appear in another marked construction, identifying antitopics. In antitopic constructions, the nuclear clause is followed by a referring expression which reconfirms the identity of a continuing topic. In (20) the speaker was discussing her childhood. There was a brief explanation of the Depression, but the overall topic remained her family. The sentences which followed continued this topic.

(20) Antitopic construction: Watshenní:ne' Sawyer, speaker

'We were poor growing up.
But then everybody was poor then.
Nobody had any money.
It is what one calls 'when money was dear' in our language.
The Depression.'

Néktsi	*ionkwater'swí:io*	***nì:'i.***
but	our luck was good	**the 1**

'But we were still lucky, **us**.'

'We had a home.
We had food.'

The prosody of Mohawk antitopic constructions is distinctive. Antitopics are usually pronounced with a relatively flat pitch contour, often creaky voice, and slower rhythm.

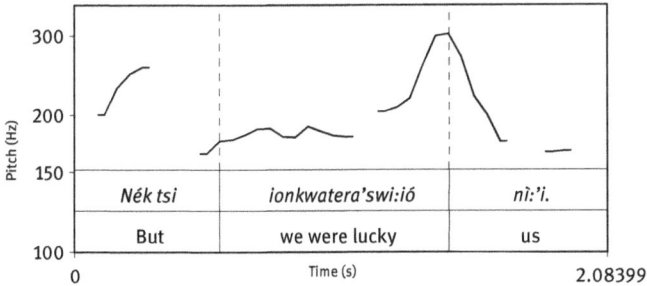

Figure 15. Antitopic construction

(The pitch rise at the end of *ionkwatera'swí:ió* 'we are lucky' is part of a general pattern whereby if the stressed syllable of a word is open and the tone rising, the following syllable is pronounced with a further rise in pitch, when it is followed immediately within the prosodic phrase by another word).

The information status of referents identified by free pronouns in antitopic constructions is quite different from that of referents in focus or topicalization constructions. They do not represent new information, they show no contrast, and they refer to a continuing larger topic rather than a shifted one.

8 Isolated pronouns

Free pronouns appear in still other types of constructions. They are used to identify a referent when there is no verb to support a prefix. This use can be seen in the comparative construction in (21).

(21) Isolated free pronoun: Watshenní:ne' Sawyer, speaker
 'It was a relief when they had passed through the village, because

   *Tho   nihontária'kskwe'   tsi **ni:'**   ní:io*   ...
   there so they used to be hungry as   **the 1** so it is
   'they were as hungry as **us**... '

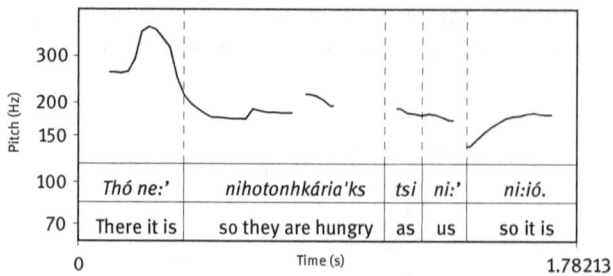

Figure 16. Isolated free pronoun in comparative construction

Another example of a free pronoun is in the negative construction without a verb to host a prefix in (22): 'not me'.

(22) Isolated free pronoun: Josie Day, speaker
'I used to wonder why my uncle Sens'

*Shakoien'okòn:'a tioateriseríhare'   k   **ni'**   iáh.*
his children   there they their stocking hung and **the 1** not
children hung up their stockings and not **me**.'

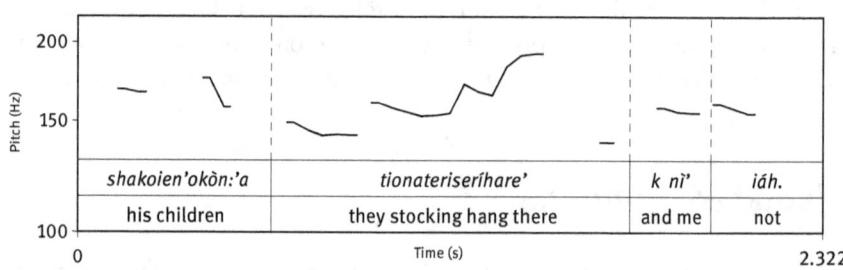

Figure 17. Isolated free pronoun in negative construction

A third example is in (23) in the clause 'it was you', literally 'that you'.

(23) Isolated pronoun: Minnie Hill, speaker

Wa'koniatkáh tsi **í:se'**.
I saw you that **2**
'I saw that it was **you**.'

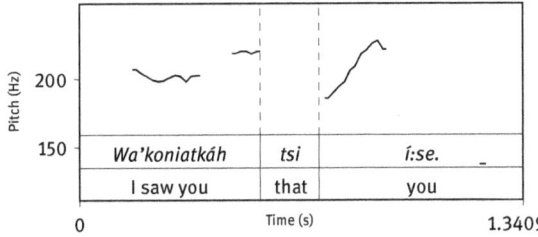

Figure 18. Isolated free pronoun in equational construction

A fourth example is in (24), where the speaker is echoing the sentiment of the previous speaker.

(24) Isolated pronoun: Josephine Horne, speaker
'I feel strongly about the language.'

Í: ò:ni'.
1 also
'**Me** too.'

Such examples show that the free pronouns do not necessarily indicate contrast.

9 The free pronouns

The Mohawk free pronouns thus serve a variety of functions. They are sometimes emphatic or constrastive, but not always. They occur in distinct constructions marking basic focus, contrastive focus, non-focus contrast, topic shift, antitopic, and a variety of functions in verbless contexts, that is, clauses without a verb to host a prefix, seen here in comparative, negative, equational, and parallel constructions. The same free pronoun can even occur more than once within a sentence with different functions. The sentence in (25) contains a topicalization construction, with topicalized *í:'i* 'I' and pitch reset before the nuclear clause, and a non-focused contrastive *ní:* 'myself'. As explained above, the article *ne* marks the second, though not the first appearance of the pronoun.

(25) Topicalization and non-focal contrast: Watshenní:ne' Sawyer, speaker

'There were three of us children in the family, two of them boys.
One boy was called *Kahionwa'kérha'* [Canoe Floating on the River].
And one boy was called *Tiohatéhkwen* [Parting of the Road].'

Tánon' **í:'** Watshenní:ne'   **ní:**   ióntiats.
and   1   she name carries **the 1** one calls me
'And **I**, I am called Namebearer **myself**.'

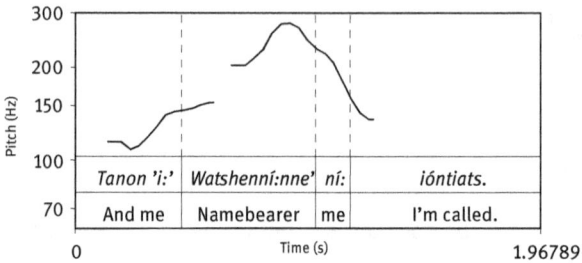

Figure 19. Multiple free pronouns

10 Conclusion

The free pronouns in Mohawk thus do not serve a single, unified function. A syntactic analysis under which they are considered the only basic arguments of their clauses, and the prefixes mere agreement, runs into problems at every turn. The free and bound markers do usually 'agree', in that they both reflect features of a common referent. But free pronouns make many fewer distinctions than the prefixes, so they would make poor controllers. They are, furthermore, absent much more often than they are present. Ascribing their absence to a kind of 'pro-drop' mechanism, whereby they are deleted when reference is otherwise clear, would be at odds with their actual distribution; when they occur, reference is usually otherwise clear from the obligatory prefixes on the verb. Furthermore, they do not serve a unified function in terms of information structure. They identify referents in basic focus, contrastive focus, non-contrastive focus, topicalization, antitopic, and a variety of verbless constructions.

If, however, we shift our attention to the prefixes and the mechanisms by which they tend to develop over time, an explanation for the differences between the two sets emerges. The most common mechanisms by which affixes come into being involve processes of grammaticalization. Recurring constructions consisting of an unstressed function word adjacent to a content word can become routinized by speakers, processed as chunks during speech. Word boundaries within the construction may fade, and the function word may ultimately become an affix. Such a scenario could well underlie the structure of the modern Iroquoian verb. It is likely that unstressed free pronouns, representing given core arguments in clauses with unmarked information structure, were regularly positioned immediately before the verb, an order which continues within the verbal morphology. Their high frequency, their constant position adjacent to the verb, their unmarked information structure, and their corresponding lack of prosodic prominence would set the stage for fusion with the following verb. Pronouns that were not regularly positioned adjacent to the verb and that carried marked prosody would not be subject to such developments.

In some languages with both free and bound markers, the two sets are still etymologically related, as in French, but this need not be the case. Both sets of markers may evolve over time, as individual forms are added, lost, and replaced. In Mohawk, the modern first person free pronoun is *i:'i*, but the first person singular and exclusive prefixes are all based on *k-*, and the inclusive prefixes *t-*, none containing the vowel *i*. The modern third person free pronouns are transparently complex morphologically, based on a root *-onha* 'alone', with third person prefixes: *a-ónha* 'it/she/her' (NEUTER/ZOIC), *aka-ónha* 'one/she/her' (GENERIC/FEMININE), *ra-ónha* 'he/him/his', *ion-ónha* 'they/them/their' (FEMININE/ZOIC), and *ron-ónha* 'they/them/their' (MASCULINE). These forms are apparently newer than the prefixes and, unlike most of the prefixes, are not cognate across the family. The Iroquoian prefix paradigm also did not necessarily take shape all at once (Mithun to appear). Only one basic third person prefix category can be reconstructed for Proto-Iroquoian, undifferentiated for gender, plus an indefinite or generic category 'one'. A distinct masculine prefix category can be reconstructed only to the Northern Iroquoian branch of the family. The extension of indefinite forms to certain women occurred even later and is in fact still an ongoing process in Mohawk, slowly making its way through the elaborate transitive prefix paradigm.

So what characterizes the modern Mohawk free pronouns as a group? They are simply an assortment of forms that do not share in the positional and prosodic patterns that would be conducive to fusion with a host, patterns that typically underlie the development of found forms. They occur outside of the nuclear clause, in marked focus, topic, or antitopic positions, scattered throughout the clause, or in contexts without a following verb. They show distinctive prosody and are not usually part of the same prosodic phrase as the verb in the clause. The prefixes, by contrast, are apparently descended from pronouns in unmarked information structures that regularly occurred immediately before the verb without special prosodic prominence. Differences between the Mohawk free and bound forms may ultimately be best understood in terms of the mechanisms behind their development.

Abbreviations

1 first person, 2 second person, 3 third person, AGT agent, AL alienable, APPL applicative, BEN benefactive, DU dual, FACT factual, FI feminine-indefinite gender, FZ feminine-zoic gender, INAL inalienable, IRR irealis, M masculine, N neuter, PAT patient, PFV perfective, PL plural, PRF perfect, Q question marker, SG singular, STAT stative.

References

Mithun, Marianne. 2003. Pronouns and agreement: The information status of pronominal affixes. *Transactions of the Philological Society* 101(2). 235–278.

Mithun, Marianne. To appear. Gender and culture. In Greville Corbett (ed.), *The Expression of Gender*. Berlin & Boston: De Gruyter Mouton.

Olson, Cliff. 1992. Gumawana (Amphlett Islands, Papua New Guinea): Grammar sketch and texts. *Papers in Austronesian Linguistics* 2. 251–430.

Siewierska, Anna. 2004. *Person*. Cambridge: Cambridge University Press.

Siewierska, Anna & Dik Bakker. 2005. The Agreement Cross-Reference Continuum: Person marking in FG. In Kees Hengeveld & Casper de Groot (eds.), *Morphosyntactic Expression in Functionial Grammar*, 203–247. Berlin & New York: De Gruyter Mouton.

Siewierska, Anna & Dik Bakker. 2006. Bi-directional vs. uni-directional asymmetries in the encoding of semantic distinctions in free and bound person forms. In Terttu Nevalainen, Juhani Klemola & Mikko Laitinen (eds.) *Types of Variation. Diachronic, Dialectal and typological interfaces*, 21–50. Amsterdam: John Benjamins.

Johanna Nichols
The origin and evolution of case-suppletive pronouns: Eurasian evidence

1 Introduction

The pronoun systems of Eurasia are more diverse and unusual than might appear at first glance. This paper began in an attempt to apply concepts from Anna Siewierska's work on person (2004, 2011) to a typological analysis of puzzling aspects of pronominal systems especially in Eurasia, in the hope of better describing the considerable morphosyntactic differences that separate the often phonologically similar forms of different languages. As it happens, the resultant structural description also reveals a geolinguistic distribution of types that lets a more general Eurasian linguistic prehistory take shape.

Case-suppletive pronouns are ones that have two distinct roots in their case paradigms, as in the examples in (1).

(1) The nominative and one oblique case form of first person singular independent pronouns in selected case-using languages of Europe, the Caucasus, and Siberia.

	Nominative	Oblique[1]	
Proto-Indo-European (Indo-European)	*eĝō / eĝ⁽ʰ⁾om	*me / mē	(ACC)
Dutch (Indo-European)	ik	mij	(OBJ)
Bulgarian (Indo-European)	az	mene	(ACC)
Georgian (Kartvelian)	me	čemi	(GEN)
Botlikh (Nakh-Daghestanian)	den	iškur	(ERG)
Tundra Nenets (Uralic)	mənyº	syiqmº	(ACC)

---

[1] A list of abbreviations can be found at the end of the article.

The sources of the split stems in (1) vary from family to family. In Indo-European and Kartvelian the suppletion is ancient, reconstructed to the protolanguage. The Botlikh ergative is unique in its family, and of unknown origin. The Tundra Nenets accusative form reconstructs to the branch level (Samoyed) and has a non-pronominal etymology (discussed again below).

Since only case suppletion is at issue here (and not suppletion for number, honorificity, etc.), below I will simply speak of *suppletion* and *suppletive paradigms* (and suppletive stems, forms, etc.). (For more precise terminology and theoretical grounding see Siewierska & Bakker, this volume). In examples I will mechanically retain the names for cases used in grammatical descriptions, since the exact functions of the cases are never at issue. Since case suppletion often divides nominatives from other cases, and since one of the important trajectories of change discussed below is importation of new nominatives into existing paradigms, I will use the cover term *oblique* for cases other than nominative. (Following Kibrik 2003:147 and previous descriptive work, Creissels 2009, and others including my own past work, I use *nominative* for the case identical to the citation form, whether that is the S/A case of accusative languages or the S/O case of ergative languages).

As will be argued below, suppletive pronominal paradigms often arise when the original nominative is replaced by a word that was not originally part of the paradigm and in many instances was not pronominal and not person-related in origin. Sometimes these originate as intensifiers of one kind or another (for intensifiers see Siewierska 2004: 67–73); sometimes they are emphatic forms; sometimes they are avoidance or honorific or formal terms; sometimes they are general strong forms (for some of the formations of these see Kibrik 2011: 147–157); and sometimes their origins are unknown. Grammars do not always give enough detail to be certain of the origin or function, and of course for reconstructed protoforms the exact functions are even less clear. Since a general label is needed for such forms I will call them *extrinsic* (forms, words, stems, etc.) to indicate that they are not, or originally were not, part of the pronoun paradigm itself. (Though the synchronic and perhaps even historical facts may one day be better known for most languages, I suspect that a general term will always be needed to cover the range of words available in principle to be plugged into pronoun paradigms).

2 Typology of suppletive pronoun paradigms and histories

This section surveys the kinds of suppletion and non-suppletion that I have found in pronoun paradigms.

2.1 Non-suppletion: invariant pronoun forms

In the head-marking West Caucasian family, personal pronouns lack case and appear in a single invariant form. The first and second person pronouns have what are known as short vs. long forms, but these are not separate case forms. (Nor are the long forms, apparently, intensifiers or otherwise grammatically different from the short forms; they appear to be stylistic and/or dialect variants).

(2) Kabardian (Matasović 2010: 25)

	SG	PL	long:	SG	PL
1	sa	da		sara	dara
2	wa	fa		wara	fara

(3) Abkhaz (Hewitt 1989: 48)

	SG	PL		
1	sa(rà)	ħa(rà)	exclusive	ħart
2 M	wa(rà)	šwa(rà)		
F	ba(rà)	"		

2.2 Non-suppletion: one-stem paradigms

In many languages with cases, pronouns have a single stem, i.e. are non-suppletive. Examples are the second person singular pronouns in most Indo-European languages, e.g. Russian:

(4) 2SG
NOM ty
ACC tebja
GEN tebja
DAT tebe
INSTR toboj
PREP tebe

There is vowel ablaut in the paradigm and a -*b*- extension in the oblique cases, so the stems have some allomorphy but no suppletion.[2]

All pronouns are non-suppletive in most of the western Uralic languages, e.g. Finnish:

(5) Finnish (Baltic Finnic; Eliseev 1993: 100). Selected cases.

	1SG	2SG
NOM	*minä*	*sinä*
GEN	*minu-n*	*sinu-n*
ACC	*minu-t*	*sinu-t*
PART	*minu-a*	*sinu-a*
ADESS	*minu-lla*	*sinu-lla*
ILLAT	*minu-un*	*sinu-un*

2.3 Suppletion with no known origin

The Indo-European and Georgian examples shown in (1) have suppletion that reconstructs to the protolanguage with no traceable origin; whatever created the suppletive paradigm is lost in time.

2.4 Suppletion due to phonological change

Ordinary sound change can produce allomorphs that, once the conditioning environment is obscured, end up being suppletive. An example of incipient suppletion is Mongolic languages, where the first person singular forms on the left in (6) result from the non-suppletive forms on the right:

(6) Proto-Mongolic and Pre-Proto-Mongolic (Janhunen 2003: 18)

NOM	*bi-	<	**bi
GEN	*min-		**binü
ACC	*nama		**bima

---

[2] At least not suppletion in the sense defined above (different roots). Allomorphs like these might be called weak suppletion or partial suppletion, but because there is a more or less segmentable extension I will not treat them as suppletive. Semi-segmentable extensions like these are not uncommon in pronominal oblique stems but are generally not at issue here.

The relevant sound changes are distant nasal assimilation (in the genitive and accusative), dissimilation of the first of two *m*'s (in the accusative), and vowel assimilation (in the accusative). That the nominative and genitive are related by a regular alternation is synchronically evident, and even for the divergent-looking accusative the first two of the sound changes are still present in phonotactic constraints and make the relatedness of the stems evident.

In Eastern Armenian, the first person singular paradigm preserves the ancient Indo-European suppletion shown in (1), while the second person is synchronically suppletive due to later sound change: the forms in k^h- regularly reflect Indo-European *two-/twe- (Ajello 1998: 218–219, Matasović 2009: 20). (The forms of Classical Armenian are nearly the same).

(7)   Eastern Armenian. Selected cases.

	1SG	2SG
NOM	es	du
GEN	im	$k^h o$
DAT = ACC	inj	$k^h ez$
ABL	injnic^h	k^heznic^h
INSTR	injnov	k^heznov
LOC	injnum	k^heznum

In Nakh-Daghestanian (also known as East Caucasian), a root consonant can be reconstructed for the personal pronouns but the rest is still to be worked out. The pronouns had two stem shapes, *CV- and *VC-, probably for different cases but this too is unclear. The combination of regular sound changes and positional effects on initial vs. medial consonants has produced some instances of synchronic suppletion, shown boldface in (8). (For Nakh-Daghestanian pronouns see Schulze 1999, Schrijver 2009, Nichols 2012a).

(8) Nakh-Daghestanian. C = gender-agreeing consonant; "=" is the boundary adjacent to a gender agreement marker (following the convention of Kibrik & Kodzasov 1988–1990 and other work).
Bold = synchronic suppletion due to sound change; underlined = due to morphological change (discussed later below).

	1SG			2SG		
	NOM	OBL.1	OBL.2	NOM.	OBL.1	OBL.2
Proto-ND	*-_dz_- / *-_d_-			*-_ghʷ_-		
Nakh: Ingush	so	aaz		ho	ʕa <	*aħ
Avar		dun	di-		mun	_du_-
Andic: Andi	din	din	di-	min	min	_du_-
Tsezic: Hinuq	de	de	di-	me	me	_debe_-
Lak	**na**	**ttu**-		ina	wi-	
Dargi	nu	nuni	di-	ħu	ħuni	ħe-
Dargi: Kubachi	du	dudi-	di-	u	udi-	i-
Lezgi	zun	za-		wun	(wu)na-	
N. Tabasaran	izu	zas		iwu	jaw	
Tsakhur	zy	jiz-y=n		**ghu**	**was-y**=	
Archi	zon	C=is		un	wit	
Udi	zun	bez		**hun**	**wi**	

2.5 Suppletion due to fusion of clitic

In some Western Armenian varieties a former proclitic preposition has fused to the pronouns to form the accusative:

(9) Cilician Western Armenian (Karst 1901: 224; s.a. Wilhelm 2008)

	1SG	2SG
NOM	yes	tu / tum
ACC	z-is	z-kʰ i̯ez
GEN	im	kʰo
DAT	inj	kʰ i̯ez

In Classical Armenian this z- was a widely used clitic preposition (Wilhelm 2008: 296), so forms like the accusatives in (9) would have been transparent; but in modern varieties, though the accusative initial z- is identical in pronouns of all three persons and segmentable in that respect, the degree of fusion brings the accusative form close to suppletive.

2.6 Suppletion due to morphological analogy

In the Nakh-Daghestanian forms shown in (8) above, the italicized oblique forms in the second person have been reshaped on the analogy of the first person forms. The original forms probably had a non-nasal consonant such as /w/ or /ɣw/ which was in danger of becoming inaudible before the /u/ vocalism (for these forms see Nichols 2012a). In the Avar-Andic-Tsezic branch the nominative (±ergative) *m*- could presumably have been extended to overcome this impasse, but this has not happened; rather (and surprisingly), the initial of the first person was extended to the second person. The result was the appearance of suppletive stems in the second person.

2.7 Suppletion due to intrusion of extrinsic form

The Botlikh first person singular ergative shown in (1) is isolated in all of Nakh-Daghestanian; compare the Botlikh forms to those of several close sisters shown in (10).

(10) First person singular in selected Andic (Nakh-Daghestanian) languages. =C is a gender agreement suffix (agreeing in gender with the head noun of a possessive construction). Bold: the unique Botlikh ergative.

	NOM	ERG	GEN	DAT
Andi	*din/den*	*din*	*di=C*	*di-*
N. Akhvakh	*dene*	*de-*	*di=C*	*di-*
Chamalal	*de=C*	*dennu*	*di=C*	*di-*
Botlikh	*den(i)*	**iškur**	*di=C*	*di-*
Godoberi	*den*	*den*	*di=C*	*di-*
Karata	*den*	*den=a*	*di=C*	*di-*
Bagwalal	*deⁿ*	*den*	*di=C*	*di-*

The origin of the Botlikh ergative is mysterious (Schulze 1999). It must be an extrinsic word in origin, recruited into the pronominal paradigm for reasons having to do with the pragmatics of first-person agentive reference and thereby creating a suppletive paradigm.

2.8 Generic pronoun bases

A generic base is a non-pronominal root or stem which itself has no lexical category of person but serves as the base for one or (usually) more equivalents to independent pronouns, acquiring its person-number categories from inflection. Siewierska 2004: 19–21 calls them *generic pronoun roots*, but in some languages they appear to be not simplex roots but derived stems, so I use *base* as a looser term.

The clearest examples of generic bases come from head-marking languages of the Americas, e.g. Lakhota and Cree:

(11)   Lakhota (Siouan; Rood & Taylor 1996: 454, 458)

	EMPHATIC	CONTRASTIVE
1SG	miyé	míš
1PL	ųkíye	ųkį́š
2	niyé	níš
3	é	íš

(12)   Cree (Algonquian; Wolfart 1996: 424; colon for his raised dot)

1SG	ni:ya	INCL	ki:ya:naw	1PL	ni:yana:n
2SG	ki:ya			2PL	ki:yawa:w
3SG	wi:ya			3PL	wi:yawa:w

The prefixes Lakhota *mi-, ųkį-*, Cree *ni-, ki-*, etc. are also those used for possessive inflection of nouns. The stems *-íye, -íš; -ya-* are generic bases.

Outside of some of the Uralic languages to be reviewed in section 5, generic bases are not common in Eurasia. They arguably occur to a limited extent in languages of the Chukchi-Kamchatkan family:

(13)   Telqep Chukchi (Dunn 1999: 65)

	NOM	OBL stem
1SG	yəyəmo	yəyəm-
2SG	yəto	yəyət-
1PL	muri	mury-
2PL	turi	tury-

(14)   Itelmen (Georg & Volodin 1999: 125)

	NOM	LOC	DAT
1SG	kəmma	kəmmank	kəmmanke
2SG	kəzza	knink	knanke
1PL	muzaʔn	mizwink	məzwanke
2PL	tuzaʔn	tizwink	tizwanke

Chukchi ɣəyə-, Itelmen kə- could be analyzed as a singular generic base, followed by a person marker – except that neither *m* nor *t/z* is a singular person marker in other forms of Chukchi or Itelmen (for analysis of the person marking on verbs see Fortescue 2003, Comrie 1980). In the plurals these elements are identifiable as person markers in verb conjugation, and the plural pronouns do not call for analysis as a generic base.

Ainu has a prototypical generic base:

(15) Ainu (Isolate; Shibatani 1990: 31)

    1SG   *ku-ani*
    2SG   *e-ani*
    3SG   *ani*

where *ku-*, *e-*, 3SG *ø-* are subject agreement prefixes of verbs and *-ani* is a nominalized form of the verb 'exist' (Shibatani 1990: 31, 28). There is a corresponding plural form of the verb used as generic base of the plural pronouns.

An additional possible example is the pronouns of West Caucasian in (2)–(3) above: the long forms *sara*, etc. consist of the possessive prefixes *s-*, etc. plus what may be a generic base; alternatively, these could simply be a suffix *-ra* attached to the independent pronouns. Chirikba (1996: 394, 397) reconstructs **sa(-ra)*, etc. without comment on the *-*ra*.

2.9 None of the above

The pronominal case system of Hungarian, shown in (16), is distinctive.

(16) Hungarian (Uralic: Ugric branch). Selected case paradigms and other forms (in orthography). Boldface: See text. The parenthesized endings on the 1sg and 2sg accusative forms are optional (and not frequent).

a.

	Noun 'house'	1SG	2SG
NOM	*ház*	*én*	*te*
ACC	*ház-at*	*en-ge-m(et)*	*té-ge-d(et)*
DAT	*ház-**nak***	***nek**-em*	***nek**-ed*
INSTR	*ház.**zal***	***vel**-em*	***vel**-ed*
INES	*ház-**ban***	***benn**-em*	***benn**-ed*

b. Postposition:

a ház mellett	mellett-em	mellett-ed
the house beside	beside-1SG	beside-2SG
'beside the house'	'beside me'	'beside you'

c. Possessive:

1SG ház-am	2SG ház-ad
house-1SG	house-2SG
'my house'	'your house'

In Hungarian the accusative is formed by adding a possessive suffix to a variant of the nominative stem, and the other oblique cases of pronouns consist of a stem carrying the case meaning (but no person-number meaning) followed by a person-number suffix. The same suffix marks pronoun objects of postpositions and possessors of nouns. The oblique *stems* of the pronouns are cognate to the case *suffixes* of nouns; both are postpositional in origin. (The postpositions, in turn, go back to case-suffixed relational or spatial nouns). There is a sizable theoretical literature on the synchronic status of the Hungarian forms. Most recently, Spencer & Stump (2014) argue that the Hungarian "cases" are actually postpositions – postpositions lacking any uninflected free form (unlike the free postposition *mellett* in (16b), which does occur in uninflected form as an independent word: see the example with noun object in (16c)). The "case suffix" of the noun then is actually the conjunct (or dependent or compounding) stem of the postposition. On that analysis, there are no oblique stems of pronouns; person-inflected postpositions (in conjunct form) step in for the oblique cases and in the paradigm have the status of generic bases. On a strict traditional analysis there is a case paradigm with a different oblique stem for every case,[3] so the pronoun paradigms are multiply suppletive. However, not only their structure but also their diachronic evolution is different from that of ordinary suppletive stems, as can be better seen in sister languages of Hungarian discussed below.

2.10 Typology

I can now propose tentative terminology and definitions for a typological distinction that runs through the examples reviewed here. The category of person is *lexical* if it is mostly instantiated in independent root words which have person

---

[3] Some of the cases share the same postpositional root, e.g. *-ba/-be* illative, *-ban/-ben* inessive, where the non-root part is etymologically a former case suffix.

as part of their lexical meaning; it is *inflectional* if it is mostly realized in inflectional morphology such as argument agreement on verbs.[4] The polar lexical type of person system is found in conservative Nakh-Daghestanian languages such as Ingush, many Pama-Nyungan languages such as Dyirbal, or Japanese, where there is no person marking whatever on verbs or nouns and person is found only in personal pronouns, which are lexemes. In most such languages the singular and plural forms of pronouns have no formal similarity, so that person is not formally factored out in the root or stem shapes. The polar inflectional type is found in many head-marking languages (such as Abkhaz, Kabardian, Lakhota, and Cree mentioned above) with head-marked person agreement in several word classes (on verbs, possessed nouns, adpositions) and no root lexemes with person as part of their meaning (separate personal pronouns are lacking, and in their place the languages use a person-inflected generic base). Inflectional person is almost entirely head-marking, which explains why the inflectional person type is frequent in head-marking languages.[5]

This typology is not a dichotomy but a scale, and most languages are at non-polar positions. European languages, for instance, are more lexical than inflectional in their person marking, but have inflectional person agreement on verbs (a common situation, as the majority of the world's languages have verb agreement with one argument, regardless of other typological considerations: Dryer 2005, Kibrik 2011: 102). Languages with minimal inflectional morphology can nonetheless be positioned at different points on the scale: Chinese has lexical person, though in factoring out person from number in its pronouns it is one step removed from the polar lexical type; Thai, with its large set of extrinsic surrogate pronouns but arguably no true pronouns, does not have lexical person, though with its general lack of agreement it has no inflectional person either; in thoroughly mixing person with honorific and deferential categories it is a step removed from polar inflectional person systems. Ainu has a relatively modest morphology, but its agreement morphology is for person (two verb arguments) and its personal pronouns use a generic base which takes person inflection, so it is an inflectional-person language.

---

4 I agree with Kibrik (2011: 204–231) that the term *agreement* is often a misnomer, but with this proviso I use it anyway where it is traditional.
5 The distinction and the terminology *lexical* and *inflectional* are not novel here; Cysouw (2003: 311–315) uses the terms in much the same sense, and Kibrik (2011: 102–104) points out the cross-linguistic near-perfect coincidence of bound pronominals, person, and head marking. What is new here is placing not paradigms or constructions but whole languages on the continuum, and also the geographical and historical correlations discusssed in sections 5 and 7 below.

3 Evolution of suppletive pronoun paradigms in the west

This section reviews all the processes I have found leading to the formation of suppletive paradigms.

3.1 Untraceable

As mentioned in section 1, the suppletive first person forms of Indo-European and Kartvelian are inherited from the respective protolanguages; the origin of the suppletion is unrecoverable.

3.2 Sound change

As mentioned in section 2.4, ordinary sound change can produce stem allomorphs whose etymological unity is eventually obscured.

3.3 Morphological change

See sections 2.5–2.6 for examples of ordinary fusion and analogy that eventually obscure the etymological unity of forms.

3.4 Recruitment of extrinsic forms as nominatives

Here are two pieces of evidence for how extrinsic forms can be recruited into case paradigms. The first is the Nakh-Daghestanian interrogative pronouns 'who', 'what' (Nichols 2012b). The 35 or more Nakh-Daghestanian daughter languages are fairly consistent in reflecting inherited stems in the oblique cases, but in their nominatives they exhibit a striking variety of unrelated stems (Nichols 2012b: Table 2). This alone is evidence that the nominatives are secondary. Evidence that these may have come from extrinsic forms comes from the Nakh branch, where the nominative exhibits the initial *m-* common to most of the Nakh interrogatives, evidence that the nominative has been recruited from a different interrogative series. The Nakh nominative functions frequently as a clefting form. Though the ergative of 'who', as in (17a) from Ingush, is not ungrammatical, the strongly preferred alternative is a clefting construction with a nominative as in (17b):

(17) Ingush (Nakh-Daghestanian: Nakh)

    a. *Hwan(uo) yz dead?*
       who.ERG   it   D.do-NONWIT.PAST-D
       Who did it?

    b. *Mala=v yz dear?*
       who=v.be   it   D.do-NOMLZR
       id., lit. 'Who is it that did it?'

The nominative in this function is a predicate nominal and typically bears focus and/or emphasis, which makes it a natural target for replacement by an intensifier or emphatic form. Though I do not have evidence of change in progress (such as alternation between an inherited nominative and an innovative extrinsic form, where the extrinsic form is favored in predicate nominal function), I suggest that this is a common origin for intrusive nominatives.

The second example is the circum-Baltic expression German *was ... für*, Russian *čto... za*, Polish *co... za*, Lithuanian *kas... par*, etc. 'what kind of'. Structurally it is a discontinuous modifier (the ellipsis marks the position of a copula and an optional subject, usually a demonstrative pronoun 'it', 'this'). Semantically it starts out as an emphatic interrogative, widening the interrogation beyond the domain that might otherwise be assumed: 'what on earth', 'whatever (kind)'. I believe that in all of these languages this interrogative is used most often as modifier of a predicate nominal, which is nominative. Certainly this is true for Russian, where a corpus survey shows that the great majority of its uses are as semantically emphatic and as modifier of predicate nominal:[6,7]

---

[6] All examples from the Russian National Corpus (www.ruscorpora.ru), accessed June 4, 2012. Full examples and sources are in the Appendix. In (18)–(21), *èto* 'this' is subject and the *čto... za...* construction is predicate nominal; in (22)–(23) *èto* is topic and the *čto... za...* phrase is subject. All these Russian examples have the copula in the present tense, where its form is zero. The copula is overt in other tenses, e.g.:

  Čto èto byli za zvuki, nikto ne znaet ...
  what this were-PL for sound-PL nobody NEG knows
  Nobody knows what kind of sounds these were ...

As is usual in Russian, the copula agrees not with the subject (singular *èto* 'this') but with the predicate nominal (*zvuki* 'sounds').

[7] When this phrase is included in dictionaries its citation form is with the nominative, giving the impression that the preposition *za* governs the nominative in this usage. It does not; no preposition in Russian governs the nominative. Rather, *čto ... za* is a discontinuous modifier whose second component is etymologically but not synchronically a preposition, and the case of the noun phrase it modifies is determined by that noun phrase's own syntax.

(18) Čto èto za štuka   takaja,   ne vyjasneno
     what this for thing.NOM such.NOM not clarified
     What kind of thing this is isn't clear.

(19) Čto èto za derev'ja?
     what this for trees.NOM
     What kind of trees are these? (Context: a surreal scene with strange trees).

But it can also be a fairly ordinary taxonomic question 'what kind':

(20) **Čto èto za kolebanija**   i   kakov ix   period?
     what this for oscillations.NOM and what their period
     What kind of oscillations are these and what is their period?

(21) **Čto èto za rastenie?**
     what this for plant.NOM
     What plant is this? (Context: child shows branch to teacher)

In addition to modifying a predicate nominal, in a few examples it modifies a nominative subject:

(22) Poslušaj, **čto èto za kampanija**   pošla nasčet   domov?
     listen   what this for campaign.NOM went concerning houses
     Listen, what kind of campaign has started up about the houses?

or an accusative direct object:

(23) **Čto èto za bumagi**   vam   ostavil Pečorin?
     what this for papers.ACC you.DAT left   Pechorin
     What (sort of) papers did Pechorin leave you?

(24) **Čto za čeloveka**   videla Evgenija Aleksandrovna noč'ju
     what for person-ACC saw   E.NOM   A.NOM   at_night
     What kind of person Evgenia Aleksandrovna saw last night...[8]

---

[8] In this example there is no copula or subject in the čto za, which is therefore unquestionably a modifier of čeloveka 'person'. The status of the copula and subject in the other examples needs work, but basically they are optional where čto za modifies an S or O and required where it modifies a predicate nominal.

Thus Russian *čto … za,* basically an emphatic modifier of predicate nominals, has begun to overlap with the adjectival interrogative *kakoj* 'what kind, what one', expanding into part of the latter's semantic range and into its highest-ranked cases and most accessible argument roles. This is my only good example so far of how such change proceeds, but I take it to justify this hypothesis: Extrinsic forms can enter pronominal paradigms as nominatives, and after entering the paradigm may expand their forms and functions.

4 Structure and evolution of pronoun paradigms in the east

Apart from the Uralic family to be discussed in the next section, I have found no examples of case-suppletive pronouns in eastern Asia. Rather, pronoun paradigms there are invariant (e.g. Yukagir, Tungusic languages, Japanese, Korean, Mandarin and the isolating Southeast Asian languages) or utilize generic bases (Ainu and the Chukchi-Kamchatkan languages illustrated in section 2 above). A number of East Asian languages can be said to lack independent pronouns: either they use generic bases or, as in Thai and some other Southeast Asian languages, they have a variety of words usable as pronouns for various honorific and non-honorific effects (Siewierska 2004: 228–235). Japanese and Korean have different pronouns for different levels of formality or deference (Shibatani 1990: 371, Sohn 1999: 207). Absence of a dedicated, closed lexical class of independent pronoun roots might be said to be an East Asian phenomenon more generally.

The paradigms of Mongolic and Turkic languages, exemplified by Mongolian in section 2 above, show effects of sound changes such as distant nasal assimilation and other assimilation, which can sometimes make the forms synchronically non-transparent, eventually leading to suppletion. Historically, however, both families appear to have had invariant pronoun paradigms.[9]

---

[9] As is pointed out by proponents of an Altaic superfamily (which includes Tungusic, Turkic, and Mongolic as its core), the reconstructable pronoun paradigms of those three families are nearly identical. The distant nasal assimilation illustrated for Mongolic in (6) above has also affected most Turkic languages and one Tungusic language, Nanai, so the secondary modern forms are also very similar.

5 Pronoun paradigms in Uralic

The Uralic family, which spreads across northern Eurasia from Scandinavia and central Europe to western Siberia, exhibits a variety of paradigm types and evident diachronic morphological processes several of which have no parallel elsewhere in Eurasia. The family serves as a microcosm of sorts, spanning the easternmost and westernmost paradigm types, and because it is well reconstructed it can provide reliable evidence for those diachronic processes.

To contextualize the pronoun forms in the linguistic geography of Uralic, see the improved traditional family tree in (25) and a recently proposed one in (26). In both trees branching structure mirrors almost perfectly the distribution of the languages from west to east across the north of Europe, from northwestern Scandinavia (Saami) to western Siberia (Ugric, Samoyed). Hungarian is a recent emigrant, geographically detached from the Ugric branch.

(25) Uralic family tree (upper branches only), based largely on Janhunen 2009: 65. Boldface: branches in which there are traces of Hungarian-like pronoun paradigms.

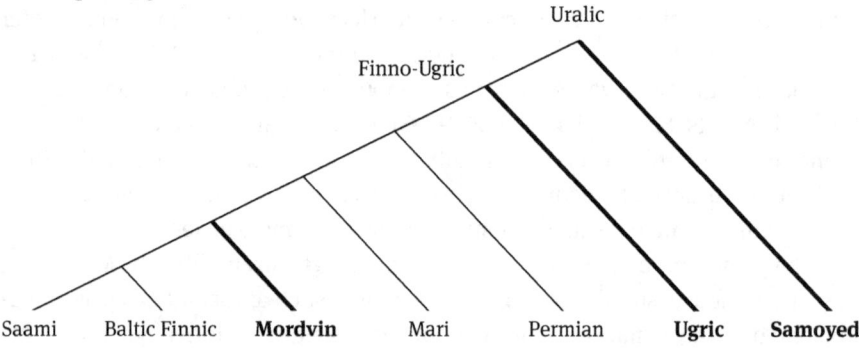

(26) Another proposed tree (based on Häkkinen 2012). Conventions as above.

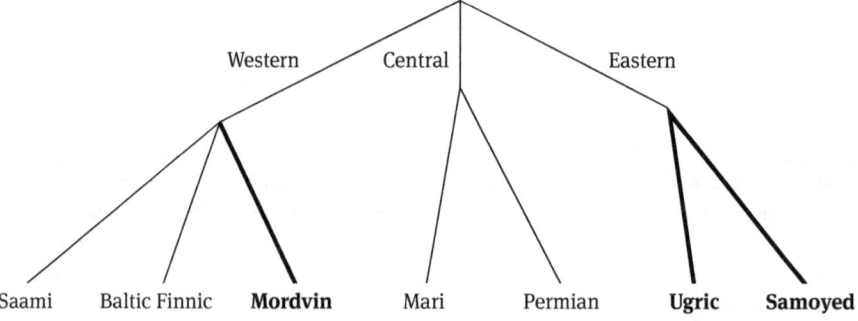

On either tree structure the evidence of the Hungarian-like paradigm has a phylogenetically diverse distribution that makes it reconstructable to Proto-Uralic. (It is not grounds for subgrouping, however, since as argued below it is evidently an archaism).

5.1 Hungarian-style paradigms

The distinctive pronoun paradigms – or perhaps better non-paradigms – of Hungarian were illustrated in (16) above. This is the most transparent exemplar of its type. (27) shows an inventory of forms from Mansi, the closest sister of Hungarian.

(27) Mansi (Uralic: Ugric branch; Keresztes 1998: 410, 413; s.a. Riese 2001: 30–31). Case paradigms (selected cases). The dative and comitative cases are called lative and instrumental respectively for nouns. ng = velar nasal. Double vowel = long. Underlined = possessive suffix.

	Noun 'pot'	1SG	2SG
NOM	puut	am	nang
ACC	puut	aan-əm	nang-ən
DAT	puut-n	aan-əm-n	nang-ən-n
ABL	puut-nəl	aan-əm-nəl	nang-ən-nəl
COM	puut-əl	aan-əm-təl	nang-ən-təl

In the Mansi pronouns the oblique stem is a possessed form (with 1sg -əm, 2sg -ən), and the possessive suffix is followed by the case suffix (this is the normal order for possessive and case suffixes in Ugric possessed nouns). The first person singular has a synchronically suppletive stem with nominative *am*, oblique *aan*, of which the nominative stem contains first person *m* which has been lost in the oblique stem by regular sound change.[10] The formation of the nominative and accusative is much as in Hungarian, but that of the other case affixes is entirely different from Hungarian: in Mansi there are very ordinary case suffixes, identical in nouns and pronouns, and pronouns are distinctive only in that their oblique base is formed with possessive morphology.[11]

---

[10] The 1sg root nominative *am*, oblique *aan*- is cognate to Hungarian nominative *én*, accusative *en-ge-m*. The Mansi *-n-* is suffixal, and internal *-m-* is regularly lost. Some Mansi dialects preserve the *-m-* in the nominative. See Gulya (1976: 290). The initial vowel is traditionally regarded as a deictic or emphatic element (Liimola 1963: 214, with references).

[11] Not all dialects have the person suffix in all oblique forms (Liimola 1944: 39–40 gives some dialect ablatives without it).

5.2 Languages with non-suppletive pronouns

All of the more westerly Uralic languages except Mordvin have straightforward non-suppletive pronouns in which the pronoun case endings are much the same as those of nouns and are attached to a stem which is also the stem of the nominative. Finnish (Baltic Finnic) pronominal paradigms are in (5) above.

(28) Hill Mari (Kovedjaeva 1966: 244, 246). ə̈ = higher or more fronted schwa.

	Noun 'mother'	1SG	2SG
NOM	äva	mə̈n'	tə̈n'
GEN	äva-n	mə̈n'ə̈n	tə̈n'ə̈n
DAT	äva-lan	mə̈lanem	tə̈lanem
ACC	äva-m	mə̈n'ə̈m	tə̈n'ə̈m

(29) Komi (Permian; Lytkin 1966: 287, Hausenberg 1998: 312–313). Underlined: possessive suffixes. Branch sister Udmurt is morphologically almost identical (Csúcs 1998: 282, 287).

	'companion'	1SG	2SG
NOM	jort	me	te
GEN	jort-lön	men-a<u>m</u>	ten-a<u>d</u>
ABL	jort-lys'	men-s'y<u>m</u>	ten-s'y<u>d</u>
DAT	jort-ly	men-y<u>m</u>	ten-y<u>d</u>
ACC	jort, jort-os	men-ö	ten-ö
INSTR	jort-ön	me-ön	te-ön
COM	jort-köd	me-köd	te-köd
PRIV	jort-tög	me-tög	te-tög

In the Komi forms note that, in those cases where the pronouns have stem-final -n-, the pronoun case endings differ from those of nouns and are followed by possessive suffixes. In the other cases, pronoun stems without -n- add the regular noun case endings directly. (Third person pronouns, which are demonstratives rather than true original pronouns, decline like nouns throughout). The cases taking possessive morphology in the pronouns are are those whose endings begin with -l- in nouns. The same situation obtains in Hill Mari (28), except that the -l- element is also found in the pronouns. The *-l- formative is likely to be a postposition in origin (Tepljashina & Lytkin 1976: 145), which suggests that the possessive suffix descends from the person inflection of the postposition and antedates the fusion of the postposition to the noun or pronominal stem. The root-final -n- on the pronouns may then have been an adnominal case ending and what is now the pronoun root may once have been a preposed appositive to the person suffix on the postposition. The cases without the -n- are then non-postpositional cases.

Alternatively, since the -n- is also found in the accusative, which has no person element, *-n- may have been a derivational element that converted an uninflectable pronoun into an inflectable word, i.e. an element that changed the word class or lexical category of the pronoun, converting it to a noun or noun-like word. Only secondarily did the bare nominative stem become case-inflectable, as in the instrumental, comitative, and privative. This analysis is consistent with evidence from languages discussed below that the early Uralic independent pronouns were not words of the same lexical category as most of the modern pronouns (where the independent pronouns are root words with pronominal meaning and more or less noun-like syntactic behavior and inflection).[12]

In one of the Ugric languages, Khanty, illustrated in (30) by the Tremjugan dialect, the pronouns are non-suppletive but some of the case endings of pronouns differ from those of nouns, and some case endings of pronouns contain possessive suffixes.[13] Note especially the dative and ablative cases in (30), which have case suffixes followed by possessive suffixes, the opposite order from possessed nouns in Ugric (see the Hungarian possessed nouns in (16) above). The order suggests that the case endings are in origin not a sequence of case and possessive but person-inflected postpositions which were added to the base; or, alternatively, the postposition initially stood alone and the optional preposed appositive or intensifier later fused to the postposition and was reanalyzed as the root of a case form.[14] In Khanty as in Komi we have a mix of complex case suffixes added to a longer stem (in several of the cases in (30)) and a simple suffix added to the bare stem (in the locative).[15]

---

12 The same -n appears in the nominative forms in several Uralic languages, including Mari shown in (28) here, Moksha Mordvin in (32), and Selkup in (35).
13 The dialect diversity of Khanty is considerable, and at least some dialects can be considered separate languages. The formation of oblique cases is also diverse in the dialects, and different morphological (and not just phonological) processes need to be reconstructed for some of them. This shows that the development of the oblique case paradigm was relatively recent, postdating at least some of the Khanty divergence.
14 Nichols (1973) and Comrie (1980) discuss the ordering of case and possessive suffixes in Uralic nouns but not pronouns. The Khanty pronoun paradigms support their finding (which is also the traditional claim) that the order Case + Possessive is archaic in Uralic; but the complex way in which the suffixes are worked into the pronoun paradigms suggests that the topic is worth another look.
15 Tremjugan is an eastern dialect. In another eastern variety described by Filchenko (2007: 84–90), oblique case formation is as it is in Mansi: all oblique cases have a stem extension -m-, and all case endings are added directly to that. In some northern dialects there are only three cases (nominative, accusative, dative) and all others are rendered with adpositional phrases, a situation similar to that of Hungarian pronouns.

(30) Tremjugan Khanty (Ugric; Abondolo 1998: 367, 369; his segmentation, hyphens, and zeroes). Selected cases. Underlined: possessive suffixes.

	Noun 'house'	1SG	2SG
NOM	kååt	mää	nöng
ACC	kååt	mään-t	nöngaa-t
DAT/LAT	kååt-aa	mään-tee-<u>m</u>	nöngaa-tii-Ø
APPROX	kååt-naam	mään-tee-<u>m</u>-nääm	nöngaa-tii-naam
LOC	kååt-nə	mää-nə	nöng-nə
ABL	kååt-ii	mää-niingt-ee-<u>m</u>	nöng-ngiingt-ee
COM	kååt-naat	mään-tee-<u>m</u>-näät	nöngaa-tii-naat

Thus, in the Permian and Ugric branches, pronouns with non-suppletive stems exhibit some distinctive morphology where the formation of oblique cases is more complicated than simply adding endings to stems. In particular, possessive suffixes figure in some of the case suffixes as does a root-final -*n*. I have suggested that both of these may have had something to do with converting the pronoun from a non-inflectable part of speech to one that could inflect for case. Unfortunately, none of the Uralicist literature I have seen on the derivation of case endings and oblique stems mentions such issues as the word class of pronouns, the internal syntax of constructions with *-*n*- and/or person morphology, or types of agreement markers (syntactic, pronominal, or ambiguous, in the terms of Siewierska 2004: 126).

5.3 Uralic languages with suppletive paradigms and generic bases

Examples from Mansi (Ugric) are in (27) above. Unlike Khanty and Komi ((29), (30) above), where some oblique stems have possessive affixation and/or different endings from the noun cases, in Mansi the oblique stem is a possessed form throughout the paradigm (possessive suffix underlined):

(31) Aan-ə<u>m</u>-n
1SG-1SG-DAT
'to me'

The consistency of the Mansi formation implies that the possessive morphology converted the pronominal base into something sufficiently nominal to carry case inflection. The ordering Possessive suffix + Case suffix, used in all the oblique cases, is the regular order for possessed nouns in Ugric languages (contrast the situation in Khanty, (30) just above, where the possessive suffix, when present, follows part or all of the case morphology). Mansi and Hungarian ((16) above) are closely related, and the most parsimonious reconstruction is one where their independent pronoun roots originally had only nominative, accusative, and adnominal (possessive) functions (as is still the situation in Hungarian). All other cases were formed later and independently, by Hungarian recruiting inflected postpositions and Mansi adding possessive morphology to the pronominal stem to make it case-inflectable.

The Mordvin languages construct their case paradigms much as Hungarian does, with a different postpositional stem for each case of pronouns and mostly the same adpositions suffixed to the nouns. The Mordvin paradigms are less transparent than Hungarian, however, so the cognacy of noun and pronoun case endings is not as obvious at first glance.

(32) Moksha (Mordvin; Feoktistov 1975: 290, 308). Underlined: possessive suffixes. Pronouns lack the ablative.

	Noun 'vein'	1SG	2SG
NOM	san	mon	ton
GEN	san-o-n'	mon'	ton'
DAT	san-o-ndi	t'ei-_n'e_	t'ei-_t'_
ABL	san-da		
INES	san-ca	eso-_n_	eso-_t_
ELAT	san-cta	esto-_n_	esto-_t_
ILLAT	san-c	ezo-_n_	ezo-_t_
TRANSLAT	san-ks	laco-_n_	laco-_t_
COM	san-ška	eška-_n_	eška-_t_

In the Mordvin languages the oblique pronouns can also have a preposed appositive genitive: dative *mon-d'ei-n'e,* inessive *mon'-co-n,* etc. When these are added the resultant paradigm is a one-stem one, at first glance like that of Finnish. However, the possessive suffixes in the oblique case endings are unlike the Finnish paradigm and point to a more complex history of stem formation than the Finnish paradigm appears to have.

Three Samoyed languages, representing the major subbranches, have generic bases in their pronoun systems: Tundra Nenets, Nganasan, and Selkup.[16] Tundra Nenets, shown in (33), has two non-nominative stems.

---

[16] A recent breakdown of Samoyed has Nganasan separating first, followed by the severely underattested Mator and then by the split of the remainder into Northern and Southern Samoyed (Janhunen 1998: 458–459). For a flatter classification see Salminen 1994–2012. Either way, languages with generic bases cover all the available high-level phylogenetic diversity in the branch (Mator, unfortunately, has only the nominative and genitive 1SG-2SG pronouns attested: Helimski 1997: 147).

(33) Tundra Nenets (Samoyed; Salminen 1998a: 537, 540, 1998b:30, 1997; Tapani Salminen, p.c.). ° = schwa. Noun, 1SG possessed form of that noun, and personal pronouns. Hyphenated suffixes are case for the unpossessed noun and possession (or case-possession in that order) for the possessed noun and pronouns. The possessed noun paradigm shows that the pronouns end in person forms, not case forms.

	'tent'	'tent-1SG'	1SG	2SG
NOM	myaq	myaq-m°	mɘny°	pidə-r°
ACC	myad°-m	myaq-m°	syiq-m°	syi-t°
GEN	myad°-h	myaq-n°	syiq-n°	syi-t°
DAT	mya-t°h	mya-kə-n°	nyaa-n°	nyaa-nt°
LOC	mya-k°na	mya-k°na-n°	nya-na-n°	nya-na-nt°
ABL	mya-kəd°	mya-k°də-n°	nya-də-n°	nya-də-nt°
PROSEC	myaq-m°na	myaq-m°na-n°	nya-mna-n°	nya-mna-nt°

The nominative pronouns are used only for emphasis "and can in that role occur also before the accusative and genitive forms as well as the postpositional forms" (Salminen 1997: 131–132; postpositional forms are the dative, locative, and ablative), which I take to mean that the nominative is an intensifier of the appositive type, making no case distinctions and modifying a noun or pronoun in any case.

The 1sg nominative is the pan-Uralic 1sg form, and the 2sg nominative *pid* is a generic base (originally a noun 'body, self') also used in the third person. Tereschenko 1993: 334 cites alternative 2sg forms based on *xərt*, which is a reflexive pronoun (Hajdú 1988: 15). Thus two different extrinsic forms have entered the paradigm as second person nominatives, ousting the original nominative that is still attested elsewhere in Samoyed.

The accusative and genitive pronouns are traced to a nominal stem meaning 'form, likeness, image' (Janhunen 1977: 70–71, Hajdú 1988: 15) (found also in the accusative of Selkup, another Samoyed language: see below; also cognate to the *-ge-* in the Hungarian 1sg and 2sg accusatives of (16a) above: Helimski 1982, Aikio 2006). The dative, locative, and ablative are based on a postposition *nya-* 'at' (Salminen 1998: 540), so they are analogous in their formation to the Hungarian oblique cases, except that that stem is not found in the case suffix of the corresponding noun cases. As their final element they have a possessive suffix in the oblique form (i.e. the allomorph used on a noun in an oblique case) (for the forms see Salminen 1997: 125–126). Thus, for the oblique cases, noun and pronoun forms are entirely unrelated.

Therefore Tundra Nenets can arguably be said to have no pronoun roots. The nominatives appear to be caseless intensifiers rather than true nominatives; and in any event the second (and third) person forms are transparently non-pronominal in origin. The non-nominative forms are built on non-pronominal stems, and their person meaning is carried by the possessive suffix. These paradigms are similar to the Hungarian ones, except that there is only one postpositional stem and (as in Mordvin but unlike Hungarian) the corresponding noun cases do not use the pronoun stem as the case ending.

Nganasan, shown in (34), has only one generic base, an evident cognate to the Tundra Nenets non-core oblique stem and with the same functions. Pronouns, but not nouns, have nominative/accusative/genitive syncretism, and that syncretic form is the inherited Proto-Uralic pronoun.

(34)　Nganasan (Samoyed; Helimski 1998a: 498, 501; my hyphens).
　　　Possessive suffixes underlined.

	'skin, hide'	1SG	2SG
NOM	kuhu	mənə	tənə
ACC	kubu-(m)	”	”
GEN	kubu-(ŋ)	”	”
LAT	kubu-tə	na-nə	na-nt<u>ə</u>
LOC	kubu-tənu	na-nu-n<u>ə</u>	na-nu-nt<u>ə</u>
ELAT	kuhu-gətə	na-gətə-n<u>ə</u>	na-gətə-t<u>ə</u>
PROLAT	kuhu-mənu	na-mənu-n<u>ə</u>	na-mənu-nt<u>ə</u>

The other cases of pronouns consist of a postposition (more properly a case-inflected relational noun) plus possessive suffix (Helimski 1998a: 497–500), more transparent than the Tundra Nenets analogs.

The Selkup accusative -ši-m/-ši-ntï is cognate to the Tundra Nenets accusative-genitive base, but Selkup has but no analog to the postpositional base of Nenets and Nganasan.

(35)　Selkup (Samoyed; Helimski 1998b: 558, 564)

	'God, heaven'	1SG	2SG
NOM	nom	man	tan
GEN	nuun	man	tan
ACC	nuum	(ma)ši<u>m</u>	(ta)ši<u>ntï</u>
INSTR	nopsä	massä	tassä
CAR	nomkåålïk	matkåålïk	tatkåålïk
TRANS	nuutqo	matqo	tatqo
DAT/ALL	nuunïk	mäkkä ~ matqäk	täntï ~ tatqä<u>ntï</u>

Apart from the accusative, the paradigm is a regular one-stem one, and when the optional initial *ma-* or *ta-* is present in the accusative that too is a regular member of the one-stem paradigm (albeit with an accusative ending that differs from the regular accusative and contains a possessive suffix).

The other Samoyed languages have generalized a single stem for the whole paradigm, either by doubling all case forms with an appositive nominative as Enets has done:

(36) Enets (Samoyed; Tereščenko 1966: 447)

	1SG	2SG
NOM	*modi, mod'*	*u:*
GEN	*mod' sin'*	*u: sit*
ACC	*mod' si*	*u: sit*
DAT	*mod' non'*	*u: nod*
LOC	*mod' nonen'*	*u: nod*
ABL	*mod' noðon'*	*u: noðod*
PROLAT	*mod' noonen'*	*u: nooned*

(note that the second element of each Enets form is obviously cognate to the Tundra Nenets form) or by making the nominative stem inflectable and adding the regular case endings to it as Selkup appears to have done in several of its oblique cases (see (35) above). Either of these two developments can eventually lead to loss of suppletion.

5.4 Typological overview of Samoyed

A general Samoyed structural pattern can be detected in all this. There are three pronoun stem types: a nominative, at least sometimes an extrinsic form in origin and at least in Tundra Nenets an intensifier in function, that can double the person marker of any case but cannot take case inflection; a generic base recruited as an accusative stem (Tundra Nenets *syi(q)-*, Selkup *-ši-m, -ši-ntï*) which can take possessive marking, so that the set of nominative and accusative stems is suppletive; and another generic base (Nenets *nya-*, Enets *no-*, Nganasan *na-*), postpositional in origin, which takes case and possessive suffixes (in that order, which is the usual order for Samoyed). The essence of the system in its most extreme form is that pronouns have no case inflection; extrinsic words have been recruited as inflectable stems, and/or possessive morphology derives inflectable noun stems from pronoun roots. This same structure is reflected in Hungarian and Mordvin and, in view of its dispersal across the Uralic family tree and its rarity worldwide, must be archaic rather than an independent parallel innovation.

Now, was the original Samoyed nominative a true nominative which has changed its function, detaching from its paradigm to become an appositive intensifier, i.e. an extrinsic word, as in Tundra Nenets? Or was it an extrinsic form that was recruited into the pronoun paradigm as nominative? Only the latter development is consistent with the usual trajectory of grammaticalization (for this in the development of person markers see Siewierska 2004: 246–268). It is also indicated by the Tundra Nenets second and third person nominatives based on *pid-* and similar dialect variants, and Enets 2sg *u:* in (36) just above, which have clearly non-pronominal origins. But since the Tundra Nenets first person nominative is also an appositive intensifier and is not secondary but continues the Proto-Uralic form, then if the second trajectory is correct the only reconstructable Proto-Uralic nominative personal pronouns were really intensifiers and extrinsic forms rather than members of a case paradigm. This would make the widespread Eurasian pronominal pattern of first person *m-*, second person *t-*, *s-*, etc. look less well embedded in Proto-Uralic pronouns than has generally been assumed. (It was present in possessive suffixes and verb agreement suffixes, however).

5.5 Proposed typological history of Uralic pronouns

The changes and structural types described above can be boiled down to the following four diachronic typological stages:

(1) The earliest stage, perhaps Proto-Uralic: Person is a purely inflectional category; there are no lexical personal pronoun roots. There must have been intensifiers and/or other extrinsic forms, and the forms traditionally reconstructed as the Proto-Uralic nominatives must have originally been such forms. In the most radical terms, this would mean that the roots now reconstructed as Proto-Uralic personal pronouns were in fact not personal pronouns but extrinsic forms of some kind.[17] Whatever those extrinsic forms were, they could not take case inflection (unlike nouns, which had a modest case paradigm).

(2) Person begins to become a lexical category. Personal pronouns take shape and a de facto case array for them is assembled out of person-inflected words (such as generic bases and postpositions) and extrinsic forms recruited as nominatives. The early phase of this stage is visible in Samoyed, discussed

---

[17] Kulonen (2001) also argues that the modern personal pronouns are secondary at least in the Ob-Ugric languages (Khanty, Mansi), since their initial *n-* is in her view derived from verb inflection.

above.[18] A more developed stage appears in Hungarian. Though person is partly a lexical category in Hungarian, the oblique case system could be described as one where, when there is competition, case is more easily accorded lexical status than person is.

(3) The de facto case array is reanalyzed as a case paradigm. An appositive nominative or genitive begins to be generalized as a lexical person root and former postpositions fuse to it, so that the erstwhile appositive becomes the root of an oblique case form. The early phase of this process is visible in Mordvin; the later stage is present in Baltic Finnic, Saami, and Permian. In the late stage, independent pronouns are noun-like words in their syntactic behavior and their case paradigms.

Importantly for understanding the history of suppletion, the de facto case array turns into a bona fide case paradigm without ever producing true case suppletion.

What can be reconstructed for Proto-Uralic person typology is not de facto case arrays or multiply suppletive paradigms with specific postpositional or generic bases, but simply the absence of lexical person. Formation of a de facto case array is a fairly straightforward and perhaps even common consequence of the type, assuming the language has any tendency to develop cases at all (and Proto-Uralic did have a reconstructable small system of case endings). Most languages with strongly inflectional, non-lexical person do not develop cases and therefore give no evidence of this process.

6 Loss of suppletion

Suppletion is most often lost by generalizing one of the stems. The Indo-European 1sg suppletive paradigm is extremely tenacious, but it has been removed in two branches: Indo-Iranian and Celtic. Most Indic languages and several Iranian ones have 1sg nominatives in *m-*, e.g. Hindi *main*, Shina *ma*; Persian *man*, Kurdish *min*. (Since not all the languages have this innovation, it is not a single Proto-Indo-Iranian innovation but separate ones in various daughter languages or subbranches). In Celtic, Irish has 1sg nominative *mise* and Welsh *mi*. All of these represent extensions of the oblique stem, ousting the old nominative.

---

18 The frequently non-pronominal origin of nominatives in Samoyed suggests that perhaps *siC < *kit, the protoform of the Nenets-Selkup accusative-genitive base (Janhunen 1977: 70–71; my *C stands for some unspecified stage in the transition from Proto-Samoyed *t to the modern alternation set of glottal stop, /t/, and /d/), may have been a nominative as well, until new nominative forms were recruited.

In Kartvelian, three of the four languages have reflexes of 2sg nominative *sen, genitive *sh(w)en (e.g. Mingrelian *si, skan-*), while Georgian has removed this suppletion by generalizing the oblique stem to the nominative: nom. *shen*, gen. *shen-i*.

Uralic languages have followed two different ways of removing or forestalling suppletion, as discussed above. One is to double the person marker or person category of oblique pronoun cases with an independent pronoun form that is formally a possessor (nominative in Ugric languages and Enets [Samoyed], genitive in Mordvin). This possessor is necessarily preposed (following the consistently head-final word order of most Uralic languages). As was discussed in connection with Moksha Mordvin ((32) above), if the preposed possessor becomes default or obligatory, the oblique pronoun form is prone to fuse to it. The obligatory possessor is then reanalyzed as the root and the result is a single root throughout the paradigm.

The other means of removing or forestalling suppletion in Uralic is to make the nominative stem directly inflectable and add case endings to it. In Mansi ((27) above) it looks as though possessive morphology added to the pronoun stem makes it inflectable as a noun, with case suffixes. But this is not true everywhere; in Komi some oblique pronoun cases take possessive suffixes and some do not, and in those that do not the pronoun root is directly case-inflectable. In Khanty ((30) above), most of the oblique pronoun cases add a noun case ending to a suffixed stem whose last element is a possessive suffix, but the locative case adds the regular noun ending directly to the pronoun root. These shorter forms of Komi and Khanty may be later additions to the case paradigm, and regardless of the relative chronology of their formation they show that over time the pronoun roots of these languages have become case inflectable.

It is notable that the de facto case arrays still attested in Mordvin, Hungarian, and some Samoyed languages have not settled into stable suppletive paradigms like those of Indo-European and Kartvelian. Rather, they add a preposed adnominal intensifier and, when that becomes fused to the rest and is reanalyzed as the root, turn into non-suppletive stems.

7 Conclusions

Despite what would seem to be welcoming conditions for the rise of case-suppletive pronoun systems, Hungarian-style arrays of postpositional forms do not readily develop into suppletive stems. Rather, when we have evidence for their formation, suppletive stems are produced by recruiting extrinsic words into existing case paradigms, initially as surrogate nominatives.

Other historical processes reflect typological geography more than structural tendencies. The lexical and inflectional types of person markers form a cline in Eurasia, with inflectional person dominating in the east (of those illustrated here, most clearly Ainu and the Chukchi-Kamchatkan languages). In the Tungusic and Turkic languages inflectional person is strong; there are lexical pronouns, but their roots are similar or identical to those of the inflectional endings. Mongolic languages, at least Proto-Mongolic and conservative modern varieties, have no person agreement, so their person is lexical. In western Eurasia, most languages have lexical person. The picture is more complex in the Caucasus, where person is in origin lexical in Nakh-Daghestanian, inflectional in West Caucasian, and mixed in Kartvelian (there the independent pronoun forms are lexical, inflectional person agreement with two or three arguments is well developed in the verb, but there are no possessive affixes). There is relatively little leakage of types across family boundaries in the Caucasus, suggesting that types are fairly stable.

Which is more stable cross-linguistically, nominative stems or oblique stems? The question cannot be properly answered without a worldwide survey, but the material given here shows expansions of both nominative and oblique stems and recruitment of new forms as both nominatives (usually from extrinsic words) and obliques (usually from postpositions). Neither stem type has obvious claim to greater stability.

Suppletive systems and those with oblique generic bases have some tendency to undergo regularization to a single stem, but such changes are not numerous. The Indo-European suppletive 1sg paradigm is quite stable (at attested rates of change it would take considerably more than another 6000 years for it to disappear from most branches), and the Uralic system of oblique generic bases, though more prone to regularization than the Indo-European suppletion, is still durable enough to leave evidence sufficient for reconstruction despite the considerable age of Uralic.

And in general changes in pronominal paradigms and changes of person type are not rapid. Despite the many opportunities for morphological change offered in the long histories of Indo-European and Nakh-Daghestanian, these families have not undergone appreciable changes of pronominal type. In Uralic, in contrast, if the reconstruction offered here is correct, most languages have undergone major changes, shifting to the lexical-person type. But this is because of the position of Uralic vis-à-vis the east-west geographical cline of inflectional to lexical person categories. In Uralic the lexical type has come to predominate in the west, while the conservative east and the protolanguage have a much more East Asian typological cast. Early eastern affinities are also consistent with recent work which, though it varies somewhat on where it places the center of the Proto-Uralic dispersal, agrees on a more eastern origin for Pre-Proto-Uralic (Janhunen

2009, Häkkinen 2012; Parpola 2012). The pronominal typological facts suggest that the Uralic languages have moved westward and/or the typological boundary has moved eastward, though they cannot say which of these is correct.[19]

Appendix

Examples (18)–(24) in orthography with more context and with sources, and the example from note 6. All are cited from the Russian National Corpus (www.ruscorpora.ru).

(18´) **Что это за штука такая,** не выяснено, но в науке она несомненно присутствует [Даниил Гранин. Зубр (1987)]
What kind of thing this is isn't clear, but it's certainly known to science.

(19´) Нигде Зыбин не видел ничего подобного. — **Что это за деревья?** — спросил он. — А мёртвые, — ответил парень.— Задушенные. [Ю. О. Домбровский. Факультет ненужных вещей, часть 1 (1978)]
Zybin had never seen anything like this. "**What kind of trees are these?**" he asked. "Dead ones," answered the boy. "Smothered."

(20´) **Что это за колебания** и каков их период? [Владимир Лукашик, Елена Иванова. Сборник задач по физике. 7–9 кл. (2003)]
What kind of oscillations are these and what is their period?

(21´) Вдруг ко мне подбегает девочка, показывает веточку и спрашивает: «**Что это за растение?**
[коллективный. Переписка с читателями // «Наука и жизнь», 2007]
Suddenly a little girl runs up to me and shows me a branch and asks, "**What plant is this?**"

(37) (not included above)
Что это за женщина там, наверху, смеётся, что за мужчина рядом,... [Василий Аксенов. Пора, мой друг, пора (1963)]
What woman is laughing up there, what man is next to her ...

---

[19] Work in the library of the Max Planck Institute for Evolutionary Anthropology, Leipzig made possible an efficient initial survey of the Uralic literature. I thank Daniel Abondolo for advice on the Ugric material, Tapani Salminen for Tundra Nenets, and Juha Janhunen for comments on the Uralic section.

(22′) — Послушай, **что это за кампания пошла** насчёт домов?
[Фазиль Искандер. Должники (1968)]
Listen, **what kind of campaign started up** about the houses?

(23′) — Максим Максимыч, — сказал я, подошедши к нему, — а **что это за бумаги вам оставил Печорин?**
[М. Ю. Лермонтов. Герой нашего времени (1839–1841)]
"Maksim Maksimych," I said, going up to him, "**what kind of papers did Pechorin leave you?**"

(24′) Было бы очень неплохо, если бы вы сумели выяснить, **что за человека видела Евгения Александровна** ночью на лестничной площадке. [Н. Леонов, А. Макеев. Гроссмейстер сыска (2003)]
It would be very good if you could explain what kind of person Evgenia Aleksandrovna saw last night on the landing.

(38) (from note 6)
Что это были за звуки, никто не знает …
[Лягушки // «Мурзилка», 1999]
What sort of sounds these were no one knew …

Abbreviations

1 first person, 2 second person, 3 third person, ABL ablative, ACC accusative, ADES adessive, APPROX approximative, CAR caritative, COM commitative, CONTR contrastive, D gender agreement category, DAT dative, ELAT elative, EMPH emphatic, ERG ergative, FEM feminine, GEN genitive, ILLAT illative, INCL inclusive, INES inessive, INSTR instrumental, LAT lative, LOC locative, MAS masculine, NEG negator, NOM nominative, NOMLZR nominalizer, NONWIT non-witnessed, OBJ objective, OBL oblique, PART partitive, PL plural, PREP prepositional, PRIV privative, PROLAT prolative, SG singular, TRANSLAT translative, V gender agreement category.

References

Abondolo, Daniel. 1998. Khanty. In Daniel Abondolo (ed.), 358–386. London: Routledge.
Abondolo, Daniel (ed.). 1998. *The Uralic Languages*. London: Routledge.
Aikio, Ante. 2006. New and old Samoyed etymologies, 2. *Finnisch-Ugrische Forschungen* 59(1–3). 9–34.
Ajello, Roberto. 1998. Armenian. In Paolo Ramat & Anna Giacolone Ramat (eds.), *The Indo-European Languages*, 197–227. London: Routledge.

Chirikba, Viacheslav A. 1996. *Common West Caucasian: The reconstruction of its phonological system and parts of its lexicon and morphology.* Leiden: Research School CNWS, Leiden University.
Comrie, Bernard. 1980. The order of case and possessive suffixes in Uralic languages: An approach to the comparative-historical problem. *Lingua Posnaniensis* 23. 81–86.
Creissels, Denis. 2009. Uncommon patterns of core term marking and case terminology. *Lingua* 119(3). 445–459.
Csúcs, Sándor. 1998. Udmurt. In Daniel Abondolo (ed.), 276–304. London: Routledge.
Cysouw, Michael. 2003. *The Paradigmatic Structure of Person Marking.* Oxford: Oxford University Press.
Dryer, Matthew S. 2005. Expression of pronominal subjects. In Martin Haspelmath, Matthew Dryer, David Gil & Bernard Comrie (eds.), *World Atlas of Language Structures*, 410–413. Oxford: Oxford University Press.
Dunn, Michael John. 1999. *A Grammar of Chukchi.* Ph.D. dissertation, Australian National University.
Eliseev, Jurij Sergeevich. 1993. Finskij jazyk. In Ju. S. Eliseev, K. E. Majtinskaja & O. I. Romanova (eds.), *Jazyki mira: Ural'skie jazyki*, 90–114. Moscow: Nauka.
Feoktistov, A. P. 1975. Mordovskie jazyki. In V. I. Lytkin, K. E. Majtinskaja & Károly Rédei (eds.), *Osnovy finno-ugorskogo jazyoznanija: Pribaltijsko-finskie, saamskie i mordovskie jazyki*, 248–345. Moscow: Nauka.
Filchenko, Andrey Yury. 2007. *A grammar of Eastern Khanty.* Ph.D. dissertation, Rice University.
Fortescue, Michael. 2003. Diachronic typology and the genealogical unity of Chukotko-Kamchatkan. *Linguistic Typology* 7. 51–88.
Georg, Stefan & Alexander P. Volodin. 1999. *Die itelmenische Sprache: Grammatik und Texte.* Wiesbaden: Harrassowitz.
Gulya, János. 1976. Morfologija obsko-ugorskix jazykov. In V. I. Lytkin, K. E. Majtinskaja & Károly Rédei (eds.), *Osnovy finno-ugorskogo jazykoznanija: Marijskij, permskie i ugorskie jazyki*, 277–341. Moscow: Nauka.
Hajdú, Péter. 1988. Die samojedischen Sprachen. In Denis Sinor (ed.) *The Uralic languages: description, history and foreign influences*, 3–40. Leiden: Brill.
Häkkinen, Jaakko. 2012. Early contacts between Uralic and Yukaghir. In Tiina Hyytäinen et al. (eds.), 91–101.
Hausenberg, Anu-Reet. 1998. Komi. In Daniel Abondolo (ed.), 305–326. London: Routledge.
Helimski [Xelimskij], Eugene A. 1982. *Drevnejshie vengersko-samodijskie jazykovye paralleli: Lingvisticheskaja i ètnogeneticheskaja interpretacija.* Moscow.
Helimski, Eugene A. 1997. *Die matorische Sprache.* (Studia Uralo-altaica, 41). Szeged: Dept. of Altaic Studies, University of Szeged.
Helimski, Eugene A. 1998a. Nganasan. In Daniel Abondolo (ed.), 480–515. London: Routledge.
Helimski, Eugene A. 1998b. Selkup. In Daniel Abondolo (ed.), 548–579. London: Routledge.
Hewitt, B. George. 1989. Abkhaz. In B. George Hewitt, ed., *The Northwest Caucasian Languages*, 39–88. Delmar, NY: Caravan Books.
Hyytiäinen, Tiina, Lotta Jalava, Janne Saarikivi & Erika Sandman (eds.), *Per Urales ad Orientem: Iter Polyphonicum Multilingue* (Festschrift for Juha Janhunen). Helsinki: SUST.
Janhunen, Juha. 1977. *Samojedischer Wortschatz: Gemeinsamojedische Etymologien.* (Castrenianumin toimitteita, 17). Helsinki: Helsinki University.
Janhunen, Juha. 1998. Samoyedic. In Daniel Abondolo (ed.), 457–479. London: Routledge.
Janhunen, Juha. 2003. Proto-Mongolic. In Juha Janhunen (ed.), *The Mongolic Languages*, 1–29. London: Routledge.

Janhunen, Juha. 2009. Proto-Uralic – what, where, and when? *The Quasquicentennial of the Finno-Ugrian Society*. 57–78. (Suomalais-Ugrilaisen Seuran Toimituksia, 258). Helsinki: Finno-Ugric Society.
Janhunen, Juha. 2013. Personal pronouns in core Altaic. In Martine Robbeets & Hubert Cuyckens (eds.), *Shared Grammaticalization: With special focus on the Transeurasian languages*. Amsterdam: Benjamins, in press.
Karst, Josef. 1901. *Historische Grammatik des Kilikisch-armenischen*. Strassburg (Reprint, Walter de Gruyter, 1970): Trübner.
Keresztes, László. 1998. Mansi. In Daniel Abondolo (ed.), 387–427.
Kibrik, Aleksandr E. 2003. *Konstanty i peremennye jazyka*. St. Petersburg: Aleteija.
Kibrik, Aleksandr E. & S. V. Kodzasov. 1988. *Sopostavitel'noe izuchenie dagestanskix jazykov: Glagol*. Moscow: Moscow University.
Kibrik, Aleksandr E. & S. V. Kodzasov. 1990. *Sopostavitel'noe izuchenie dagestanskix jazykov: Imja. Fonetika*. Moscow: Moscow University.
Kibrik, Andrej A. 2011. *Reference in Discourse*. Oxford: Oxford University Press.
Kovedjaeva, E. I. 1966. Gornomarijskij jazyk. In V. I. Lytkin & K. E. Majtinskaja (eds.), 241–254.
Kulonen, Ulla-Maija. 2001. Zum *n*-Element der zweiten Personen besonders im Obugrischen. *Finnisch-Ugrische Forschungen* 56(1–3). 151–174.
Liimola, Matti. 1944. Zu den wogulischen Personalpronomina. *Finnisch-Ugrische Forschungen* 28(1). 20–56.
Liimola, Matti. 1963. *Zur historischen Formenlehre des wogulischen, I. Flexion der Nomina*. (Suomalais-ugrilaisen seuran toimituksia, 127). Helsinki: Suomalais-ugrilainen Seura.
Lytkin, V. I. 1966. Komi-zyrjanskij jazyk. In V. I. Lytkin & K. E. Majtinskaja (eds.), 281–299.
Lytkin, V. I & K. E. Majtinskaja (eds.). 1966. *Jazyki narodov SSSR 5: Finno-ugorskie i samodijskie jazyiki*. Moscow: Nauka.
Matasović, Ranko. *A grammatical sketch of classical Armenian*. MS, University of Zagreb. (www.ffzg.unizg.hr/~matasov/armenian2.pdf; accessed May 27, 2012)
Matasović, Ranko. 2010. A short grammar of East Circassian (Kabardian). MS, University of Zagreb. (http://www.ffzg.hr/~rmatasov/KabardianGrammar.pdf; accessed March 2012)
Nichols, Johanna. 1973. Suffix ordering in Proto-Uralic. *Lingua* 32(3). 227–238.
Nichols, Johanna. 2012a. The history of an attractor state: Adventitious *m* in Nakh-Daghestanian. In Tiina Hyytäinen et al. (eds.), 261–278.
Nichols, Johanna. 2012b. Selection for *m: T* pronominals in Eurasia. In Lars Johanson & Martine Robbeets (eds.), *Bound Morphology: Copies or Cognates?*, 47–70. Leiden: Brill.
Parpola, Asko. 2012. The problem of Samoyed origins in the light of archaeology: On the formation and dispersal of East Uralic (Proto-Ugro-Samoyed). In Tiina Hyytäinen et al. (eds.), 287–298.
Riese, Timothy. 2001. *Vogul*. Munich: Lincom Europa.
Rood, David S. & Allan R. Taylor. 1996. Sketch of Lakhota, a Siouan language. In Ives Goddard (ed.), *Handbook of North American Indians: Languages*, 440–482. Washington: Smithsonian Institution.
Salminen, Tapani. 1994–2012. Uralic (Finno-Ugrian) languages. (http://www.helsinki.fi/~tasalmin/fu.html)
Salminen, Tapani. 1998. Nenets. In Daniel Abondolo (ed.), 516–547.
Salminen, Tapani. 1998. *Morphological Dictionary of Tundra Nenets*. (Lexica Societatis Fenno-ugricae 26). Helsinki: Finno-Ugric Society.
Salminen, Tapani. 1997. *Tundra Nenets Inflection*. Helsinki: Suomalais-ugrilainen Seura.

Schrijver, Peter. 2009. Why Indo-Europeanists should know more about East Caucasian. MS, Universiteit Utrecht.
Schulze, Wolfgang. 1999. The diachrony of personal pronouns in East Caucasian. In Helma van den Berg (ed.), *Studies in Caucasian Linguistics*, 95–111. Leiden: Leiden University.
Shibatani, Masayoshi. 1990. *The Languages of Japan*. Cambridge: Cambridge University Press.
Siewierska, Anna. 2004. *Person*. Cambridge: Cambridge University Press.
Siewierska, Anna. 2011. Person marking. In Jae Jung Song (ed.), *The Oxford Handbook of Linguistic Typology*, 322–345. Oxford: Oxford University Press.
Siewierska, Anna & Dik Bakker. 2013. Suppletion in person forms: the role of iconicity and frequency. This volume.
Sohn, Ho-Min. 1999. *The Korean Language*. Cambridge: Cambridge University Press.
Spencer, Andrew & Gregory Stump. 2014. Hungarian pronominal case and the dichotomy of content and form in inflectional morphology. *Natural Language and Linguistic Theory*, to appear.
Tepljashina, T. I. & V. I. Lytkin. 1976. Permskie jazyki. In V. I. Lytkin, K. E. Majtinskaja & Károly Rédei (eds.), *Osnovy finno-ugorskogo jazykoznanija: Marijskij, permskie i ugorskie jazyki*. Moscow: Nauka.
Tereschenko, N. M. 1966. Èneckij jazyk. In V. V. Vinogradov (ed.), *Jazyki narodov SSSR, vol. 3: Finno-ugorskie i samodijskie jazyki*, 438–457. Moscow: Nauka.
Tereschenko, N. M. 1993. Nenecskij jazyk. In Ju. S. Eliseev, K. E. Majtinskaja & O. I. Romanova (eds.), *Jazyki mira: Ural'skie jazyki*, 326–342. Moscow: Nauka.
Wilhelm, Christopher. 2008. The development of classical Armenian prepositions. In Dennis Kurzon & Silvia Adler (eds.), *Adpositions: Pragmatic, Semantic, and Syntactic Perspectives*. Amsterdam: Benjamins.
Wolfart, H. Christoph. 1996. Sketch of Cree, an Algonquian language. In Ives Goddard (ed.), *Handbook of North American Indians, 17: Languages*, 390–339. Washington, DC: Smithsonian Institution.

Anna Siewierska and Dik Bakker[1]
Suppletion in person forms: the role of iconicity and frequency

1 Introduction

As is well known, the expression of inflectional categories in personal pronouns is often irregular. Whereas with nouns a given inflectional category may be rendered by an affix attached to a lexical stem, with pronouns often no segmentation into discernible stem and affix is possible. By way of example, compare the English *cat* vs. *cat+s* and *I* vs. *we* in regard to the expression of number. Such formal irregularity coupled with semantic regularity as in the case of *I* vs. *we* is commonly referred to as suppletion (Dressler 1985; Melčuk 1994: 358; Veselinova 2006; Corbett 2007). We too will use this term, though we are fully aware of its varying interpretations and the controversies surrounding its application with respect to oppositions in pronominal paradigms, which will be briefly discussed in Section 2.

The frequent occurrence in languages of suppletion in person paradigms is typically attributed to the high textual frequency of personal pronouns. At least since Nida (1963: 265), all forms of irregularity including suppletion have been tied to high textual frequency. The argument is not just that high textual frequency produces irregularity (though it may contribute to its emergence simply due to frequency-driven phonological erosion), but rather that it precludes or at least impedes subsequent regularization. In other words, whereas irregularity displayed by less frequent items is unstable due to the pressure of analogical levelling over generations of speakers, highly frequent items, being well entrenched and easily accessible, resist such levelling (cf. e.g. Croft 2003; Tomasello 2003; Bybee 2010). There are also scholars (e.g. Ronneberger-Sibold 1980; Werner 1987; Harnisch 1990) who adduce actual functional benefits to suppletion in high-frequency items including personal pronouns. These benefits include: the communicative advantages of short frequent forms (under the assumption that supple-

---

[1] This article was completed days before Anna and I went on the fateful journey from which she was not to return. It is therefore the last article of the many on which we have worked together. It goes without saying that any thought of real interest it might contain stems from her. I wish to thank the colleagues present at the Leipzig Workshop in the memory of Anna for their comments, above all Martin Haspelmath. Obviously, all remaining errors and shortcomings are mine.

tive forms are shorter), direct rather than rule-based access to frequent forms, and the perceptual advantage of maximally differentiated forms. As argued by Pike (1965), these advantages accrue to suppletion of closed as opposed to open class items since only in the former case is there no need for a productive morphological rule.

The observations made in the literature regarding suppletion in pronominal paradigms have not been confined to its frequent occurrence. It has also been noted that the distribution of suppletion differs depending on both the inflectional category and person involved. Thus suppletion is seen to be more common in the expression of number than in the expression of case, and it seems to favour the first and second person over the third (see e.g. Dressler & Barbaresi 1994; Corbett 2000: 62–66; Siewierska 2004: 48). For scholars who consider suppletion to be just a non-functional residue of diachronic change, the existence of these asymmetries in the distribution of suppletion in person pronouns is of little interest. By contrast, for those who view suppletion as potentially having a functional dimension, asymmetries in its distribution and especially the factors underlying them constitute an important research question.

While we do not exclude the possibility that the asymmetries in suppletion in personal pronouns may be due to idiosyncratic aspects of paradigmatic structure, as argued most convincingly by Maiden (2004) for the distribution of suppletion in the Romance verbal paradigms, in this article we would like to consider the case for a functional motivation of suppletion among personal pronouns. The most promising functional explanation we are aware of centres on the notion of iconicity and its various instantiations. Broadly speaking, the notion of iconicity encapsulates a correspondence between form and meaning (Peirce 1932). Within the domain of morphology, iconicity is understood as expressing the expectation that the structure of language reflects the structure of meaning in some way or other (c.f. Mayerthaler 1981; Haiman 1985a,b; Dressler 1985; Croft 2003). This basic principle has been extended in various ways to account for finer grained aspects of the semantic and formal composition of words.

An extension of special importance in the context of the present discussion of suppletion is Bybee's (1985: 24–25) Principle of Relevance, which specifies that affixes that are semantically more relevant to the meaning of the stem, should have a greater morpho-phonemic effect on the stem than the affixes which express less relevant meanings. In the case of verbal inflectional categories, for example, the Principle of Relevance predicts that fusion of the verbal stem with aspect, tense and mood affixes would be more frequent and to a higher degree than with number and person affixes. And this does indeed appear to be so (see e.g. Bybee 1985; Cinque 1999). As for the nominal inflectional categories of number and case, since number clearly affects the meaning of nominals much more strongly than does case, number being an inherent category of nominals and case possibly only a contextual one, the Principle of Relevance predicts that there should be considerably more fusion between a nominal stem and number affixes than between the stem and case affixes. When transferred to personal pronouns, the prediction thus is that suppletion in the expression of number should be more common than in the expression of case.

Bybee's Principle of Relevance is not sensitive to the lexical features of the stem; in other words it makes no predictions with respect to the lexical distribution of stem alternations with a given inflectional category. Therefore while it provides a potential explanation for the greater likelihood of suppletion in number as compared to case, it has nothing to say about the asymmetries in the amount of suppletion for first, second and third person. An explanation for such asymmetries has been sought also in the preference for an iconic relationship between meaning and form, however, in this instance with respect to the degree of transparency between the two. While transparency is normally understood as implying that transparent meanings should be encoded by transparent forms, the converse is also seen to hold, i.e. the encoding of non-transparent meaning by non-transparent form. Taking this expectation as their point of departure, Dressler & Barbaresi (1994) argue that suppletion in number should strongly favour the semantically nontransparent pairings of person and number above the semantically more transparent ones. The former, as we know, relate to the first and, to a somewhat lesser extent, second person, which in the non-singular are rarely interpreted as involving two or more speakers or hearers, respectively (Lyons 1968: 277). Rather they tend to express groups of referents which include the speaker and the hearer. The groupings associated with the non-singular first person are: speaker and addressee (1+2); speaker, addressee and other (1+2+3); or speaker and one or more others (1+3 (+3)). The groupings relevant to the second person are of the addressee and one or more others (2+3 (+3)). The third person non-singular, by contrast, is semantically much more transparent as simply more than one other is involved, just as most often is the case with non-singular NPs. Given the semantic opacity of the first and second person non-singulars and the relative transparency of the third person non-singular, Dressler & Barbaresi suggest that suppletion in number should favour the first person over the second, and both over the third.[2]

---

[2] Interestingly in this context, Hampe & Lehmann (this volume) observe that the frequency of the semantically 'odd' partially coreferential singular- plural pairs occurring as subject and object of the same verb, are much more frequent for first person than for second (third person pairs are not studied). This might be interpreted as support for the view that the semantic opacity with respect to singular and plural is greater for the first person than for the second.

The differences in how number is interpreted with the three persons are not paralleled by the interpretations of case. The interpretation of the accusative relative to the nominative appears to be the same for the first person as for the second as for the third. Accordingly, if Dressler & Barbaresi's explanation for the differences in the distribution of number relative to person are broadly correct, not only should there be far less suppletion in the expression of case with person than with number, as also predicted by Bybee's Principle of Relevance, but also the instances of suppletion that do occur should not exhibit the same preference for suppletion with the first person over the second over the third.

The efficacy of iconicity-based explanations for the patterns of structural encoding such as the above has been recently put into question by Haspelmath (2006, 2008), who argues that many iconicity-based explanations for asymmetrical marking patterns find a better account in terms of textual frequency.[3] As already mentioned, high textual frequency is widely recognised as the major factor underlying the frequent occurrence of suppletion in grammatical categories such as personal pronouns in general. Whether it can also be seen as underlying the discussed asymmetries in suppletion between number and case, and differences between the three persons is by no means clear. Needless to say, the possibility of a frequency-based explanation for the above is predicated on there being significant differences in frequency in the use of personal pronouns inflected for number as opposed to case, and the frequency of these inflections with first person forms as compared to second and third person ones. Interestingly enough, while the available frequency literature on the language internal use of personal pronouns reveals that there are indeed significant differences in the frequency of use of individual person pronouns, whether these differences are in line with a frequency-based account of the distribution of suppletion remains to be established.

To the best of our knowledge, neither the asymmetries in the distribution of suppletion in personal pronouns discussed above nor the viability of the functional explanations that have been invoked to account for them have ever been systematically investigated at any larger scale. The present article seeks to do so by examining in detail the distribution of number and case suppletion in free person pronouns, in particular differences between the respective persons in a cross-linguistic sample of 488 languages, and by confronting the results with both the iconicity-based and frequency-based explanations. The article is organized as follows. In section 2 we briefly review some of the controversies surrounding

---

3 Actually, Haspelmath (2008) distinguishes six types of iconicity: Iconicity of quantity, complexity, cohesion, paradigmatic isomorphism, syntagmatic isomorphism, and contiguity. Only the first three are assumed to be better explained by a frequency account.

the notion of suppletion and its application to pronominal paradigms. Section 3 presents the language and areal composition of our cross-linguistic sample and of the sub-samples– languages with marked number and with marked case – that we have derived from it. Then, in section 4 we describe in detail how we have applied the typology of suppletive encoding to the person paradigms in the languages in the sample. Two methods of doing so will be described, which together should provide a robust and replicable classification of these complex data. In sections 5 and 6 we consider to what extent the asymmetries in suppletive encoding of number and case in the three persons stemming from our sample are in conformity with the iconicity-based explanations for this phenomena captured in Bybee's Relevance Principle and Dressler & Barbaresi's transparency-based (or rather: opacity-based) explanation. In section 7, we consider the data on suppletion from the perspective of the predictions following from the textual frequency of the relevant personal pronouns. As we have frequency data only for a few languages, and the interpretation of these data is far from straightforward, our comparison of the frequency-based account of suppletion in personal pronouns relative to the iconicity-based one will necessarily be more suggestive than conclusive. Finally, in section 8 we conclude the discussion with some remarks on the potential interplay between the two types of functional explanation.

2 Suppletion and person forms

Like so many other terms in linguistics, suppletion is not a homogenous notion. In traditional historical linguistics (see e.g. Rudes 1980) a distinction is made between morpho-phonologically irregular forms, which are the product of phonological change, and suppletive forms which are the result of what is sometimes referred to as incursion (see e.g. Maiden 2004: 241; Corbett 2007: 13), i.e. the invasion into a paradigm of outside forms. In other words, suppletive forms are necessarily etymologically unrelated on this older view. Nowadays, since speakers cannot be assumed to be aware of the diachronic origins of the forms they encounter, this restriction is rarely adhered to, and the term suppletion is used both for forms which are phonologically distinct by virtue of incursion and by virtue of just phonological change.[4] Needless to say, since we know next to nothing about the diachronic origins of pronouns in most languages, an investigation such as the current one is only possible if the source of the phonological irregularity of

---

4 Bobaljik (2012) and presumably other adherents of Distributive Morphology are a notable exception as they treat suppletion as categorically different from irregular phonological change.

the suppletive form is not at issue. Thus, rather than viewing suppletion as combining maximal semantic regularity with extreme phonological irregularity, following Corbett (2007) and many others, we see it as part of a cline of irregularity and itself as being scalar (see further below).

2.1 Number as an inflectional category of personal pronouns

Suppletion is typically conceived of as a relation between stems within an inflectional paradigm.[5] Thus in order to be considered as suppletive the relevant forms must be involved in an inflectional alternation. There is no question as to personal pronouns being viewed as inflected for case provided the language exhibits this inflectional category. Accordingly, the English *I* vs. *me* or Polish *ja* vs. *mnie* are uncontroversially treated as suppletive. The situation with number, however, is far less clear. As discussed in the introduction, number with first and second personal pronouns is interpreted somewhat differently than with nouns. Whereas the non-singular of a noun is typically interpreted as involving more than one token of the entity denoted by that noun, and the same holds for third person pronouns, first and second person non-singulars are rarely interpreted as denoting more than one speaker or hearer, but rather receive group or associative readings. This lack of semantic transparency in their interpretation is precisely what Dressler & Barbaresi (1994) expect to be reflected iconically in their form by means of suppletion. There are scholars, however, who argue that the associative readings found with first and second person pronouns indicate that number is not an inflectional category for first and second person pronouns at all. Moreover, since, say, *I* and *we* do not express an opposition in number, the forms in question cannot be seen as suppletive. Rather, they should be viewed as distinct lexemes on a par with, say, *speaker* and *group*. A robust defence of the traditional view whereby number is an inflectional opposition within all personal pronouns is presented by Corbett (2005). We are in full agreement with his position, and mention here only two of the most important arguments for it that he cites. The first concerns formal marking, namely the fact that there are languages in which first and second person pronouns take exactly the same number affixes as third person forms and sometimes even as nouns. A case in point is that of Mizo, a Tibeto-Burman language of the Kuki-Chin group, in which the plural of all three persons consists of the singular stem with the suffix *-ni*, as shown in (1).

---

[5] Some scholars e.g. Mel'čuk (1994) and Markey (1985) extend the term to also include derivational and even lexical relationships (e.g. Bhat 1967).

(1)   Mizo (Murthy & Subbarao 2000: 778)

	SG	PL
1	kei	ke+ni
2	nang	nang+ni
3	ani	an+ni

The second argument relates to the associative interpretations of the first and second person non-singular. Corbett points out that associative readings of non-singular forms are not in fact restricted to first and second person pronouns but rather also occur with nouns. In fact the distribution of these associative readings is governed by the position of an item on the animacy hierarchy, as first observed by Smith-Stark (1974), and subsequently documented extensively in Moravcsik (1994, 2003), and especially Corbett (2000). Thus, first and second person pronouns are not exceptional in manifesting special interpretations when inflected for number. Further, the associative interpretations found with first and second person pronouns are only one type of a range of complex readings which non-singular number may induce. In sum, there is no reason to deny the presence of a number opposition in first and second person pronouns on either morphological or semantic grounds.

2.2 Types of suppletion

The suppletion found in the marking of number and case with personal pronouns may be seen as falling into two types: total suppletion and stem suppletion. Total suppletion, which is typically considered to be the prototypical instance of suppletion, is an opposition between forms that are phonologically different from each other and are not segmentable into a stem and an affix. Total suppletion is illustrated in (2) on the basis of case marking in Polish.

(2)   Polish

	NOM	ACC
1SG	ja	mnie
2SG	ty	ciebie
3SG.F	ona	ją
3SG.M	on	jego
3SG.N	ono	go

In stem suppletion, on the other hand, there is an alternation of stems which are segmentable from the affixes with which they occur. A good example of stem suppletion is given in (3) from Mangghuer, a Mongolic language spoken in China, where the addition of the plural suffix -si is accompanied by a change of the stem of the first person from bi to da, and of the second person from qi to ta.

(3)   Mangghuer (Slater 2003: 314)

	SG	PL
1	bi	da+si
2	qi	ta+si
3	gan	gan+si

The forms involved in both total and stem suppletion may display various degrees of phonetic similarity to each other. Forms which exhibit no phonological similarity to each other at all are said to be strongly suppletive, and those which do display some phonological similarity as being weakly suppletive (see e.g. Dressler 1990: 36–37; Nübling 2000: 228; Corbett 2007).The examples of total suppletion with respect to case in Polish shown earlier in (2) and stem suppletion with respect to number in Mangghuer illustrated in (3) are clear instances of strong suppletion. It is more difficult to be confident about instances of weak suppletion without knowing well the phonological rules of a language. Since weakly suppletive stems share some common phonetic material, the possibility exists that there is a synchronic phonological rule linking the stems in question, in which case they would not qualify as suppletive. For example, in English the opposition between the strong verbs such as *think* and *thought* is typically seen as an instance of weak suppletion as there is no synchronic rule which links the two (though diachronically there is). However, rules may be devised not only for such cases but even for instances of strong suppletion, as shown by Comrie (1989). Thus, forms classified as being weakly suppletive must be viewed with some caution. A potential instance of total weak suppletion is that of the number opposition in the first person in Oromo, a widely spoken Cushitic language of Ethiopia, illustrated in (4).

(4)   Harar Oromo (Owens 1985: 98)

	SG	PL
1	na	nu
2	si	isi+ní
3M	isá	isáa+ni
3F	isíí	

A corresponding example of weak stem suppletion is that of the case opposition in the first person in Northern Vogul, shown in (5).

(5)   Northern Vogul (Riese 2001: 30)

	NOM	ACC
1SG	am	an+əm
2SG	naŋ	naŋ+ən
3SG	taw	taw+e

The distinction between strong suppletion, weak suppletion and a phonologically conditioned alternation is not always easy to draw. Strong suppletion is often associated with incursion and weak suppletion with phonologically conditioned historical changes. However, incursion can also result in weak suppletion, as in the case of Catalan, where the verb 'give' exhibits a stem alternation between *do* originating from the Latin *donare* 'donate' and *dam/dat*, originating from the Latin *dare* 'give' (Maiden 1992). And phonological change may lead to strong suppletion, as in the case of the English *am* and *is* from the Proto-Indo-European *esmi and *esti (Juge 1999: 186).

In section 4 we will provide a detailed discussion of how we have applied the above typology to the person forms in our sample, as well as a second, independent measure of phonological distance between two forms. To facilitate the discussion, we will assume the following terminological conventions. We will consider two forms as involving **strong suppletion** if they have no phonological material in common other than what may be taken to be coincidental. If there is some non-arbitrary phonological overlap between the relevant forms, they will be viewed as examples of **weak suppletion**. If two stems are identical, apart from possible regular phonological variation, they will be classified as **regular**. Finally, two forms may be completely **homophonous**, in which case they are classified as such.

3 The sample

In order to determine to what extent the patterns of suppletion and affixal marking involve combinations of persons consistent with the respective hypotheses under scrutiny here, personal pronouns stemming from a large sample of languages need to be considered. We collected data for a convenience sample of 488 languages of the world, which we will call S488, and which will be used as the default sample below. From this sample, using the sampling method presented in Rijkhoff & Bakker (1998) and the language classification of the Ethnologue version 15 (Ethn15; Gordon 2005) we extrapolated a subsample of 350 languages (S350) that will be employed to check the typological nature of some of our claims and observations. The languages of both samples are listed together with their genealogical affiliation in the Appendix. An idea of the makeup of the sample can, however, be deduced from the areal distribution of the languages shown in Figure 1, in which the macro-areas are essentially those used by Dryer (1989). The representation is in percentages of both samples.

In terms of the sampling technique used, the Americas and Australia are underrepresented in S488, and Eurasia, New Guinea and Southeast Asia & Oceania are overrepresented.

When we compare the distribution of the languages in both samples on the basis of the larger macro-areas proposed by Nichols (1992), we get the distribu-

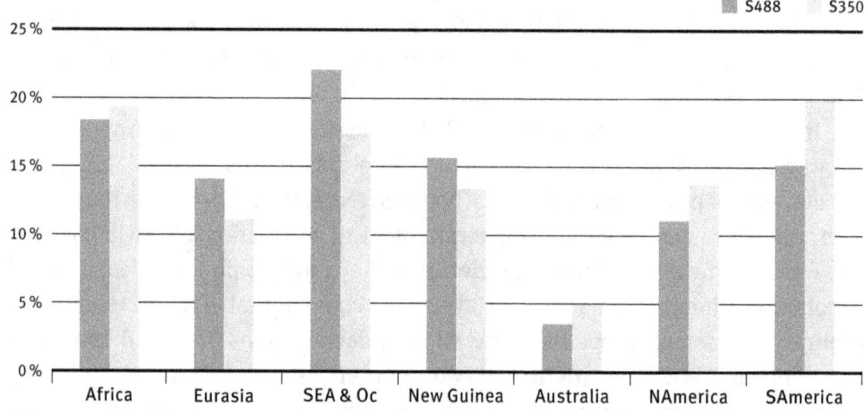

Figure 1. Distribution of the sample languages per macro-area (Dryer 1989)

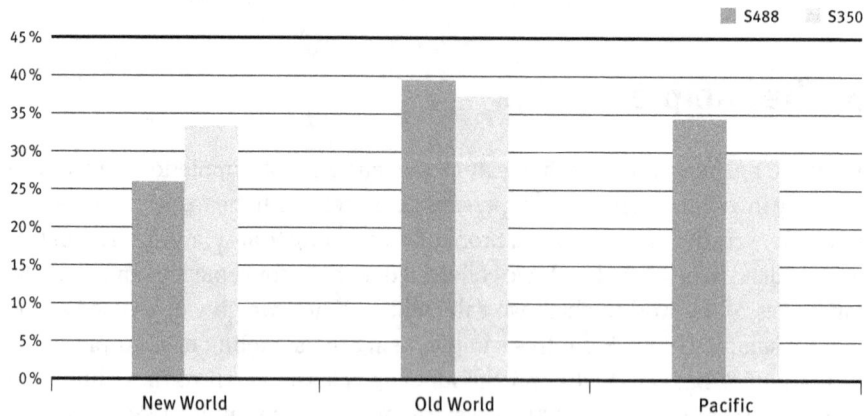

Figure 2. Distribution of the sample languages per macro-area (Nichols 1992)

tions found in Figure 2. As to be expected, we now have a clear underrepresentation of the New World, while the Old World, and more so the Pacific are overrepresented.

Of the 488 languages in the overall sample, 12 do not exhibit any number marking in their independent pronouns. Thus, for our investigation of the distribution of suppletion with respect to number the S488 sample is reduced to 476 languages, and the S350 sample to 340 languages. The final sample for case marking is considerably smaller than this. We were able to establish a differentiation between Nom/Abs and Acc/Erg in at least one of the three singular person forms for only 178 languages of S488, and for only 131 languages of S350. All the above is indicated in the language list in the Appendix.

4 The coding of suppletion

As mentioned in section 2.2. distinguishing between total and weak suppletion, on the one hand, and weak suppletion and regular phonological alternations on the other, is fraught with difficulty. A degree of arbitrariness is inevitable especially when dealing with large amounts of data, and languages with whose phonology and diachrony one is not very familiar. We have made every attempt to minimize the level of arbitrariness and maximize the degree of confidence that can be adduced to our classification of the data by employing a multi-method approach. However, before outlining the methods employed, a few words about the organization of the data are in order.

4.1 The organization of the data

For each pronominal paradigm, we entered between 2 forms (for Acoma) and 20 forms (for Ani) per language out of a theoretical total of 110, using the phonological representations of the sources consulted, typically descriptive grammars. Table 1 gives an overview of the numbers of forms selected for the respective person, number and case categories. The figures indicate the numbers of languages manifesting the corresponding forms. Alternative realizations, say of the 1SG NOM, within a language, were counted only once. When a given person-number category was further subcategorized, for example into M(asculine) vs. F(eminine) vs. N(euter), these forms were counted instead of the more general categories 1st, 2nd and 3rd. The same applies to the In(clusive)-Ex(clusive) distinction in the Pl(ural), Du(al) and Pauc(al). The empty cells in the Table 1 correspond to combinations that were not attested in any of the languages in our sample.

Table 1. Person forms in the S488 sample

		1ST	1M	1F	2ND	2M	2F	3RD	3M	3F	3N
SG	NOM/ABS	472	6	6	463	23	23	343	119	114	40
	ACC/ERG	177	1	1	175	3	3	129	48	46	17
PL	—	283	5	5	454	12	9	394	54	45	23
	IN	188			2						
	EX	184			2						
DU	—	59	7	3	107	6	6	101	12	9	2
	IN	87									
	EX	80									
PAUC	—	4	1	1	18	1	1	17	1	1	
	IN	16									
	EX	17									
Total		4,416	1,567	20	16 1,221	45	42	984	234	215	72

Case forms were recorded only in the singular, and only for the opposition Nom(inative)-Acc(usative) or Abs(olutive)-Erg(ative), with the absolutive corresponding to the nominative and the ergative to the accusative, in accordance with markedness conventions. In the absence of a case system, the relevant form was coded as Nom. Gender distinctions other than the typical masculine vs. feminine ones were subsumed under the more common M vs. N. While for the overwhelming majority of languages we obtained complete paradigms, there were a few which had to remain incomplete.

Among the person forms, there were many with uncommon phonemes, expressed by a symbol outside the standard Ascii range as found on the regular computer keyboards.[6] The analysis program that we developed, written in a standard programming language, does not have a built-in representation mechanism for the higher (> 255) unicode characters. Therefore in order to maintain as much phonological detail as possible, we transferred the database to its hexadecimal unicode representation, substituting a phoneme by a unique number. This transformation has no influence whatsoever on the results discussed below, so we will

---

[6] We are aware of the fact that grammars may vary strongly with respect to the notational system used for phonological representation, especially in the case of grammars older than several decades, when typewriters and printing techniques did not always provide much opportunity for precise reproduction. Developing a unified representation system for the languages in our database was beyond the scope of the present text, and the competence of the authors. The fact that we will compare mainly forms within the same language neutralizes most of the problem, since only internal consistency counts in such a case.

continue talking in terms of phonemes. The representations in the database also contain indications of morpheme boundaries, separating stems from number and case affixes, as well as tone, coded by means of a number added to the syllable in question, as in (6) below, from Izon, a Niger-Congo language from Nigeria.

(6) Izon (Williamson 1965: 114)

    SG1:   *arí5*   PL1: *wónì4*
    SG2:   *árì4*   PL2: *ọmínì4*
    SG3:   *arí5*   PL3: *ọmínì5*

4.2 Measuring the degree of suppletion

We are not aware of any generally accepted method to measure the amount of phonological likeness between two word forms from the same language, or across languages. Therefore, in order to minimize the potential bias that relying on one method might introduce, we applied two independent, and very different strategies, one rather subjective and the other completely objective.

4.2.1 The subjective method

Applying the global suppletion scale introduced in section 2.2, we assessed the overlap for all relevant form pairs 'on face value', and from a purely synchronic angle, without taking into consideration any information about (possible) diachronic morpho-phonological developments of the languages involved. Both authors compared and coded independently of each other the degree of overlap between the first, second and third person singular and their respective plural forms, on the one hand, and the nominative and accusative singular forms for the three persons on the other hand. This was done using a system of seven codes which we applied on the basis of our linguistic intuitions. All conflicting or otherwise doubtful assignments were discussed, and a compromise was established, iteratively leading to greater consistency in the coding.

    According to our coding system, a pair of forms is considered to be a case of *strong total suppletion* (TS) when the forms share no phonological material whatsoever, apart from what could be seen as a coincidence. When there is some overlap that seems to be not coincidental, then this pair is coded as showing *weak total suppletion* (TW). More often than not, this is the case when the forms share the first syllable or the first few phonemes. When one or both of the forms are morphologically marked for number and/or case we compare only the stems, in the same way that we compare full forms. When these are the same, we have *regularity* (RG). When the stems are completely different we have a case of *strong stem suppletion* (SS). And when there is some non-coincidental overlap between the two stems, we have a case of *weak stem suppletion* (SW). A special case are languages with independent person forms consisting of a person affix attached to an invariable stem as in Baruya, a Trans New Guinea language from Papua New Guinea, and exemplified in (7) below. For these forms, we ignored the invariable stem and looked only at the variable affixes, treating them like stems. So, Baruya first person is coded as SW, and second and third person as SS.

(7) Baruya (Lloyd 1989: 103)

SG1:	*ni-mino*	PL1:	*ne-mino*
SG2:	*gi-mino*	PL2:	*sari-mino*
SG3:	*ga-mino*	PL3:	*ku-mino*

In a few cases our sources did not provide enough information for us to decide whether the small differences between two stems were in fact the result of synchronically regular phonological alternations– then they would be RG – or of the insertion of epenthetic phonological material. For these we introduced the category *marginal stem suppletion* (SM). Finally, two forms may be completely homophonous (HM). Table 2 presents an example of each of the seven types of relationships between person forms that we coded.

Table 2. Coding the different kinds of suppletion

suppletion			example				
TYPE	STRENGTH	CODE	LANGUAGE	FORM1		FORM2	
Total	Strong	TS	Ari	SG3.M:	*nó*	PL3:	*ketá*
	Weak	TW	Awa Pit	SG2:	*nu*	PL2:	*u*
Stem	Strong	SS	Cavinena	SG1:	*ike*	PL1:	*ekw-ana*
	Weak	SW	Kodava	SG2:	*niini*	PL2:	*nii-gal*
	Marginal	SM	Tzutujil	SG3:	*jaaʔ*	PL3:	*jaʔ-eeʔ*
Regular		RG	Miskito	SG3:	*wĭtĭn*	PL3:	*wĭtĭn-nănĭ*
Homophone		HM	Kayah Li	SG3:	*ʔa*	PL3:	*ʔa*

4.2.2 The Levenshtein method

Given the obvious drawbacks of the above intuitive method of classification, we introduced a second method of measuring the amount of suppletion between two person forms, this time a completely mechanical and objective, and thus fully reproducible one. This alternative method involves calculating the similarity between two forms in a language on the basis of the algorithm proposed by Levenshtein (1966). In its original, most simple form, the Levenshtein Distance (LD) between two forms is the number of steps– changes, additions, deletions – necessary to transform one row of elements (in this case: phonemes) into the other. This leads to a figure anywhere between 0 (no transformations whatsoever, complete equivalence) and n, where n is the length of the longest of the two forms (all elements transformed, maximum difference). Instead of using LD in its basic form, we adopted the normalized version as proposed by the ASJP project (cf. Brown et al. 2008; Bakker et al. 2009). This project seeks to classify the languages of the world precisely by applying the Levenshtein method to the Swadesh lists of over 6,000 languages and dialects. The normalized version, LDN is derived from LD by dividing it by the length of the longest of the two forms, and then multiplying the result by 100, leading to a value between 0.0 (equivalence) and 100.0 (maximum distance).[7] The application of LDN to the pairs in Table 2 gives the results presented in Table 3.

Table 3. LDN values for word pairs

LANGUAGE	FORM1		FORM2		LDN	Code
Ari	SG3.M:	*nó*	PL3:	*ketá*	100.0	TS
Cavinena	SG1:	*ike*	PL1:	*ekw-ana*	66.7	SS
Awa Pit	SG2:	*un*	PL2:	*u*	50.0	TW
Kodava	SG2:	*niini*	PL2:	*nii-gal*	40.0	SW
Tzutujil	SG3:	*jaaʔ*	PL3:	*jaʔ-eeʔ*	25.0	SM
Miskito	SG3:	*wītīn*	PL3:	*wītīn-nănī*	0.0	RG
Kayah Li	SG3:	*ʔa*	PL3:	*ʔa*	0.0	HM

The standard LDN score, as exemplified in Table 3, is based on a segmental comparison of the two forms in question. We will label this version LDN$_{phon}$. For its calculation, each pair of phonemes that is compared contributes either 0 (the same phoneme) or 1 (a different phoneme) to the overall score. According to this

---

[7] A further operation is applied to compensate for the basic phonological overlap within a language. For details see Bakker et al. 2009.

procedure, /a/ is as different from /e/ as it is from /p/. Since this tends to overestimate the phonological difference between two forms, sometimes considerably, we added some refinement to our comparison procedure. For each of the phonemes currently found in our database we established its representation in terms of phonological features. This puts us in the position to compare pairs of feature sets rather than pairs of phonemes. Such sets will often show a certain overlap, especially in the case of two vowels or two consonants. Instead of always leading to a value 0 (equal) or 1 (different), any pair of phonemes that is compared on the basis of their respective feature sets will contribute a fraction to the total, which is rendered by the quotient (Number of features different / Total number of features compared). This expression has 0 and 1 as its limits, but it typically has a value between the two. In general, this way of measuring LDN will lead to a lower total value for the distance between two forms, which we will label LDN_{ftr}. The set of features we currently use for this operation may be found in the leftmost column in Table 4 below. It also includes some examples of the representations of four rather common phonemes. The features in Table 4 are the ones used in the P-base project (Mielke 2008). Although this set is quite basic, we believe that it provides enough dimensions for our current purpose.

Table 4. Phonological feature set and some representations

Feature	/p/	/g/	/a/	/i/
CONSONANTAL	+	+	–	–
HIGH	–	+	–	+
BACK	–	+	+	–
LOW	–	–	+	–
ROUND	–	–	–	–
SONORANT	–	–		
ANTERIOR	+	–		
CORONAL	–	–		
VOICE	–	+		
CONTINUANT	–	–		
NASAL	–	–		
STRIDENT	–	–		

Using the features in Table 4 we have defined a basic list of 31 consonants and 7 vowels in terms of this feature set. In fact, this is the list in use by the ASJP project mentioned earlier. All other phonemes in the database are coded in relation to how close they are to a phoneme in the basic list. So, all phonemes in the list A = [a, à, á, â, ã, ä, å, ă, ą, ā̰, ã̱] are phonologically represented as the first element of the list, i.e. /a/. When comparing phonemes, we assign the maximum value 1.0 in case the value for their consonantal feature is different. So /p/ and /a/ will differ by 1.0. When two phonemes are in the same consonantal category, we compare the remaining set of relevant features, and determine the distance according to the formula given above. So, the distance between /p/ and /g/ is (4/11) = 0.36, and the distance between /a/ and /i/ (3/4) = 0.75. In the case of two phonemes that stem from the same set but are not identical, as for /à/ and /ã/ from set A defined above, we add one feature to the total, and stipulate 1 feature difference. Thus, all phonemes in the list A defined above will differ (1/5) = 0.2. This makes them less distant from each other than any other pair of vowels, which will score at least (1/4) = 0.25.[8]

Not surprisingly, the values for LDN_{phon} and LDN_{ftr} are rather different. For the 1,390 singular vs. plural pairs in our database, the mean value of the segment-based LDN was 60.3, while for the feature-based value it is only 38.6. Nonetheless, there turns out to be a very high correlation between the two, namely a Pearson correlation of 0.829 (p < .01). For the 533 pairs involving case, the correlation was even higher, at 0.900 (p < .01). However, it must be noted that in individual instances the values for the two measurements can be very different. Table 5 presents some striking examples.

Table 5. Differences between the LDN phoneme and feature values

Language	Form 1	Form 2	LDN_{phon}	LDN_{ftr}	LDN_{mean}
Breton	SG1: me	PL1: ni	100.0	12.8	56.4
Bukiyip	SG3.M: enan	PL3.M: omom	100.0	21.7	60.9
Amele	SG1: ija	PL1: ege	100.0	28.0	64.0
Basketo	SG1: ta	PL1: nu	100.0	38.3	69.2
Warao	SG2: ihi	PL2: yatu	100.0	49.0	74.5

The differences between the two LDN values are particularly large when the forms under comparison have the same Consonant-Vowel pattern, as in the first four examples in Table 5 above. In such cases, the feature method 'profits' from the C-C and V-V correspondences. In most instances the two methods lead to largely the same (relative) outcome, and it is not immediately clear which one should

---

[8] Other calculi have been proposed to measure the morpho-phonological distance between members of a paradigm. A very fine-grained method is introduced by Corbett et al (2001), who investigate regularity in Russian nominal paradigms. Their method contains seven levels of measurement, running from suppletion to full regularity. It assigns a greater weight to differences in stems than affixes, and counts both segmental and stress contrasts. Since it assigns weights to complete paradigms, and includes information not always available to us for all languages in our database, we think our simpler method of comparison between form pairs is to be preferred here.

be preferred. But for cases like the ones in Table 5, a more stable and realistic result can be obtained by taking the average of the two scores, i.e. the LDN_{mean}, as shown in the right-hand column in Table 5. Such a step compensates for the most extreme differences between LDN_{phon} and LDN_{ftr}. Therefore, in the following sections we will use LDN_{mean} as the default LDN value, while the two contributing values LDN_{phon} and LDN_{ftr} will be used occasionally for comparison.

As for the subjective method of classification discussed in section 4.2.1, we will regularly check the results based on the LDN values with the categories that we assigned ourselves. Some idea of the correspondences between the two systems can be gathered from a consideration of the data in Table 6, which compares the LDN_{mean} scores for the 1,390 singular-plural pairs in our database with our subjectively-assigned categories.

Table 6. Correspondences between the two measurements: Number

Code	Pairs	LDN_{mean}	Standard Deviation	Minimum	Maximum	Range
Stem Strong	111	72.9	12.8	46.8	100.0	53.2
Total Strong	624	70.3	13.4	34.6	100.0	65.4
Stem Weak	104	40.8	13.9	18.1	84.0	65.9
Total Weak	304	37.3	12.7	9.6	78.7	69.1
Stem Marginal	28	27.3	11.0	11.5	52.5	41.0
ReGular	201	1.3	5.5	0.0	33.3	33.3
HoMophone	18	0.0	0.0	0.0	0.0	0.0
TOTAL	1,390	49.4	28.3	0.0	100.0	100.0

As Table 6 shows, there certainly does not exist a clear 1:1 relationship between the two systems in the sense of code groups corresponding to non-overlapping ranges on the LDN_{mean} scale, with clear cut-off points. However, the mean values for LDN are very close for both types of strong suppletion (72.9 and 70.3, respectively), and for both types of weak suppletion (41.2 and 37.4), while the overall means for strong and weak suppletion (70.7 and 38.4) are a third of the scale removed from each other. The mean for the marginal stem category SM is considerably lower than the SW value, as it should be. The score for the regular cases is extremely low indeed, at 1.3, and HM, as per definition, has 0.0 for all pairs concerned. The standard deviations are relatively low, and rather constant over the categories. However, the minimum and maximum values do have a considerable overlap between the strong and weak categories. But the extreme cases– a relatively low value for 'strong' and a high value for 'weak'– are rather rare, as the standard deviations already suggest.

For the 533 pairs in our database that have a case distinction, more or less the same state of affairs holds, with the overlap between the strong and the weak categories even less than for number. We submit that these facts provide a sound basis for the use of the suppletion scale as a secondary instrument, next to the LDN_{mean}, for the analysis of the pronominal data, to which we will turn in the next section.

At this point, however it might be interesting to compare the figures for the several types of pronominal number suppletion to those of another relatively large-scale sample on plurality in independent person forms. Daniel (2011) looked at pronominal plurality in 261 languages, of which 200 correspond to the basic sample as established by Dryer & Haspelmath eds. (2011). The comparison can only be very partial, and has to be impressionistic to some extent, since Daniel only takes into consideration first and second person forms, and in case the two plurals are derived in different ways, categorizes a language according to the way plural is coded for first person only. In his sample, 11 languages (4.2%) have no plural form, roughly the same as our figure, especially if we assume that cases of homophony are included in Daniel's percentage. Furthermore, he distinguishes six categories with respect to the way singular and plural forms differ from each other. If we generalize this to three, by skimming over the subcategories that indicate whether the plural affix is the general nominal one or a pronoun specific one, then we come to the totals in Table 7 below. Note that the percentage for Regular in the column for Daniel (2011) is a maximum, since only a subset of the languages concerned are said to have exactly the same stem for both singular and plural. No distinction is made by Daniel for the degree of suppletion, only the type.

Table 7. Comparison with data from Daniel (2011)

TYPE	Daniel (2011) (n = 250)	Our 1st Person (n = 476)
Regular	26.8%	8.2%
Stem Suppletion	27.6%	17.8%
Total Suppletion	45.6%	74.0%

If we assume that a certain amount of cases that are counted as Regular by Daniel would be going to (Stem) suppletion according to our standards, there is still a vast difference between the respective percentages. The relative frequencies tend to go in the same direction. However, we measure much more suppletion than Daniel does, especially of the Total kind. We assume that this is at least partially due to the way the samples are constructed.

5 Analyzing the data: Number

Our database contains a total of 4,416 paradigm slots, an average of 8.8 per language, of which we will consider only those relating to the singular vs. plural distinction. In 328 slots there were two or more alternative forms available. For these, we have decided to select the form that was presented as the first alternative in the source. In general, it is the shortest or most regular form. For each of the three persons we will use either the general Nom(inative)/Abs(olutive) form or, if there is a gender distinction, the masculine form. For the Pl(ural), we use either the single general form or, if there is a distinction in clusivity, the Ex(clusive). Of the 488 languages in our database, 448 languages (92%) have three singular-plural pairs according to this selection criterion, one for each person. This subset, which is of particular interest here, will be called S448 below. Furthermore, 19 (4%) languages have only two pairs, and 8 (2%) only one pair. Finally, 12 languages (2.5%) have no number distinction in their independent pronouns.[9] In all, we identified 1,390 Sg-Pl pairs as already introduced in Table 6 above. The overall figures for the encoding of number over the three person categories are presented in Table 8. The number of different pairs (in terms of presence or absence of gender) that make up the three global person-number groups are given in the second column; we will come back to the individual pairs later.

Table 8. LDN and equivalence categories for Person-Number pairs

Person	Different Pairs SG-PL	N of pairs	Mean LDN	Homoph	Regular	Weak Suppl	Strong Suppl
1ST	5	473	56.1	.01	.07	.28	.64
2ND	5	467	50.4	.01	.14	.32	.53
3RD	4	450	41.2	.02	.23	.35	.40
TOTAL	14	1,390	49.4	.01	.15	.32	.53

The mean LDN value for the first person is considerably higher than for the second person, and for the latter much higher than the one for the third person. Over the whole relevant subset of languages, the relations between the three pairs of LDN values – 1st vs 2nd; 1st vs 3rd; and 2nd vs 3rd person – correlate highly ($p < .01$). This can

---

[9] There is one language, Ani (Khoisan; Botswana), that has both a clusivity and a gender distinction in the second person plural, and therefore would contribute four pairs, but we will select only one pair per person to facilitate the comparison between languages.

be summed up by saying that, in terms of LDN_{mean} values, pronominal number distinction is subject to the suppletion hierarchy in (8).

(8)   Person1 > Person2 > Person3

This state of affairs receives support from the relative contribution per person to the four equivalence categories given in the four rightmost columns of Table 8. To determine these fractions we aggregated the figures for the three types of weak suppletion (SM/SW/TW) and those for the two types of strong suppletion (SS/TS). For all three persons the percentage of homophony is equally low, as this indeed occurs very infrequently. The amount of weak suppletion seems to be rather equal as well for the three persons. The greatest contribution to the difference between the persons stems from the low amount of regular forms for first person (7%) as opposed to the high amount for third (23%), counterbalanced by a high amount of strong suppletion for first (64%) and a relatively low amount for third person (40%). Second person takes an almost perfect intermediate position for these two categories. The bias in the distribution is significant at the .005 level, and gives independent support to relation (8). This situation is illustrated by the graphs in Figure 3 below, where we combine the scores for the four equivalence categories for each person by straight lines.

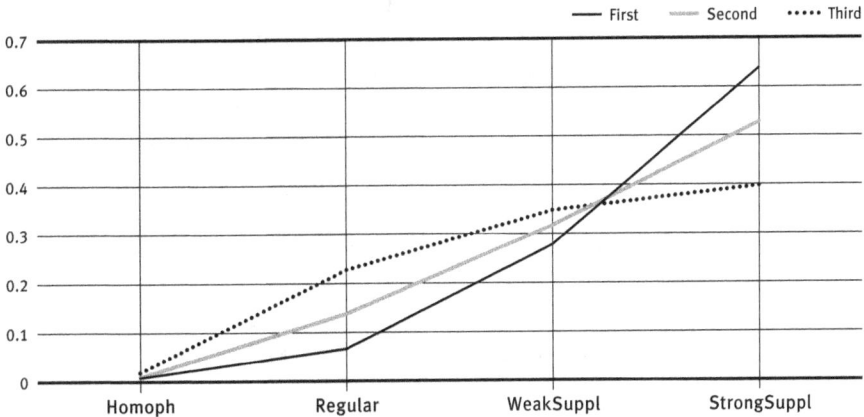

Figure 3. Graphic representation of equivalence categories for Number

Nonetheless, what we are dealing with here appears to be a tendency rather than a strict rule. The iconicity-based explanation for the distribution of asymmetries in number suppletion for the respective persons may be seen as compatible with the range of distributions captured in (9), with A corresponding to the strictest interpretation of the iconicity principle, and D to the weakest.

(9) A: Person1 > Person2 > Person3   n = 98 (22%)
    B: Person1 ≥ Person2 > Person3   n = 108 (24%)
    C: Person1 > Person2 ≥ Person3   n = 125 (28%)
    D: Person1 ≥ Person2 ≥ Person3   n = 161 (36%)

The figures on the right in (9) depict the number of languages in the S448 sample that comply with the distributions captured in A through D. We see that in 98 languages (or 22%) does the distribution of number suppletion conform to the strictest interpretation of the iconicity principle, i.e. that the first person exhibits more suppletion than the second and the second more than the third. This relatively low figure improves slightly if we allow the degree of suppletion to be equal either between the first and second person, as captured in (9.B), or between the second and third person, as captured in (9.C). Under the weakest interpretation of the iconicity principle, which allows for equality between both the first and second person and the second and third, as shown in (9.D), a little over a third of the languages in the sample (36%) are consistent with a pattern that might derive from the iconicity principle. It has to be noted that of these 161 languages, 24 have a value 0.0 for all three Sg-Pl pairs since the paradigm is regular. This leaves us with 137 (31%) 'real' cases.

The above results are somewhat surprising since the mean LDN values of the three persons given earlier looked rather suggestive with respect to there being more languages in the sample with person paradigms directly reflecting an increase in the degree of transparency in the encoding of number relative to person in accordance with the hierarchy in (8). A significantly better coverage of languages in the sample can only be achieved if we relax the interpretation of the iconicity principle even further, i.e. if we abandon the requirement that the first person should be more suppletive than the second, and juxtapose the first and second person together relative to the third, as in the two hierarchies below.

(9) E: Person1, Person2 > Person3   n = 197 (44%)
    F: Person1, Person2 ≥ Person3   n = 252 (56%)

Interestingly, even now only in the case of the weaker of the two hierarchies, (9.F) which allows for any distribution of degree of suppletion in number relative to person other than that of the third person being higher than the first and second, do more than 50% of the languages in the sample comply. The only counterexamples to F are paradigms in languages such as Xokleng (Macro-Ge; Brazil) in (10), and the 'worst case' type as in Maranungku (Australian) in (11).

(10) Xokleng (Urban 1985: 167): PRS3 > PRS1 > PRS2

 SG1: ẽŋ PL1: ãŋ
 SG2: a PL2: a
 SG3.M: tã PL3: ɔŋ

(11) Maranungku (Tryon 1970: 16): PRS3 > PRS2 > PRS1

 SG1: ngany PL1.EX: nga-tya
 SG2: nina PL2: ni-tya
 SG3: nankuny PL3: wi-tya

In the sample there are 47 languages of type (10), 34 of type (11), and another 115 languages for which third person scores higher than either first or second person but lower than the other.

The above analyses notwithstanding, the distribution of the languages in our sample over the diminishing constraint sets A to F might still be seen as providing support to an iconicity-based explanation of the formal differences between the respective Sg-Pl pairs, as long as they diverge significantly from chance distributions, and in the right direction. In order to test whether this is indeed so, we ran a large number of simulations over the same dataset, randomly drawing the LDN values for the three persons independently from the subset of 448 languages with three Sg-Pl pairs, and thus combining three pairs that originate from different languages, thus simulating a situation in which the three pairs are independent from each other. The results are given in Table 9, which also repeats the original figures from (9) for comparison. The third column gives the mean number of languages per simulation for which the relation in the first column holds.

Table 9. Comparison original sample versus random simulation

Relation	Original sample (448 languages)	Simulations (n = 30,000)	Probability Simulations > Original
A	98 (21.9%)	103.7	.709
B	108 (24.1%)	105.6	.363
C	125 (27.9%)	120.5	.304
D	161 (35.9%)	123.9	.000
E	197 (44.0%)	198.2	.525
F	252 (56.3%)	224.0	.000

We established that the means for the LDNs and the corresponding variance are virtually the same for both calculations, as of course they should be.[10] In short, the distribution of the random triplets over the six relation categories A–F does not differ much from that of the original data. In fact, in the case of two of the hierarchies –A and E– the number of languages included is even greater, and more than half of the simulations surpass the original counts in these cases. The scores for the hierarchies B and C are close, with over 30% of the simulations scoring higher. Only for the hierarchies D and F do we find considerably higher numbers for the original data. Arguably, only these two might be of further interest, with D as the most interesting candidate since it is stronger than F both statistically and in its potential implication for language. But note again that the number of languages for D would be reduced to 137 (31%) if we took out the languages with regular paradigms. Under such stricter interpretation the simulation would score such that there are more languages in the simulations than in the original data in around 5% of the cases.

For now, let us leave aside the LDN values, which have on the whole provided only partial support for the iconic basis of the distribution of suppletion over person with respect to number, and consider whether more favourable results may emerge from our subjectively determined categories. In order to determine to what extent the languages in the sample conform to the predictions of the iconicity principle in its various degrees of strength when interpreted in terms of the subjective criteria, we merged these into three individual categories: the two types of strong suppletion were collapsed into the category High, the three types of weak suppletion into Middle, and the regular cases plus the homophonies into Low. Using these three categories, the distribution corresponding to pattern A, the strongest version of the hierarchy in (8), would be H/M/L. At the other extreme, F, we would find all patterns that would have no category in any position that would be higher than its predecessor. Thus, M/M/M would fit F, but not M/L/M. Given the overlap between the respective categories this tripartite division is, of course, a less robust scale of measurement than the LDN based one. Our application of this scale to the languages in the sample with respect to each of the six interpretations A to F of the iconicity principle is shown in (12); the percentages of the LDN-based groupings are included on the right for ease of comparison.

---

[10] We give the figures here for interest's sake. Person1: mean 56.21– variance 639.8 (original sample) vs 56.23–636.8 (simulations); Person2: 50.02–778.9 vs 50.04–777.1; Person3: 40.99–881.6 vs 41.06–880.3.

(12) A: 1 > 2 > 3   13 (3%)   22%
      B: 1 ≥ 2 > 3   119 (27%)   24%
      C: 1 > 2 ≥ 3   66 (15%)   28%
      D: 1 ≥ 2 ≥ 3   326 (73%)   >   36%
      E: 1, 2 > 3   123 (28%)   44%
      F: 1, 2 ≥ 3   353 (79%)   >   56%

A comparison of the two sets of data reveals that for interpretations A, C and E the subjectively based frequencies are (even) lower than the LDN-based ones. For interpretation B, which allows the first and second person to be in the same category, provided that both are in a higher category than the third person, the scores are more or less the same as for the LDN based approach. For the weaker interpretations, there is a dramatic increase in coverage when we allow the third person to be in the same group as the first and/or second (D, F). Disregarding differences between just the first and second person, as in E, has a negative effect. So, it is again interpretations F, and above all D, that stand out.

Finally, we disregard all languages that have a homophony, regularity or stem suppletion in any of the three persons, and look only at those languages that have three instances of total strong (TS) or total weak (TW) suppletion. These may be seen as the least constrained languages with respect to their person forms, since no higher order pattern is paradigmatically 'forced' upon any of them. We will call these type T languages, since all three persons have a TS or TW relation between singular and plural. This turns out to be a substantial subset, containing 240 of the 448 relevant languages (i.e. 54%).[11] However, even among these languages we do not find strong support for the iconicity hypothesis. In fact, the scores for the relations A to E turn out to be consistently lower than for the overall group, and only the weakest category F sees a higher representation for type T languages than in the random simulation.

We have seen that the distribution of suppletion in number, whether measured subjectively or objectively, does not conform to any but a rather watered down interpretation of the iconicity principle. Only in a fifth of the languages in the sample does the first person exhibit a strictly higher level of suppletion than the second, and the second person a strictly higher degree than the third. This being so, the question arises whether there is still a reason to assume that the iconicity principle plays a distinctive role in the shaping of person forms. One possi-

---

[11] The seven 'subjective' categories TS, TW, SS, SW, SM, R and H as defined in section 4.2.1 could be generalized to four meta-categories T, S, R and H. Of the 64 potential patterns for the three persons that may be derived from them, only 31 occur among the 448 relevant languages in our sample, with a very skewed distribution.

bility may be that the asymmetrical distribution of suppletion in number relative to person is an areal phenomenon. Let us see whether this is indeed the case.

The distribution of the LDN values for the 448 languages with a value for all three persons relative to the three macro-areas distinguished by Nichols (1992) is presented in Table 10.

Table 10. LDN values per Macro-area (Nichols 1992)

Area	Languages	1st	2nd	3rd	Mean
NewWorld	112	51.5	34.3	28.4	38.1
OldWorld	181	58.6	52.7	43.0	51.5
Pacific	155	56.8	58.2	47.7	54.2
TOTAL	448	56.2	50.0	41.0	49.1

What strikes one immediately is the considerably lower mean value for suppletion in the New World. The differences are highly significant ($p < .001$) on a T-test for all three persons and on the overall mean in relation to the Old World, and for second and third person and the overall mean in relation to the Pacific. The Old World and Pacific differ only for the second person ($p = .05$). Given that the differences for the New World are mainly caused by the rather low values for second and third person, these 112 languages are potential candidates for higher scores on the relations of (9) above. This expectation is borne out by the data, be it only for relation D. The figures in Table 11 testify to this. We give both the figures for the 'inclusive' version of relation D (column two), which takes into consideration the languages with regular paradigms, and those for the exclusive version (column three).

Table 11. Areal distribution for relation D

	D (+Regular)	D (-Regular)	Total languages
New World	57 (51%)	45 (40%)	112
Old World	56 (31%)	50 (28%)	181
Pacific	48 (31%)	42 (27%)	155
TOTAL	161	137	448

The distribution is significant at the .005 level for the inclusive version, but only at the .05 level for the exclusive one. The inclusive version of relation D for the New World is the only relation that surpasses 50% of the relevant languages. It is the only relation that surpasses the total for random simulation in more than

99.9% of the cases (n = 30,000). A more specific test on the basis of Dryer's (1989) 7-way areal classification also shows significance at the .005 level for the inclusive version. Here, both North America (relation D applies to 57%) and South America (47%) stand out on the high side, and Africa (18%) and Australia (23%) on the low side.

Yet another check that we made is genealogical. Since the 448 languages in the database with a number form for all three persons are distributed over 109 different language families as distinguished by the Ethnologue, only a few groupings contain enough languages to enable any observations to be made. When we take into consideration only families with five or more languages in the sample, only one family stands out, namely Indo-European, with 11 out of 26 languages (42%) complying with relation A. However, this turns out to be due to genealogical overrepresentation, and a potential repetition of the same pattern. In the genealogically controlled sample of 350 languages only 4 Indo-European languages comply with relation A, which is fully in line with the overall distribution. In this subsample we found that relations A and E have scores more or less equal to the simulated set, relation B scores somewhat higher, relation C scores consistently higher with $p < .04$, and only relation D (for 38% of the languages) and relation F (55%) do better than $p < 0.005$. This may strengthen the case for D and F somewhat.

Finally, we checked the six relations A-F on the basis of the sample presented in Bybee (2005). This is a very conservative sample in the sense that great care is taken not to include languages that might derive affixes from the same etymological source, a category that is assumed to be very resistant to change. As a result, the sample contains only 26 languages, one per phylum in Voegelin & Voegelin (1977), which is taken as the guiding classification. Only six of these languages (Abkhaz, Cantonese, Guaymi, Kanuri, Karok and Tok Pisin) are also in our sample. The other 19 we replaced by the language from the same phylum in our sample that was closest to the Bybee language genealogically. Since one of these– Ojibwa, replacing Cheyenne– does not have a plural form for 2nd and 3rd person, we ended up with a sample of 25 languages. The LDN values for the three Sg-Pl pairs turn out to be even more separate from each other than for our overall sample: Person1 51.0 (overall 56.1); Person2 41.3 (50.4); and Person3 32.0 (41.2). This clearly confirms the tendency, observed for the whole database, of a greater formal distinction Sg-Pl for first than for second, and for second than for third person. Given these even greater differences, it does not come as a surprise that the percentages of languages for all relations A-F are higher for the Bybee sample than for our S448 set, and as a consequence the probabilities that a random sample scores better are considerably lower for most relations. This may be clear from the figures in Table 12.

Table 12. Comparison sample data versus random simulation

Relation	Bybee Sample (n=25)		Original data (n=448)	
	Languages	Probability Simulations > Sample	Languages	Probability Simulations > Original
A	7 (28%)	.165	98 (22%)	.709
B	8 (32%)	.078	108 (24%)	.363
C	10 (40%)	.162	125 (28%)	.304
D	15 (60%)	.002	161 (36%)	.000
E	12 (48%)	.082	197 (44%)	.525
F	19 (76%)	.007	252 (56%)	.000

But even if the figures for the small Bybee sample seem to be more in support of an iconicity explanation, this is still convincingly the case only for relations D and F. And even in the case of the weakest of all, F, a quarter of the languages does not follow an iconicity-based pattern. It can therefore hardly count as a universal. The strongest relations, A-C, still only apply to a minority of the languages (<< 50%).

In sum, we have seen that, across the languages in our sample, there is a strong overall tendency for a relatively high degree of suppletion between the singular and plural for first person forms, a lower degree for second person ones, and a yet lower one for third person forms. This is evident on the basis of both the 'objective' LDN approach and our 'subjective' equivalence estimate. However, these differences between the persons do not translate necessarily into implicational patterns in individual languages. The strongest version of a hierarchical relation, labelled A, applies to only 98 (22%) of the languages in our sample, and not much more in both the genealogically controlled subsample S350 (23%) and Bybee's sample (28%). Only relatively weak versions of a hierarchical relation between the three pairs, the ones we have labelled D and F, and which allow for equality between the scores for the three persons, provide stronger support for the role of iconicity in this domain. Around 36% of the languages in our S448 sample comply with relation D, 38% in our genealogically controlled S350 sample, and 60% in Bybee's 25 language sample. If we disregard the languages in our overall sample for which the paradigm is regular, we are left with around 31% for this relation. This is better than chance, and seems to suggest that iconicity could be seen as a force at work in shaping these paradigms. However, the facts and figures do not seem to be convincing enough to propose iconicity as the sole factor behind the formal differences between the three person forms with respect to number, at least not for all languages. It might however provide a partial explanation, as one of the forces at work in shaping number forms in person paradigms. Other factors might be leveling, i.e. the tendency to regularity, and frequency. Or the current situation may be determined to a high degree by phonological processes, which, over time leave more overlap between two forms in one language, where we still see correspondences between a singular and a plural form, than in another, where we observe suppletion. Such factors may play a different role in different languages and/or at different diachronic stages of the development of person paradigms, even differently for the respective person categories. Particularly illustrative of such a scenario are the examples in Nichols (this volume), who gives an in depth, historical treatment of case suppletion in person forms in several Eurasian language families. This might explain the areal and genealogical effects that we have observed.

As a final test of the potential effects of iconicity on the distribution of suppletion in number, we will compare suppletion in number to that of suppletion in case, where iconicity is not supposed to play a role of any significance.

6 Analyzing the data: Case

As already discussed in the introduction, Bybee's (1985) Principle of Relevance predicts that suppletion in case should be considerably less frequent than suppletion in number. And as we shall see below, this is indeed so. Our interest in suppletion in case, however, lies in the extent to which it displays the same person distinctions as suppletion in number. Since there have been no claims in the literature with respect to any iconic motivation for the existence of suppletion in case, the identification of the same person-based preferences for suppletion with case as with number would further undermine any iconicity-flavoured explanation for suppletion in number. Conversely, if suppletion in case exhibits no person distinctions, or favours the third or second person rather than the first, iconicity will emerge as a potentially credible, be it weak determinant of the distribution of suppletion in number as opposed to case. Let us see what the data hold.

As stated earlier, case is considerably less frequently expressed in personal pronouns than number. Only 178 of the languages (36.5%) in our sample have either a Nom(inative)-Acc(usative) or Abs(olutive)-Erg(ative) case opposition in their person pronouns, and even fewer languages, 165 (33.8%) have the distinction for all three persons. Taking only the singular forms into consideration, we established a total of 518 Nom-Acc or Abs-Erg pairs, selecting the forms for the masculine gender in persons manifesting such distinctions. The LDN_{mean} values per person of these forms as well as their distribution over our (generalized) equivalence categories are presented in Table 13.

Table 13. LDN and equivalence categories for Person-Case pairs

Person	N of pairs (SG)	Mean LDN	Homoph	Regular	Weak Suppl	Strong Suppl
1ST	173	39.6	.04	.36	.27	.33
2ND	171	29.9	.07	.44	.34	.15
3RD	174	26.9	.09	.45	.28	.18
TOTAL	518	32.2	.07	.42	.29	.22

A comparison of these figures with those for number in Table 8 reveals that the LDN values for case are considerably lower than those for number; the overall mean, of 32.2, is not much more than half of that for number. Thus, the Nom-Acc (and Abs-Erg) pairs are on the whole much less phonologically differentiated from each other than the corresponding Sg-Pl forms. This is confirmed by the distribution over the four equivalence categories. While for number around 85% of the pairs were at least weakly suppletive, and over 50% even strongly suppletive, for case almost half of the pairs are regular or even homophonous. The same observations hold for the individual persons. The mean LDN values are all 14 to 20 percentage points lower than for number. However, the relative order between the figures in Table 13 suggests that relation (8) from the previous section, repeated below could to some extent also be reflected in suppletion for case.

(8)   Person1 > Person2 > Person3

Indeed, on a T-test, the difference for the mean LDN of case pairs between 1st person, on the one hand, and 2nd as well as 3rd on the other hand, is significant, at least at the .02 level. However, the difference between 2nd and 3rd person is not. But whatever differences there are between the persons from the LDN perspective, they almost disappear when we compare the scores for our four equivalence categories. Although 1st person scores somewhat higher in the strong suppletion column, and somewhat lower in the regular column, these differences are not significant at $p = .05$.

Given the above, there turns out to be only little reflection of relation (8) with respect to suppletion in case. This is further confirmed by the simulations for all six interpretations A–F of (9), the results of which are presented in Table 14.

Table 14. Comparison of the original sample versus random simulation

Relation	Original data (165 languages)	Simulations (n = 30,000)	Probability Simulations > Original
A	22 (13%)	25.9	.814
B	28 (17%)	27.7	.459
C	38 (31%)	49.1	1.000
D	85 (52%)	62.3	.000
E	44 (27%)	43.1	.463
F	104 (63%)	94.8	.002

For four out of six relations, the scores for the data are not better – for A and C even worse – than for the random samples. The only exceptions are again relations D and F, which do considerably better, as they did for number. In this case, however a relatively high number of languages have a regular stem for all three persons.

The areal patterns follow those of number in the sense that all three areas have a pattern that globally follows (8). Again, the New World has considerably lower scores than the Old World. However, the Pacific now takes an intermediate position rather than being more or less equal to the Old World. Table 15 provides the relevant figures.

Table 15. LDN values per area (Nichols 1992)

Area	Languages	1st	2nd	3rd	Mean
NewWorld	40	27.3	21.6	16.7	21.9
OldWorld	97	48.9	34.2	32.4	38.6
Pacific	41	30.5	28.4	24.3	24.3
TOTAL	**178**	**39.6**	**29.9**	**26.9**	**32.2**

On the whole we can say that case shows the same global tendencies as number, be it in a much weaker sense than the latter, while there seems to be not much difference between 2nd and 3rd person. Furthermore, there is much more regularity for the case than we found for the number paradigm.

We may interpret the fact that there is some suppletion for case forms where we would not expect it as further weakening the position of iconicity as an explanatory factor for the distribution of suppletion in number relative to person. After all, if similar global trends are found with respect to case as to number, and no iconicity based explanation could be advanced for the former, it is not immediately clear to what extent it should be invoked for the latter. We would then have to come up with other factors that might explain the still considerable numbers of languages for which relation D holds. Alternatively, we might still maintain iconicity as an explanatory factor, under the following assumptions. Firstly, we may reassess the role of Bybee's Principle of Relevance. Counter to what we assumed earlier on, we would suggest that case markers such as Nom and Acc are not merely markers of accidental contextual relations. In so-called accusative languages, Nominatives mark Subjects and Accusatives mark Objects, which are indeed syntactic categories. But in the by far most frequently occurring active sentences, the role of Subject is typically played by an Actor, and the role of Object by an Undergoer, both macroroles as defined by Van Valin & LaPolla (1997: 139f). These are semantic, not syntactic categories, and they are directly tied to the respective referents in the speech situation represented by the utterance at hand. The difference between the Actor and Undergoer functions may be so crucial pragmatically, especially when it concerns the first person, i.e. the speaker herself, that they may have given rise to specialized forms for both role types, just like non-prototypical plurality might give rise to idiosyncratic plural forms, again especially for first person. Second and third person would then be equally less sensitive for these semantic role distinctions. Mutatis mutandis for Absolutive versus Ergative. And note that in many languages, one of the pair of syntactic relations– typically 'marked' Object or Ergative– are accompanied by markers, such as adpositions. Diachronically, these may have given rise to case suffixes, which, in their turn, may have eventually lost their morphological status, leading to (weakly, then strongly) suppletive forms.

Interestingly, the suppletion phenomena are not independent. We find a rather high correspondence between number and case when we look at the rather coarse-grained grouping in High, Middle and Low suppletion, as introduced in the previous section. For all three persons, the vast majority of the languages have the same suppletion class for the number and case pairs: the χ^2 values for the distributions are significant at the .005 level. This is especially so for first person, for which also the – more precise – LDN values correlate significantly. This may be indicative of the fact that either the processes leading to suppletive forms for number and case are more or less synchronized, or that iconicity plays a more central role in certain languages or families as opposed to others.

It is obvious that this scenario would hold for only part of the languages in our sample, arguably not much more than a third of them. Therefore, there must be competition from other factors in order to arrive at the rather variegated situation testified by the figures presented above. One of the candidates for this is frequency. In the next section we will have a brief look at its potential role.

7 The frequency approach

As argued already in section 1, there is little doubt as to the role of frequency as an explanatory principle for the development and persistence of suppletion in paradigms in a more general sense. However, the issue that we would like to consider now is whether frequency underlies suppletion specifically in person pronouns and if so, to what extent it constitutes an alternative explanation to iconicity for the differences in suppletion relative to person that we have documented in sections five and six.[12]

When discussing the effects of frequency on morphological form, a point of contention has been the type of frequency that needs to be considered, i.e. absolute versus relative frequency. Most studies (e.g. Schuchardt 1885; Zipf 1935; Fidelholtz 1975; Hooper 1976; Bybee & Scheibman 1999; Berkenfield 2001; and Corbett et al. 2001) consider the former to be the right choice. For example, Corbett et al. (2001) found that absolute frequencies fare much better as a predictor of irregularities in Russian nominal paradigms than relative frequencies do. They measured whether nouns for which the plural part of the paradigm showed one of eight types of irregularity, were significantly more frequent for any type in their corpus than expected. For the relative frequencies this was the case for only two irregularity types. Haspelmath (2006, 2008), on the other hand, when explaining formal differences in the coding of (in)alienability, between adjectives and their comparatives, or verbs and their derived causatives, argues that it is the relative frequencies found for the two elements of these pairs rather than their absolute token frequencies across a corpus that provide the better explanation.[13]

It seems that the two types of frequency may simply be a factor behind different kinds of phenomena. Absolute frequency is arguably behind irregularity in general, by introducing (initial) suppletion caused by the rise and maintenance of two different forms for singulars and plurals ('incursion'), and by reshaping morpho-phonologically related forms into (diachronic) suppletives over time. Relative frequency may be behind economy, with a preference for the relatively more frequent form of a Sg-Pl pair to be shorter than the less frequent one. Over time, this preference may also lead to forms becoming (diachronically) suppletive. In what follows, we will therefore consider both absolute and relative frequencies. It is important to note that there is no absolute cut off point distinguishing high

---

12 Whether one sees Frequency as an explanatory factor in its own right (e.g. Haspelmath 2008) or as one instantiation of Economy (e.g. Croft 2003) is not directly relevant for the following discussion.
13 A case for considering relative frequencies be it in connection with schemas is also presented in Hollmann & Siewierska (2007).

from low frequencies, nor whether the relative frequencies between two related forms are sufficiently different. Therefore the likelihood of suppletion developing or persisting has to be viewed in probabilistic terms.

For our comparisons we have taken into consideration only data from spoken corpora, since spoken language is the main source for the emergence and change in the shape of person forms. In performing the frequency counts we have sought to count the underlying concepts rather than the actual surface forms, in line with ideas put forward in Croft (2003: 111). Croft observes that, in discussing the singular and plural as mental constructs rather than as mere labels for linguistic forms, we should make sure that the forms considered as plural are indeed referentially plural in the specified context and not, for example, instances of pluralis majestatis or polite second person reference. Obviously, since corpus counts often span tens or even hundreds of thousands of occurrences, and the actual work is typically left to a computer program, the required type of disambiguations can only be made for fully annotated corpora. In view of the fact that only few of such corpora are currently available, we made estimates of this type of phenomenon based on 100 randomly chosen occurrences in each of the corpora that we considered. A related problem to the above, be it more tractable, is that some languages have several forms for one person-number combination while others have just one. For instance, case marking languages may have several forms for the first person singular (e.g. German: *ich* (NOM), *mir* (DAT), *mich* (ACC)) while others have just one form for all these functions (e.g. Cantonese: *ngóh*). Obviously, adding up all case forms for a person-number combination would do justice to the representation of the underlying concept (1SG), however it would overrepresent the frequency effect of the respective forms, which may in fact be very different phonologically. On the other hand, the differences between forms in a paradigm can be as subtle as the Dutch strong/weak form pairs 1SG.ACC *mij* [mɛɪ̯] vs *me* [mə], the use of which may differ only in a pragmatic sense. The most important decision that we needed to make in relation to the above was with respect to third person forms with gender distinctions. These were added up to one total for 3SG, but only provided that they were formally relatively close to each other, as for English *he* and *she*, and Spanish *él* and *ella*.[14]

---

[14] Experimental evidence with respect to activation, e.g. in McQueen et al. (1994) and Magnuson et al. (2007), seems to suggest that frequencies should be associated to pure forms rather than to more abstract notions such as first person. On the other hand, it is not clear to us to what extent the presence of person and number in verbal marking in the absence of free forms changes anything in the cognitive perception of the frequencies. In that respect, our figures may be both an underestimation and an overestimation. We think, however, that the corresponding frequencies are so high that the conclusions that we will base on them below will not be affected by these choices in a fundamental sense.

Table 16 presents the frequency data for 12 languages, with the sources from which they were derived. All these sources are spoken corpora available on line. Full references may be found at the end of the article.[15] We are aware of the fact that most of the languages in question are genealogically related, and do not represent independent cases in the typological sense. However, building a collection of relatively large spoken corpora for a sample of languages equivalent to the one we used for our typological exercise above, though a highly desirable goal, seems to be illusionary at the moment.

Since the corpora are very different in overall size, we give the frequencies in terms of occurrences per 1000 tokens, which is roughly equivalent to 5 minutes of spoken discourse. The PD column in the table indicates whether a language is fully pro-drop (Y), partially (P), or not (N).

Table 16. Corpus totals of pronouns per 1000 tokens: Number

Language	PD	Source	Tokens (x10^6)	1SG	1PL	2SG	2PL	3SG	3PL	TOTAL
English	N	BNC	4.2	40.2	8.0	20.4	11.7	19.5	10.5	110.3
Estonian	Y	MDC	.1	12.0	2.3	3.4	3.1	6.5	2.2	29.5
French	N	Beech	.1	17.4	3.4	9.1	5.5	19.2	6.3	60.9
German	N	DGD	.2	18.5	6.7	1.2	0.6	11.6	5.7	44.3
Hebrew	P	HSC	.03	29.1	3.1	16.5	1.7	21.7	6.0	78.2
Italian	Y	BADIP	.5	7.7	2.8	2.1	1.1	3.2	1.2	18.0
Polish	Y	Pelcra	.6	9.4	0.7	1.9	0.3	5.8	1.5	19.6
Portuguese	Y	Davies	1.1	18.3	3.4	0.6	0.1	4.0	0.8	27.1
Russian	P	RNC	9.6	9.7	2.8	3.2	3.5	5.2	6.0	30.3
Scots	N	SCOTS	1.1	33.7	8.9	15.7	8.8	9.8	7.9	84.8
Spanish	Y	Davies	5.1	6.0	1.0	1.1	0.1	1.9	1.0	11.1
Swedish	N	GSCL	1.4	21.3	14.5	12.1	2.0	5.7	0.7	56.2

Looking at these figures, what strikes one first are the considerable differences between the languages in the *absolute* frequencies of the respective pronouns. As to be expected, the main explanation for this turns out to be the pro-drop factor. We measured a mean of 71.1 pronouns per 1000 tokens for the non-pro-drop languages, 54.3 for the partial ones, and 21.1 for the fully pro-drop languages in the

---

[15] We are extremely grateful to the many colleagues out there on the web who were very helpful with providing access to these corpora, and with searching them. Their amicable attitude turned out to be exemplary.

corpora, i.e. around 7%, 5% and 2% of the running texts, respectively.[16] The greatest overall difference is between English with 11%, and Spanish with just over 1%. But even in the latter language, all three singular forms were found among the 100 most frequent types, all with a frequency higher than 1 per 1000 tokens. It seems to be safe to consider at least the singular forms as 'frequent' in the absolute sense for all languages concerned, since they occur at least once every few minutes of spoken discourse.

Of the singular forms, 1SG is by far the most frequent for all but one language, followed by 3SG in most of the cases, and then 2SG. For French, the order is 3SG > 1SG > 2SG. For the plural forms, we generally find the same order of the persons as for the singular. The only language that diverges more or less clearly from this pattern is Russian, with high 3PL and low 2SG values. Arguably, this is caused by the very frequent use of the third person plural form as an impersonal, possibly at the cost of the 2SG in that same function (cf. Siewierska & Papastathi 2011). We have made no attempt here to distinguish between the personal and impersonal usage of pronouns, a phenomenon that occurs in most languages, however not necessarily to the same extent for the same person-number combinations.

If we could accept that there might be minor divergences for individual languages, possibly based on differences in the way person forms are used for other functions, such as impersonality, but that do not fundamentally affect global tendencies, then the following frequency hierarchy would hold:

(13) a. 1SG > 3SG > 2SG > 1PL > 3PL > 2PL

This implies (13b) and (13c):

(13) b. SG > PL
      c. 1 > 3 > 2

If frequency were to be the major factor determining suppletion, then the amount of suppletion among the six forms across the languages in our sample of sections 5 and 6 above should echo the hierarchies in (13). In order to establish this, we turned back to our database of section 5, and calculated the LDN values for each

---

[16] The only outlier seems to be Hebrew, a language with (partial) pro drop, and which scores higher than non-pro drop French and German. But with only 26,500 tokens, the Hebrew corpus is by far the smallest, which makes statistical observations relatively unreliable. Furthermore, in general, differences may be caused by the nature of the corpora. Although all are spoken, there may be considerable differences in the use of pronouns between, e.g. informal telephone conversations and television interviews. We have not controlled for type of corpus. And there may be other factors that might create considerable differences, e.g. cultural ones.

of the six forms with respect to all the other forms in the corresponding paradigms. This provides us with a relative measure for how each form stands out within its paradigm. We found the following (the mean LDN values for the 476 languages in the sample are in brackets):

(14) 1SG (57.4) > 1PL (56.6) > 2SG (56.4) > 3SG (55.8) > 3PL (55.4) > 2PL (55.1)

The differences between the mean LDN values are rather small. Still, the ranking in (14) falls largely in step with the relative amounts of suppletion we found for the three person-number pairs in section 5, especially when we add up the values for the three persons. This would give us the relation 1 > 2 > 3 rather than the frequency based 1 > 3 > 2 order in (13c). Our conclusion must be that frequency can not be the sole, or even the most important explanatory factor for the differences in the amount of suppletion that we find for the six pronouns.

Let us now turn to the person-number pairs, and look at their *relative* frequencies. We first have to establish what we would predict in terms of suppletion as a result of differences in relative frequency, ignoring for the occasion the potential role of absolute frequency. Our assumption is that one would expect more regularity when the relative frequencies are very different, with the most frequent form of the two as the least marked, or 'zero' form, and the least frequent form the one with the additional morphology. Conversely, if suppletion would be motivated by relative frequency at all, one would expect it in case both forms occur more or less equally frequently. When we look at the actual relative frequencies for the three person-number pairs we find the proportions given in the second column of Table 17 below. The Relative Frequency Quotient (RFQ) in column two in the table is calculated as follows.

(15) $\text{RFQ} = ((f_H / (f_H + f_L)) - 0.5) * 2 \, [\, f_H > 0 \,]$

In (15), f_H is the frequency found for the most often occurring element of the pair in some corpus, and f_L the frequency of the least often occurring element. The minimum RFQ value of 0.0 indicates equal frequencies. The maximum, 1.0, is reached in case one of the two frequencies is 0. The differences between the 12 languages for which we have corpus counts are considerable, especially for second person, as the minimum and maximum values in columns three and four show. For a somewhat more balanced impression of the mean proportions, we have excluded the outliers, i.e. scores more than 1 S(tandard) D(eviation) from the mean.

Table 17. Relative frequency quotients Singular vs. Plural

Person	Mean RFQ	Minimum	Maximum
1	.57	.19 (Swedish)	.86 (Polish)
2	.69	.04 (Estonian)	.96 (Portuguese)
3	.47	.07 (Russian)	.78 (Swedish)

The figures in Table 17 would predict that we should find most suppletion for third person, less for first, and least for second, i.e. 3 > 1 > 2. If anything at all, our measurements of the suppletion levels in section five showed a tendency towards 1 > 2 > 3. The same rather negative result is found when we correlate the relative frequencies of the three person-number pairs with the corresponding LDN values for each individual language. If our hypothesis about the relation between level of suppletion and relative frequency held, then there should be a (significant) negative correlation between LDN and RFQ. Nothing of the kind was found in our data.[17] Thus, also relative frequencies do not seem to be a very convincing factor for determining the amount of suppletion among the person-number pairs of independent pronouns.

Finally, we searched for frequency effects with respect to the case forms. The corpora provided us with the figures in Table 18. As in Table 15 above, the unit is occurrences per 1000 tokens.

Table 18. Corpus totals of pronouns per 1000 tokens: Case

Language	PD	1SG	1SG.ACC	2SG	2SG.ACC	3SG	3SG.ACC
English	N	40.2	3.9	20.4	2.1	19.5	4.7
Estonian	Y	12.0	1.0	3.4	0.6	6.5	0.3
French	N	17.4	3.2	9.1	0.7	19.2	0.8
German	N	18.5	1.3	1.2	0.1	11.6	0.5
Hebrew	P	29.1	0.8	16.5	0.9	21.7	3.7
Italian	Y	7.7	4.4	2.1	2.2	3.2	7.0
Polish	Y	9.4	2.1	1.9	0.8	5.8	2.3
Portuguese	Y	18.3	4.2	0.6	0.3	4.0	9.6
Russian	P	9.7	2.0	3.2	0.8	5.2	2.8
Scots	N	33.7	3.0	15.7	1.6	9.8	2.6
Spanish	Y	6.0	5.2	1.1	1.8	1.9	5.8
Swedish	N	21.3	1.4	12.1	1.2	5.7	0.5

---

17 The correlations that we found were never significant, and even slightly positive in two out of the three cases: first person (Pearson/Kendall): .000 / .078; second person: .196 / .023; third person −.080 /−.156.

We detected the following tendencies:

(16) a. 1NOM > 3NOM > 2NOM > 3ACC > 1ACC > 2ACC
      b. NOM > ACC
      c. 1, 3 > 2

Exceptions to these implications are the predominant ACC > NOM order for the third person of the three Romance languages, and for the second person in the case of two of these, Spanish and Italian. Although a higher relative frequency for accusatives might be expected for pro-drop languages in general, and indeed is found also for the two Slavic languages, an ACC > NOM order could not be attested anywhere else in the corpora. The frequency orders of (16) would suggest suppletion values vis à vis the total paradigms for the forms in the same order, i.e. most suppletion for 1NOM and least for 2ACC, and more for NOM than for ACC. The following, however, was found for the case marking languages (the LDN values are again in brackets):

(17) 1ACC (59.9) > 3ACC (58.1) > 2ACC (57.7) > 1NOM (57.5) > 2NOM (56.5) > 3NOM (55.8)

This is clearly not a confirmation of the frequency-based order in (16a), and it definitely does not give any support to (16b). Note that the latter can not be caused by the influence of regular case markers, since only stems are compared in such cases.[18]

Following the same procedure as for the number pairs, we also established the relative frequencies for the three person-case pairs. We found the following RFQ values: 1NOM.ACC = .76 > 2NOM.ACC = .66 > 3NOM.ACC = .58. This would predict precisely a reverse 3 > 2 > 1 order in suppletion. As shown in section 6, this is certainly not the order we found for the overall LDN scores. When we look at the values for the 12 languages for which we have corpus data, we do find negative correlations for all three persons, but all of these have probability values way above the 5% level. So, also suppletion in the pronominal case forms defies a convincing frequency-based explanation.

We have to conclude from this that frequency can not be the single explanation behind the distribution of suppletion that we found for the person forms in

---

[18] Another, quite plausible explanation, pointed out by Martin Haspelmath (p.c.), may be the generally accepted fact that first and second person forms tend to be much older in a language than third person forms, which are more often 'recycled', typically by the reinterpretation of demonstratives. As a result, they may show less suppletion than second person forms, despite the fact that they are more frequent in discourse.

our sample, not even for the small subset of languages for which we have corpus data. It may, however, be a force in competition with others, arguably iconicity. We have argued that, for number, the relative frequencies would predict third person forms to have most suppletion, and second person least, i.e. more or less in the opposite direction that iconicity was assumed to work. So, we may have more suppletion for third person than we would have if iconicity were the only factor, and less for second and first person.

This would then explain the fact that, although there is a weak global tendency towards 1 > 2 > 3, there is a lot of variation among the languages in our sample. There are even a few languages that go completely counter to that tendency. With iconicity as the most prominent force overall and frequency as a secondary one, we may have a better explanation for the distribution of suppletion that we found in our sample. For the further fine-tuning of our understanding of this phenomenon we may have to appeal to factors such as pro-drop, the impersonal use of certain person forms, the existence and frequency of use of a passive, medium or inverse, the morphological type, and yet others, such as the push to regularity, or the existence of several different forms for one function. Since, with suppletion, we are mainly looking at the results of processes in the (remote) past, diachronic rather than synchronic information about the characteristics of the languages concerned is called for.

8 Concluding remarks

Our investigation of the distribution of number and case suppletion in person paradigms has shown that while there is indeed a global preference for suppletion to favor the first person over the second over the third, this is certainly not a universal in the strict sense of a typological hierarchy, or a Greenbergian kind of implication. At best, what we observe is a tendency, with many (apparent) counterexamples. But for a minority of the languages the first person does indeed exhibit more suppletion than the second and the second more than the third, 22% of the languages under a strict interpretation of such a distribution, and 36% under a more liberal view, which cannot simply be ignored, or attributed to chance. Our findings are thus reminiscent of those of Bybee (2005), who documents that there is indeed a cross-linguistic tendency in languages to use a restricted set of phonemes, especially unmarked ones, in inflectional affixes as opposed to stems, but only a weak one. Just as in our case of suppletion, the majority of the languages in her sample did not display the relevant patterning despite the unequivocal existence of such a patterning in some languages. In short, what is purported to be a universal may rather be interpreted as a tendency, apparent in some languages while obscured by competing factors in other languages. Significantly, only investigations as detailed as Bybee's (2005) and Nichols (this volume) can hope to determine what is actually going on. Ideally, we would also want to have access to a representative corpus of spoken discourse for each of the languages in our database, and for which we collected paradigmatic data. And ideally, our knowledge about the diachronic stages of the languages concerned, and above all of the history of the person forms, would be far superior to what we know today.

Our findings are also reminiscent of Bybee's with respect to the role that functional factors are likely to play in determining the existing distributions of the relevant phenomena. Bybee concludes that the distribution of phonemes in inflectional affixes vs. stems in her data is not amenable to any single explanation but rather must be attributed to multiple diachronic trends such as phonological reduction in grammaticalization, and the re-use of old affixes in creating new ones. We, too have argued that neither of the two functional factors that have been invoked in the context of suppletion with respect to personal pronouns, iconicity and frequency, suffice to account for the distribution of suppletion in person paradigms that we have documented.

The primary functional factor that we considered was iconicity, more specifically the hypothesis that the greater semantic opacity of the first person non-singular as compared to the second, and the second as compared to the third should be accompanied by corresponding greater morphological opacity, and thus a greater likelihood of suppletion of the first person relative to the second, and of the second relative to the third. Although the global, be it weak, trend that we found is in line with the predictions of iconicity, the same order of relative suppletion, be it a weaker version, was observed in the nominative-accusative pairs of the singular forms. In this case, no comparable iconicity-based explanation is generally assumed to be applicable. We, however speculated that the role of Relevance may be invoked here as well, which would give some extra support to the iconicity hypothesis.

The other functional factor potentially underlying suppletion that we examined was frequency. The hypothesis that the most frequent forms would be also the ones most likely to evince suppletion turned out to be even weaker than the iconicity hypothesis. Although absolute frequencies do give support to the fact that most suppletion is found in the first person singular, they would further predict that third person would be more suppletive than the second person, both in the singular and the plural, which was not what we had found on the basis of our two approaches to comparing the forms. And relative frequencies for the three person-number combinations would predict that third rather than first person would be the most suppletive pair, with second person coming last, which also goes counter to our corpus measurements. We then argued that the two forces combined, with iconicity as a primary and frequency as a secondary factor, might explain a bit better the variety in the distribution of suppletion that we found in our sample.

We are fully aware that our investigation of the impact of frequency on suppletion leaves much to be desired. We have been able to consider only corpora for a small number of languages, and the ones that we have had access to are not uniform with respect to size or type of discourse, and other factors that probably are of relevance. Furthermore, we have been somewhat opportunistic in regard to our counting procedure, which ideally should be more in line with the most recent studies of lexical processing. Finally, the push-and-pull of the presence of a (partial) paradigm in a language should be added as an independent factor, rather than just as the lower limit of suppletion.

Nonetheless, we contend that even if all the above were to be catered for, frequency is unlikely to provide a comprehensive account of the distribution of suppletion in person paradigms. Nor is the interaction of iconicity and frequency likely to suffice. The structure of person paradigms is the result of a host of interacting factors and diachronic pressures, both language internal and external, which we do not yet fully understand. We trust, however that our investigation of suppletion has shed some light on the role of two of these.

Abbreviations

1 first person, 2 second person, 3 third person, ABS absolutive, ACC accusative, DAT dative, DU dual, ERG ergative, EX exclusive, F feminine, IN inclusive, M masculine, N neuter, NOM nominative, PAUC paucal, PL plural, SG singular

References

Bakker, Dik, André Müller, Viveka Velupillai, Søren Wichmann, Cecil Brown, Pamela Brown, Dmitry Egorov, Robert Mailhammer, Anthony Grant & Eric W. Holman. 2009. Adding typology to lexicostatistics: a combined approach to language classification. *Linguistic Typology* 13(1). 167–179.
Berkenfield, Catie. 2001. The role of frequency in the realization of English *that*. In Joan Bybee & Paul Hopper (eds.), 281–308.
Bhat, D. N. Shankara. 1967. Lexical suppletion in baby talk. *Anthropological Linguistics* 9(5). 33–36.
Bobaljik, Jonathan David. 2012. *Universals in Comparative Morphology*. Cambridge, MA: MIT Press.
Brown, Cecil H., Eric W. Holman, Søren Wichmann & Viveka Velupillai. 2008. Automated classification of the world's languages: A description of the method and prelimary results. *STUF* 61. 285–308.

Bybee, Joan. 1985. *Morphology. A study of the relation between meaning and form*. Amsterdam: John Benjamins.
Bybee, Joan. 2005. Restrictions on phonemes in affixes: A crosslinguistic test of a popular hypothesis. *Linguistic Typology* 9(2). 165–222.
Bybee, Joan. 2010. *Language, Usage and Cognition*. Cambridge: Cambridge University Press.
Bybee, Joan & Joanne Scheibman. 1999. The effect of usage on degrees of constituency: the reduction of *don't* in English. *Linguistics* 37. 575–596.
Bybee, Joan & Paul Hopper (eds.). 2001. *Frequency and the Emergence of Linguistic Structure*. Amsterdam: John Benjamins.
Cinque, Guglielmo. 1999. *Adverbs and Functional heads. A Crosslinguistic Perspective*. New York: Oxford University Press.
Comrie, Bernard. 1989. *Language Universals and Linguistic Typology*. Oxford: Basil Blackwell.
Corbett, Greville. 2000. *Number*. Cambridge: Cambridge University Press.
Corbett, Greville. 2005. Suppletion in personal pronouns: theory vs. practice and the place of reproducibility in typology. Linguistic Typology 9(1). 1–23.
Corbett, Greville. 2007. Canonical typology, suppletion, and possible words. Language 83(1). 8–42.
Corbett, Greville, Andrew Hippisley, Dunstan Brown & Paul Marriott. 2001. Frequency, regularity and the paradigm: A perspective from Russian on a complex relation. In Joan Bybee and Paul Hopper (eds.), 201–226.
Croft, William. 2003. *Typology and Universals*. Cambridge: Cambridge University Press.
Daniel, Michael. 2011. Plurality in Independent Personal Pronouns. In Matthew S. Dryer & Martin Haspelmath (eds.) *The World Atlas of Language Structures Online*. Munich: Max Planck Digital Library, chapter 35. (http://wals.info/chapter/35; accessed on 2013-02-24).
Dressler, Wolfgang. 1985. On the predictiveness of natural morphology. *Journal of Linguistics* 21. 321–337.
Dressler, Wolfgang. 1990. Sketching submorphemes within natural morphology. In Julian Mendez Dosuna & Carmen Pensado (eds.), 33–41.
Dressler, Wolfgang & Lavina Merlini Barbaresi. 1994. *Morphopragmatics. Diminutives and Intensifiers in Italian, German, and Other Languages*. Berlin & New York: De Gruyter Mouton.
Dryer, Matthew S. 1989. Large linguistic areas and language sampling. *Studies in Language* 13. 257–292.
Dryer, Matthew S. & Martin Haspelmath (eds.). 2011. *The World Atlas of Language Structures Online*. Munich: Max Planck Digital Library. (Available online at http://wals.info)
Fidelholtz, James L. 1975. Word frequency and vowel reduction in English. *CLS* 11. 200–214.
Gordon, Raymond G., Jr. (ed.). 2005. *Ethnologue*. 15th Edition. SIL International. (www.ethnologue.com)
Haiman, John. 1985a. *Natural Syntax*. Cambridge: Cambridge University Press.
Haiman, John. 1985b. *Iconicity in Syntax*. Amsterdam: John Benjamins.
Hampe, Beate & Christian Lehmann. 2013. Partial coreference. This volume.
Harnisch, Rüdiger. 1990. Morphologische Irregularität – Gebrauchshäufigkeit – psychische Nähe. Ein Zusammenhang im empirischen Befund und in seiner theoretischen Tragweite. In Julian Mendez Dosuna & Carmen Pensado (eds.), 53–64.
Haspelmath, Martin. 2006. Against markedness (and what to replace it with). *Journal of Linguistics* 42(1). 1–46.
Haspelmath, Martin. 2008. Frequency vs. iconicity in explaining grammatical asymmetries. *Cognitive Linguistics* 19(1): 1–33.

Hollmann, Willem & Anna Siewierska. 2007. A construction grammar account of possessive constructions in Lancashire dialect: some advantages and challenges. *English Language and Linguistics* 11(2). 407–424.

Hooper, Joan B. 1976. Word frequency in lexical diffusion and the source of morphophonological change. In W. Christie (ed.), *Current progress in historical linguistics*, 96–105. Amsterdam: North Holland.

Juge, Matthew L. 1999. On the rise of suppletion in verbal paradigms. *Berkeley Linguistic Society* 25. 183–194.

Levenshtein, Vladimir I. 1966. Binary codes capable of correcting deletions, insertions, and reversals. *Cybernetics and Control Theory* 10. 707–710.

Lloyd, Richard. 1989. Bound and Minor Words in Baruya. *Data papers in Papua New Guinea Languages Volume* 35. Summer Institute of Linguistics.

Lyons, John. 1968. *Introduction to Theoretical Linguistics*. London: Cambridge University Press.

Magnuson, James S., James S. Dixon, Michael K. Tanenhaus & Richard N. Aslin. 2007. The Dynamics of Lexical Competition During Spoken Word Recognition. *Cognitive Science* 34. 1–24.

Maiden, Martin. 1992. Irregularity as a determinant of morphological change. *Journal of Linguistics* 28. 285–312.

Maiden, Martin. 2004. When lexemes become allomorphs– On the genesis of suppletion. *Folia Linguistica* 38(3–4). 227–256.

Markey, Tom. 1985. On suppletion. *Diachronica* 2. 51–66.

Mayerthaler, Willi. 1981. *Morphologische Natürlichkeit*. (Linguistische Forschungen 28.) Wiesbaden: Athenaion.

McQueen, James M., Dennis Norris & Ann Cutler. 1994. Competition in Spoken Word Recognition: Spotting Words in Other Words. *Journal of Experimental psychology: Learning, Memory and Cognition* 20(3). 621–638.

Mel'čuk, Igor. 1994. Suppletion: toward a logical analysis of the concept. *Studies In Language* 18(2). 339–410.

Mendez Dosuna, Julian & Carmen Pensado (eds.). *Naturalists at Krems* (Papers from the workshop on Natural Phonology and Natural Morphology, Krems, 1–7 July 1988). Salamanca: University of Salamanca.

Mielke, Jeff. 2008. *The emergence of distinctive features*. Oxford: Oxford University Press.

Moravcsik, Edith. 1994. Group plural, associative plural or cohort plural. Email document LINGUIST List vol 5-681. 11 June 1994 ISSN 1068-4875.

Moravcsik, Edith. 2003. A semantic analysis of associative plurals. *Studies in Language* 27(3). 469–504.

Murthy, B. Lalitha & K. V. Subbarao. 2000. Lexical anaphors and pronouns in Mizo. In Barbara C. Lust, Kashi Wali, James W. Gair & K. V. Subbarao (eds), *Lexical Anaphors and Pronouns in Selected South Asian Languages*, 776–835. Berlin & New York: De Gruyter Mouton.

Nichols, Johanna. 1992. *Linguistic Diversity in Space and Time*. Chicago and London: The University of Chicago Press.

Nichols, Johanna. 2013. The origin and evolution of case-suppletive pronouns: Eurasian evidence. This volume.

Nida, Eugene A. 1963. The identification of morphemes. In Martin Joos (ed.), *Readings in Linguistics*, 3rd ed., 255–271. New York: American Council of Learned Societies. (Reprinted from Language 24 [1948], 414–431).

Nübling, Damaris. 2000. *Prinzipen der Irregularisierung*. Tübingen: Niemeyer.

Owens, Jonathan. 1985. *A Grammar of Harar Oromo (Northeastern Ethiopia)*. Hamburg: Buske.

Peirce, Charles. 1932. *Philosophical Writings, Vol. 2*. Cambridge: Harvard University Press.
Pike, Kenneth. 1965. Non-linear order and anti-redundancy in German morphological matrices. *Zeitschrift für Mundartforschung* 31. 193–221.
Riese, Timothy. 2001. *Vogul*. Munich: Lincom Europa.
Rijkhoff, Jan & Dik Bakker. 1998. Language sampling. *Linguistic Typology* 2(3). 263–314.
Ronneberger-Sibold, Elke. 1980. *Sprachverwendung– Sprachsystem: Ökonomie und Wandel* (Linguistische Arbeiten 87). Tübingen: Niemeyer.
Rudes, Blair. 1980. On the Nature of Verbal Suppletion. *Linguistics* 18. 655–676.
Schuchardt, Hugo. 1885. *Über die Lautgesetze: gegen die Junggrammatiker*. Berlin: R. Oppenheim.
Siewierska, Anna. 2004. *Person*. Cambridge: Cambridge University Press.
Siewierska, Anna & Maria Papastathi. 2011. Third person plurals in the languages of Europe: typological and methodological issues. *Linguistics* 49(3). 575–610.
Slater, Keith W. 2003. Mangghuer. In Juha Janhunen (ed.), *The Mongolic Languages*, 307–324. London & New York: Routledge.
Smith-Stark, T. Cedric. 1974. The plurality split. In Michael W. La Galy, Robert A. Fox and Ashton Bruck (eds.), *Papers from the Tenth Regional Meeting, Chicago Linguistic Society*, 657–671. Chicago: Chicago Linguistic Society.
Tomasello, Michael. 2003. *Constructing Language. A Usage-Based Theory of Language Acquisition*. Cambridge, MA: Harvard University Press.
Tryon, Darrell T. 1970. *An Introduction to Maranungku (Northern Australia)*. Canberra: Linguistic Circle of Canberra.
Urban, Greg. 1985. Ergativity and Accusativity in Shokleng (Gê). *International Journal of American Linguistics* 51(2). 164–187.
Van Valin, Robert D. & Randy J. LaPolla. 1997. *Syntax. Structure, meaning and function*. Cambridge: Cambridge University Press.
Veselinova, Ljuba. 2006. *Suppletion in verb paradigms: Bits and pieces of a puzzle*. Amsterdam: John Benjamins.
Voegelin, Charles F. & Florence M. Voegelin. 1977. *Classification and index of the world's languages* (Foundations of Linguistics Series). New York: Elsevier.
Werner, Otmar. 1987. Natürlichkeit und Nutzen morphologischer Irregularität. In Norbert Boretzky, Werner Enninger & Thomas Stolz (eds.), *Bochum – Essener Beiträge zur Sprachwandelforschung* IV, 289–316. Bochum: Brockmeyer.
Williamson, Kay. 1965. *A Grammar of the Kolokuma Dialect of Ijo*. Cambridge: Cambridge University Press.
Zipf, George K. 1965 [1935]. *The Psycho-Biology of Language: An Introduction to Dynamic Philology*. Cambridge, MA: The MIT Press.

Corpora

Language	Source	Web Location
English	BNC	http://www.natcorp.ox.ac.uk/
Estonian	MDC	http://www.cl.ut.ee/korpused/morfliides/
French	Beech	http://www.llas.ac.uk/resources/mb/80
German	DGD	http://dsav-oeff.ids-mannheim.de/

Hebrew	HSC	http://www.tau.ac.il/humanities/semitic/cosih.html
Italian	BADIP	http://badip.uni-graz.at/
Polish	Pelcra	http://nkjp.uni.lodz.pl/index.jsp
Portuguese	Davies	http://www.corpusdoportugues.org/
Russian	RNC	http://www.ruscorpora.ru/en/
Scots	SCOTS	http://www.scottishcorpus.ac.uk/
Spanish	Davies	http://www.corpusdelespanol.org/
Swedish	GSCL	http://www.ling.gu.se/projekt/tal/

Languages

Language Sample S488 (n=488)
NA = distinction in marking of Nom/Abs and Acc/Erg (n=178)
NN = no number marking (n=12)

Languages in italics are not part of the genealogically controlled subsample S350

AFRO-ASIATIC: *A.1*: Hausa(NA); *A.2*: Lele; *A.8*: Gude; *ARABIC*: Arabic (Egyptian), Maltese; *ATLAS*: Shilha,Tamazight; *BOLE*: Bole; *COPTIC*: Coptic; *CUSHITIC*: Angass; *DIZOID*: Dizi(NA); *GIMIRA*: Gimira(NA); *NORTH*: Beja(NA), Bilin(NA), Geez; *OROMO*: Oromo (Harar) (NA); *Rendille-BONI*: Boni; *SOUTH*: Ari(NA), Burunge, Galila(NA), Hamer(NA), Iraqw, Maale(NA); *WEST*: Basketo(NA), Hozo(NA)
ALACALUFAN: Kawesqar(NN)
ALGIC: *Ojibwa*, Passamaquoddy-Maliseet, Wiyot, Yurok(NA)
ALTAIC: Daur(NA), *Even(NA)*, Evenki(NA), Khalka Mongolian(KA), Mangghuer(NA), Turkish(NA), *Tuvin*, Udihe(NA), *Uyghur*
ANDAMANESE: Onge(NA)
ARAUCANIAN: Mapuche
ARAWAKAN: Apurinã, Arawak, Resígaro
AUSTRALIAN: Arabana(NA), Garawa(NA), Gooniyandi(NA), Gunya(NA), Kalkatungu(NA), Malakmalak, Maranungku, Martuthunira(NA), Maung, Nunggubuyu, Nyulnyul(NA), Pitjantjatjara(NA), Ungarinjin, Uradhi(NA), Wambaya, Wardaman(NA), Warlpiri(NA), Warrgamay
AUSTRO-ASIATIC: *Mon-Khmer*: Bugan, Cambodian, Car(NA), *Gorum(NA)*, Khasi, Khmu, Mon, Palyu, Ruc, Sedang, Semelai(NA), *Taoih*, *Temiar*; *MUNDA*: Kera, Mundari
AUSTRONESIAN: *ADZERA*: Adzera; *ANEITYUM*: Anejom; *ARE*: Gapapaiwa; *BALI-VITU*: Bali-Vitu; *BARIAI*: Kabana, Kove, Lusi; *CENTRAL*: Cemuhi, Kokota; *CHAMORRO*: Chamorro; *CENTRAL MALAYO POLYNESIAN*: Alune, Arguni, Buru, Dawera-Daweloor, *Kisar*, *Leti*, Manggarai, Selaru(NA), *Sikka*, Tetun, Tugun, West Damar; *EAST*: Kele, Larike; *EAST FIJIAN*: Fijian (Boumaa)(NA); *EAST MAKIAN-GANE*: Taba; *EAST UVEAN-NIUAFO'OU*: Niuafoou; *EAST VANUATU*: Ambrym (Southeast), Mwotlap, Raga; *ERROMANGA*: Sye; *FUTUNIC*: Ifira-Mele; *GELA*: Gela; *IKIRIBATI*: Kiribatese; *JAYAPURA BAY*: Tobati; *KAILI*: Uma; *KAIRIRU*: Kairiru; *KILIVILA*: Kilivila; *KORAP*: Arop-Lokep; *LABU*: Labu; *LAMENU-LEWO*: Lamenu; *LOCAL MALAY*: Indonesian; *LONGGU*: Longgu; *LOYALTY ISLANDS*: Iai, Nengone; *MALAGASY*: Malagasy(NA); *MALEKULA CENTRAL*: Vinmavis, Port Sandwich; *MARQUESIC*: Marquesan; *NIMOA-SUDEST*: Sudest;

North: *Jabem, Sakao*; PAIWANIC: Paiwan; PALAUAN: Palauan; PASISMANUA: *Kaulong*; PATPATAR-TOLAI: *Siar*; PIVA-BANONI: *Banoni*; ROTUMAN: *Rotuman*; SAN CRISTOBAL: Arosi; SAPOSA-TINPUTZ: *Taiof*; SARMI: *Sobei*; ST. MATTHIAS: Mussau; TAGALOG: Tagalog(NA); TAHITIC: Maori; TRUKIC: *Puluwat, Ulithian, Woleian*; UNCLASSIFIED: Rejang(NA); UTUPUA: *Tanimbili*; VANIKORO: *Buma*; WEST: Roviana(NA); WEST FIJIAN: *Nadrog*; WEST SANTO: *Tamabo*; WESTERN MALAYO-POLYNESIAN: Cebuano, Ida'an(NA), Ilokano, Kapampangan, Ma'anyan, Manobo Cotabato, Muna, Nias(NA), Sama (Sinama), Sasak, Tboli; XARACUU-XARAGURE: *Xaracuu*; YAPESE: Yapese; ZIRE-TIRI: *Tinrin*

AYMARAN: Jaqaru
BARBACOAN-PAEZAN: Awa Pit(NA), Tsafiki
BASQUE: Basque(NA)
CADDOAN: Wichita
CAHUAPANAN: Chayahuita
CARIBAN: Carib(NN), Hixkaryana, Macushi
CHAPACURA-WANHAM: Wari'
CHIBCHAN: Bribri(NA), Guaymi(NA), Rama(NA)
CHOCO: Epena Pedee(NA)
CHON: Selknam, Tehuelche
CHUKOTKO-KAMCHATKAN: Chukchi (Telqep)(NA)
CHUMASH: Chumash
COAHUILTECAN: Tonkawa(NA)
CREOLE: Berbice Dutch, Kituba(NA), Mauritian Creole(NA), Ndyuka(NA), Palenquero, Tok Pisin
DRAVIDIAN: Brahui(NA), Kannada(NA), *Kodava(NA),* Malayalam(NA), Tamil(NA)
EAST BIRD'S HEAD: Sougb
EAST PAPUAN: Kuot, Nasioi(NA), Santa Cruz
ESKIMO-ALEUT: Yupik(NA)
GEELVINK BAY: *Barapasi*, Saweru, Tarungare
GULF: *Atakapa, Chitimacha*, Tunica
HMONG-MIEN: Hmong Njua, Iu Mien
HOKAN: Karok, Pomo (Southeastern)(NA), Washo
HUAVEAN: Huave(NA)
INDO-EUROPEAN: Albanian(NA), Armenian (Eastern)(NA), Bengali(NA), *Bulgarian(NA)*, Breton, Catalan(NA), Chali(NA), Croatian(NA), Czech(NA), Danish(NA), French(NA), Gaelic, Greek(NA), Gujarati(NA), Icelandic(NA), *Irish, Italian(NA)*, Kashmiri(NA), Latvian(NA), Lithuanian(NA), *Pashto(NA),* Polish(NA), *Portuguese(NA), Rumanian(NA),* Spanish(NA), Swedish(NA), Talysh (Northern)(NA), Welsh(NA)
IROQUOIAN: Cherokee(NN), Mohawk
ISOLATE: Ainu (Classical), Burmeso, Burushaski(NA), Candoshi(NA), Cayuvava(NA), Itonama, Jicaque(NA), Korean, Kutenai, Kwaza(NA), Mosetén, Movima, Nahali(NA), Nivkh (Gilyak), Porome, Puinave, Trumai(NA), Waorani, Warao(NA), Yaghan(NA), Yuchi, Yurakare, Zuni(NA)
JAPANESE: Japanese(NN)
KARTVELIAN: Georgian(NA)
KATUKIAN: Kanamari
KERES: Acoma(NN)
KHOISAN: *Ani*, Nama(NA)
KIOWA TANOAN: Kiowa(NN)
KWOMTARI-BAIBARI: Momu

MACRO-GE: Bororo, Chiquitano, Kaingang, Karaja, Xokleng
MAKU: Hupde(NA)
MASCOIAN: Lengua Mascoy
MATACO-GUAICURU: Toba
MAYAN: Huastec, Jacaltec, Kekchi, Tzutujil
MISUMALPAN: Miskito
MIXE-ZOQUE: Oluta Popoluca, Zoque
MURA: Pirahã(NN)
MUSKOGEAN: Koasati
NA-DENE: Carrier, Haida(NA), Tlingit
NAMBIQUARAN: Nambiquara
NIGER-CONGO: *ADAMAWA-UBANGI:* Bai; *ATLANTIC:* Izon, Wolof; *BANTOID: Befang, Lamnso,* Limbum(NA), Vute; *BUSA:* Bokobaru; *CANGIN:* Noon; *CENTRAL NIGER CONGO:* Konni(NA); *DAGAARI:* Dagaare; *DOGON:* Dogon; *DOWAYO:* Doyayo; *EAST:* Ibibio(NA); *EDEKIRI:* Yoruba(NA); *EDOID:* Edo(NA); *IDOID:* Eloyi(NA); *IGBOID:* Igbo(NA); *KAINJI:* Clela(NA); *KISSI:* Kisi(NA); *KOH:* Koh Lakka; *KORDOFANIAN:* Katla, Krongo(NN), Tagoi; *KWA:* Akan, Chumbarung, Ewe; *KWENI-YAOURE:* Yaoure(NA); *LIBERIAN:* Grebo; *MANDE:* Jalonke, Mandinka, *Sisiqa; MOBA: Bimoba; Momo:* Mundani(NA); *NUPOID:* Gbari; *PLATEAU 1:* Doka; *SOUTHEAST:* Dagbani; *SWAHILI:* Swahili; *UKAAN:* Ukaan; *UNCLASSIFIED:* Fali; *WESTERN:* Godie; *ZANDE-NZAKARA:* Zande
NILO-SAHARAN: *BAGIRMI:* Bagirmi; *BARI:* Kuku; *BERTA:* Berta(NA); *FUR:* Fur(NA); *KANURI: Dongolese Nubian(NA),* Kanuri; *KOMUZ:* Kwama(NA); *KUNAMA:* Kunama; *LANGO-ACHOLI:* Lango; *LENDU:* Ngiti; *MABA:* Mesalit(NA); *MURLE:* Murle(NA); *NANDI:* Nandi(NA); *NGANGEA-SO:* So; *SONGHAI:* Songhai; *TESO:* Teso; *TURKANA:* Turkana(NA); *UNCLASSIFIED: Shabo(NA); WESTERN:* Nuer
NORTH CAUCASIAN: Abkhaz, Chechen(NA), *Ingush(NA), Lak(NA),* Lezgian(NA)
OTO-MANGUEAN: Copala Trique, Otomi, Popoloc Metzontla, Zapotec
PANOAN: Marubo(NA), Matses(NA), Shipibo-Konibo(NA)
PEBA-YAGUAN: Yagua, *Yava*
PENUTIAN: Nez Perce(NA), Siuslaw(NA), Takelma, Tsimshian, *Wintun(NA)*
PIDGIN: Chinook Jargon
QUECHUAN: *Quechua Ayacucho(NA),* Quechua Huanuco(NA)
SALISHAN: Coeur d'Alene, Halkomelem, Lummi
SALIVAN: Piaroa
SEPIK-RAMU: Awtuw, Chambri, Gapun(NA), Ngala, Rao(NA), Yessan Mayo(NA), *Yimas*
SINO-TIBETAN: CHINESE: Cantonese; TIBETO-BURMAN: Burmese(NA), Byangsi(NA), Chamling, Chepang(NA), Dulong, *Jinuo,* Kayah Li Eastern, Lepcha(NA), Lipo, *Lisu,* Lushai(NA), *Manchad(NA),* Qiang Southern, Tinan(NA), *Tinani(NA); UNCLASSIFIED:* Bawm, *Nisu,* Pumi Northern
SIOUAN: Catawba, Lakhota, *Tutelo(NN)*
SKOU: *I'saka,* Skou, *Vanimo*
SUBITABA-TLAPANEC: Tlapanec
TACANAN: *Araona(NA),* Cavineña(NA)
TAI-KADAI: Dong, Gelao, Thai
TARASCAN: Tarascan
TORRICELLI: Au, Bukiyip, Olo, Walman
TOTONACAN: Totonac Misantla

TRANS NEW GUINEA: *ALDELBERT RANGE*: *Mauwake(NA)*; *ANGAN PROPER*: *Kapau(NA)*; *BARAIC*: *Barai*; *BINANDEREAN PROPER*: *Suena*; *BRAHMAN*: Tauya(NA); *DUMUT*: Wambon; *EASTERN*: Una(NA); *ELEMAN*: Kaki Ae(NA); GUM: Amele; INLAND GULF: Minanibai; *KALAM-KOBON*: Kobon(NA); *KAMANO-YAGARIA*: Hua(NA); *KOIARIC*: *Koiali Mountain(NA)*; *KOWAN*: *Waskia(NA)*; *MADANG-ALBERT*: Kimaghama(NA); *MAIN SECTION*: Amanab(NA), Baruya, Binandere(NA); *MARIND PROPER*: *Marind*; MORWAP: Elseng(NN); *NIMBORAN*: Nimboran(NN); *NUMUGENAN*: *Usan*; *OKSAPMIN*: Oksapmin; *SENAGI*: Kamberataro(NA), *Menggwa Dla(NN)*; *SOUTH BIRD'S HEAD*: *Adang(NA)*; *TEBERAN-PAWAIAN*: Folopa(NA); *TRANS-FLY*: Kiwai Southern; *TURAMA-KIKORIAN*: Rumu
TUCANOAN: Barasano(NA), Cubeo(NA), Retuarã
TUPIAN: Kanoe, Karo, Munduruku, Urubu-Kaapor(NA)
UNCLASSIFIED: Birale, Yaruro(NA)
URALIC: Finnish(NA), Hungarian(NA), *Kamas(NA),* Nenets(NA), *Ostyak(NA)*, Udmurt(NA), Voghul Northern(NA)
URU-CHIPAYA: Chipaya, *Uru*
UTO-AZTECAN: Comanche(NA), Kawaiisu(NA), Pipil, *Yaqui(NA)*
WAKASHAN: Nootka
WEST PAPUAN: Hatam, Maybrat, West Makian
WITOTOAN: Bora(NA), *Witoto*
YANOMAM: Sanuma
YENISEIAN: Ket
YUKAGHIR: Yukaghir(NA)
YUKI-WAPPO: Wappo(NA)
ZAPAROAN: Iquito

Index

accusative systems, 15–18, 20, 25, 70, 73, 74, 87, 89, 227, 265, 314, 378
agreement, 1–7, 9–12, 15–33, 95–99, 101–103, 105, 107–114, 161–167, 169, 188, 197, 198, 201, 206, 207, 209–213, 217, 219, 220, 229, 231, 242, 246, 267, 284, 293, 310, 318, 319, 321, 323, 332, 337, 340
~ marker, 197, 198, 206, 207, 209, 221, 332
~ paradigms, 17, 162, 163, 165
Agreement Hierarchy, 99, 102, 103, 105, 109, 111–114
alignment, 15–33, 41–43, 46, 48, 69–71, 75–78, 80, 81, 86, 90, 227, 263–269, 273–278, 280, 281, 283–285
~ splits, 69, 70, 86
ditransitive ~, 267
hierarchical ~, 75–78, 80, 81
indirective ~, 41, 48, 265, 268, 274, 277, 280, 283
neutral ~, 266, 274, 277, 281, 283
secundative ~, 265, 268, 274–276, 284
split ~, 42, 43, 46
ambiguous agreement, 19, 207, 211
analogy, 210, 280, 319, 324
anaphora, 95, 98, 99, 103–106, 108
antitopic, 306, 307, 309–311
applicative, 264, 270, 272–275, 278–285
apposition, 71, 211, 293

bound person form, 75, 78, 95–97, 197–199, 201–203, 205, 209–211, 217, 218, 220–222
bound pronouns, 198, 201, 217, 222, 227, 229, 230, 234, 235, 293

case, 12, 15, 20, 21, 70, 89, 95, 100, 170, 172, 202–204, 207, 217, 265, 267, 269, 272, 275, 279, 283–285, 313–317, 321, 322, 324, 327, 329–339, 348–354, 357–360, 363, 365, 375–378, 380, 383, 385
causative, 264, 270–283, 285, 379
cleft constructions, 300, 301
conominal, 199, 201, 205–214, 218–222
conservative Indo-European referential system, 229, 231, 234, 238

context-induced reinterpretation, 77, 89
contrast, 106, 241, 295, 298, 300–303, 306, 307, 309–311, 320
contrastive pronouns, 218, 295, 301, 309, 320
coreference, 53–55, 61, 64, 66, 95, 99, 159–163, 165, 169–185, 187–192
corpus, 38, 40–42, 44, 120, 163, 169, 171–175, 181–187, 190–193, 240, 241, 325, 341, 379–388, 391, 392

default, 5, 7, 8, 13, 19, 126, 154, 239, 339, 355, 364
deixis, 105, 106
diachrony, 125, 357
differential object marking (DOM), 37, 48
discrepancy, 17, 18, 20, 23–29, 33
ditransitive, vi, 15, 19, 37–42, 44, 46, 47, 173, 175, 177, 178, 180, 181, 185, 263–285
double object construction (DOC), 58, 185, 263, 264, 266, 268–271, 273, 274, 276–278, 280, 283–285
dual, 27, 102, 164, 165, 220, 294, 295
Dutch, 65, 121, 137, 143, 149, 313, 380,

emphatic pronouns, 171, 217, 291, 295, 296, 309, 314, 320, 325, 327, 329
English, 17, 23, 27, 37, 42, 61, 106, 110, 111, 120, 121, 127, 129, 133, 137, 144, 147, 149, 159, 160, 162–164, 169, 170, 173, 175, 178, 180–183, 185–188, 190, 192, 197, 198, 204, 206, 207, 210, 218, 219, 228–232, 236, 237, 249, 251, 263, 266–268, 293, 304, 347, 352, 354, 355, 380–384, 391
episodic, 59, 137, 138, 140, 143, 144, 151–154
ergative systems, 15, 25, 27, 29, 30, 69–72, 87, 89, 265, 314
Estonian, 381, 384, 391
exclusive, 9, 27, 138, 139, 294, 295, 311, 315, 372
existential, 126, 128, 138, 140, 141, 147–149, 151–154

features, 1, 11–13, 15, 20, 23, 27, 30, 46, 53, 58, 96, 99–101, 105, 107, 108, 110–112,

122, 132, 136–138, 140–142, 151–153, 155, 163, 167, 168, 216, 217, 219, 229, 231, 249, 255, 349, 362, 363
first person, 2, 8–10, 18, 21, 22, 27, 75, 81, 84, 126, 163, 165, 167–174, 177–179, 181, 183, 191, 200, 235, 241, 302, 311, 313, 316, 317, 319, 324, 329, 337, 349, 350, 354, 360, 365–368, 371, 374, 378, 380, 384, 386, 387
focus, 19, 106, 107, 136, 296–303, 307, 309–311, 325
free pronouns, 163, 165, 188, 205, 206, 208, 217, 227, 229–231, 234–237, 256, 291, 292, 295–299, 301–311
French, 53, 60, 65, 100, 104, 107, 109, 110, 120, 124, 126, 128, 129, 137, 139, 143, 148, 149, 151, 163, 182, 197–200, 204, 206–208, 229, 231, 282, 311, 381, 382, 384, 391
frequency, 23, 32, 46, 48, 74, 85, 112, 172–175, 177–179, 182–184, 186, 189, 191, 192, 215, 229, 240–242, 255, 311, 347, 349–351, 365, 371, 375, 378–388
  absolute ~, 174, 379, 381, 383, 387
  relative ~, 46, 173, 175, 177, 178, 182, 186, 189, 229, 241, 365, 379, 380, 383–387

gender, 1–7, 9–13, 15, 19, 29, 57, 96, 100–102, 104, 107–110, 113, 199, 216, 217, 219, 227, 229, 235, 238, 239, 292, 311, 318, 319, 358, 366, 375, 380
generic, 53–55, 58, 60–64, 66, 85, 128, 137–139, 141, 142, 144, 151–153, 171, 292, 311
genericity, 53–66
German, 16, 20, 53, 101, 119–121, 123, 124, 136–138, 143, 144, 147–149, 163, 169, 172, 180–183, 185, 186, 188, 190, 192, 197, 198, 203, 206, 207, 210, 214, 218, 229, 230, 232, 233, 235, 242, 247–256, 265, 267, 269, 325, 380–382, 384, 391
Germanic referential system, 230, 250, 255
grammaticalization, 28, 33, 55, 59, 64, 73, 74, 80–85, 87–89, 98, 107, 125–127, 155, 163, 188, 189, 191, 192, 279, 282, 293, 310, 337, 387

Hebrew, 281, 381, 382, 384, 392
hierarchical system, 26, 27, 69, 70, 75–78, 80, 81, 86
hierarchy, vi, 11, 69–71, 74, 75, 81, 82, 86–89, 99, 102, 103, 105, 109, 111–114, 138, 159, 163, 170, 175, 182–186, 188, 189, 191, 192, 280, 353, 367, 368, 370, 374, 382, 386
homonymy, 54
hortative, 168–171, 178, 180
human theme, 37, 41

iconicity, 25, 347, 348–352, 367–371, 374, 375, 377, 378, 386–388
impersonal, vi, 53, 54, 59, 66, 119–125, 127–130, 132, 133, 136–140, 142, 143, 145, 148–151, 153–155, 198, 263, 382, 386
inclusive, 18, 27, 138, 139, 167, 294, 295, 311, 372, 373
index, 54, 60, 71, 72, 87, 95–100, 102–105, 107, 108, 111–114, 167, 188, 199, 201–217, 220–222, 392
  ~-set, 203, 204
  argument ~, 201, 202, 205, 210, 216, 217, 222
  con-~, 208
  cross-~, 95–97, 207–215, 217–222
  gramm-~, 95, 206, 207–210, 213–215, 217, 222
  pro-~, 95, 97, 208, 209, 213–215, 217, 218, 222
  solo-~, 208
indexing, 37–40, 56–57, 75, 78, 80, 95, 104, 197, 198, 201, 202, 207, 209–215, 217, 220, 222, 267, 274, 275, 284
  argument ~, 197, 198, 210, 217
indirective, 41, 48, 265–269, 272–274, 276, 277, 280, 283, 284
intensifier, 84, 314, 315, 325, 331, 334, 336, 337, 339
irregularity, 3, 190, 347, 351, 352, 379
Italian, 126, 145, 149, 155, 205, 217, 219, 381, 384, 385, 392

Levenshtein method, 361
locuphoric, 97, 114, 199, 209

Mande languages, 54, 55, 59
Mohawk, 210, 291–298, 300, 301, 305, 307, 309–311, 393
monotransitive, 37, 39, 41, 170, 175–181, 186, 265–267, 284, 285
morphology, 1, 4, 6–12, 15, 19–34, 40, 58, 59, 75, 76, 96, 167, 168, 188, 198, 219, 233, 234, 239, 241, 256, 264, 273, 282,

283, 291, 311, 318, 319, 323, 324, 328–333, 336, 339, 340, 348, 351, 353, 360, 378, 379, 383, 386, 387

Nakh-Daghestanian languages, 3, 5, 29–31, 313, 317–319, 323–325, 340
neutral, 15, 17, 18, 22, 25, 28, 29, 237, 264–269, 273–278, 280, 281, 283, 285
number, 1–5, 7, 11, 15, 19, 21, 23, 27, 82, 84, 85, 96, 101, 108, 140, 143, 144, 151, 159, 160, 163–166, 168, 178, 182, 183, 189, 191, 199, 203, 210, 216, 217, 219, 227, 229, 234, 235, 238, 239, 293, 294, 314, 320, 322, 323, 347–354, 357, 359, 360, 364–368, 370–378, 380–387, 392
 ~ distinctions, 82, 84, 183, 210, 366, 367

opacity, 349, 351, 387

paradigm, 1–12, 17, 18, 20, 23, 27, 28, 31–33, 97, 162, 163, 165, 167–169, 188, 200, 222, 240, 293, 311, 313–317, 319, 321–324, 327–340, 347, 348, 350–352, 357, 358, 363, 366, 368, 370–372, 374, 375, 377, 379, 380, 383, 385–388
partial coreference, 159, 161–163, 165, 169–179, 181–185, 187–192
person, v, vi, 1–13, 15, 17–23, 25–27, 39–41, 44, 53–55, 59–60, 64–66, 69–72, 75, 78–82, 84, 87, 88, 95–103, 105–107, 114, 119–121, 125–129, 144, 146, 155, 159–172, 174–184, 188–192, 197–212, 214, 216–222, 227–236, 238–242, 245, 246, 248, 255–257, 267, 269, 291, 292, 295, 302, 311, 313–324, 329–332, 334–340, 347–355, 357–361, 365–380, 382–388
 ~ forms, v, vi, 5, 13, 23, 40, 75, 78–81, 87, 95–98, 161, 163, 167, 188, 189, 191, 192, 197–205, 208–211, 216–222, 230, 239, 242, 319, 324, 334, 335, 347, 350–352, 355, 357, 358, 360, 361, 365, 371, 374, 375, 380, 382, 385–387
 inflectional ~, 323, 340
 lexical ~, 323, 337, 338, 340
plural, 1–5, 7–12, 18, 22, 26, 27, 40, 70, 81–90, 101, 102, 120, 121, 125–129, 140, 143, 144, 150–153, 155, 160, 163, 167, 168, 171, 173–175, 180–183, 191, 202, 294, 295, 321, 323, 349, 352, 354, 359, 363–366, 371, 373–375, 378–380, 382, 384, 387

Polish, 215, 231–233, 235, 236, 238, 239, 247, 249, 253–255, 325, 352–354, 381, 384, 392
Portuguese, 214, 215, 381, 384, 392
possession, 110, 264, 295, 334
possessive affix, 294, 202, 320–322, 329, 330–337, 339, 340
predicate nominal, 325–327
pronominal affix, 201, 213, 217
pronoun, 2–4, 11, 13, 19, 28, 37–41, 43–46, 48, 49, 51, 53–55, 57, 59, 60, 64–66, 69–74, 78, 80, 82–85, 87, 88, 95–112, 114, 119–130, 132, 133, 136–140, 142–151, 153–155, 159–163, 165, 169–175, 177–179, 181–186, 188, 189, 193, 197–199, 201, 202, 204–215, 217–219, 221, 222, 227–237, 239–242, 244–256, 291–293, 295–299, 301–311, 313–318, 320–325, 327–340, 347–353, 355, 357, 365, 366, 375, 379, 381–384, 387
 personal ~, 2, 11, 13, 84, 99–105, 107–112, 114, 136, 159, 163, 171, 173–175, 182, 189, 199, 204, 205, 210, 218, 219, 222, 228, 232, 239, 241, 248, 315, 317, 323, 334, 337, 347–353, 355, 375, 387
 subject ~, 215, 228, 229, 231–233, 235, 237, 239–242, 244–256
prosody, 291, 307, 311

random simulation, 369, 371, 372, 374, 377
recipient, 37, 170, 202, 203, 263–265, 278, 282–284
reduced reference, 227
reduced referential devices, 99, 112, 114, 199, 227–230, 233
referent, 3, 54, 60, 61, 64, 65, 71, 80, 82, 84–87, 95–97, 99–101, 103–106, 108–113, 122–124, 128, 139, 140, 144, 148, 150, 152, 153, 160, 161, 163, 165, 168, 182, 199, 202, 210, 212, 227, 229, 230, 296, 300, 303, 305, 307, 310, 349, 378

referential
 ~ category, 18, 21, 22, 26, 27, 33
 ~ hierarchy, vi, 69–71, 74, 75, 81, 82, 86–88
 ~ system, 227–231, 233–235, 238, 239, 242–250, 253–256
 ~ type, 23, 25–27,
 ~ verbal inflection, 1, 227, 231, 245

referentiality, 37, 48, 53, 119, 151, 269
regularity, 347, 352, 360, 363, 371, 375, 377, 383, 386
Relative Frequency Quotient, 383
Relevance (Principle of), 348–351, 375, 378, 387
Russian, 100, 102, 121, 122, 129, 149, 150, 206, 207, 210, 215, 227–229, 231–256, 268, 315, 325, 327, 341, 363, 379, 381, 382, 384, 392

sample, 48, 104, 136, 165, 170–172, 174, 175, 177, 178, 184, 231, 268, 295, 350, 351, 355–358, 365, 368–371, 373–375, 377, 378, 381–383, 386, 388, 392
Scots, 381, 384, 392
second person, 2–6, 8–11, 22, 23, 25–27, 33, 39–41, 44, 53–55, 59, 64–66, 69–72, 75, 78, 80–82, 97, 98, 114, 121, 146, 159, 161–163, 167–169, 172, 180, 181, 183, 184, 191, 200, 214, 239, 241, 245, 246, 291, 295, 315, 317, 319, 334, 337, 348, 349, 352–354, 365–369, 371, 372, 374, 375, 380, 383–387
secundative, 265–268, 273–277, 282–284
semantic map, 121, 125, 127, 129–131, 134–136, 149, 151, 155
singular, 1–4, 6–12, 17, 18, 20–23, 25, 27, 40, 53, 55, 59, 65, 66, 70, 78, 81–90, 104, 129, 140, 160, 163, 167–171, 173–175, 179–183, 191, 206, 214, 220, 222, 228, 233–235, 241, 294, 295, 311, 313, 315–317, 319, 321, 323, 325, 329, 349, 352, 357–359, 363–366, 371, 374, 375, 379–382, 384, 387
Spanish, 37–44, 46, 48, 101, 113, 122, 129, 149, 220, 236, 251, 380–382, 384, 385, 392, 393
Swedish, 250, 251, 381, 384, 392
suppletion, v, 314–319, 324, 327, 336, 338–340, 347–355, 357, 359–361, 363–365, 367, 368, 370–372, 374–380, 382–388
 case ~, 314, 338, 349, 350, 375, 376, 386
 coding ~, 360

 marginal ~, 360, 364
 number ~, 349, 350, 365, 367, 368, 371, 372, 375, 377, 386
 stem ~, 353, 354, 360, 365, 371,
 strong ~, 354, 355, 364, 367, 370, 376
 total ~, 353, 354, 359, 365
 weak ~, 316, 354, 355, 357, 364, 367, 370
syncretism, 2, 6, 8, 222, 335
syntactic functions hierarchy, 163, 170, 175, 183, 184–186, 188, 189, 191, 192

third person, 3–6, 8–10, 17–20, 22, 23, 25, 27, 39, 40, 64, 69–71, 75, 78, 80–82, 84, 87, 88, 97–101, 103, 105–107, 114, 120, 121, 125, 127–129, 144, 155, 159, 162, 165, 167, 169, 171, 174, 177–179, 184, 200, 219, 228, 233, 234, 238, 239, 241, 245, 246, 255, 292, 295, 311, 330, 334, 335, 337, 349, 350, 352, 359, 360, 366–369, 371–374, 378, 380, 382, 384–387
topic, 46, 53, 55, 61–64, 66, 69, 73, 74, 87, 303–307, 309, 311, 325
 ~ shift, 303, 304, 306, 309
topicalization, 303, 305, 307, 309, 310
transitivity, 268
transparency, 349, 351, 352, 368
Tucanoan languages, 4–11, 395
typological hierarchies, vi, 88, 386
typology, 15, 24, 31, 33, 53, 106, 119–121, 130, 131, 155, 197, 228, 230, 254, 263, 265, 268, 291, 293, 315, 322, 323, 338, 351, 355

universal, 31, 33, 95, 98, 99, 102, 103, 114, 167, 205, 222, 267, 281, 374, 386, 387
universal quantification, 138, 140–142, 144, 145, 150–155
universal reference, 127, 128
Uralic, 246, 313, 316, 320, 321, 327–332, 334, 335, 337–341, 395

veridical, 126, 132, 137, 138, 140, 141, 143, 144, 151–154
 non-~, 126, 137, 138, 141, 144, 151–154

www.ingramcontent.com/pod-product-compliance
Lightning Source LLC
Chambersburg PA
CBHW061341300426
44116CB00011B/1946